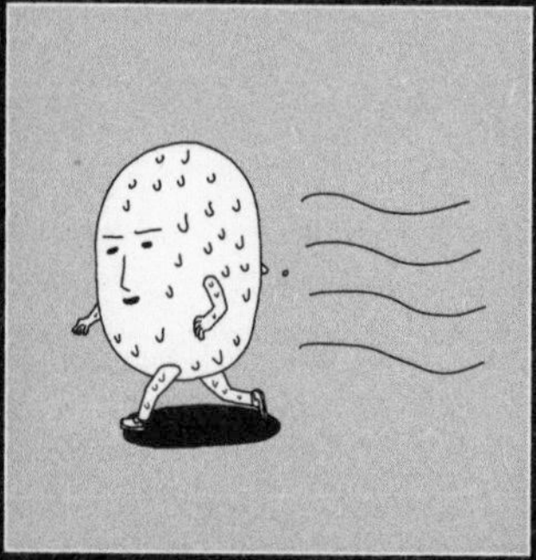

ONE

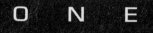

To correct my lack of exercise, I've been running outside. I want to be able to run about ten kilometers.

—ONE

Manga creator ONE began *One-Punch Man* as a webcomic, which quickly went viral, garnering over 10 million hits. In addition to *One-Punch Man*, ONE writes and draws the series *Mob Psycho 100* and *Makai no Ossan*.

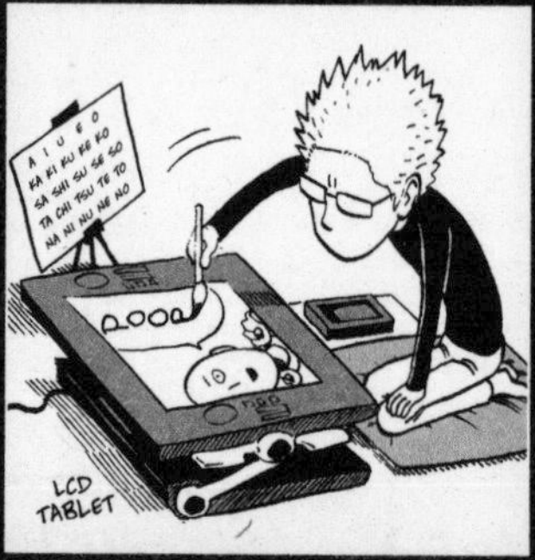
A I U E O
KA KI KU KE KO
SA SHI SU SE SO
TA CHI TSU TE TO
NA NI NU NE NO
LCD TABLET

YUSUKE MURATA

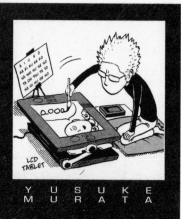

I've always had poor handwriting, so I've started practicing when I do my storyboards. The result is...finishing my storyboards four hours later.

—Yusuke Murata

A highly decorated and skilled artist best known for his work on *Eyeshield 21*, Yusuke Murata won the 122nd Hop Step Award (1995) for *Partner* and placed second in the 51st Akatsuka Award (1998) for *Samui Hanashi*.

ONE-PUNCH MAN 07

ONE + YUSUKE MURATA

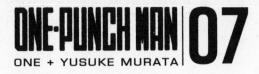

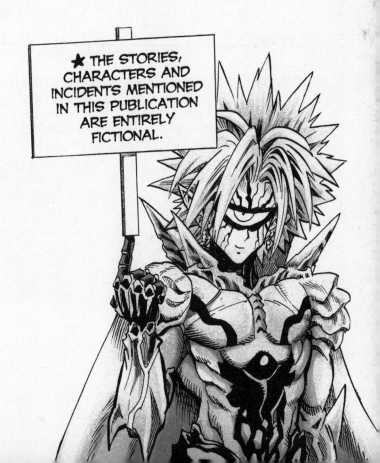

★ THE STORIES, CHARACTERS AND INCIDENTS MENTIONED IN THIS PUBLICATION ARE ENTIRELY FICTIONAL.

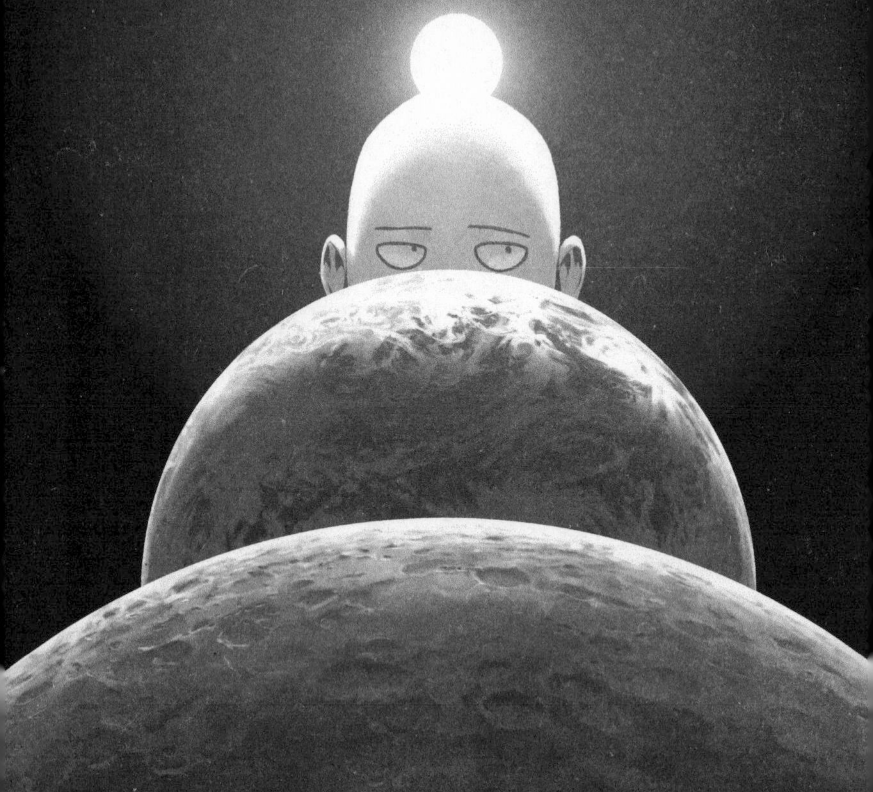

ONE

ONE - PUNCH MAN

YUSUKE MURATA

07

STORY BY
O N E
ART BY
YUSUKE
MURATA

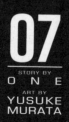

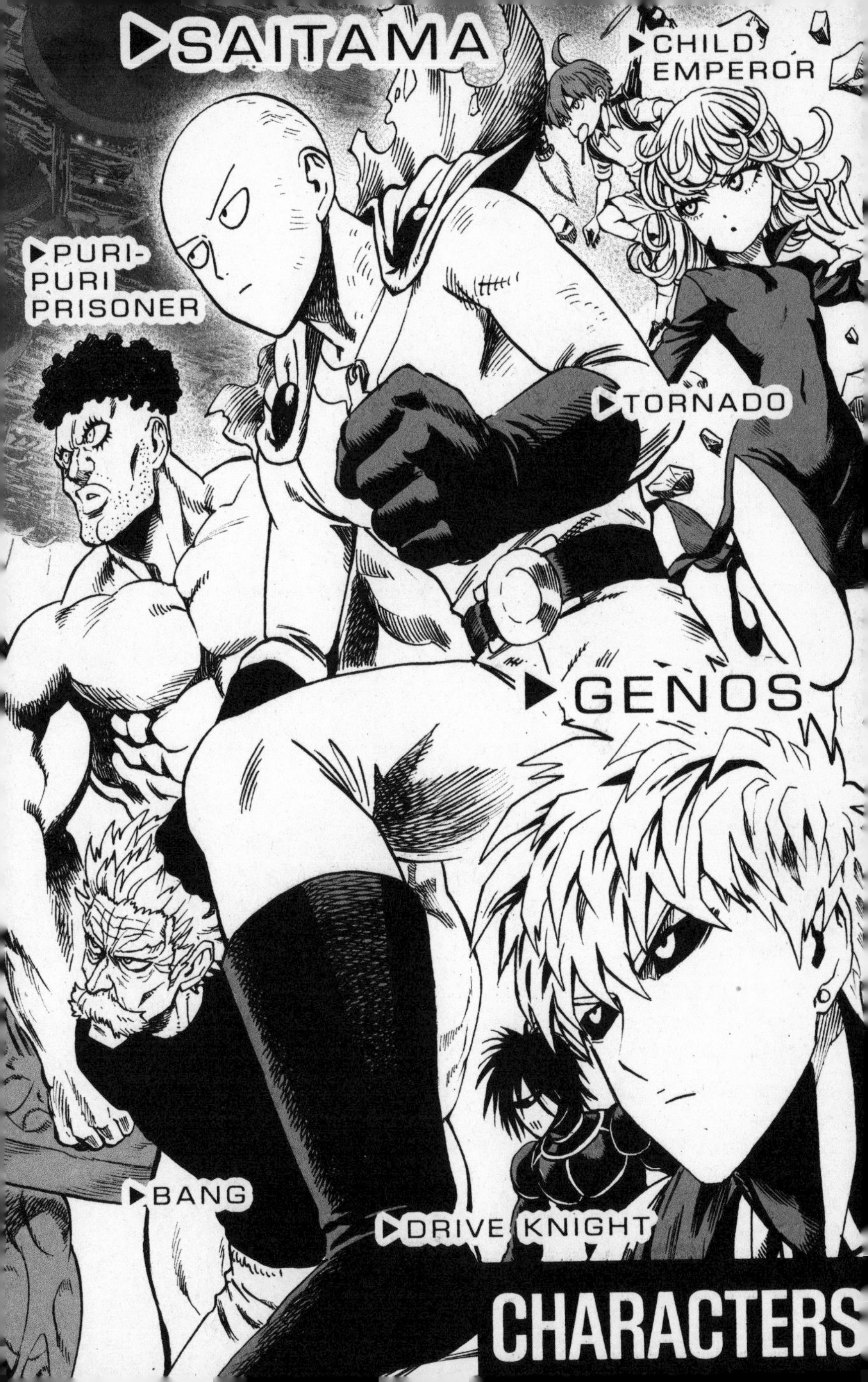
SAITAMA
CHILD EMPEROR
PURI-PURI PRISONER
TORNADO
GENOS
BANG
DRIVE KNIGHT
CHARACTERS

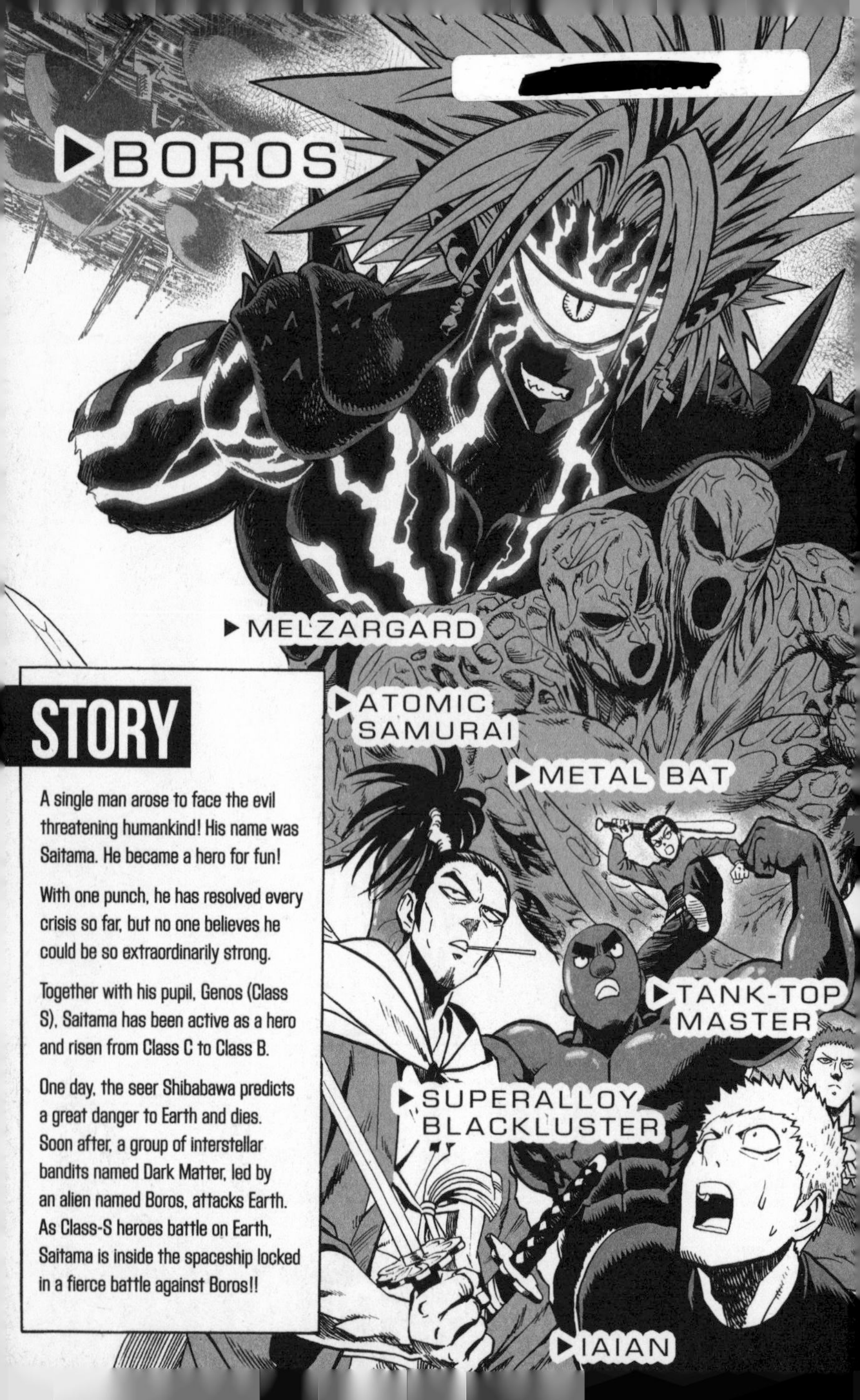
[redacted]
BOROS
MELZARGARD
ATOMIC SAMURAI
METAL BAT
TANK-TOP MASTER
SUPERALLOY BLACKLUSTER
IAIAN

STORY

A single man arose to face the evil threatening humankind! His name was Saitama. He became a hero for fun!

With one punch, he has resolved every crisis so far, but no one believes he could be so extraordinarily strong.

Together with his pupil, Genos (Class S), Saitama has been active as a hero and risen from Class C to Class B.

One day, the seer Shibabawa predicts a great danger to Earth and dies. Soon after, a group of interstellar bandits named Dark Matter, led by an alien named Boros, attacks Earth. As Class-S heroes battle on Earth, Saitama is inside the spaceship locked in a fierce battle against Boros!!

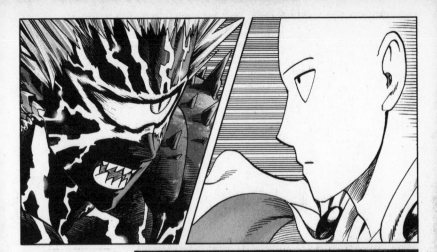

CONTENTS

ONE-PUNCH MAN VOLUME SEVEN

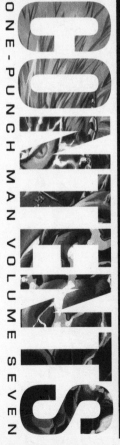

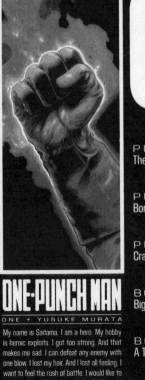

ONE-PUNCH MAN

ONE + YUSUKE MURATA

My name is Saitama. I am a hero. My hobby is heroic exploits. I got too strong. And that makes me sad. I can defeat any enemy with one blow. I lost my hair. And I lost all feeling. I want to feel the rush of battle. I would like to meet an incredibly strong enemy. And I would like to defeat it with one blow. That's because I am One-Punch Man.

07

THE FIGHT

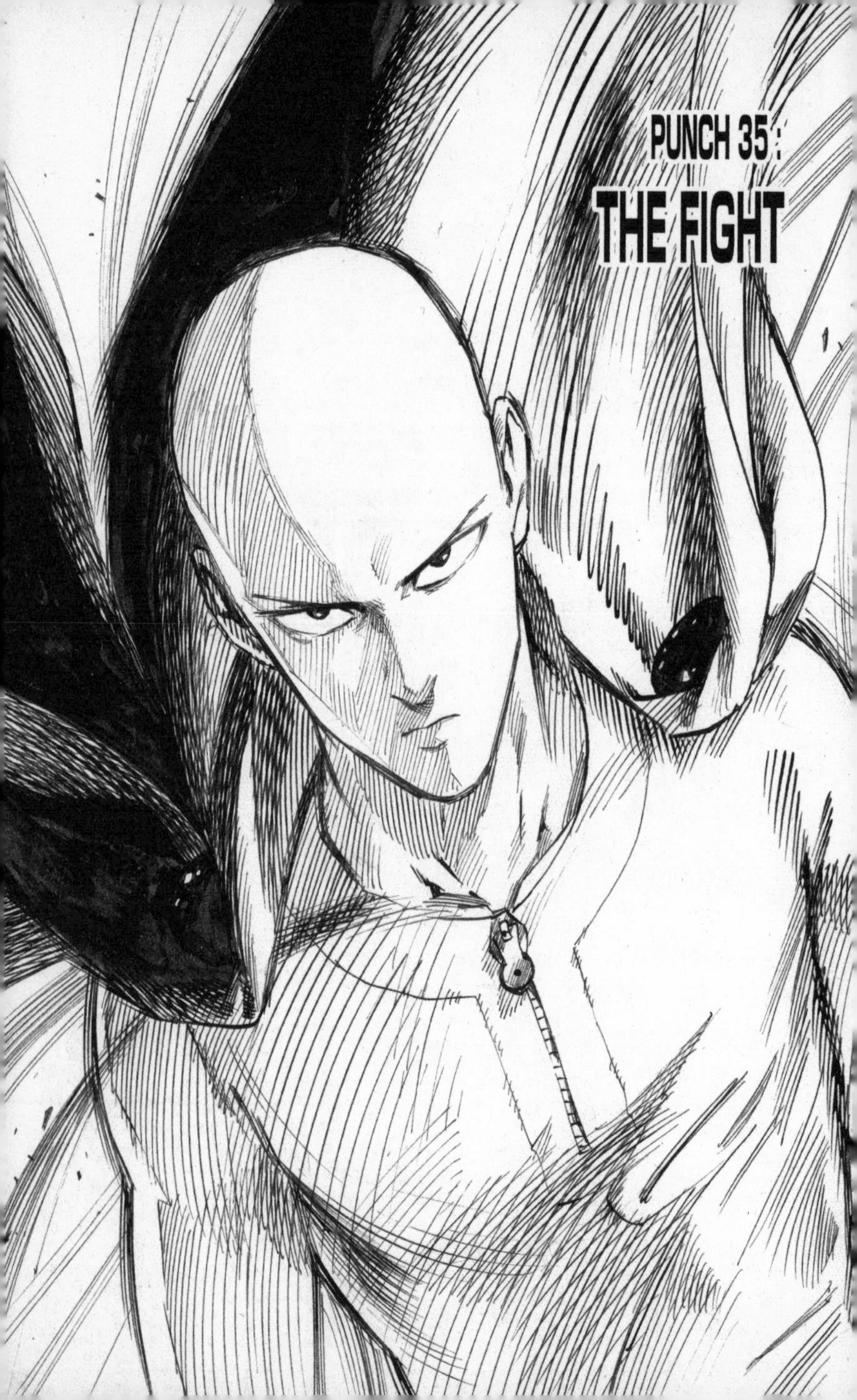
PUNCH 35 :
THE FIGHT

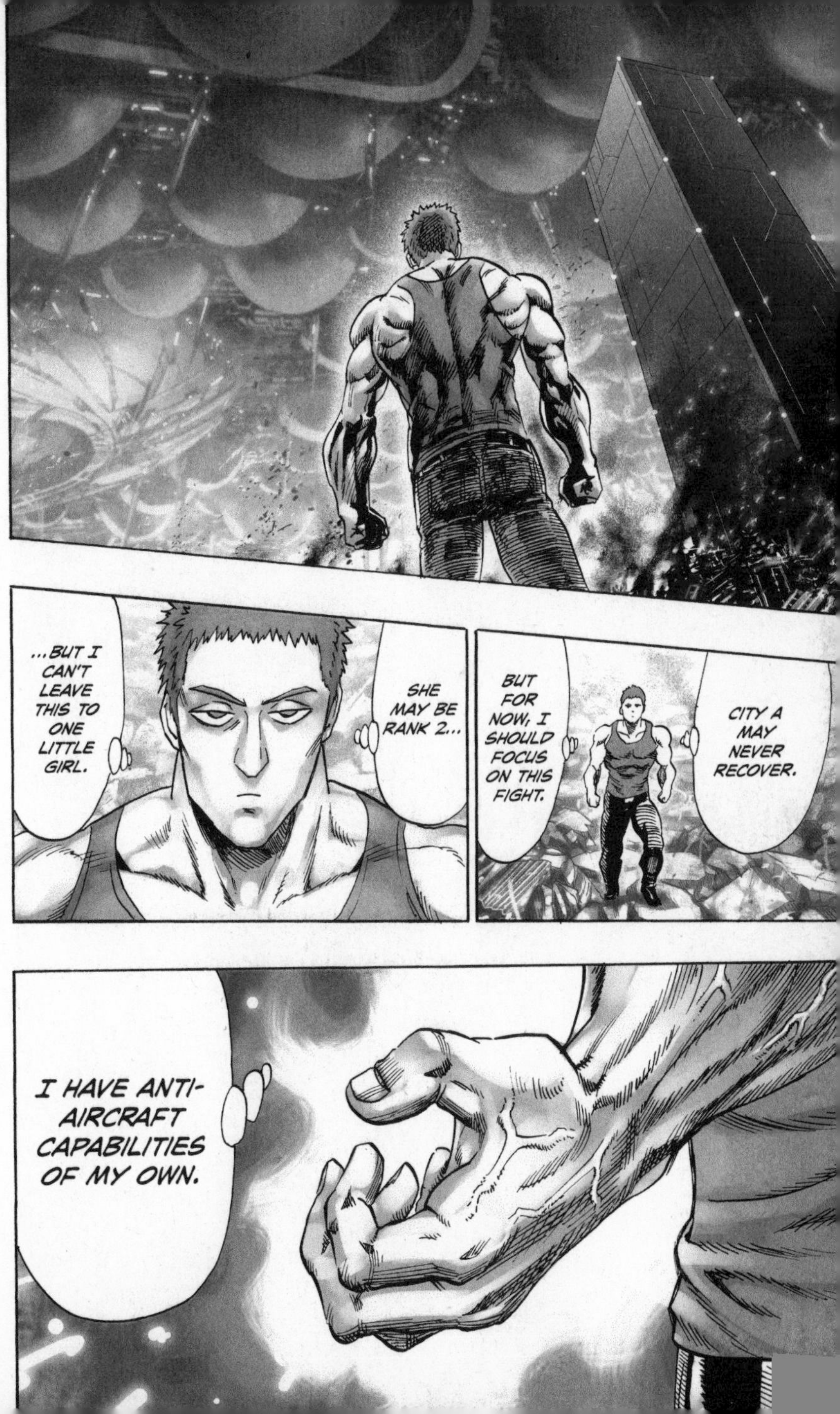
CITY A MAY NEVER RECOVER.
BUT FOR NOW, I SHOULD FOCUS ON THIS FIGHT.
SHE MAY BE RANK 2...
...BUT I CAN'T LEAVE THIS TO ONE LITTLE GIRL.
I HAVE ANTI-AIRCRAFT CAPABILITIES OF MY OWN.

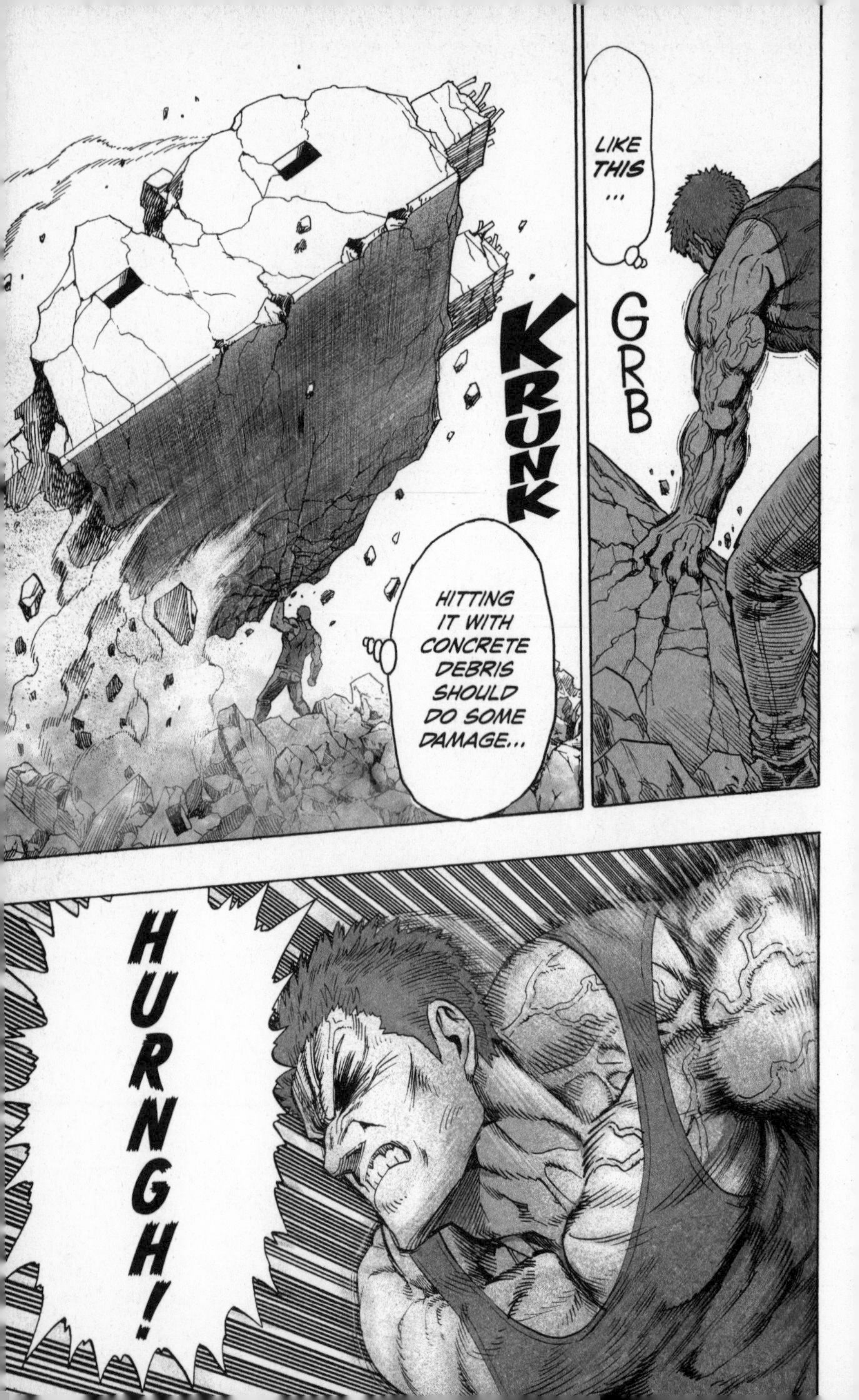
LIKE THIS ...
GRB
KRUNK
HITTING IT WITH CONCRETE DEBRIS SHOULD DO SOME DAMAGE...
HURNGH!

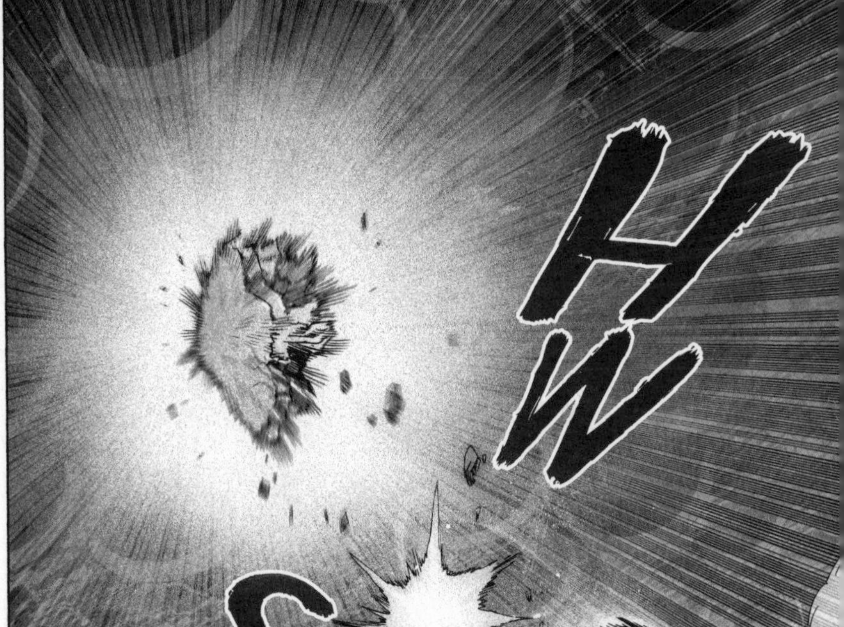

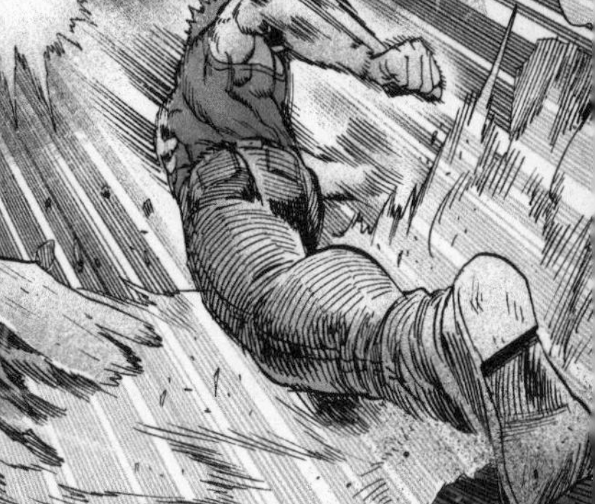
WHAT ARE YOU DOING?

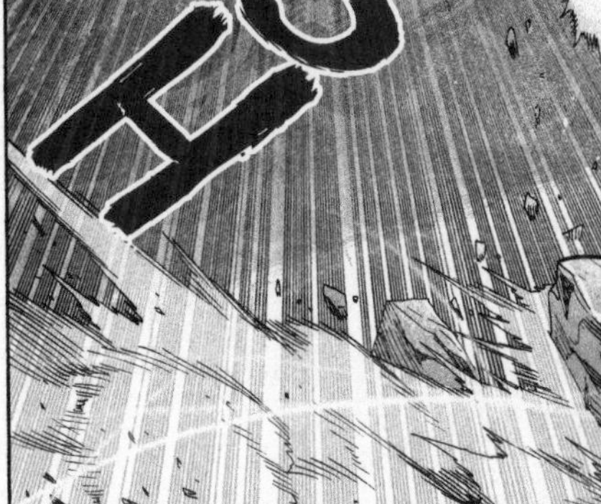
WOBBLE

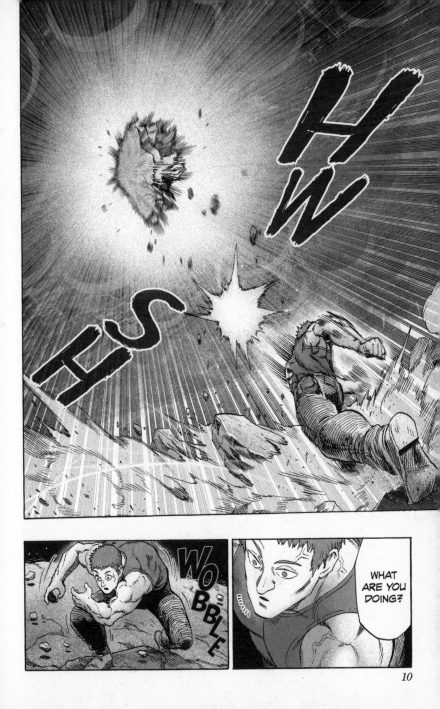

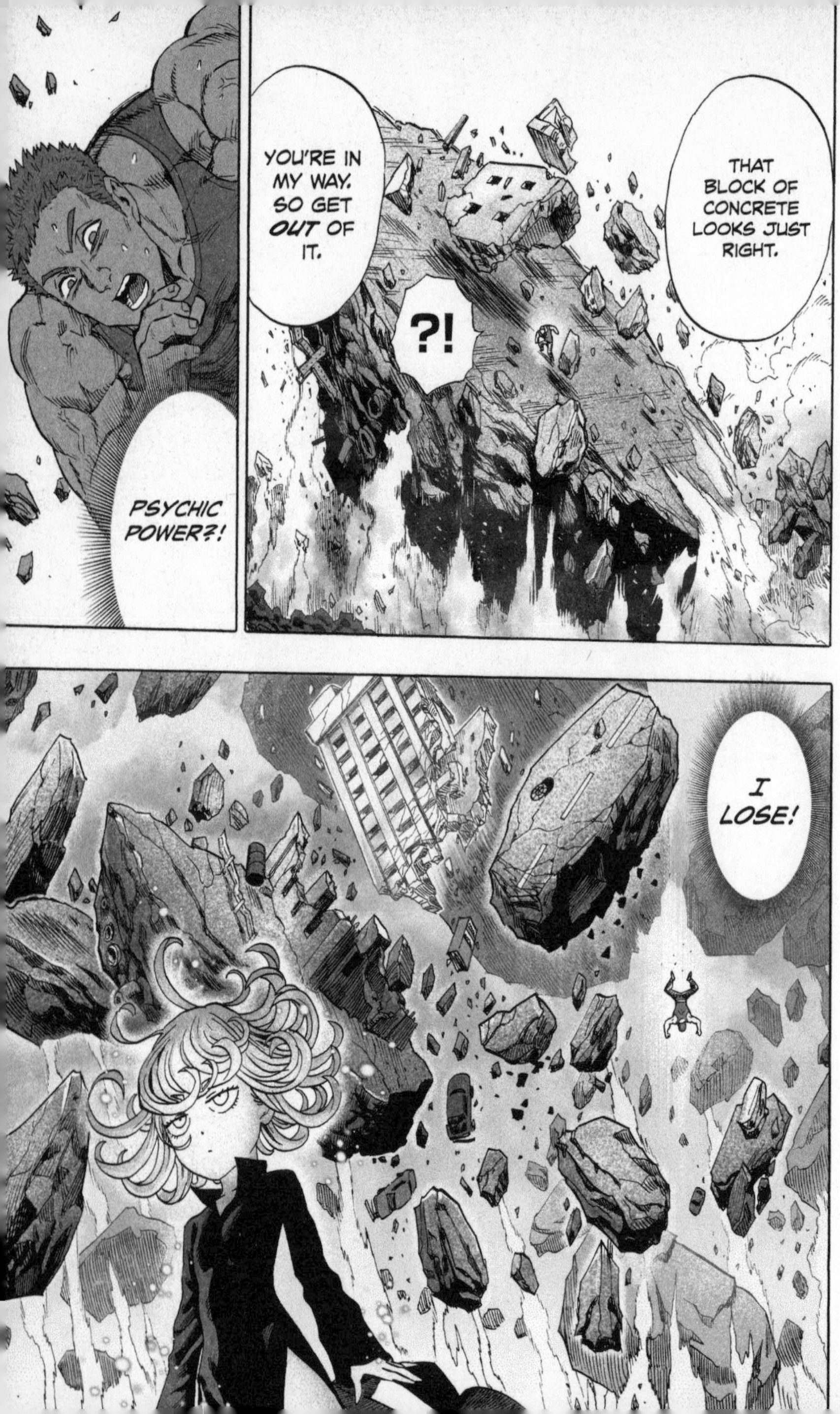
THAT BLOCK OF CONCRETE LOOKS JUST RIGHT.
YOU'RE IN MY WAY. SO GET *OUT* OF IT.
?!
PSYCHIC POWER?!
I LOSE!

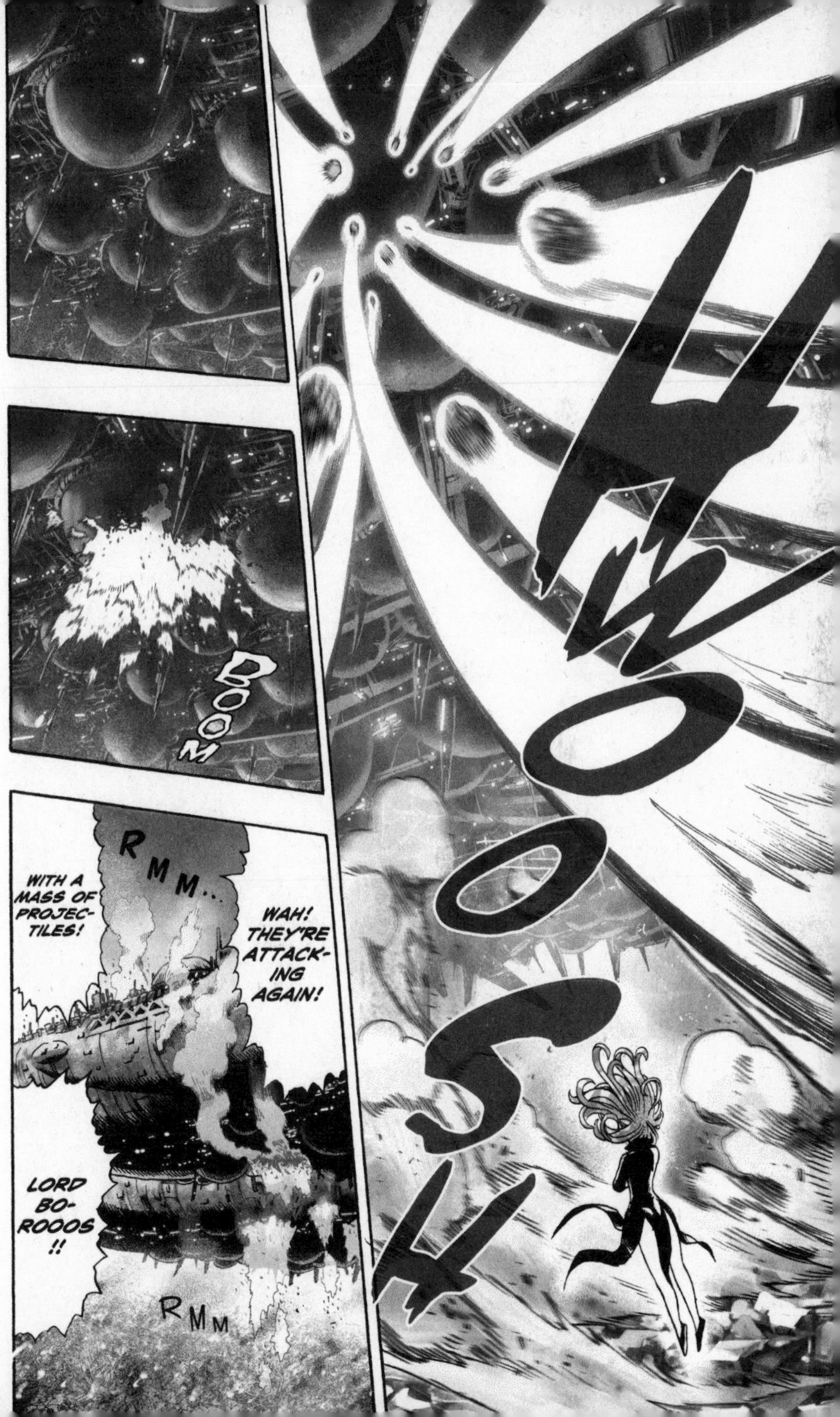

HWOOSH
BOOM
RMM...
WAH! THEY'RE ATTACK-ING AGAIN!
WITH A MASS OF PROJEC-TILES!
LORD BO-ROOOS!!
RMM

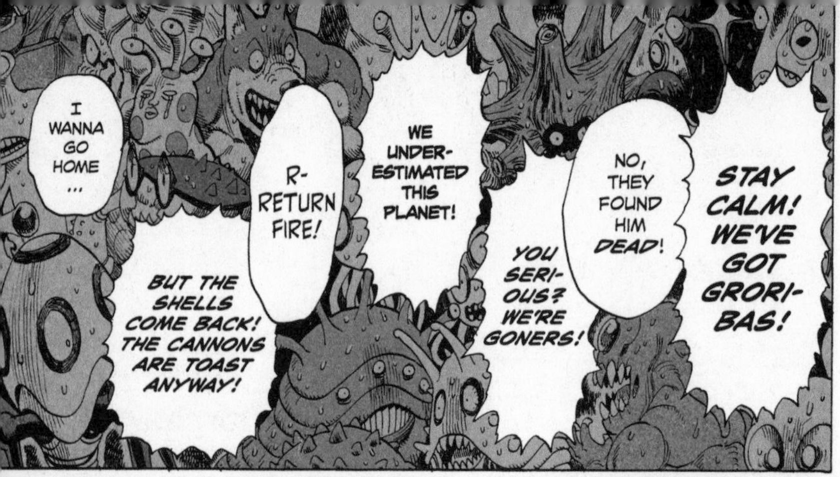
STAY CALM! WE'VE GOT GRORIBAS!
NO, THEY FOUND HIM DEAD!
YOU SERIOUS? WE'RE GONERS!
WE UNDERESTIMATED THIS PLANET!
R-RETURN FIRE!
BUT THE SHELLS COME BACK! THE CANNONS ARE TOAST ANYWAY!
I WANNA GO HOME...

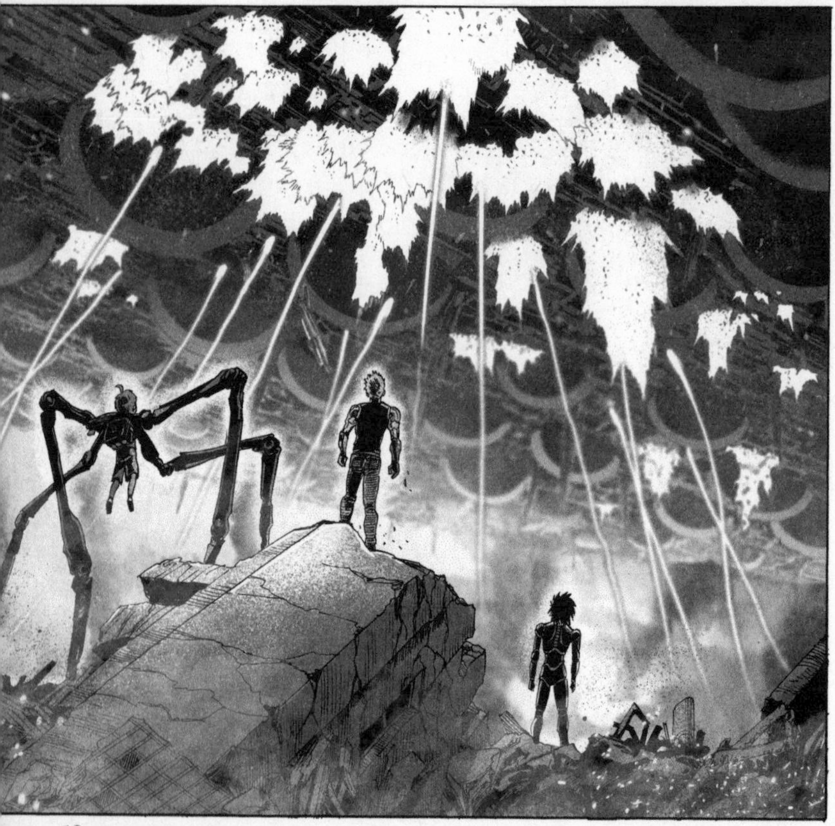

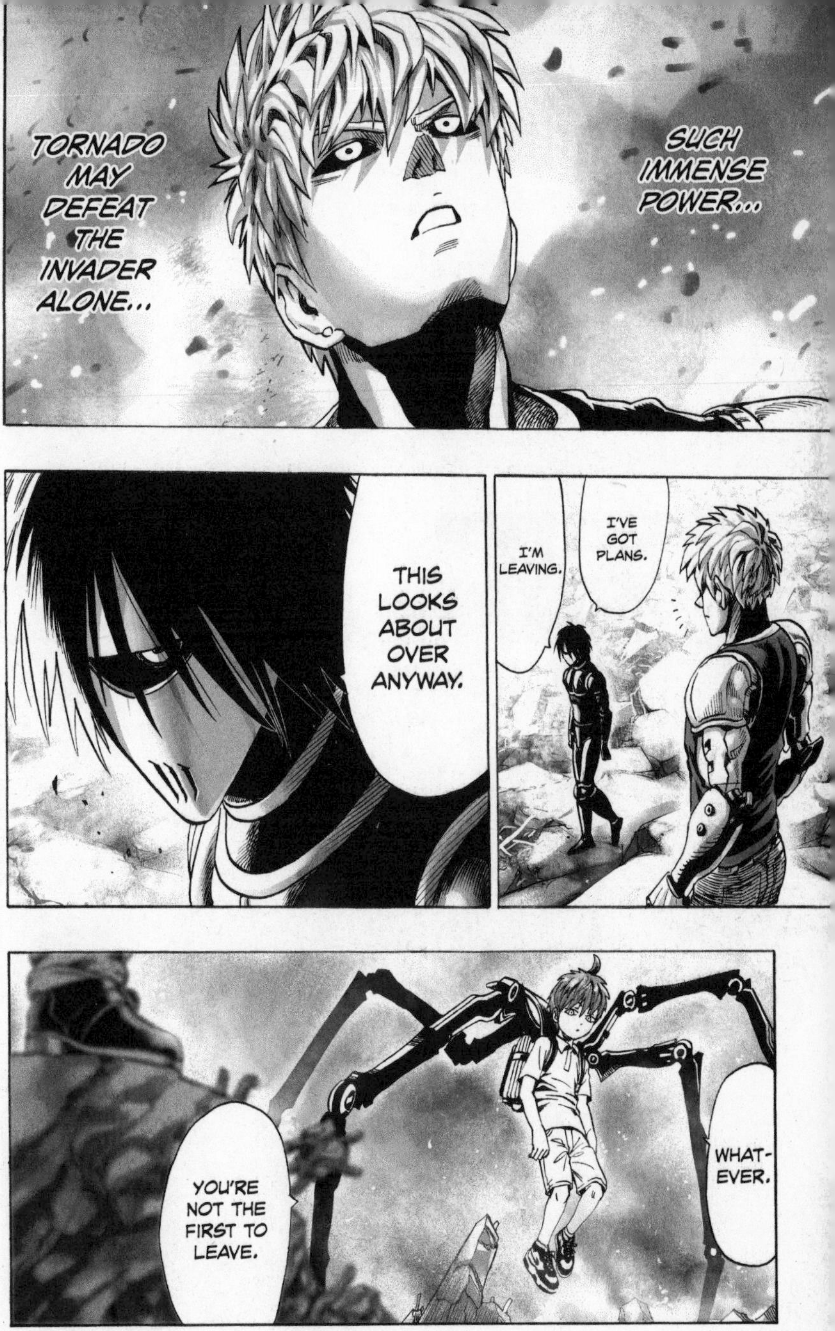
SUCH IMMENSE POWER...
TORNADO MAY DEFEAT THE INVADER ALONE...
I'VE GOT PLANS.
I'M LEAVING.
THIS LOOKS ABOUT OVER ANYWAY.
WHAT-EVER.
YOU'RE NOT THE FIRST TO LEAVE.

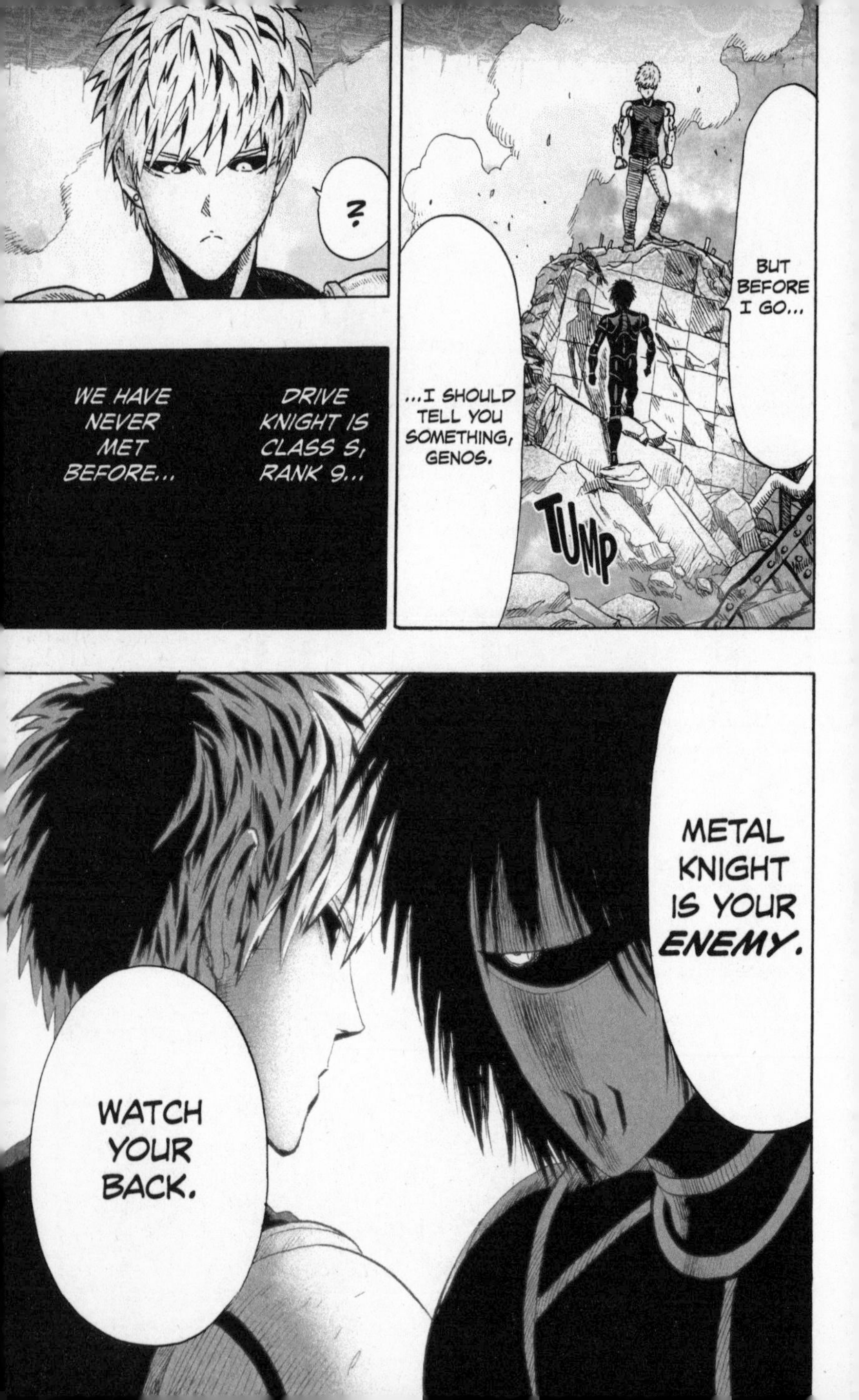
BUT BEFORE I GO...
...I SHOULD TELL YOU SOMETHING, GENOS.
TUMP
?
DRIVE KNIGHT IS CLASS S, RANK 9...
WE HAVE NEVER MET BEFORE...
METAL KNIGHT IS YOUR ENEMY.
WATCH YOUR BACK.

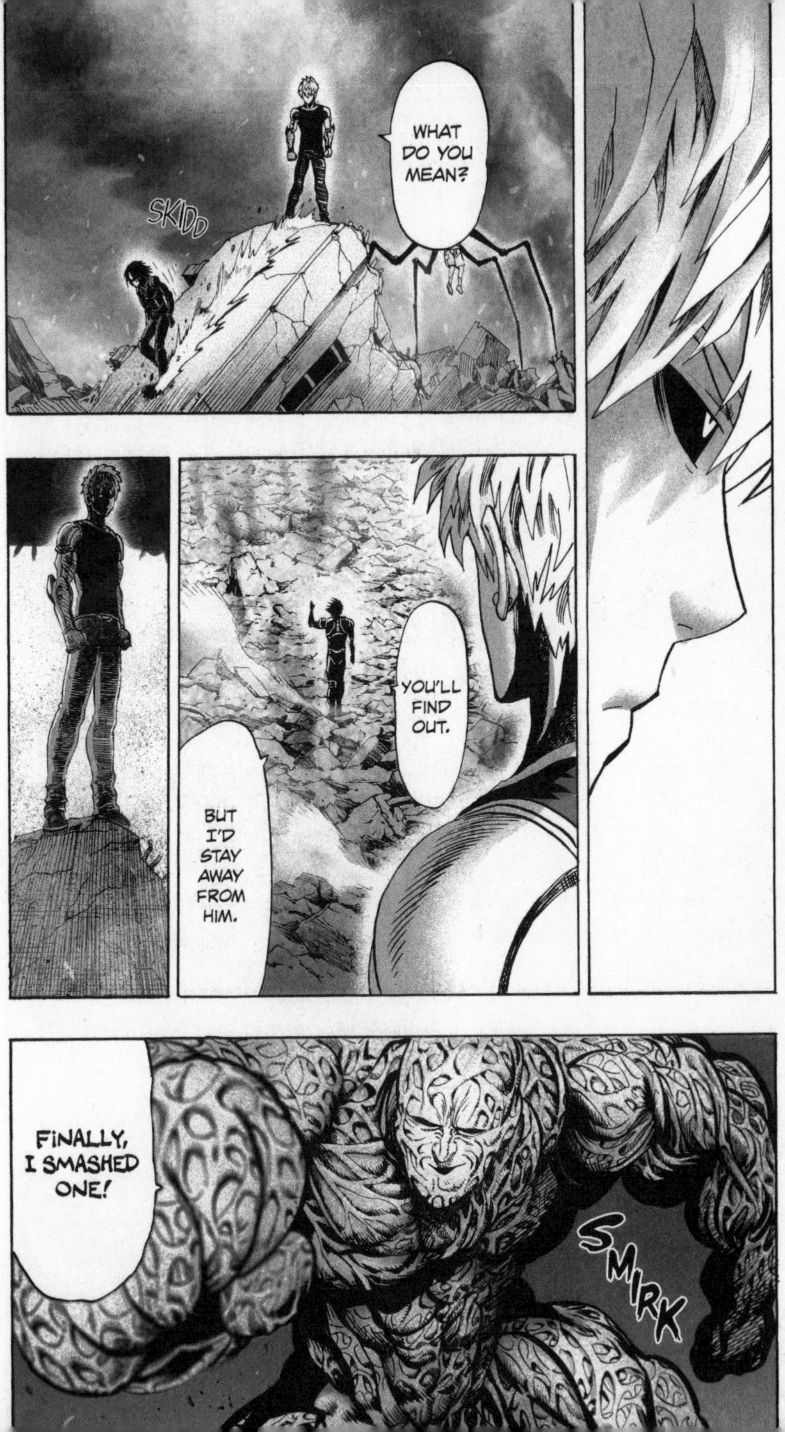
WHAT DO YOU MEAN?
SKIDD
YOU'LL FIND OUT.
BUT I'D STAY AWAY FROM HIM.
FINALLY, I SMASHED ONE!
SMIRK

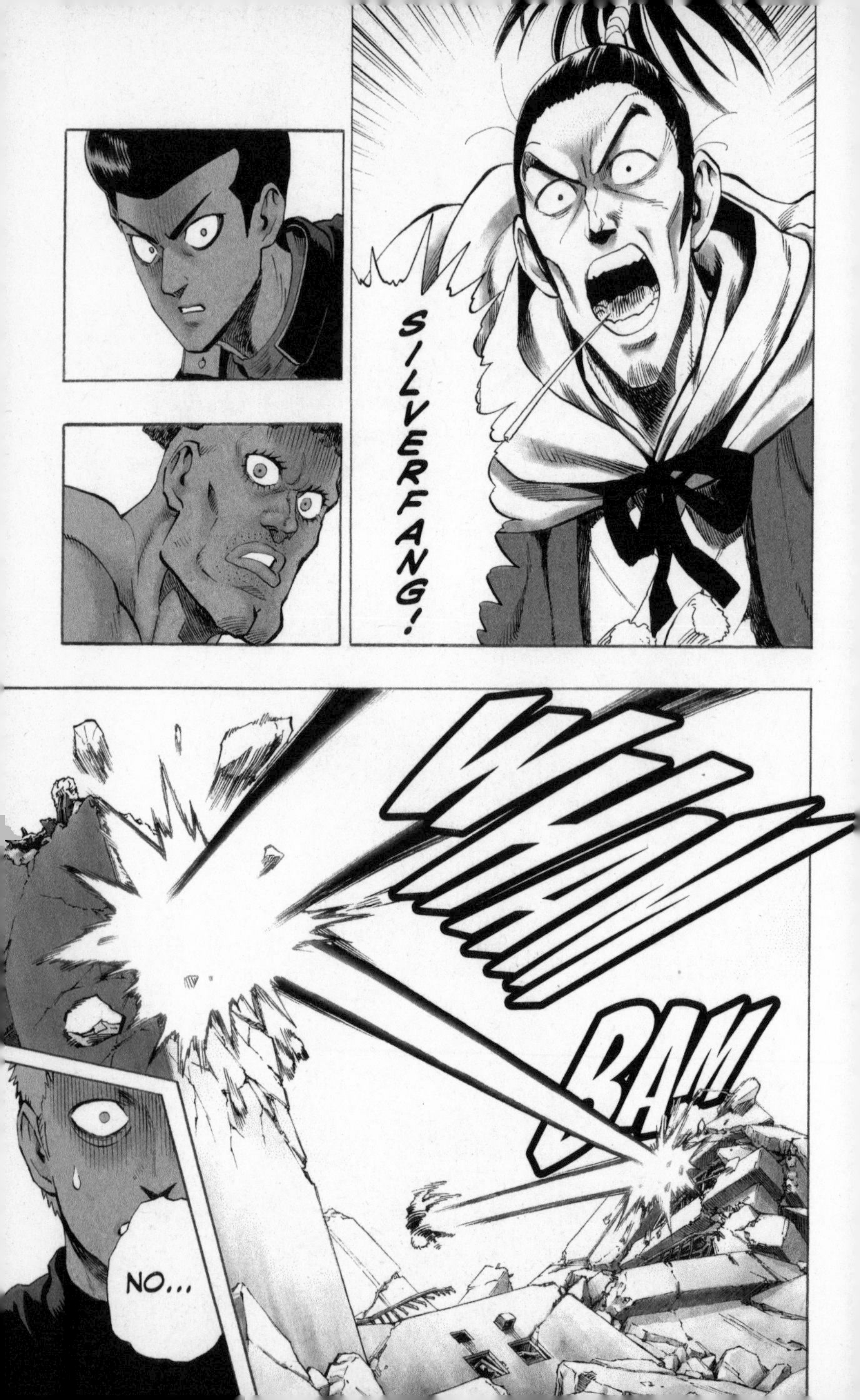
SILVERFANG!
WHAM
BAM
NO...

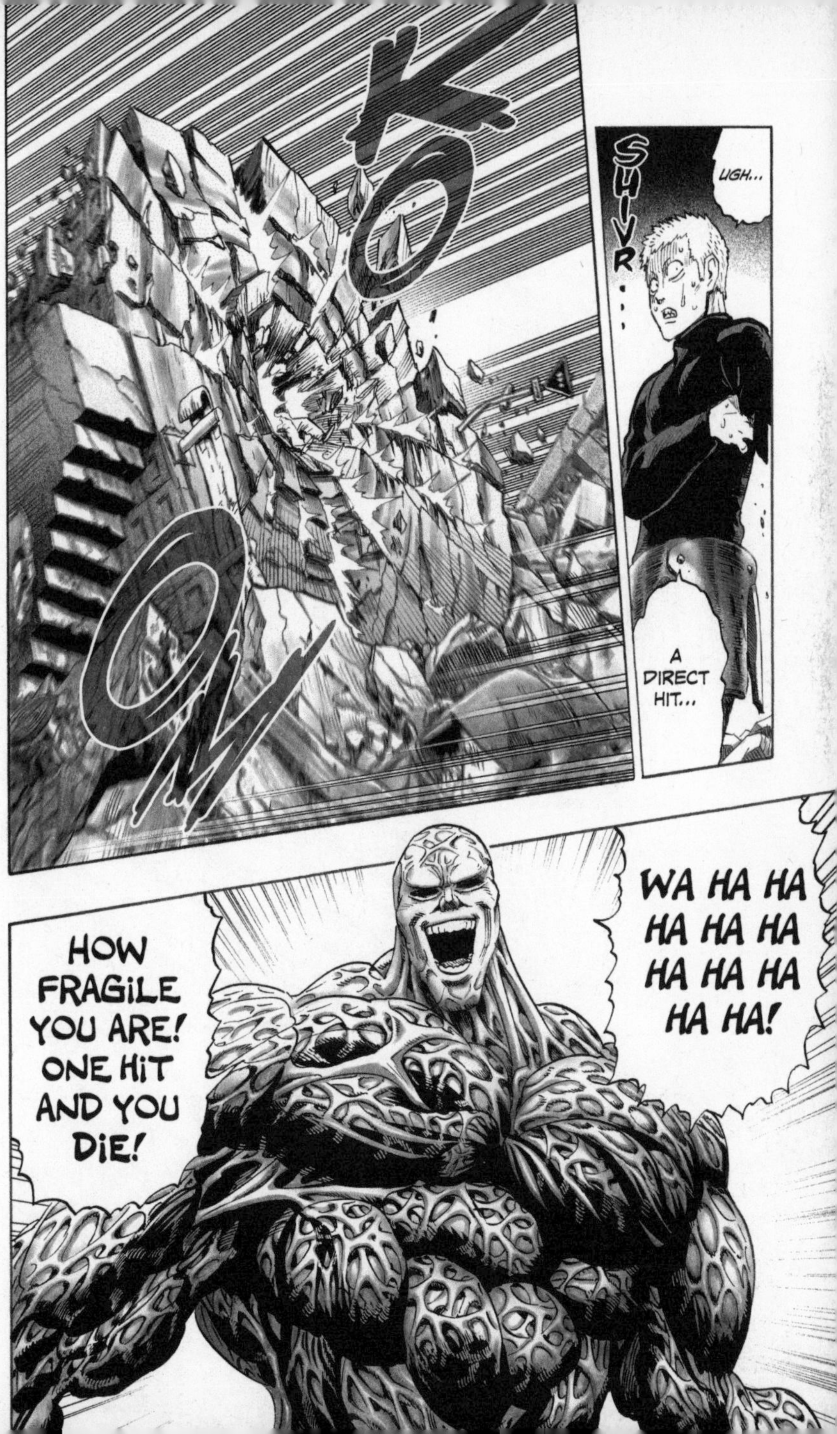
SHIVR...
UGH...
A DIRECT HIT...
KOOM
WA HA HA HA HA HA HA HA HA HA HA!
HOW FRAGILE YOU ARE! ONE HIT AND YOU DIE!

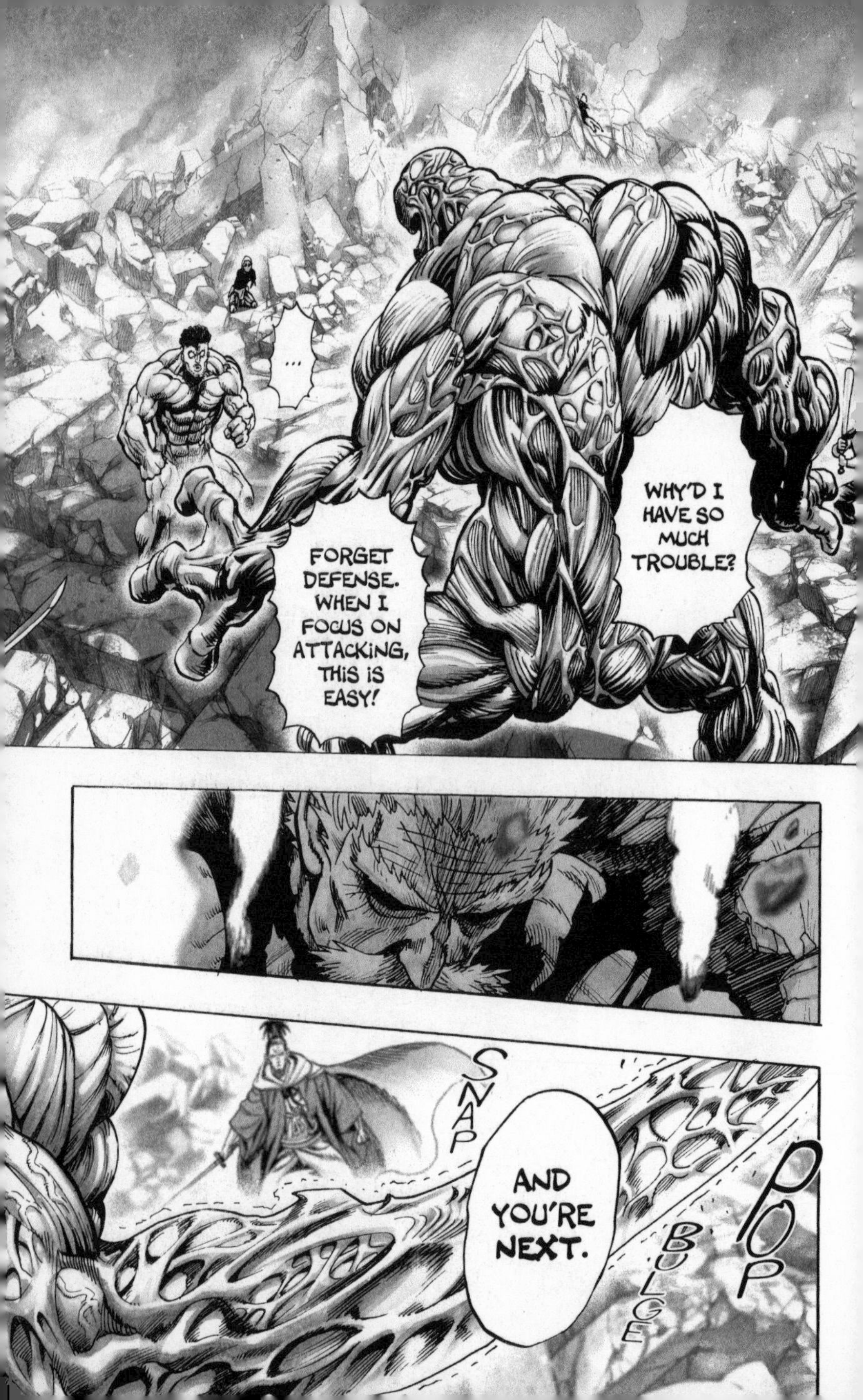
WHY'D I HAVE SO MUCH TROUBLE?
FORGET DEFENSE. WHEN I FOCUS ON ATTACKING, THIS IS EASY!
...
POP
BULGE
SNAP
AND YOU'RE NEXT.

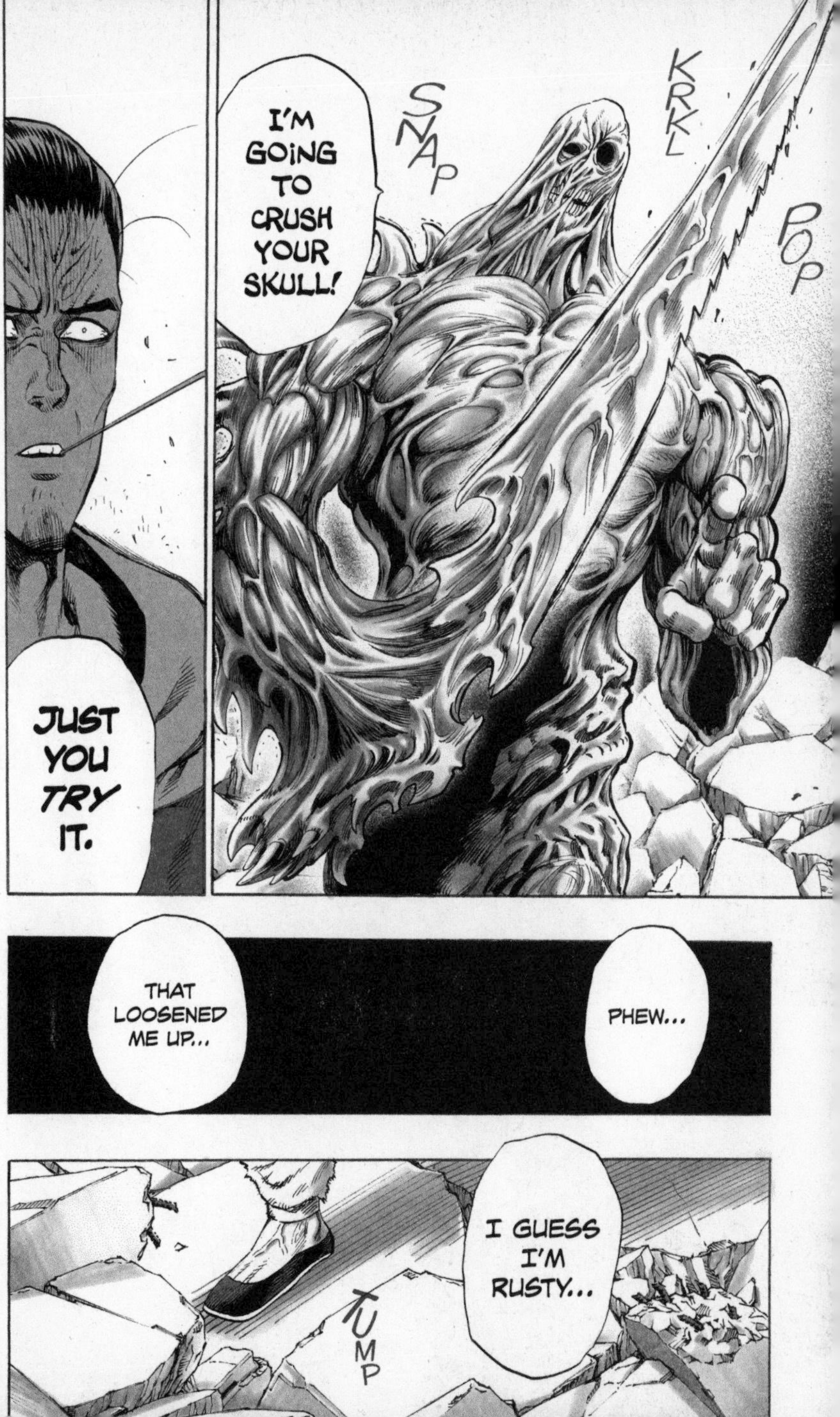
KRKL
POP
SNAP
I'M GOING TO CRUSH YOUR SKULL!
JUST YOU TRY IT.
PHEW...
THAT LOOSENED ME UP...
I GUESS I'M RUSTY...
TUMP

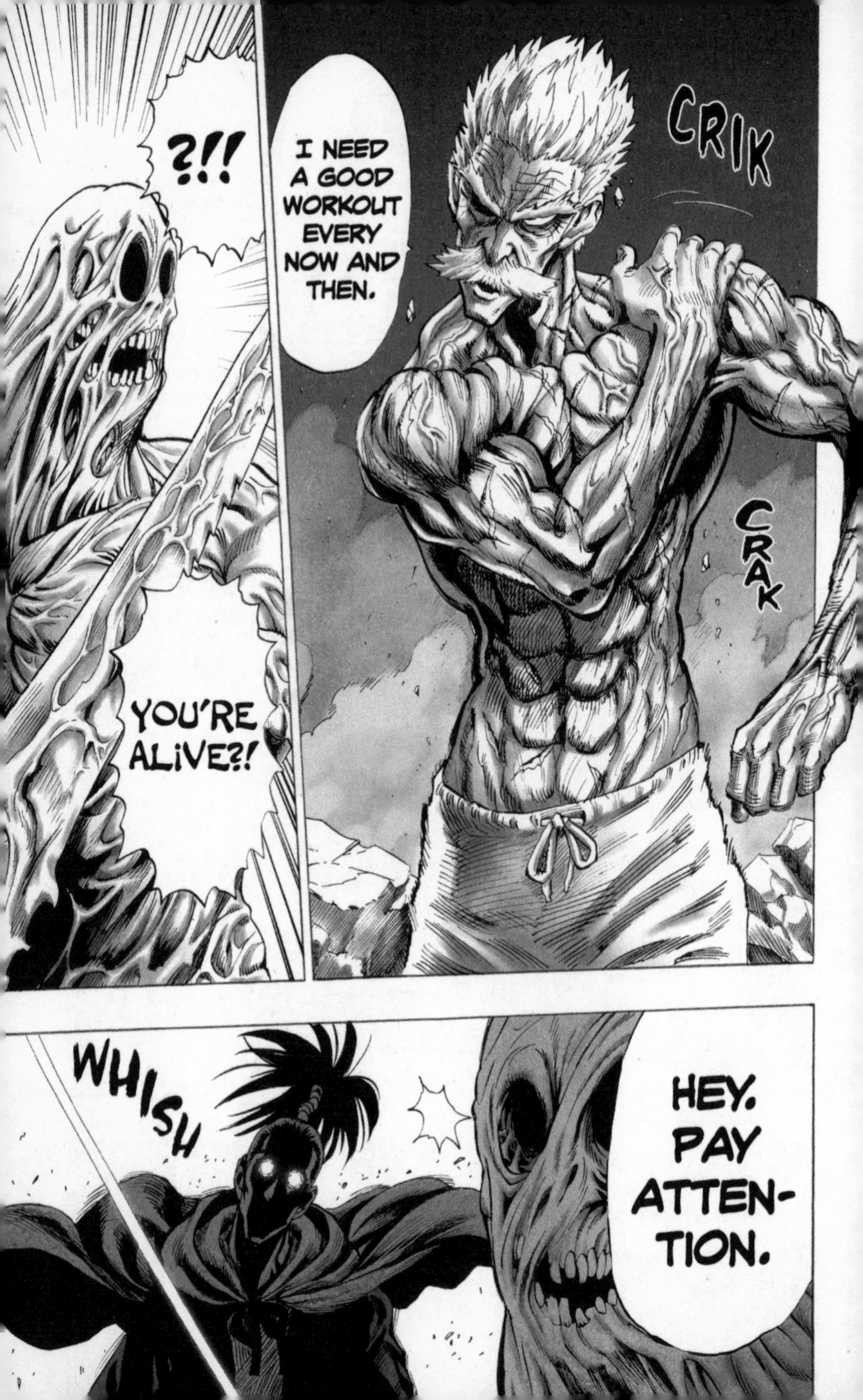
CRIK
I NEED A GOOD WORKOUT EVERY NOW AND THEN.
CRAK
?!!
YOU'RE ALiVE?!
HEY. PAY ATTEN-TION.
WHISH

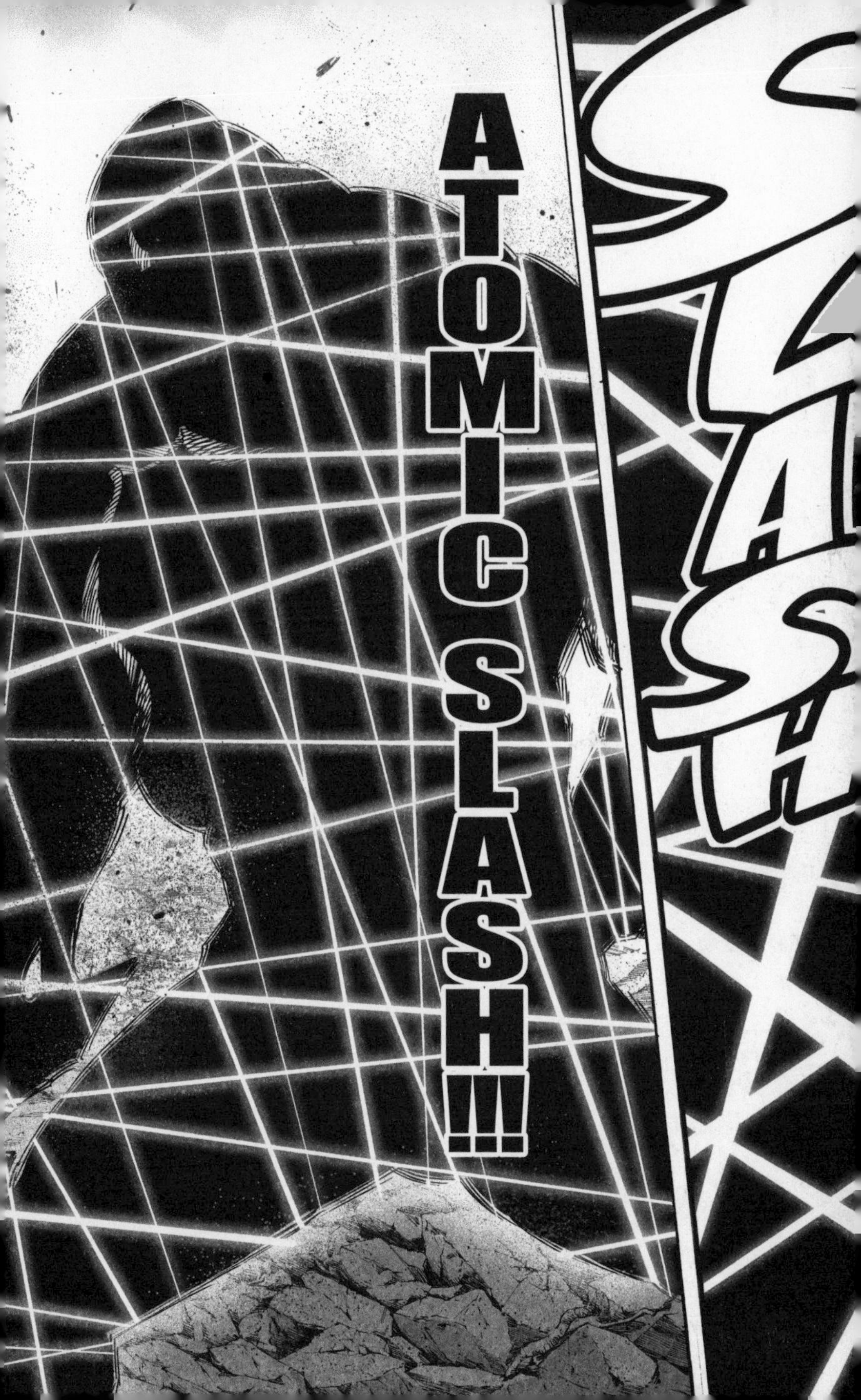
ATOMIC SLASH!!!

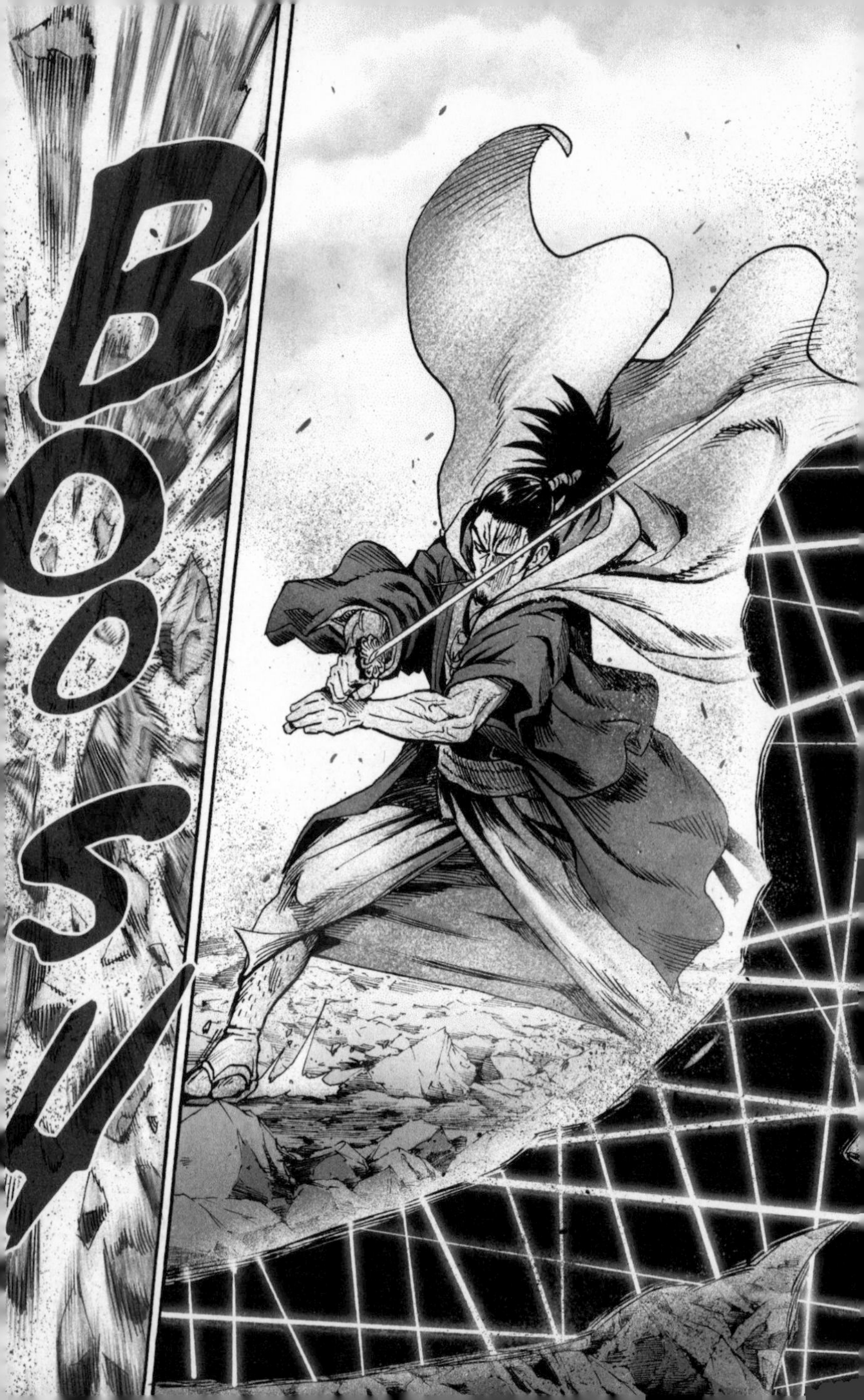
BOOSH

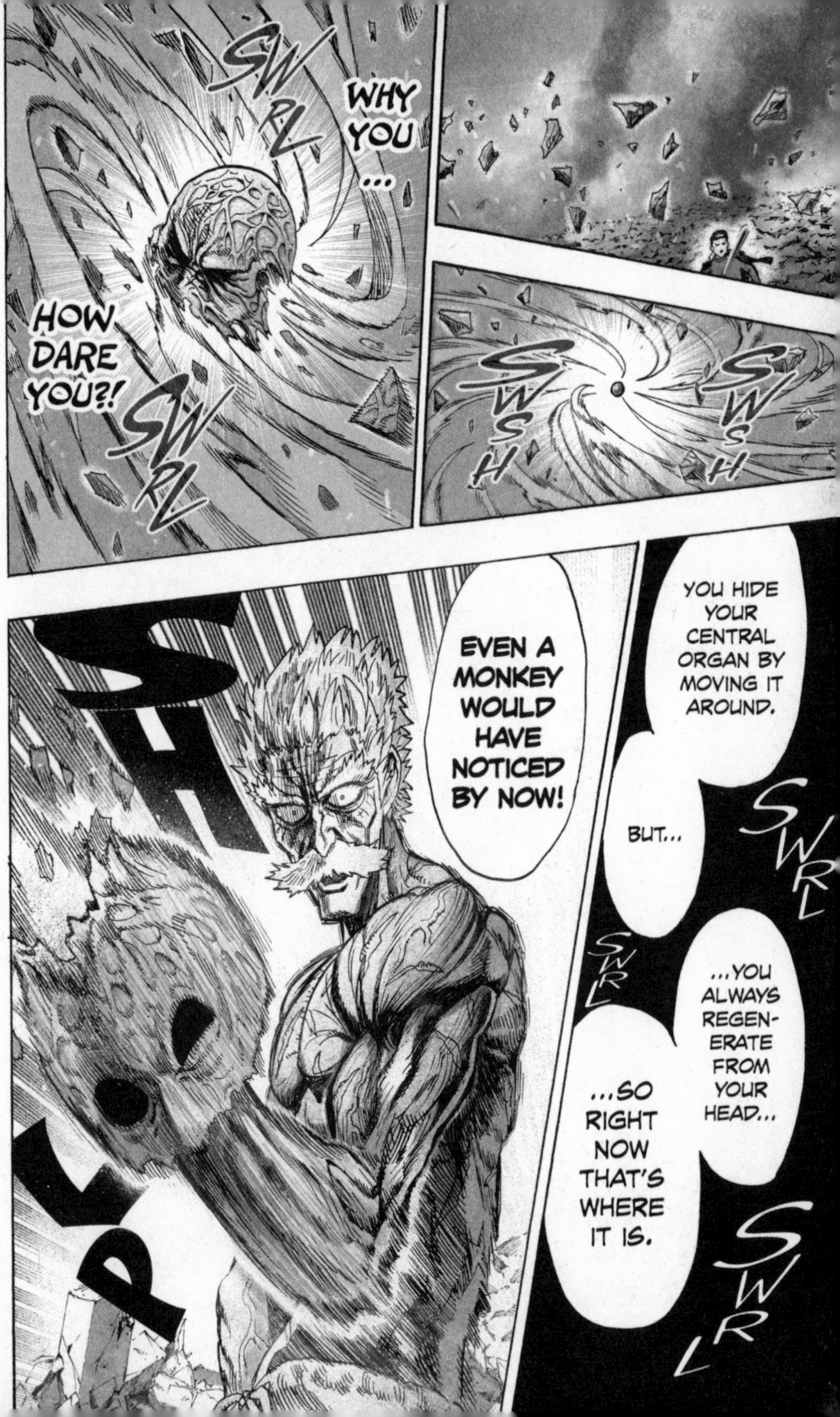
SWSH
SWSH
SWRL
WHY YOU...
HOW DARE YOU?!
SWRL
YOU HIDE YOUR CENTRAL ORGAN BY MOVING IT AROUND.
BUT...
SWRL
...YOU ALWAYS REGEN-ERATE FROM YOUR HEAD...
SWRL
...SO RIGHT NOW THAT'S WHERE IT IS.
SWRL
EVEN A MONKEY WOULD HAVE NOTICED BY NOW!

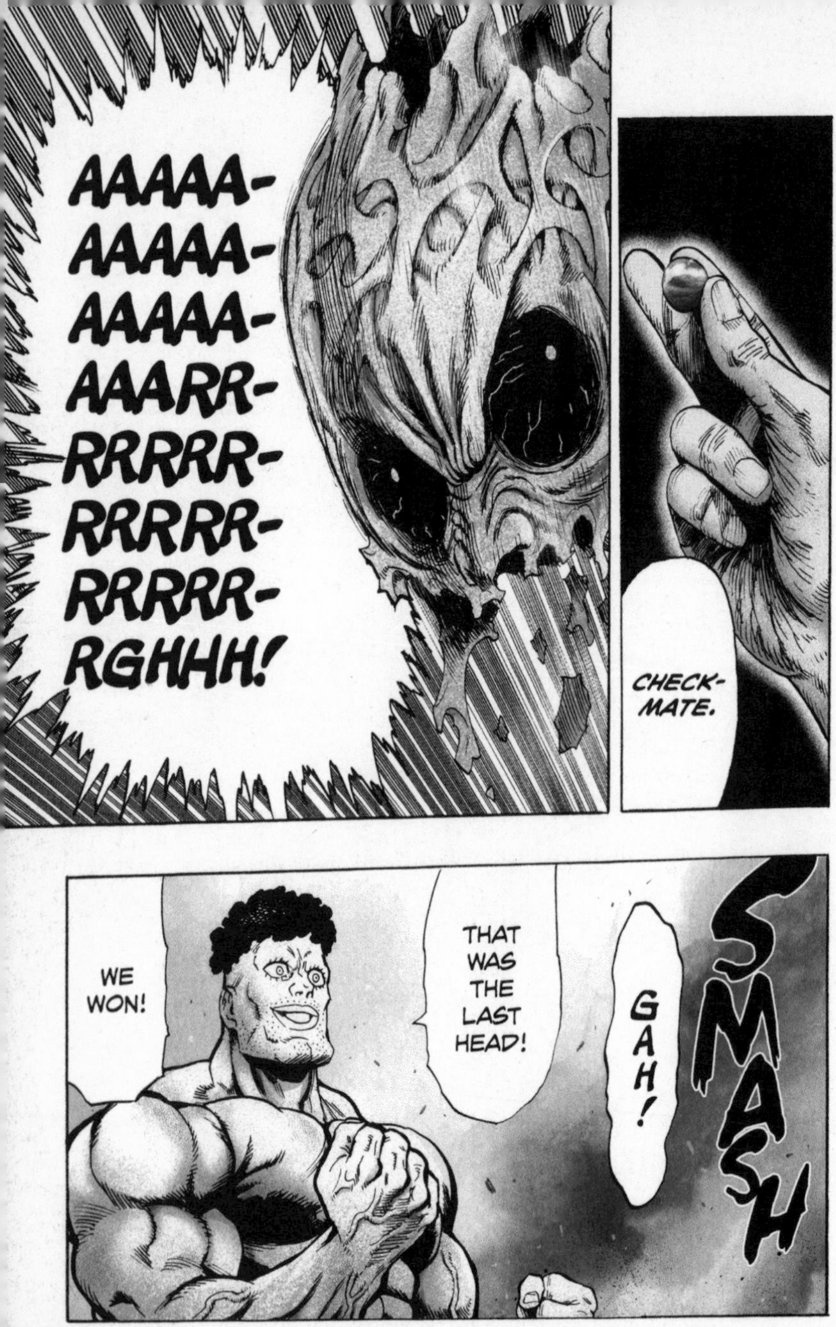
CHECK-MATE.
AAAAA-AAAAA-AAAAA-AAARR-RRRRR-RRRRR-RRRRR-RGHHH!
SMASH
GAH!
THAT WAS THE LAST HEAD!
WE WON!

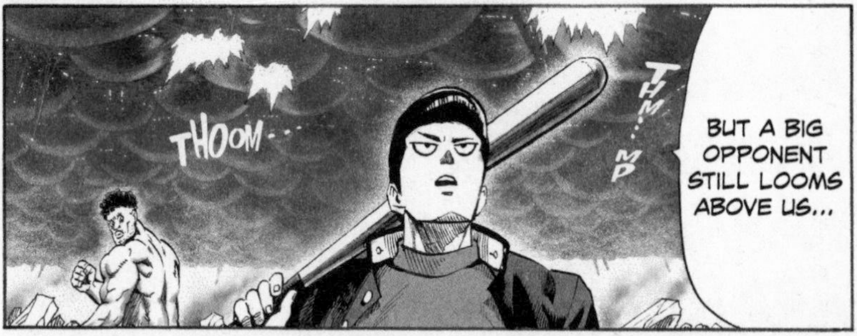
BUT A BIG OPPONENT STILL LOOMS ABOVE US...
THM... MP
THOOM...

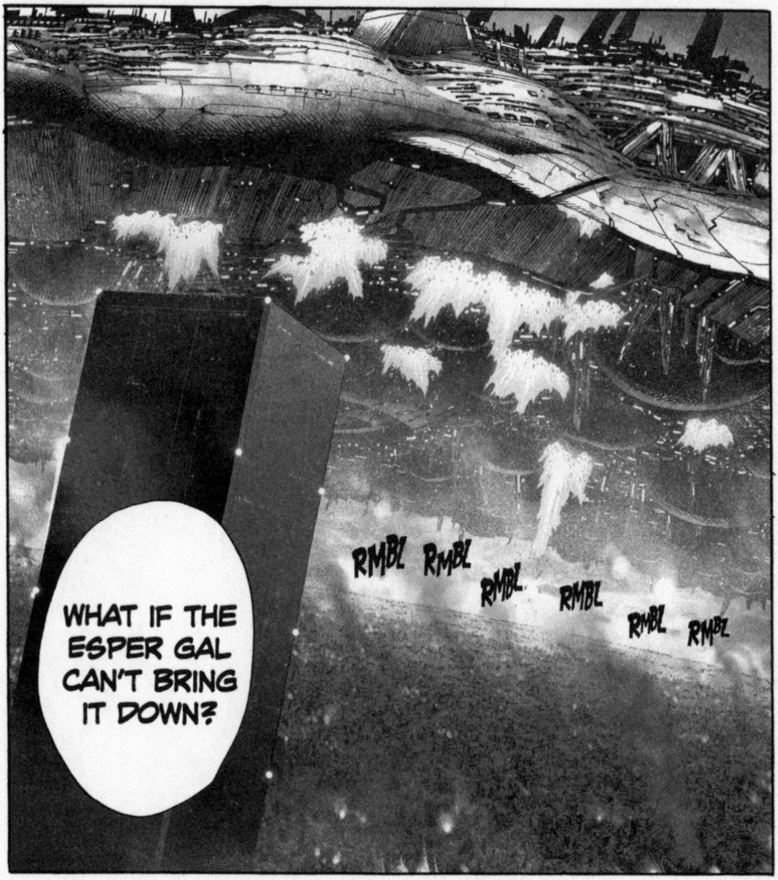
RMBL RMBL RMBL RMBL RMBL RMBL
WHAT IF THE ESPER GAL CAN'T BRING IT DOWN?

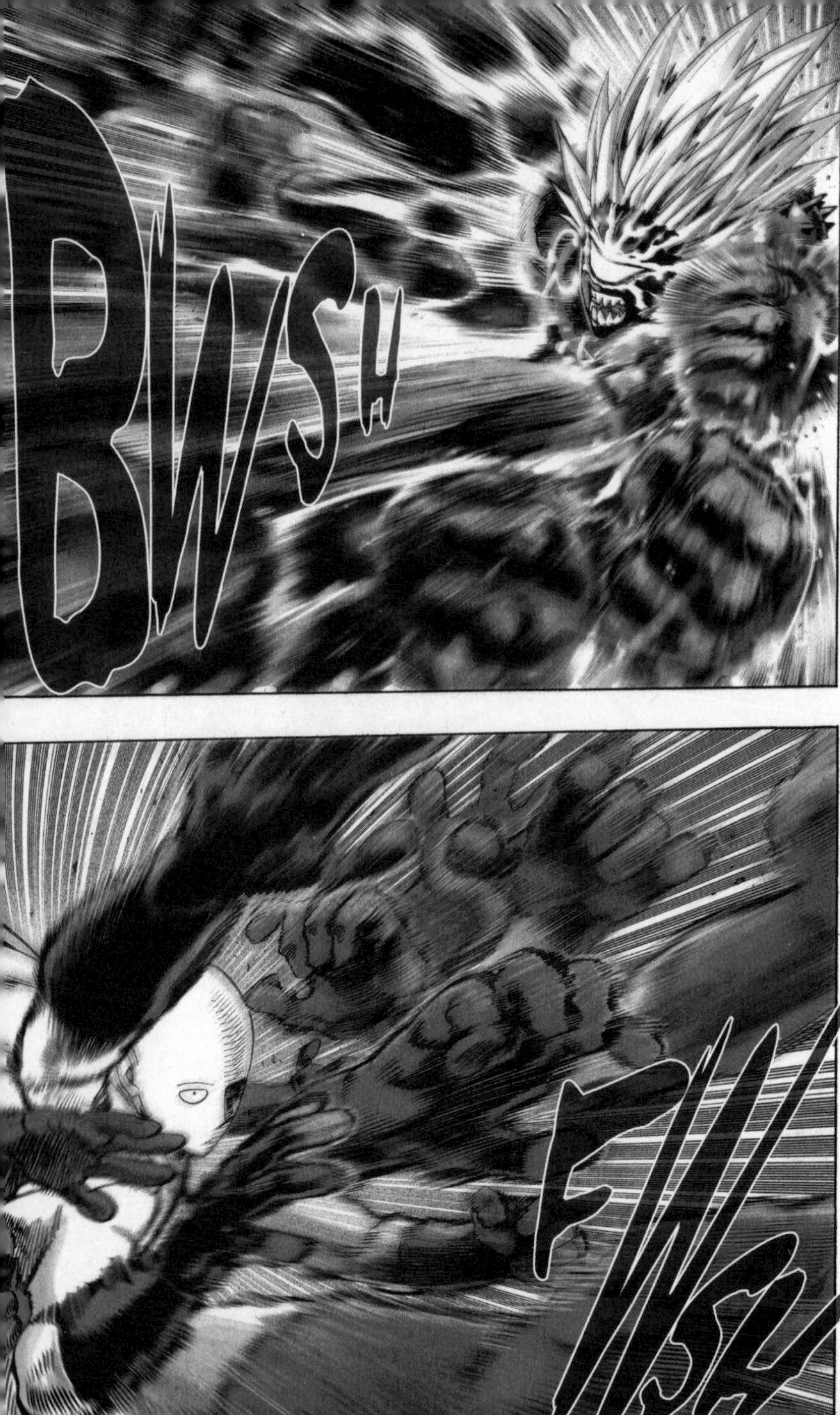
BWSH
FWSH

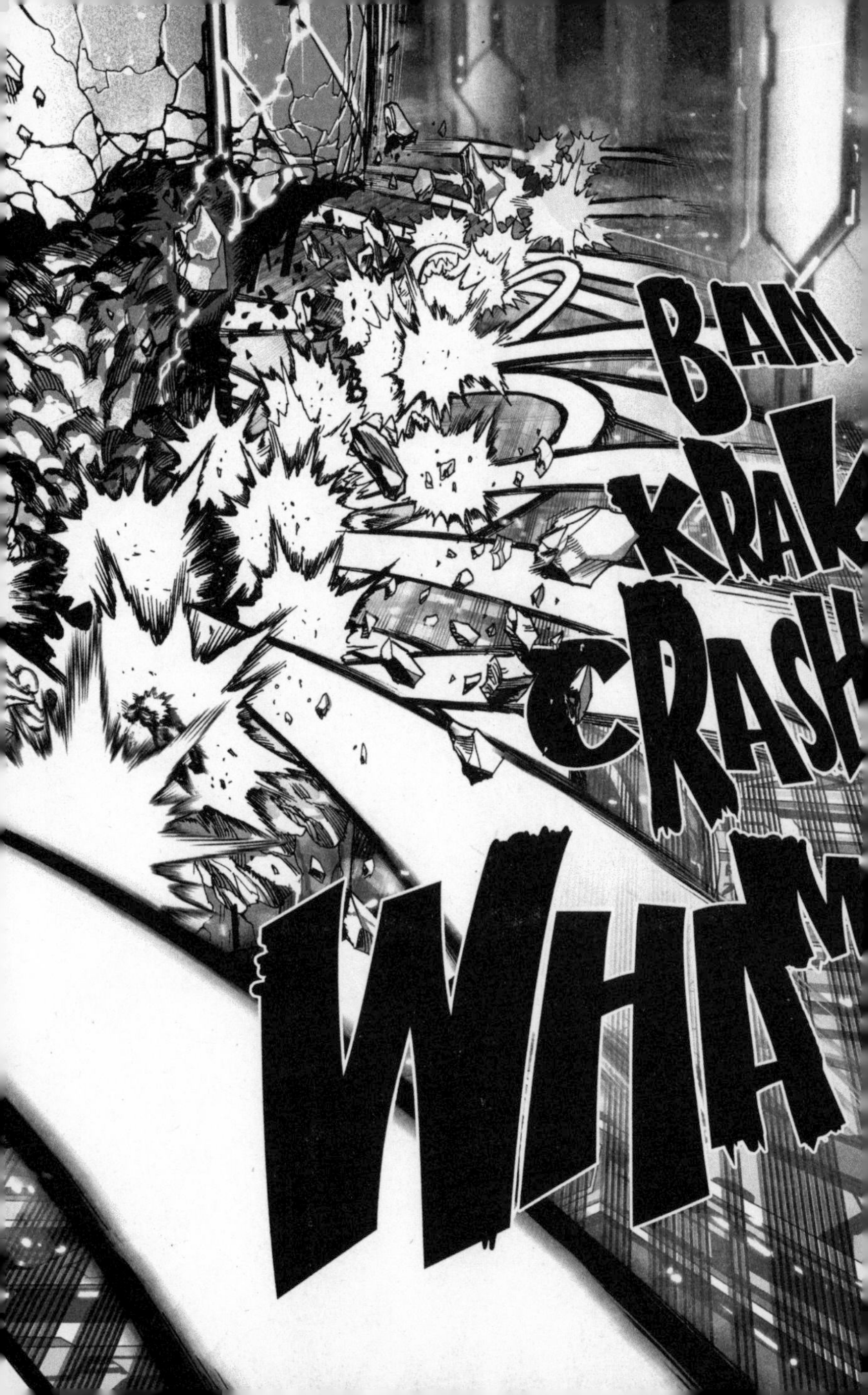
BAM
KRAK
CRASH
WHAM

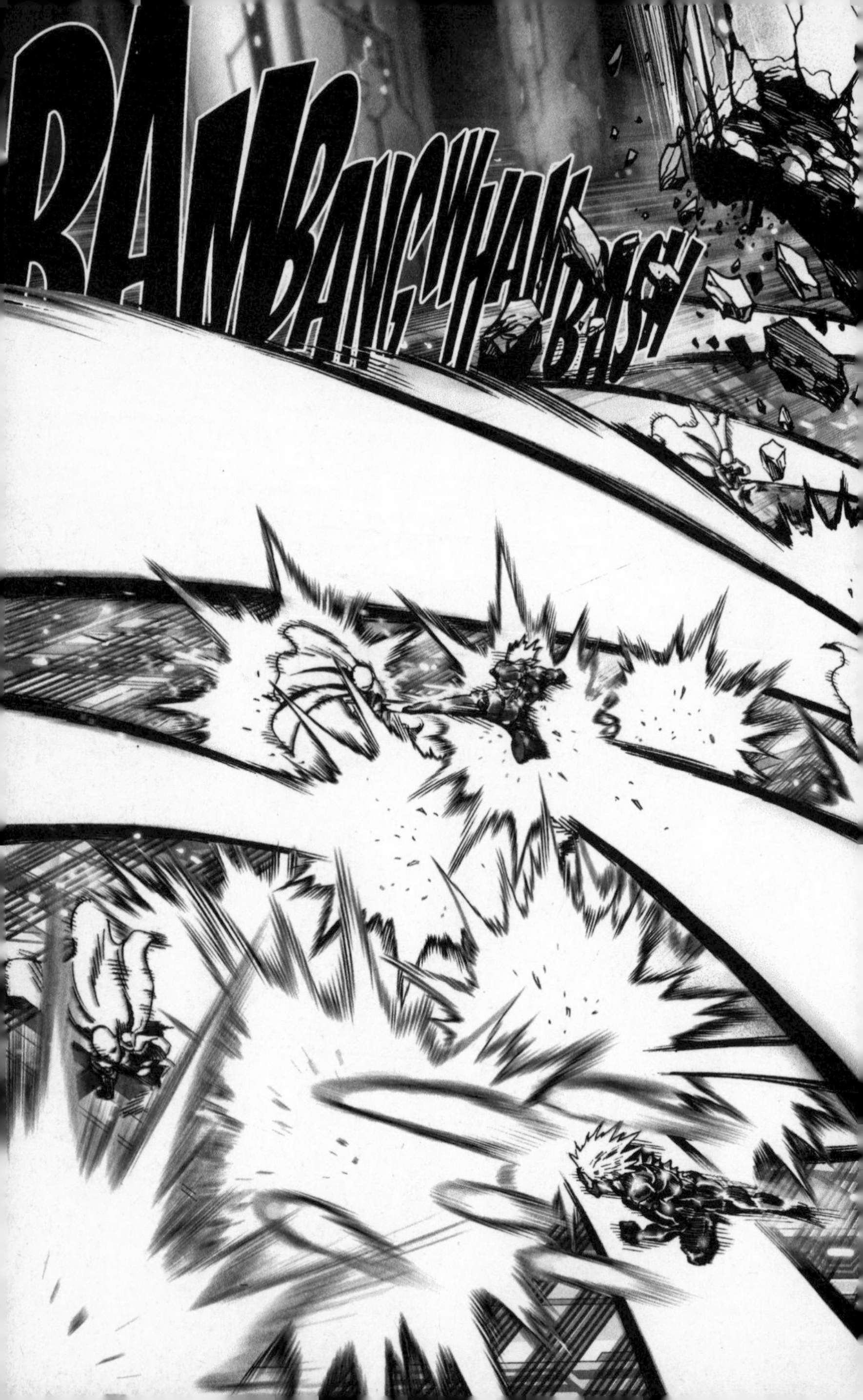
BAM
BANG
BASH

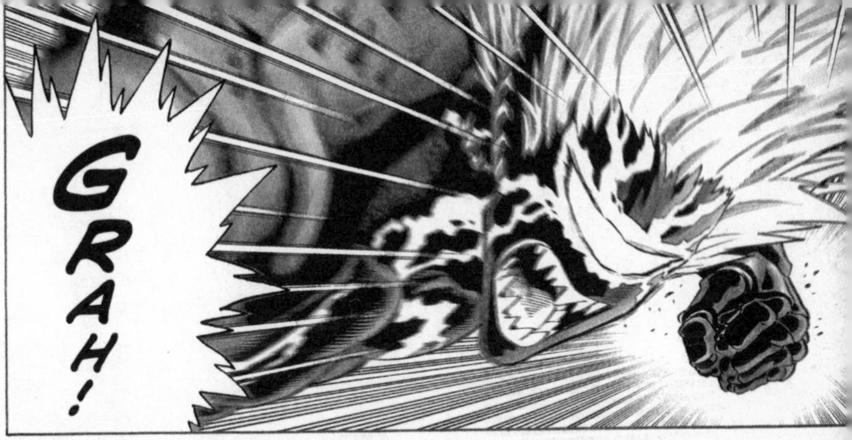
GRAH!

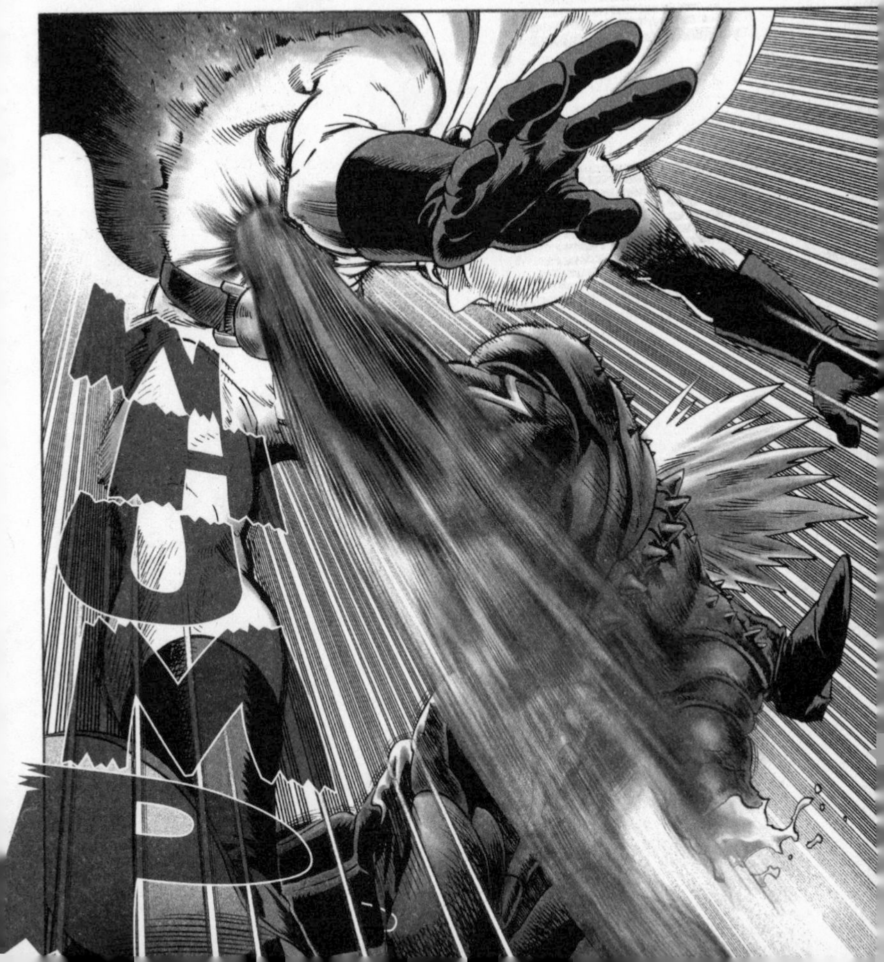
WHUMP

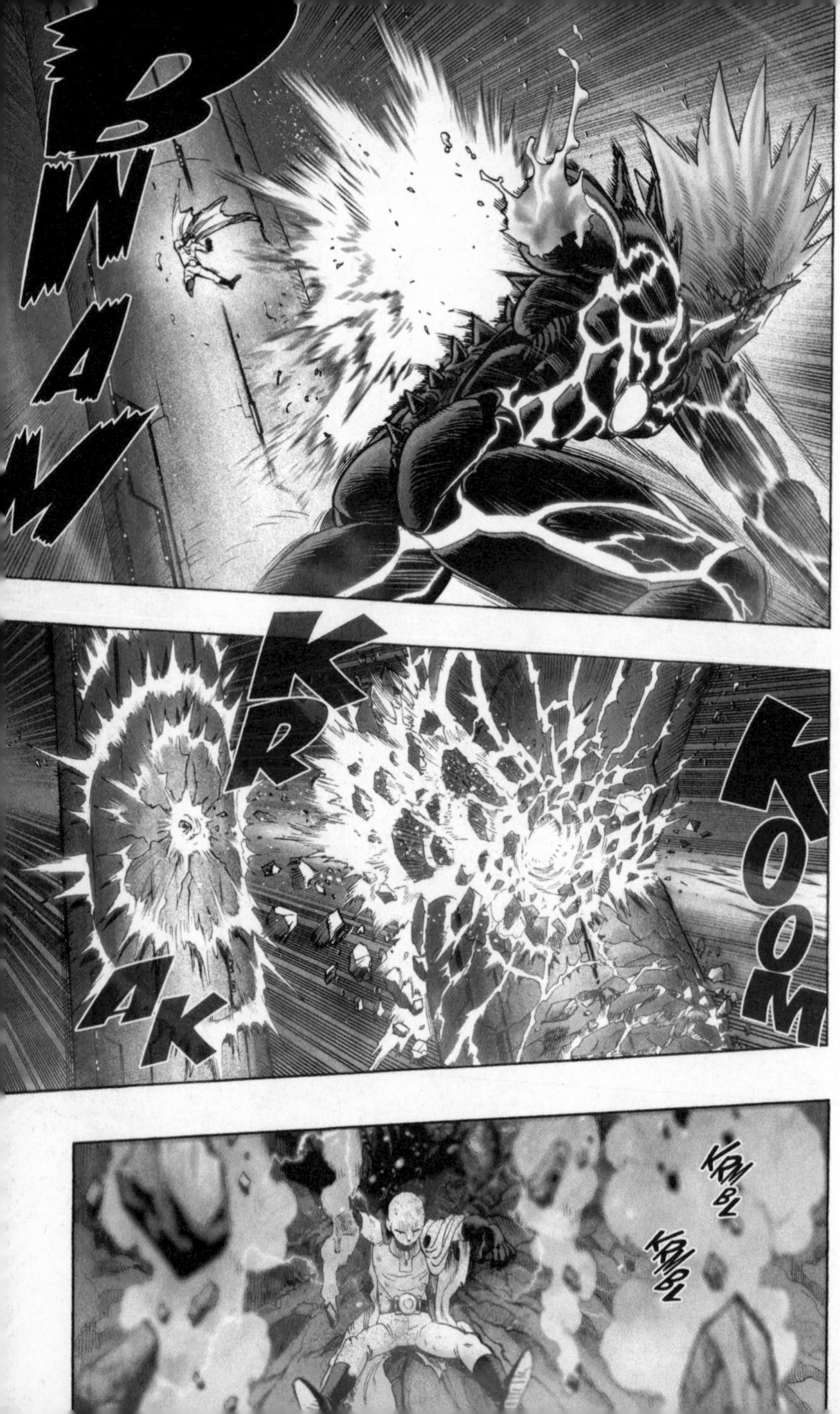
BWAM
KOOM
KRAK
KRMBL
KRMBL

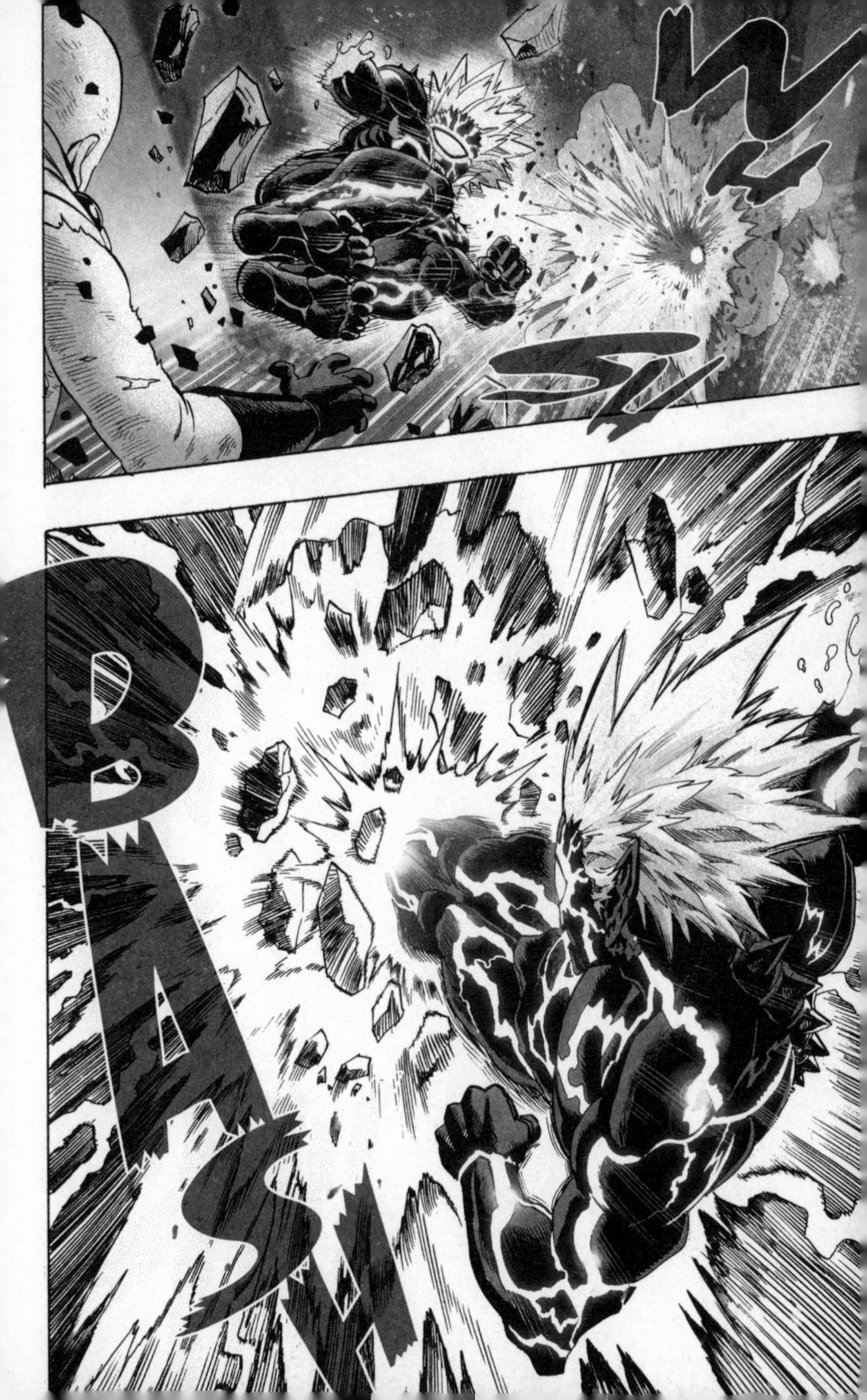
BASH

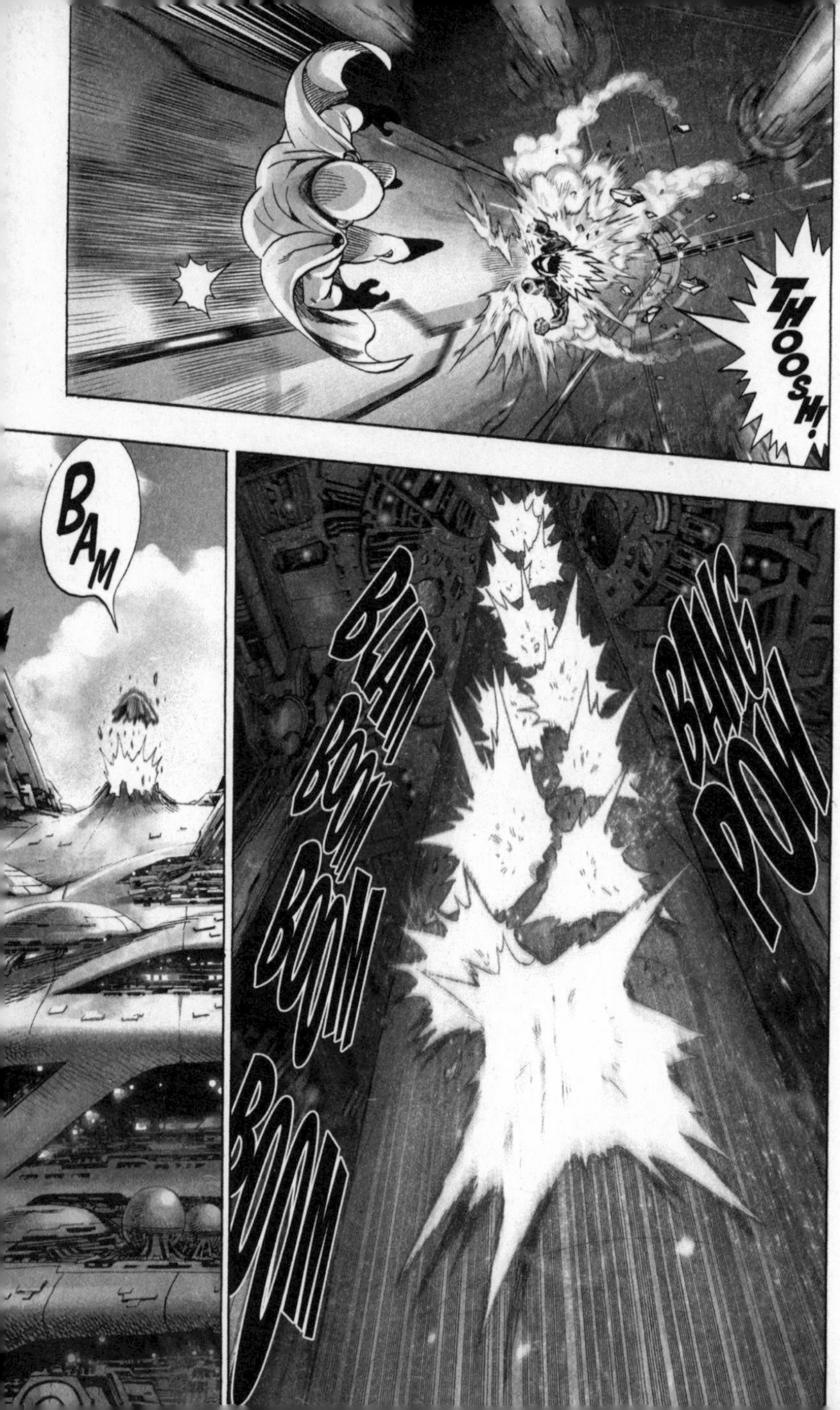
THOOSH!
BANG POW
BLAM BOOM BOOM BOOM
BAM

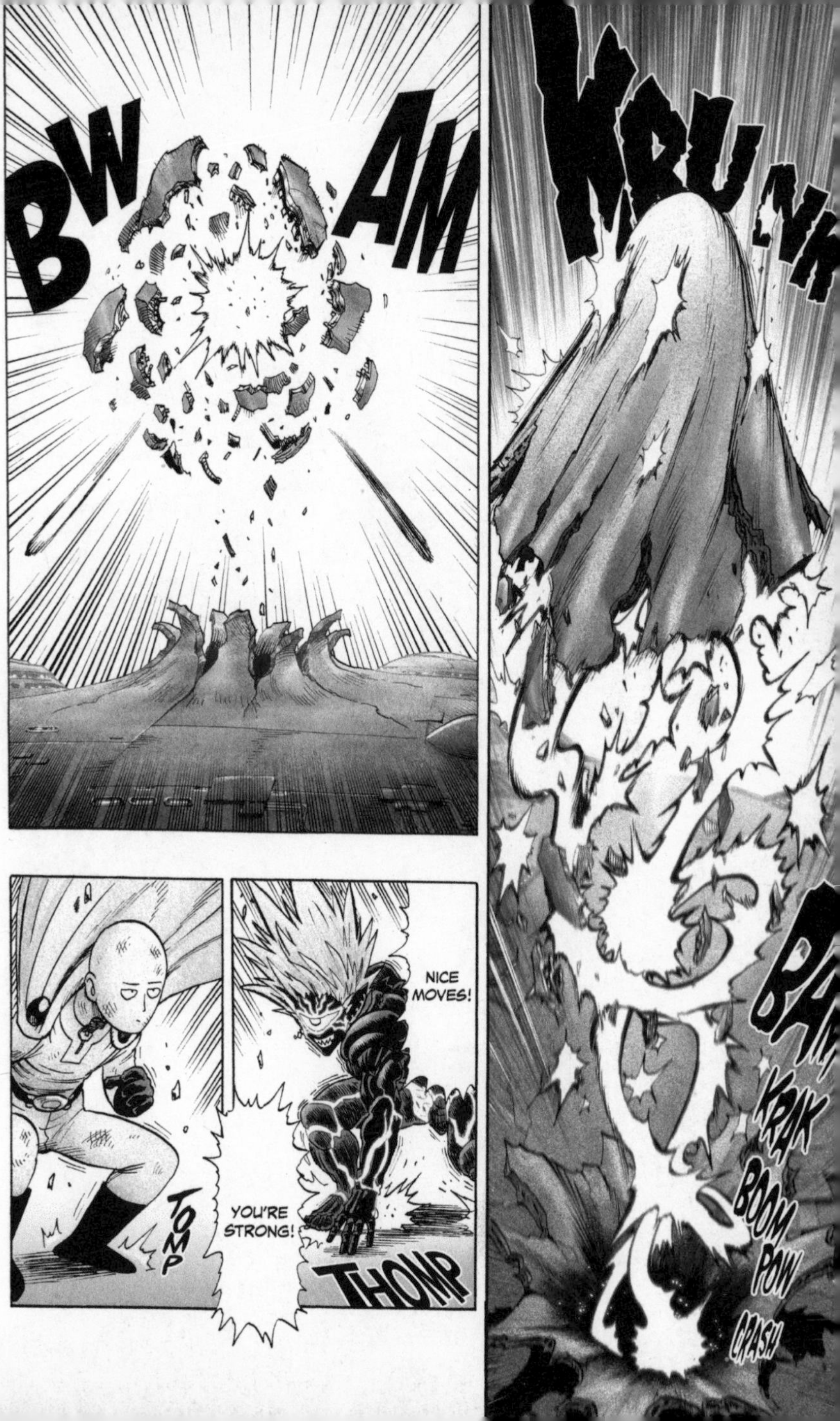
KRUNK
BA
KRAK
BOOM
POW
CRASH
BWAAM
NICE MOVES!
YOU'RE STRONG!
THOMP
TOMP

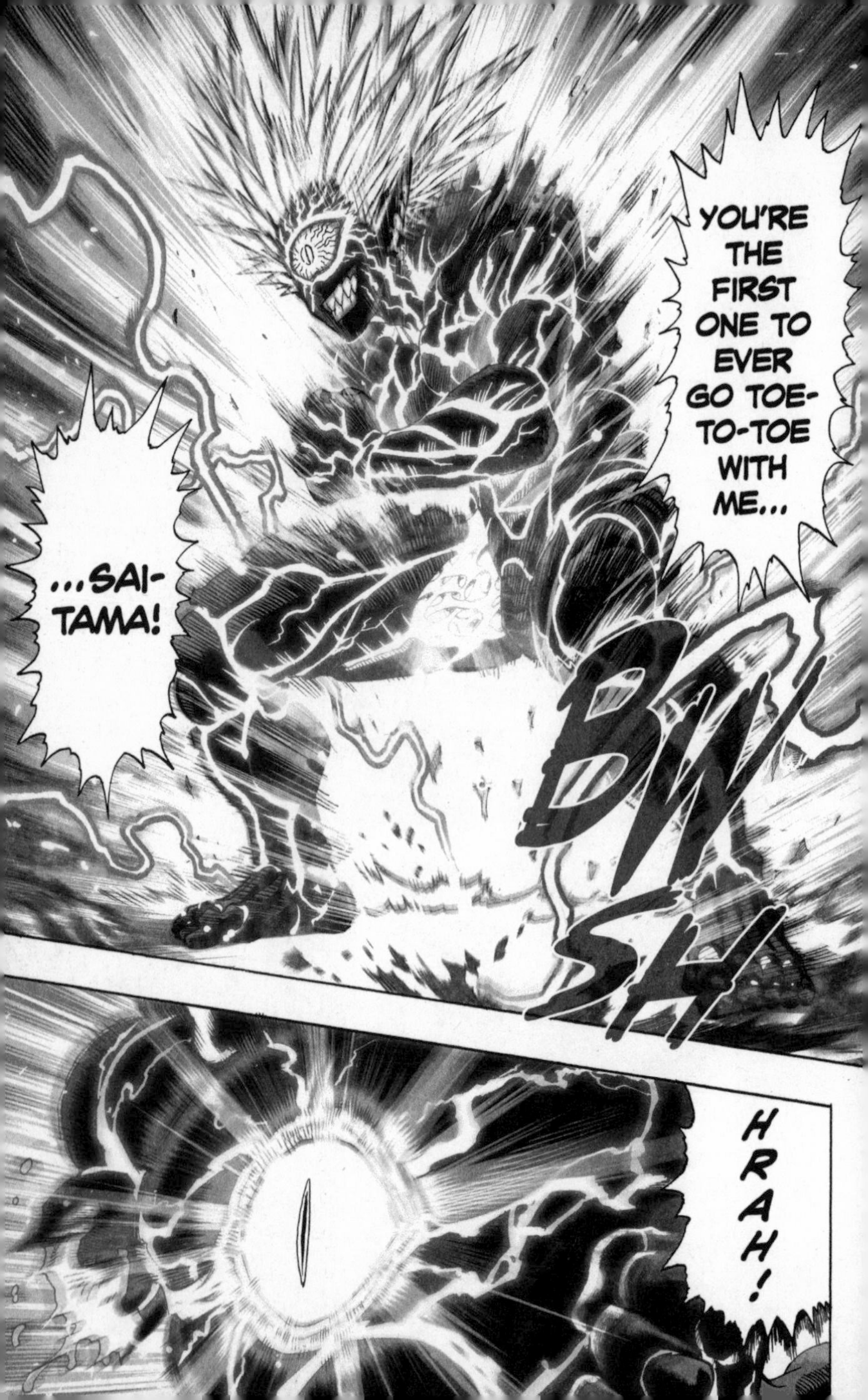
YOU'RE THE FIRST ONE TO EVER GO TOE-TO-TOE WITH ME...
...SAI-TAMA!
BWSH
HRAH!

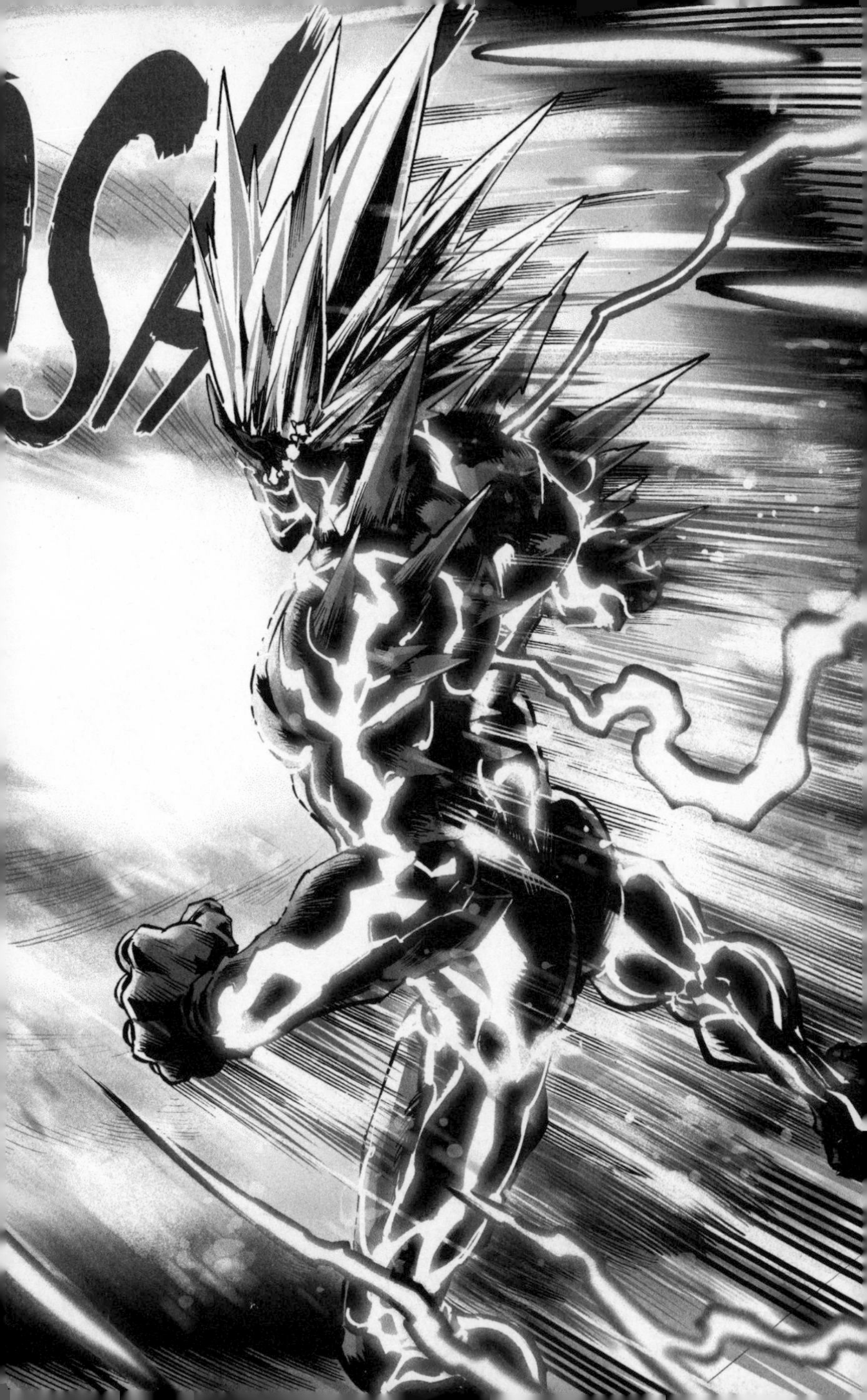

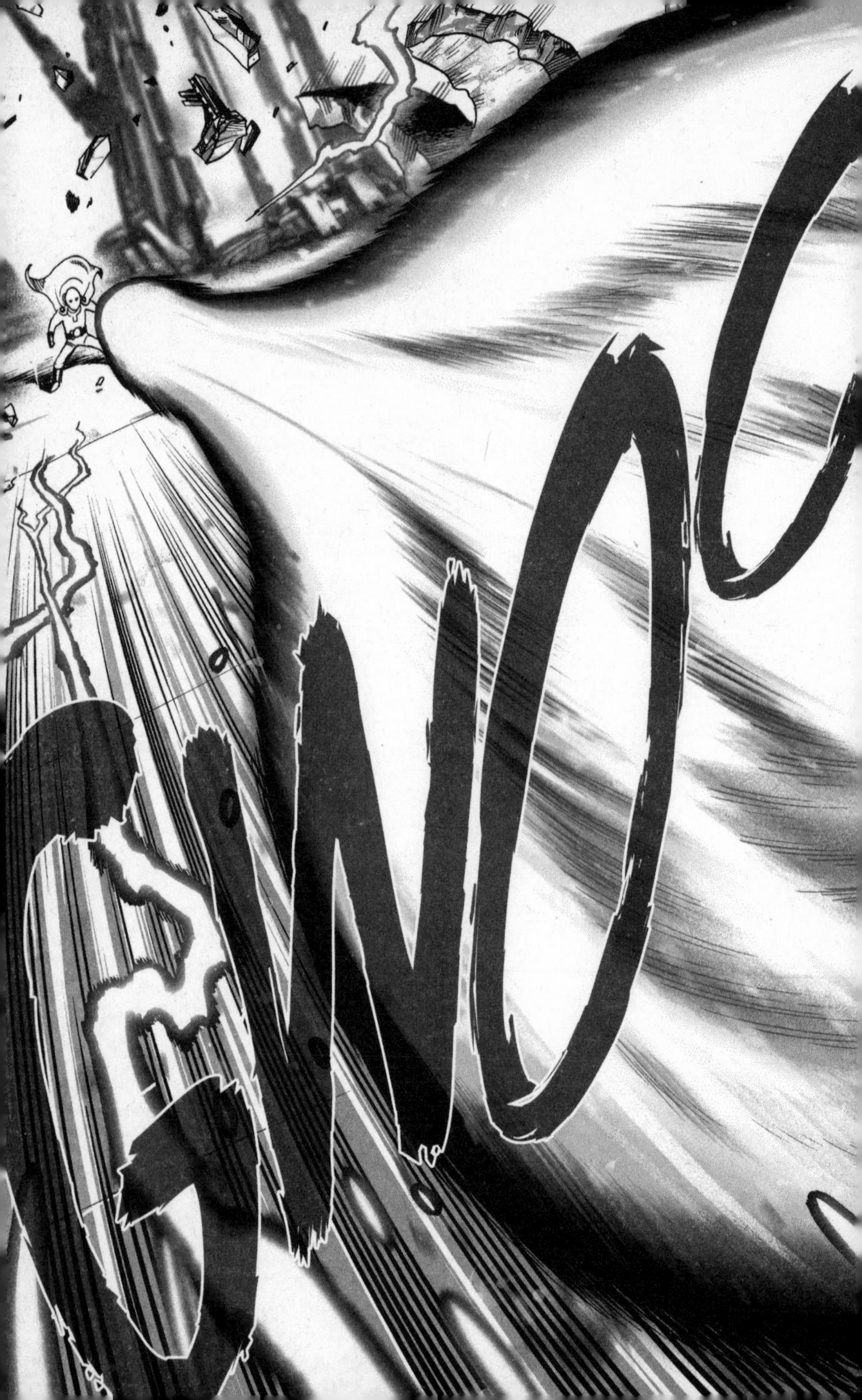

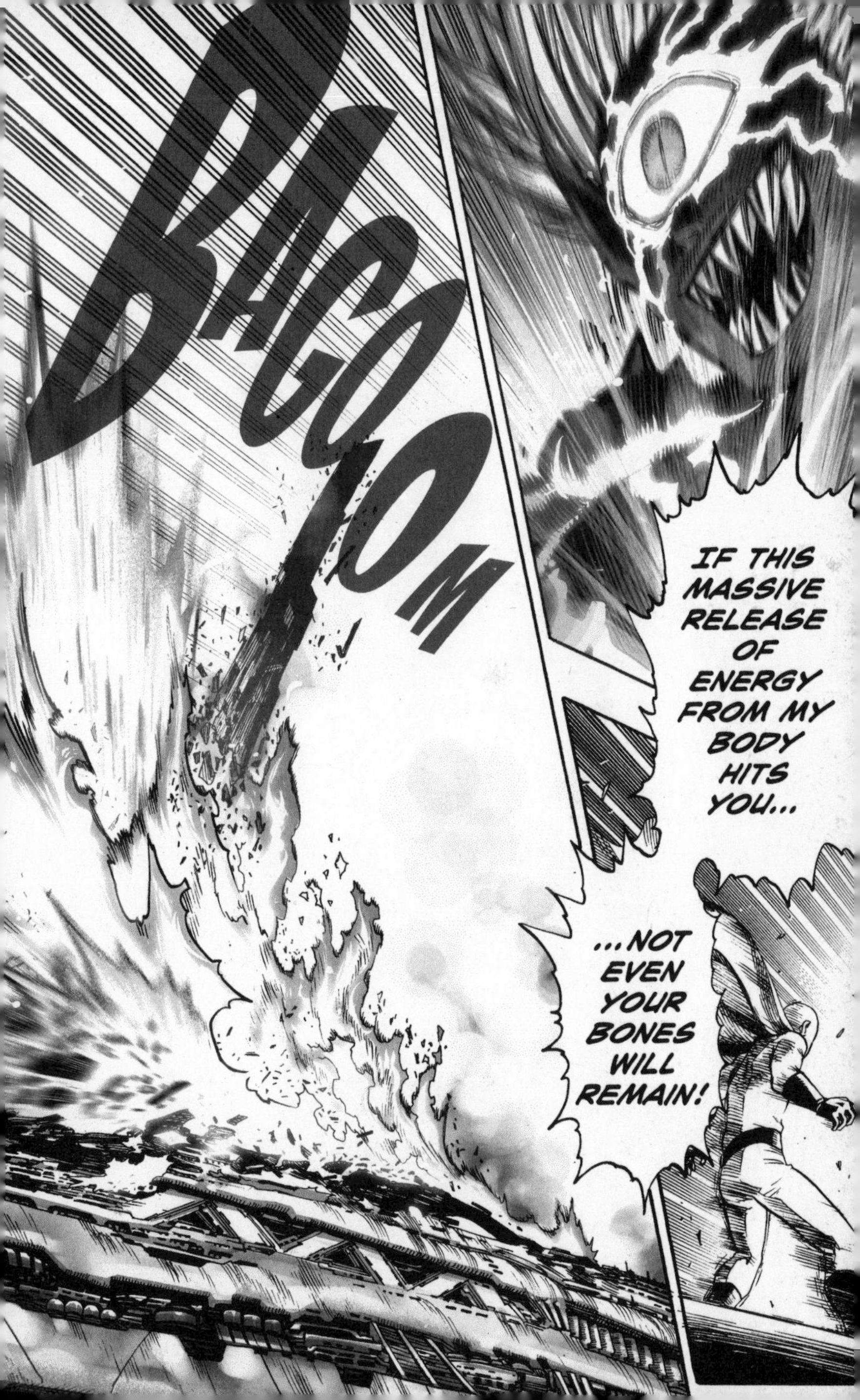
IF THIS MASSIVE RELEASE OF ENERGY FROM MY BODY HITS YOU...
...NOT EVEN YOUR BONES WILL REMAIN!
BAGOOM

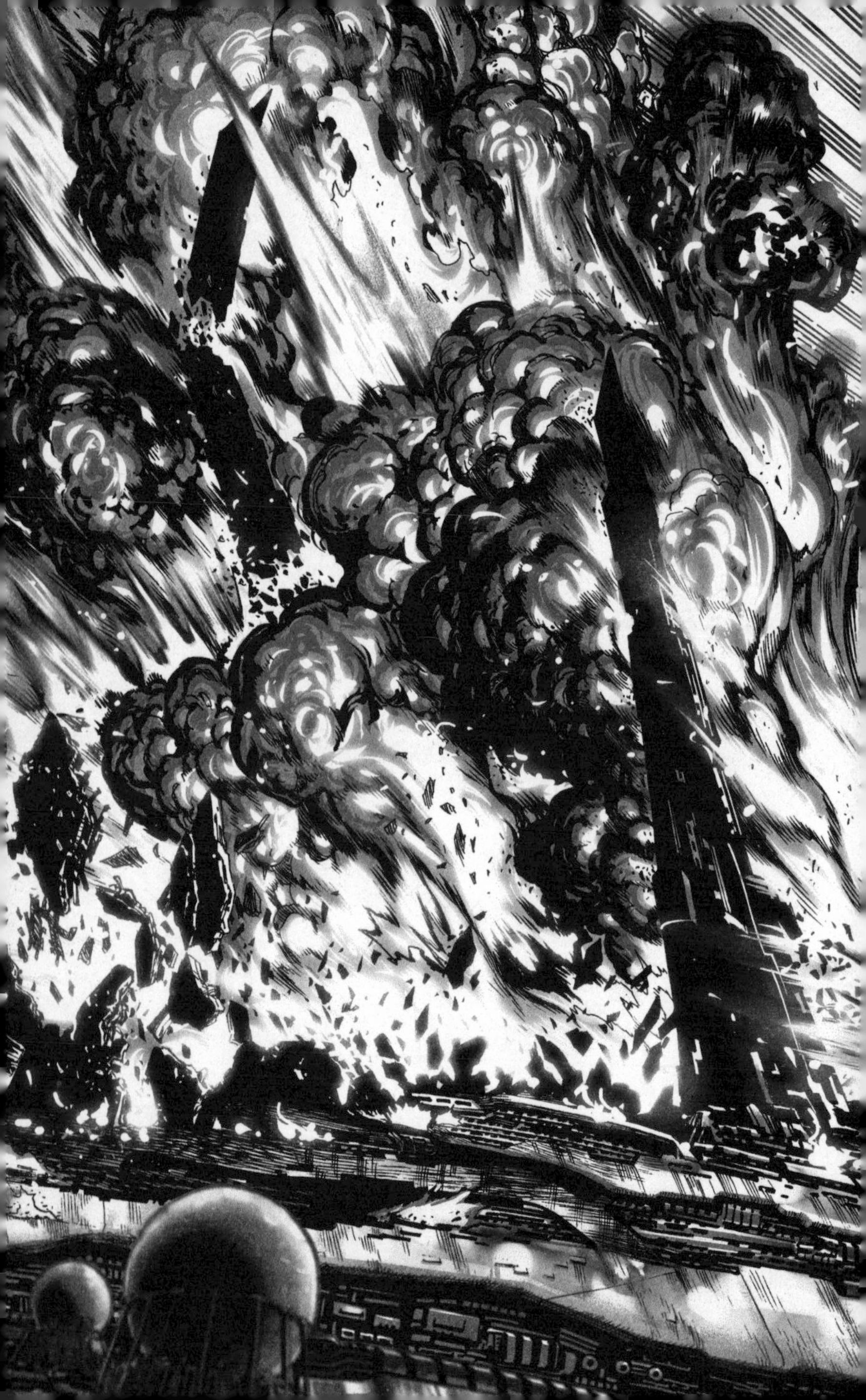

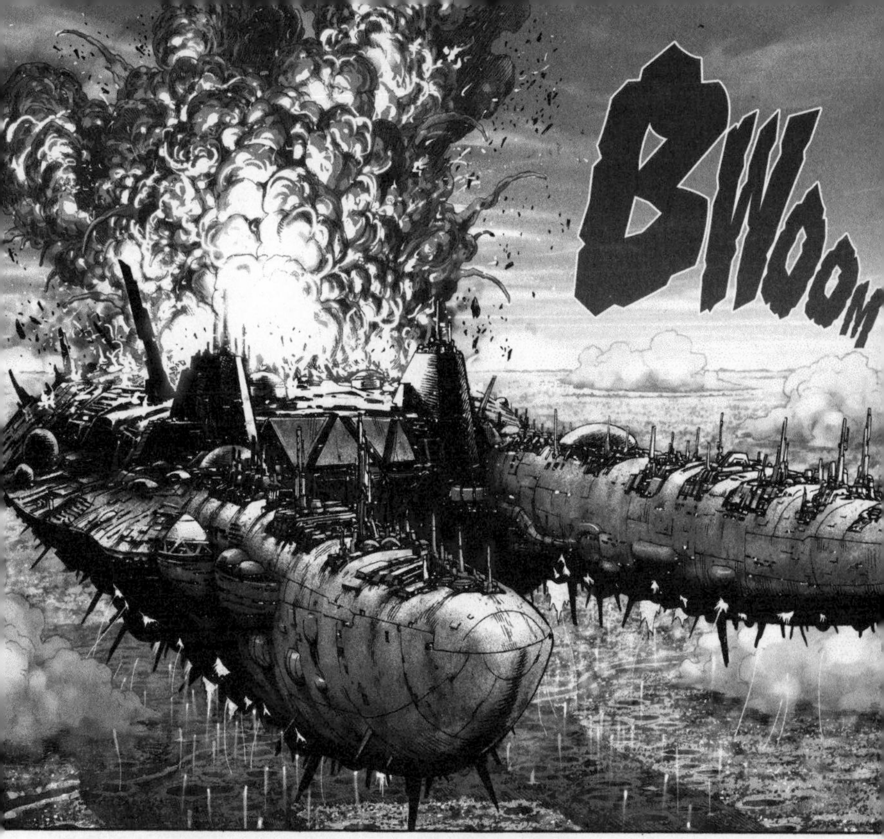
BWOOM

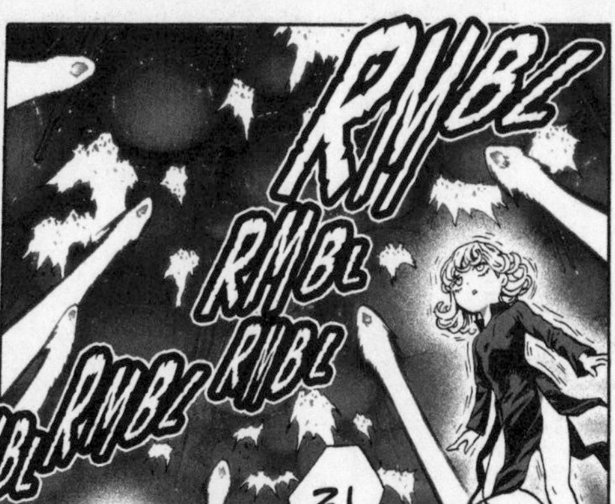
RMBL
RMBL
RMBL
?!

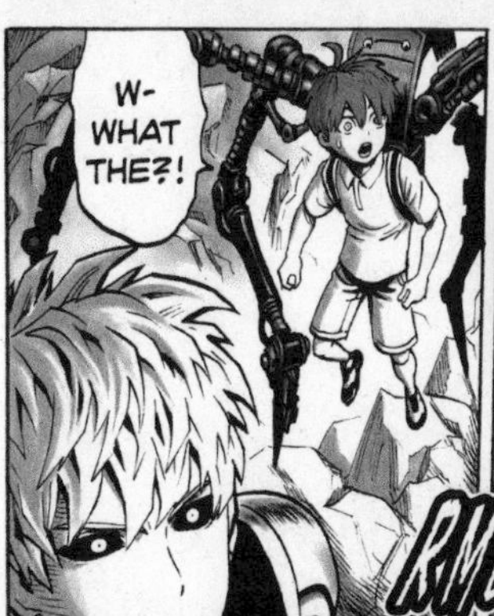
W-
WHAT
THE?!
RMBL
RMBL
RMBL

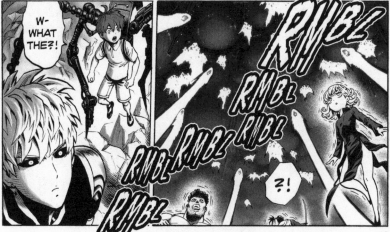

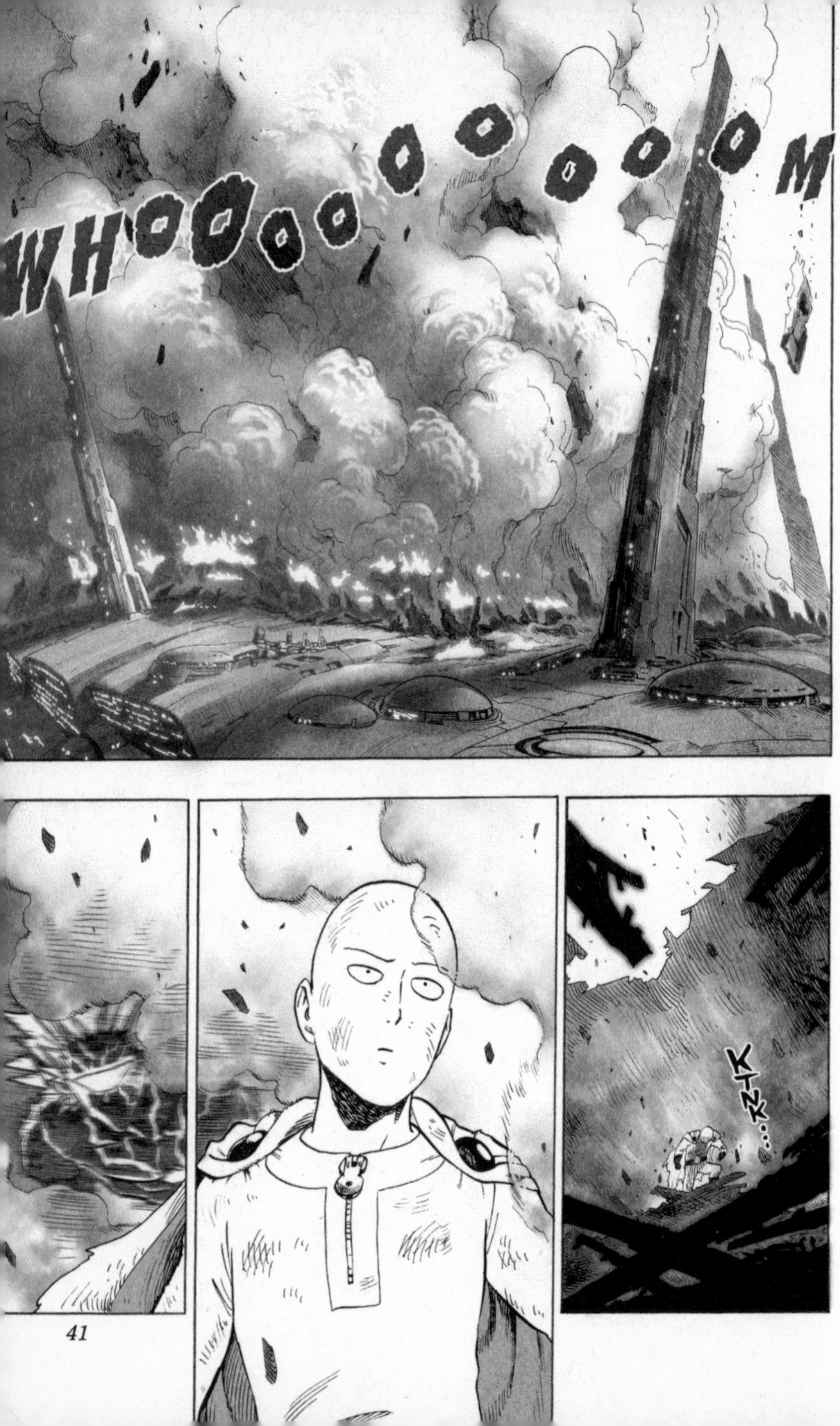
WHOOOOOOOOOOOM
KTNK...

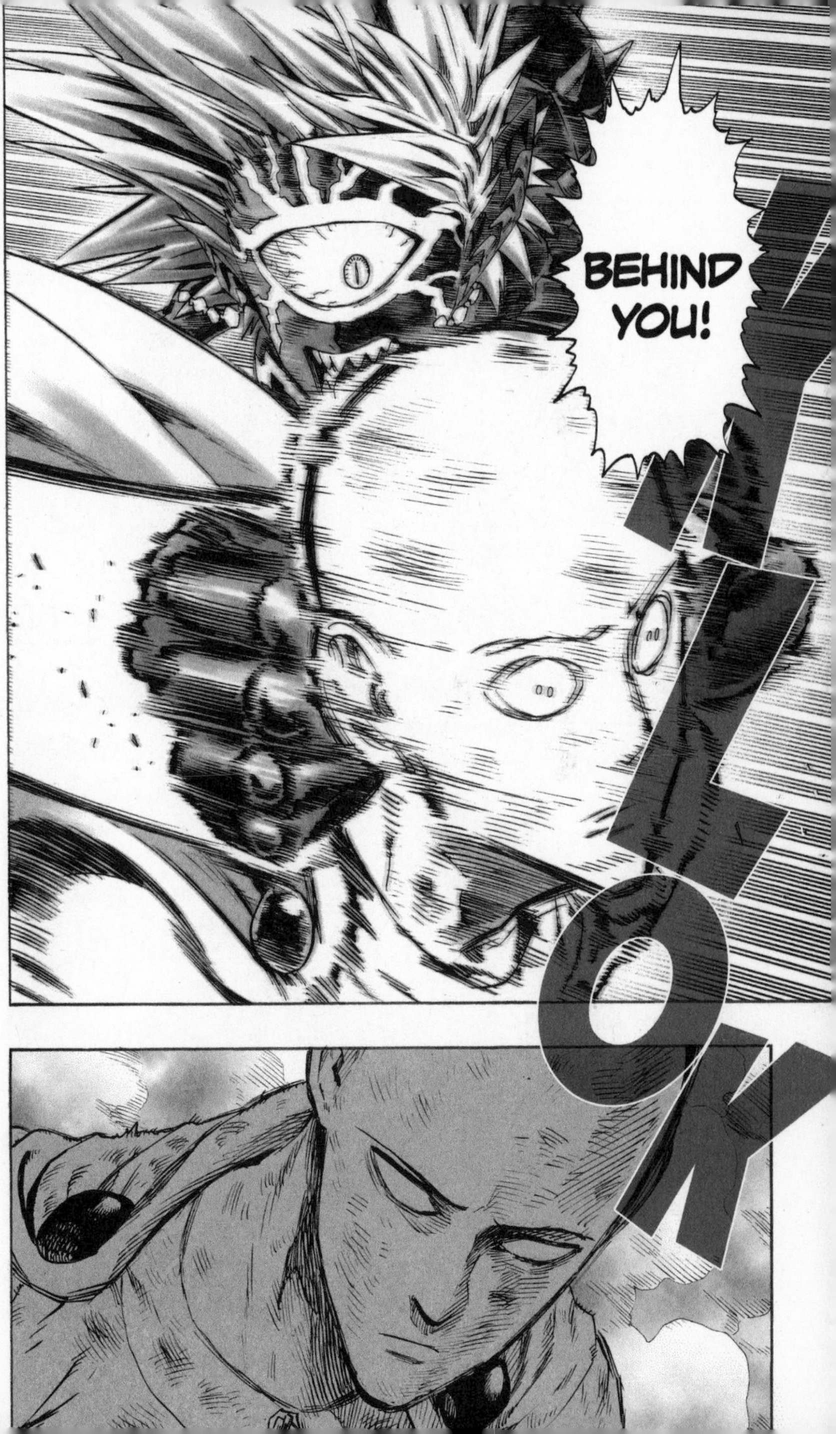
BEHIND YOU!

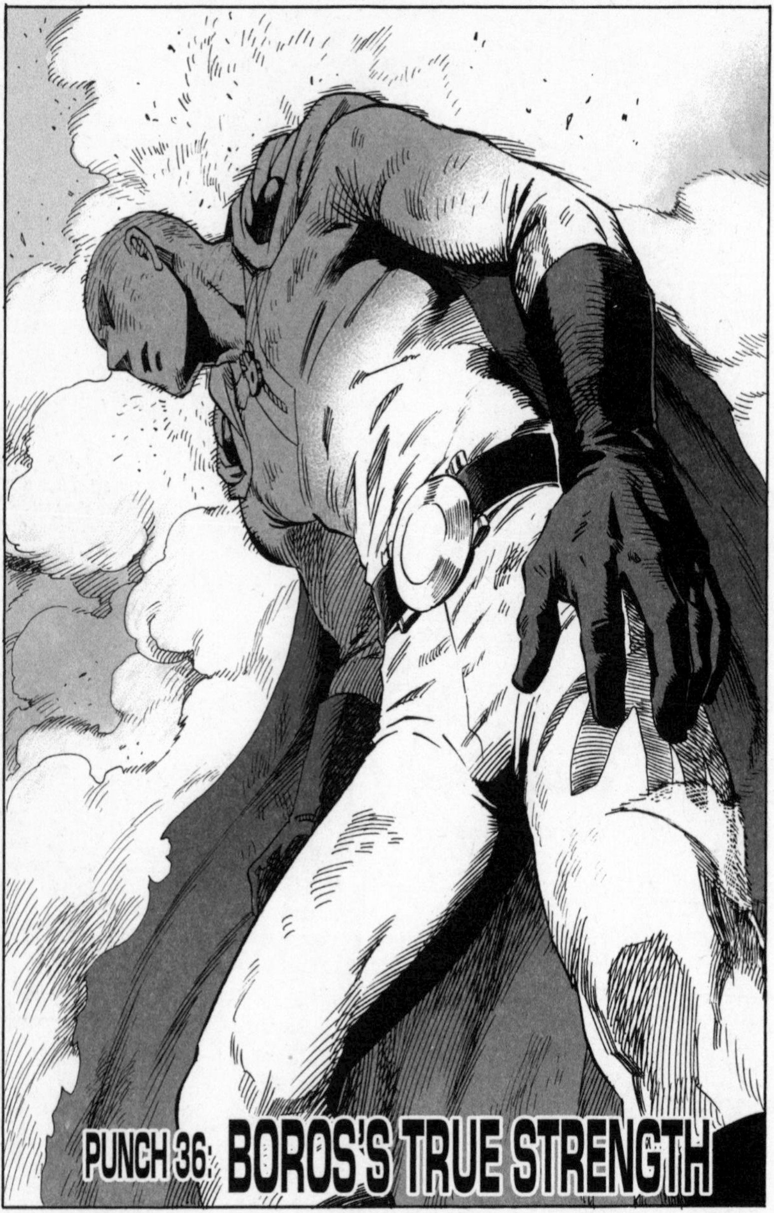
PUNCH 36: BOROS'S TRUE STRENGTH

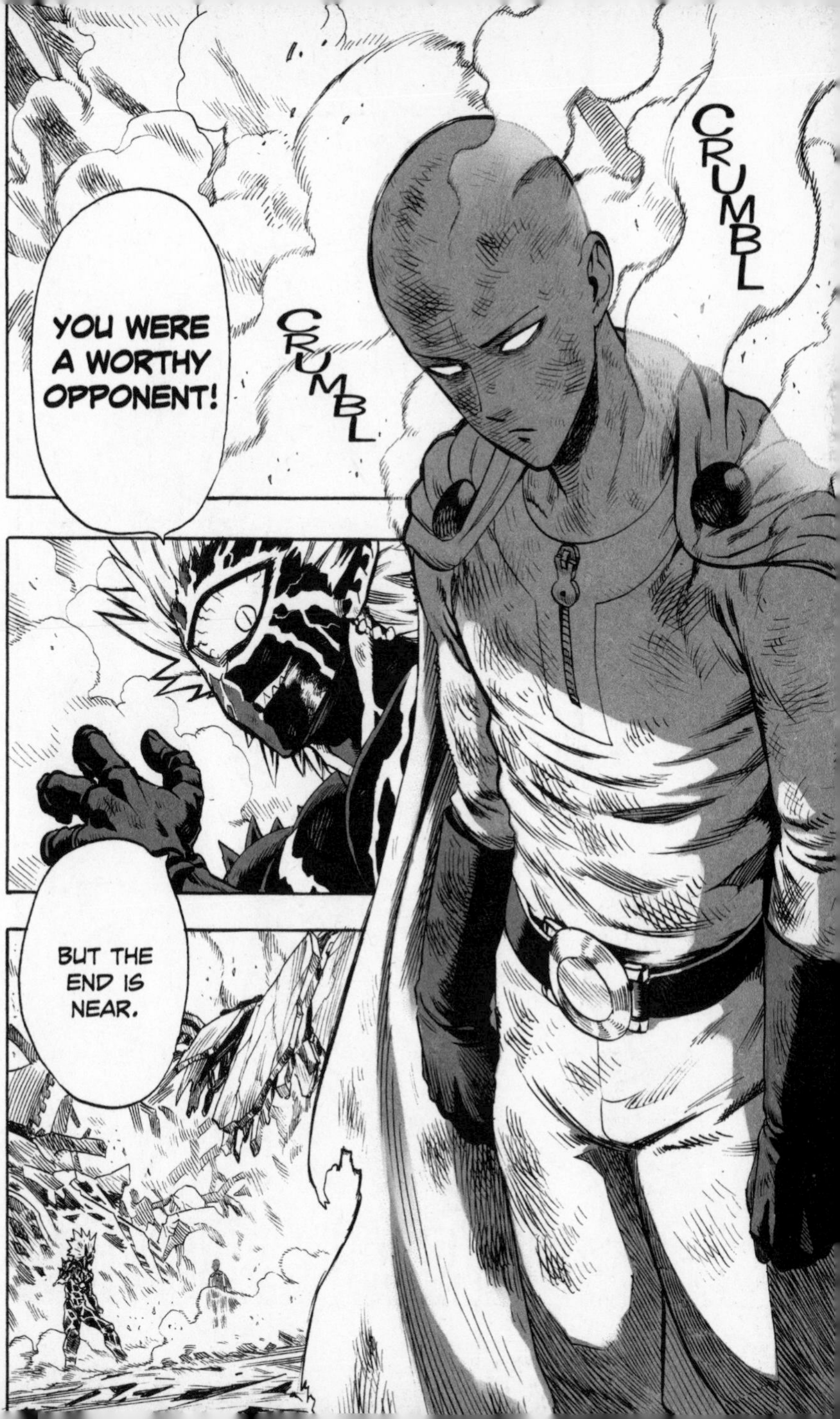
CRUMBL
CRUMBL
YOU WERE A WORTHY OPPONENT!
BUT THE END IS NEAR.

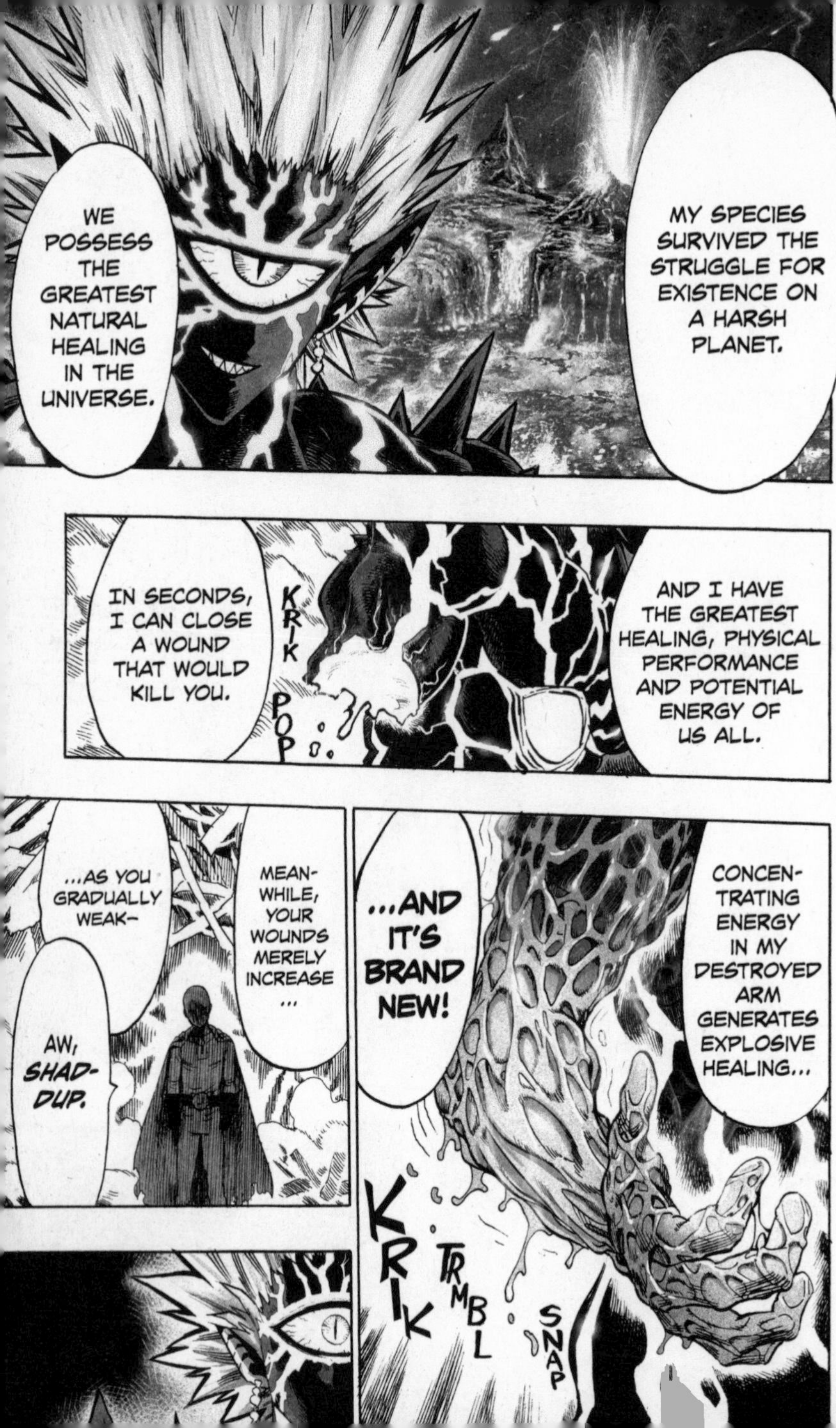
MY SPECIES SURVIVED THE STRUGGLE FOR EXISTENCE ON A HARSH PLANET.
WE POSSESS THE GREATEST NATURAL HEALING IN THE UNIVERSE.
AND I HAVE THE GREATEST HEALING, PHYSICAL PERFORMANCE AND POTENTIAL ENERGY OF US ALL.
KRIK
POP
IN SECONDS, I CAN CLOSE A WOUND THAT WOULD KILL YOU.
CONCEN-TRATING ENERGY IN MY DESTROYED ARM GENERATES EXPLOSIVE HEALING...
...AND IT'S BRAND NEW!
KRIK
TRMBL
SNAP
MEAN-WHILE, YOUR WOUNDS MERELY INCREASE...
...AS YOU GRADUALLY WEAK-
AW, SHAD-DUP.

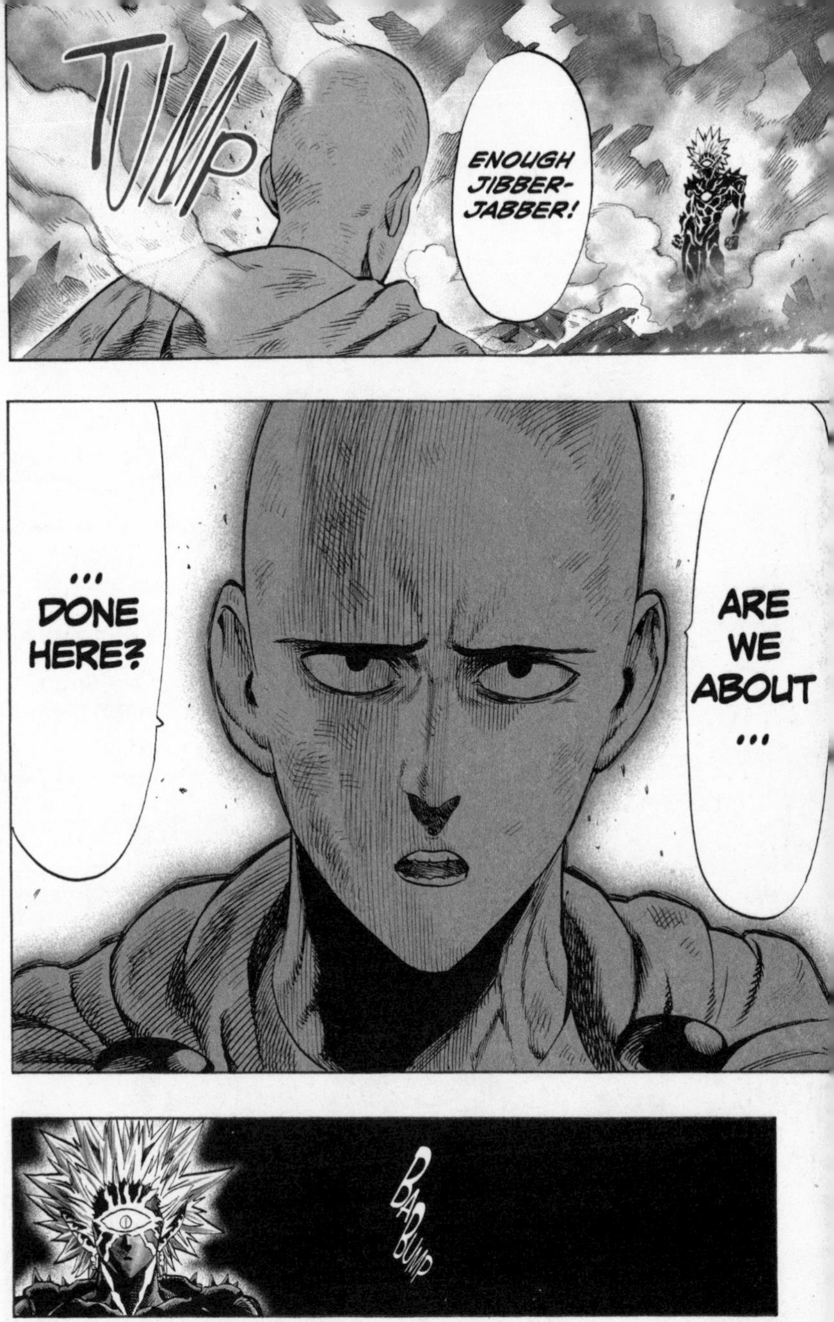
TUMP
ENOUGH JIBBER-JABBER!
ARE WE ABOUT ...
... DONE HERE?
BABUMP

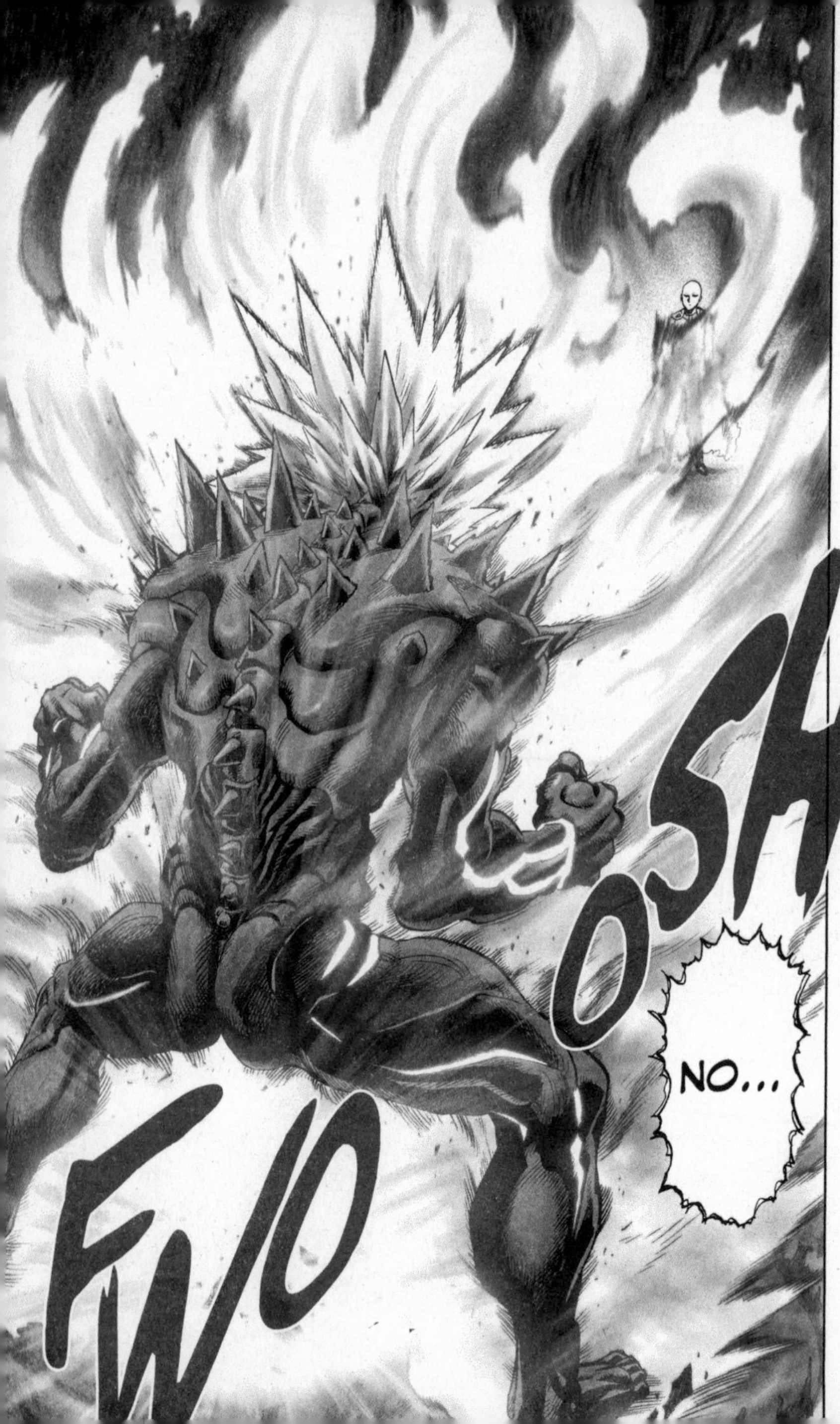
FWOOSH
NO...

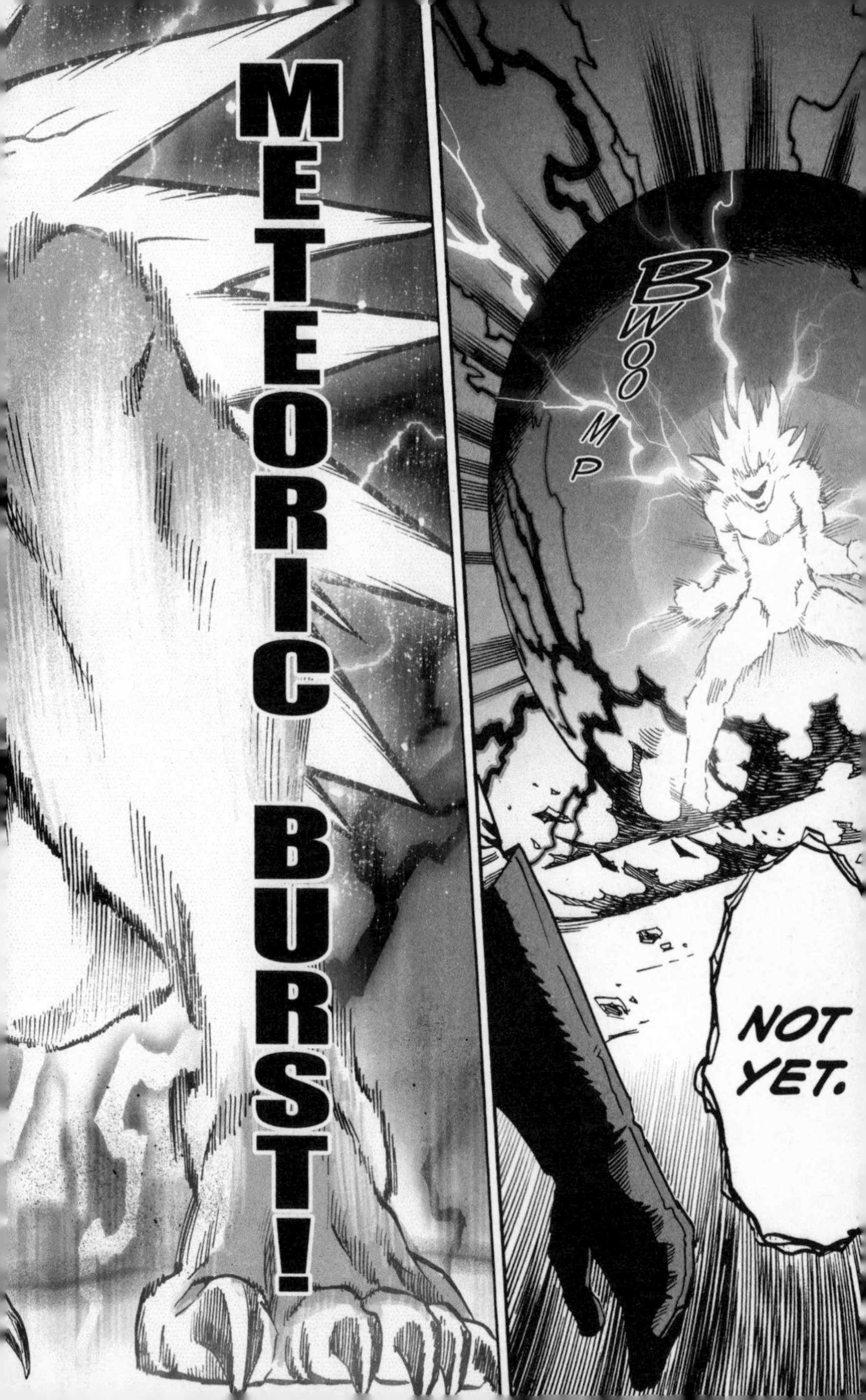
BWOOMP
NOT YET.
METEORIC BURST!

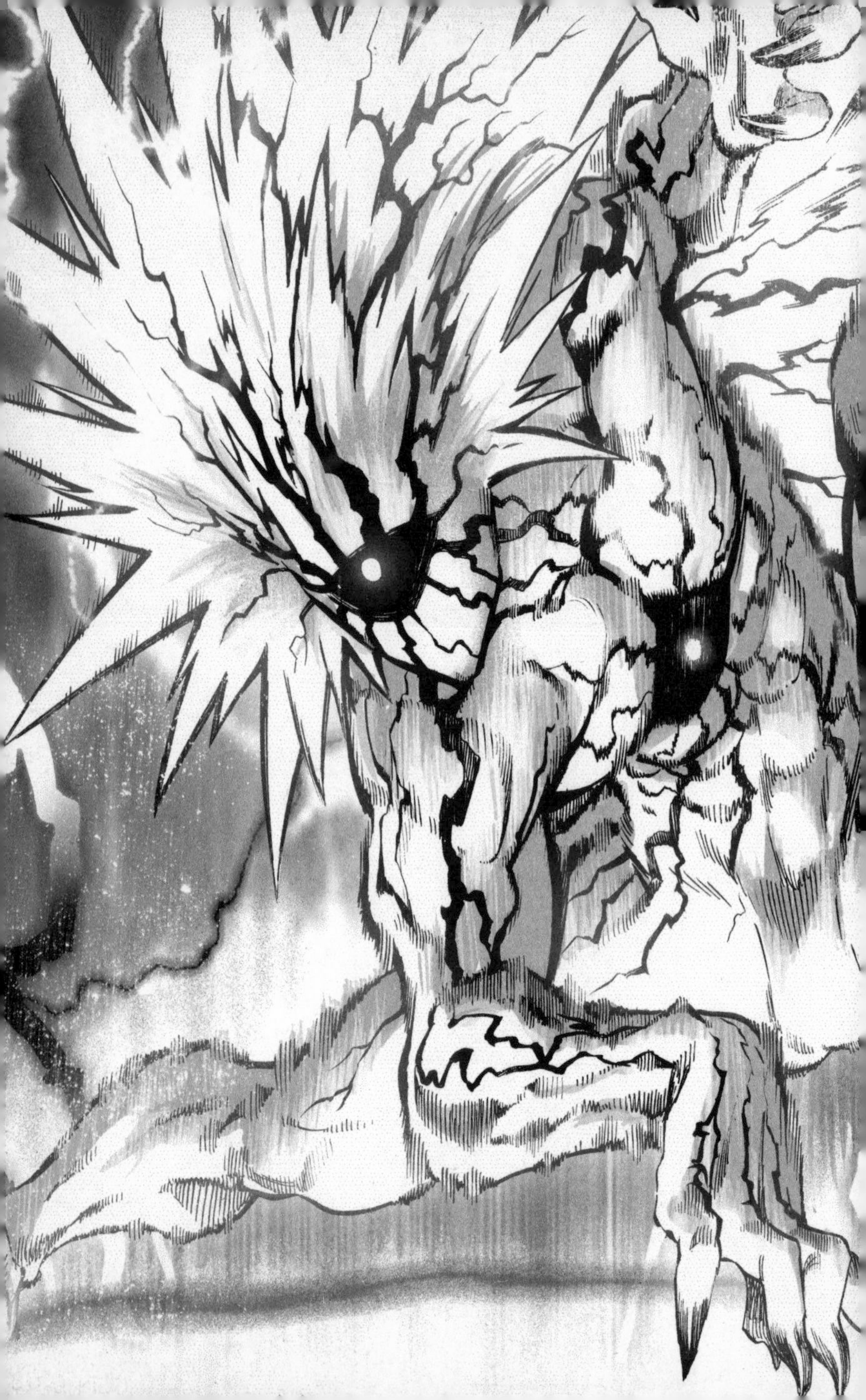

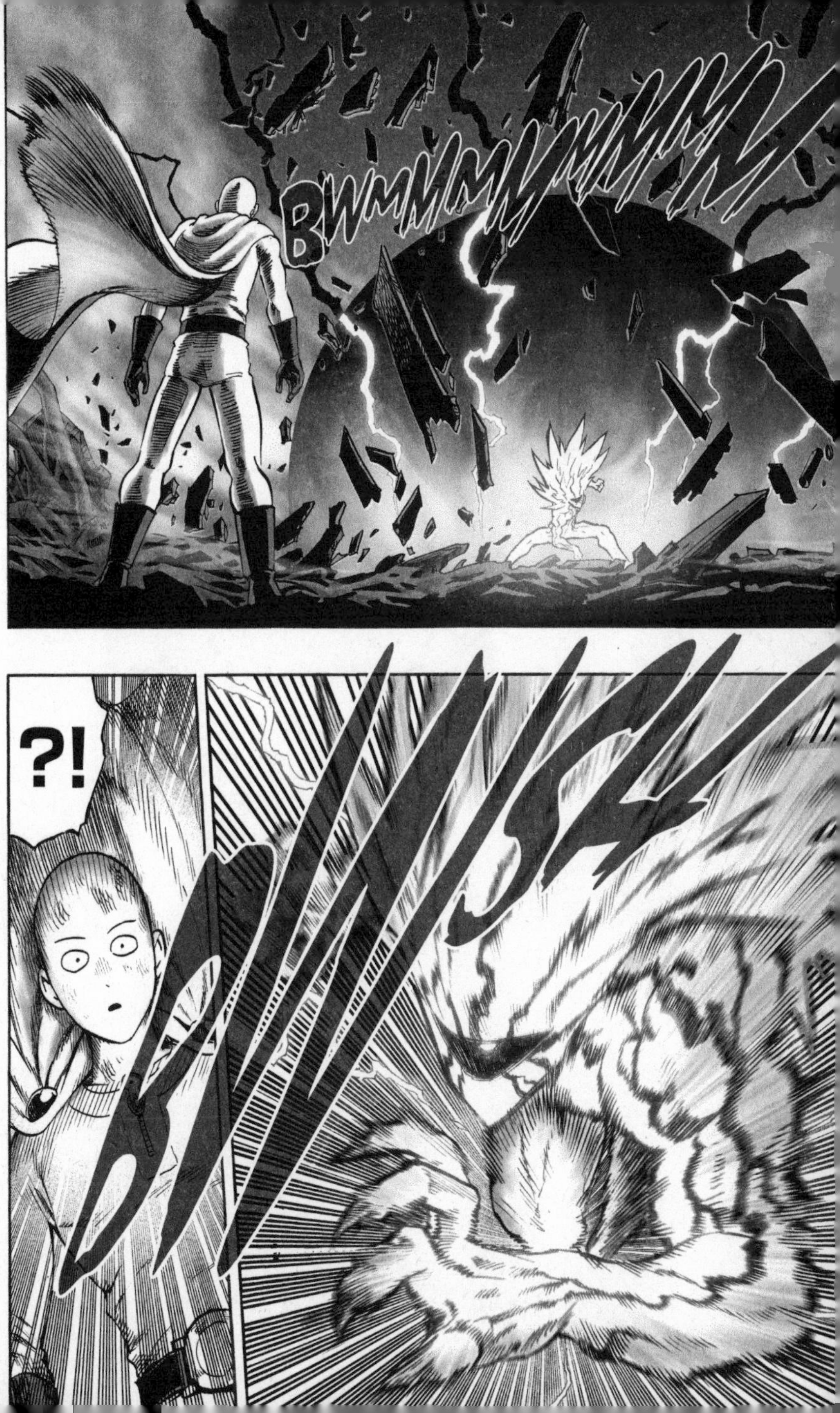
BWMMMMMMMMM
?!
SWISH

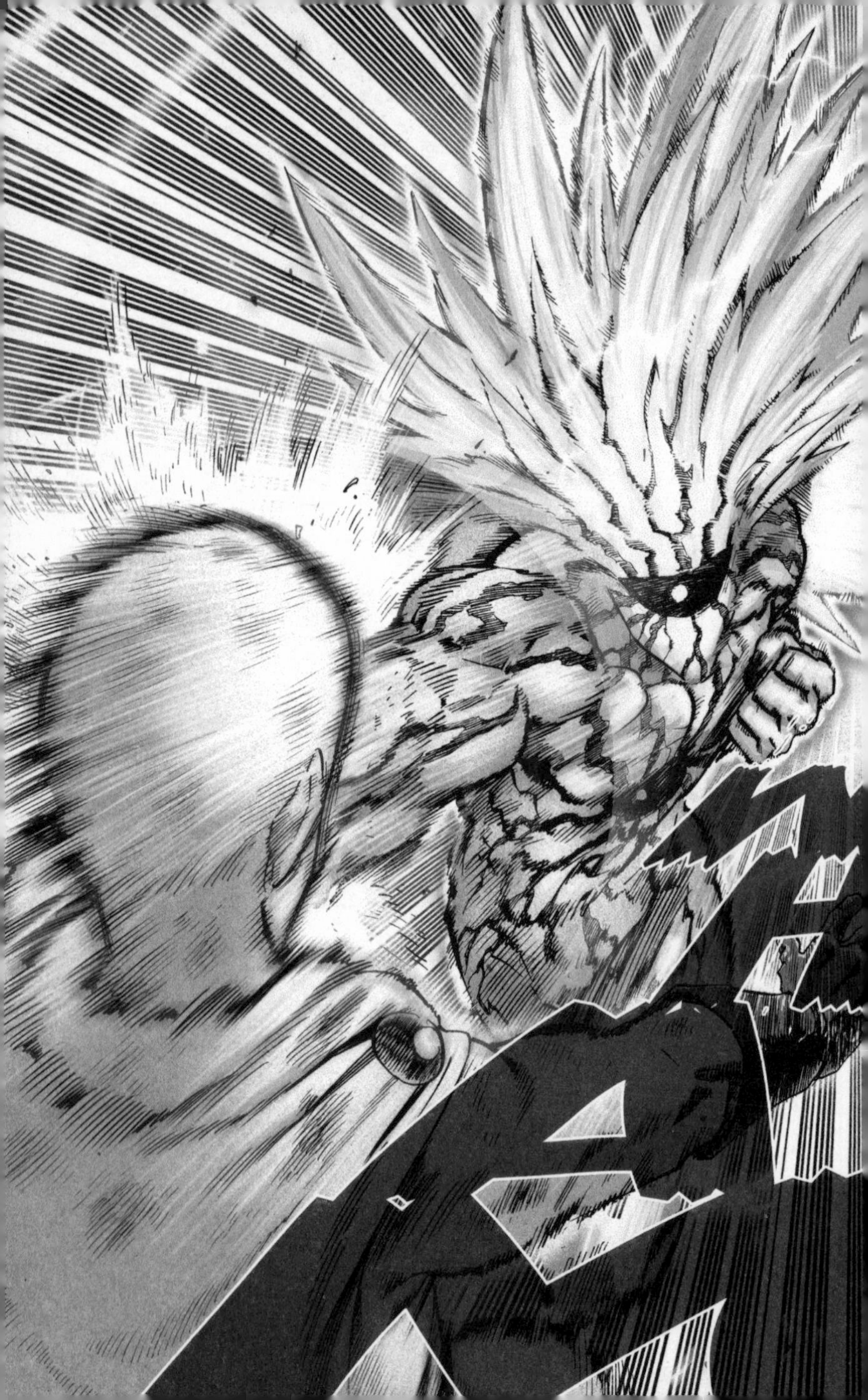

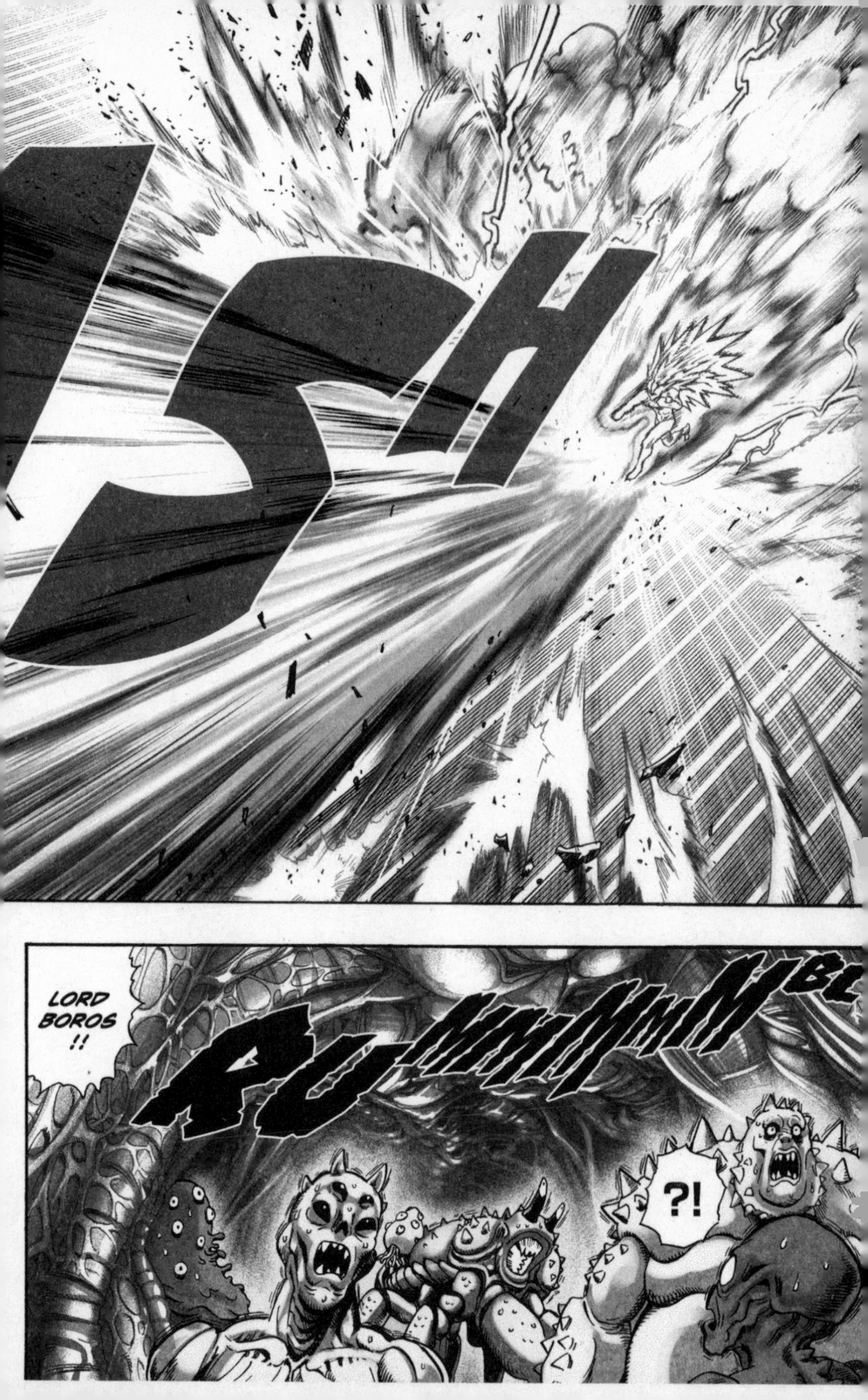

RU-MMMMMMMMMBL
LORD BOROS !!
?!

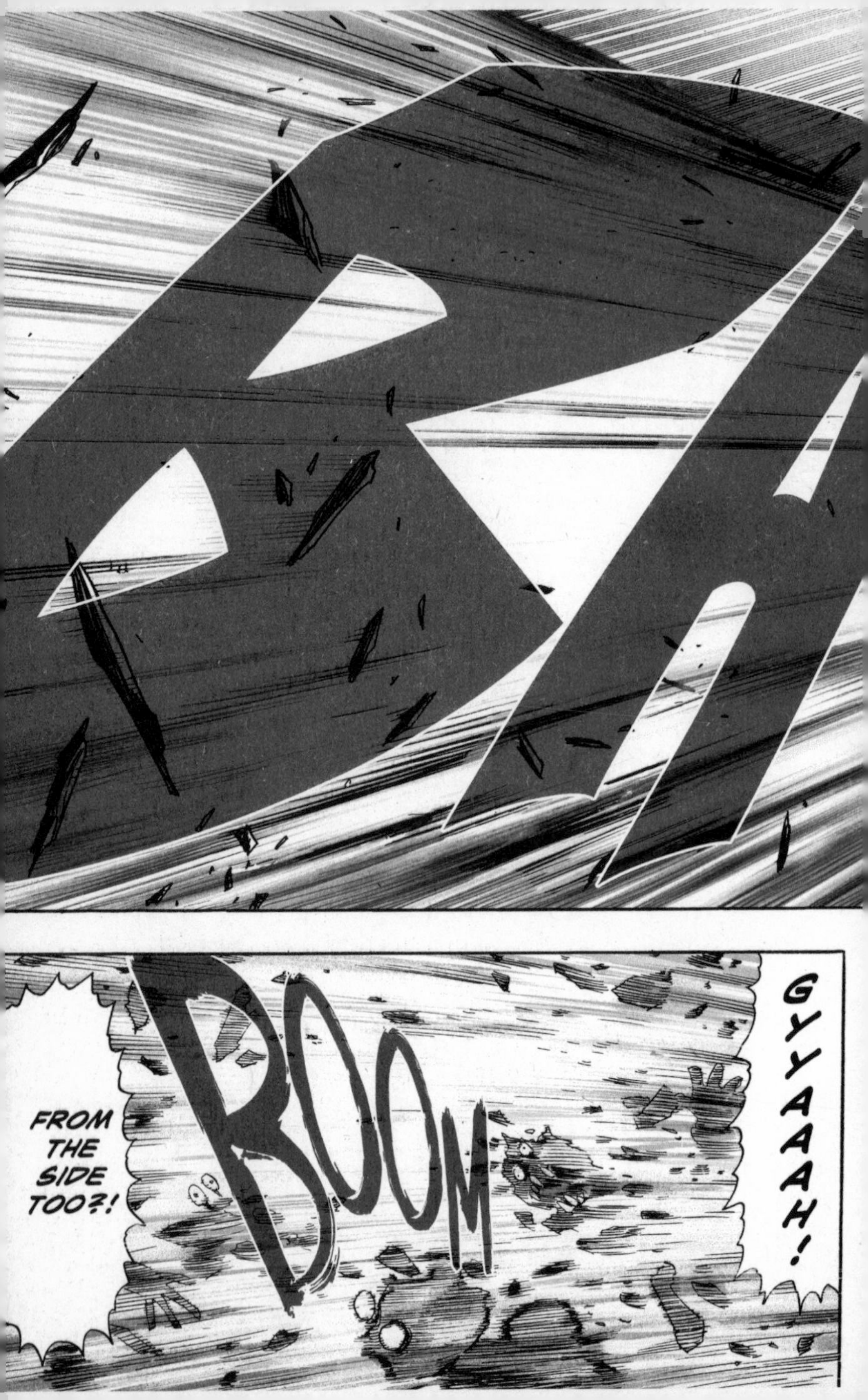
GYYAAAAH!
BOOM
FROM THE SIDE TOO?!

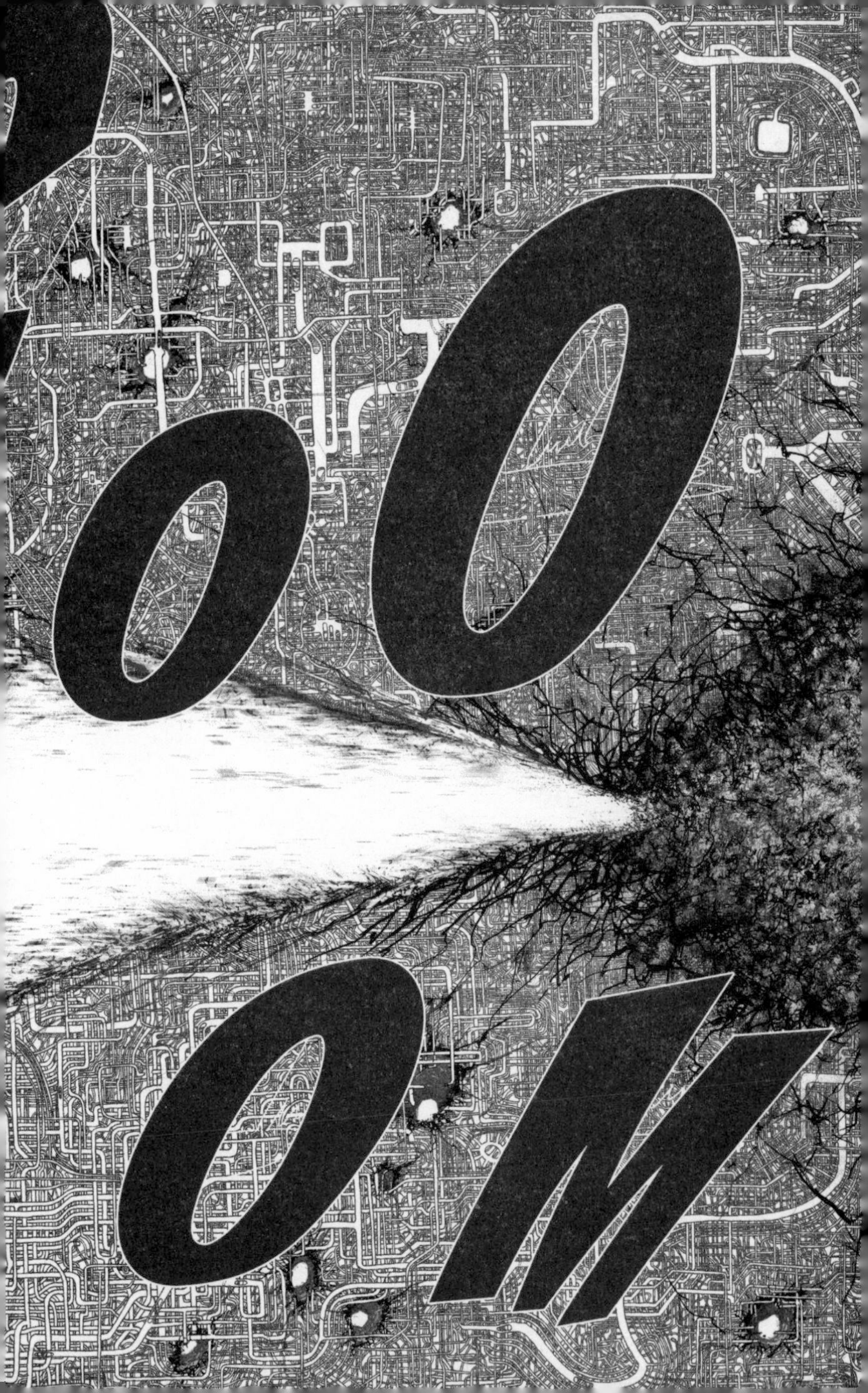
ooom

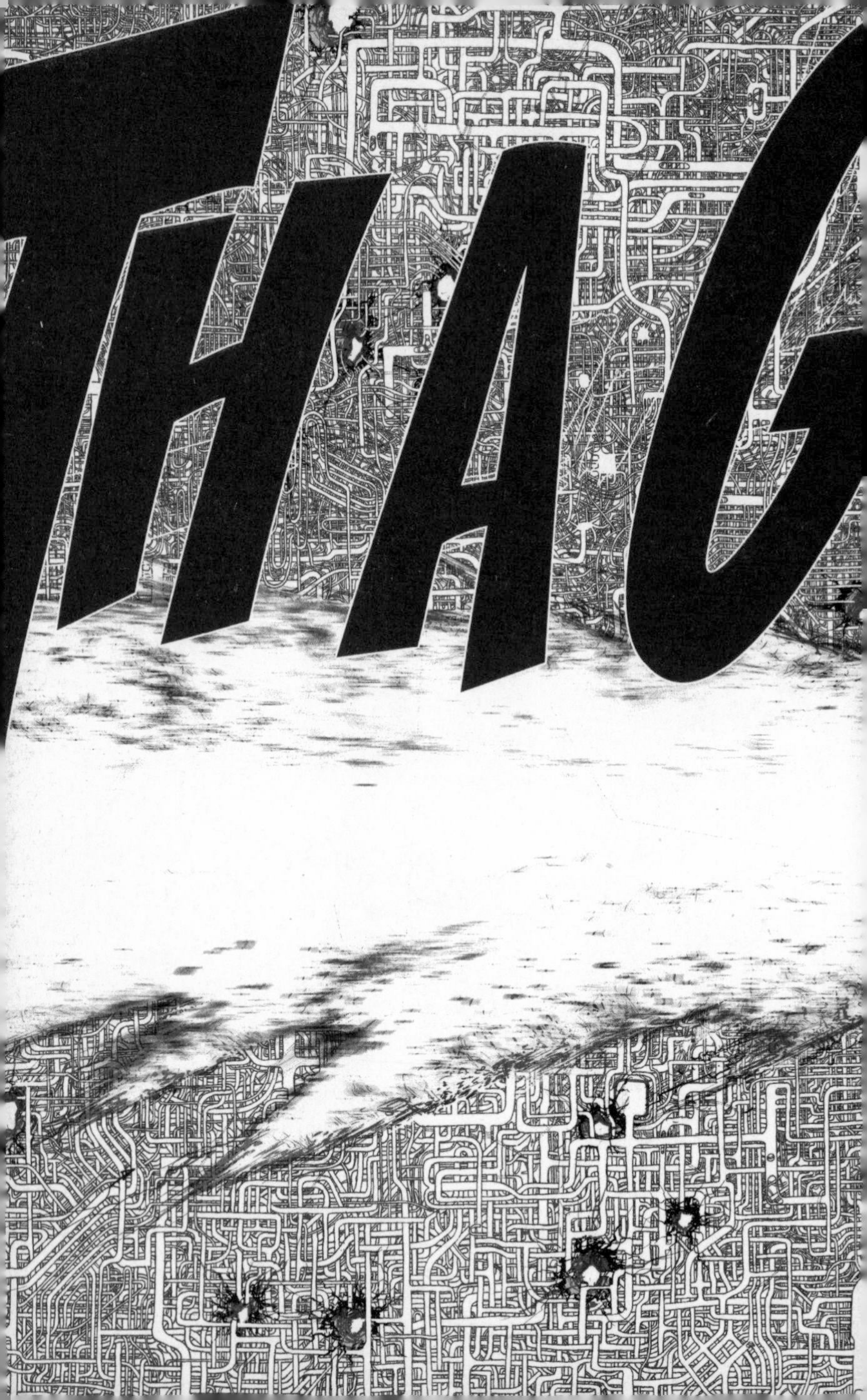
THAC

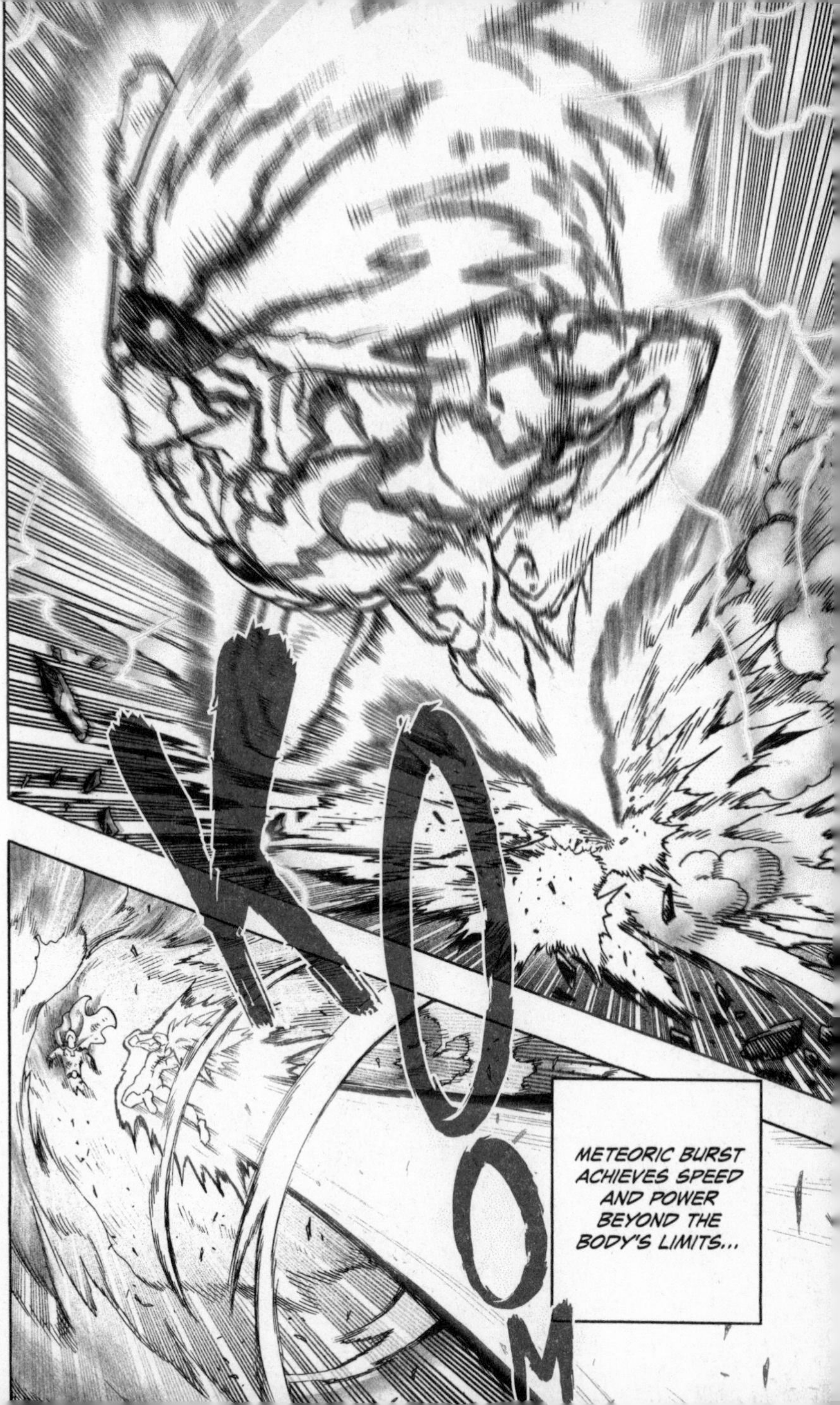
KOOOM
METEORIC BURST ACHIEVES SPEED AND POWER BEYOND THE BODY'S LIMITS...

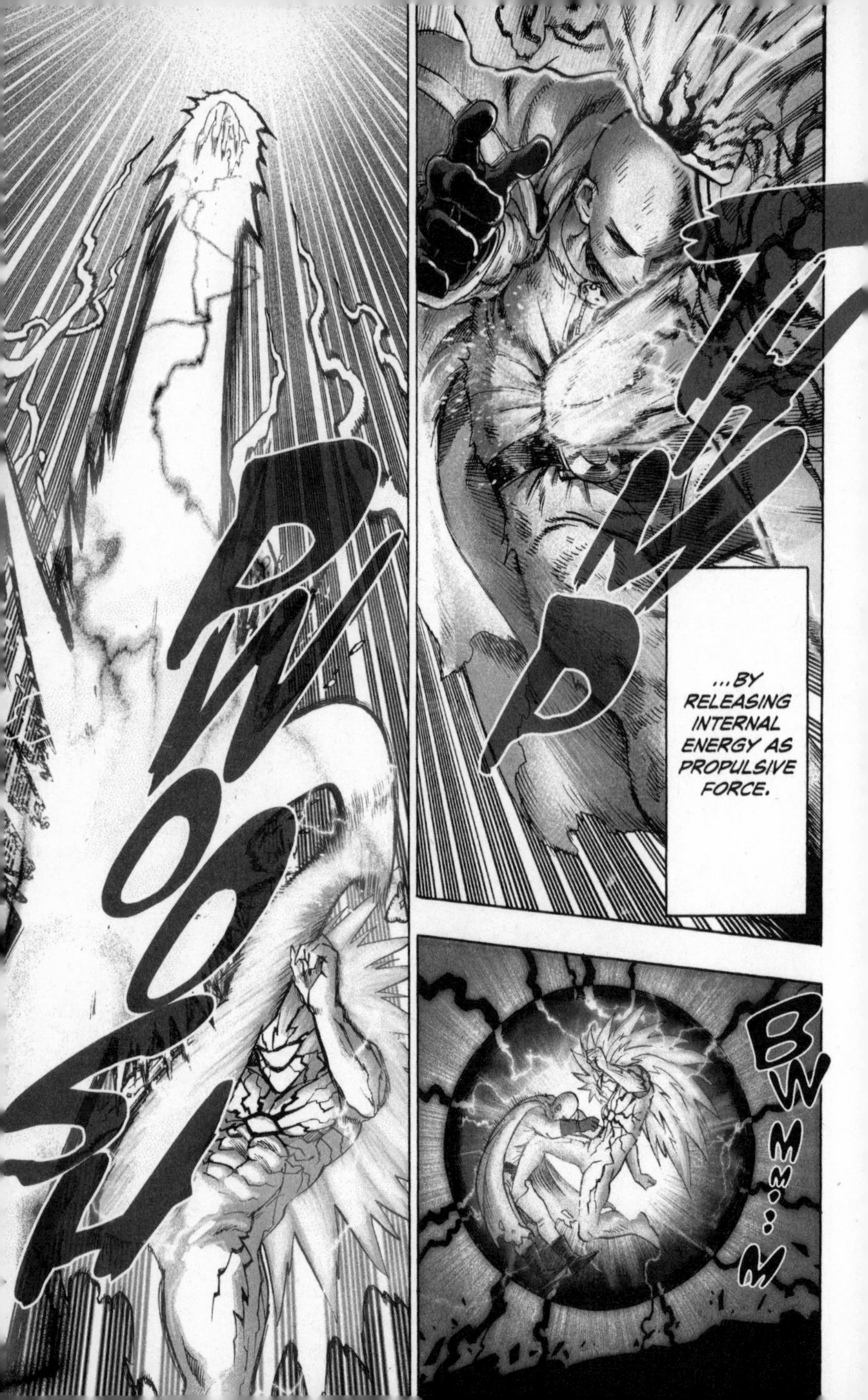
...BY RELEASING INTERNAL ENERGY AS PROPULSIVE FORCE.

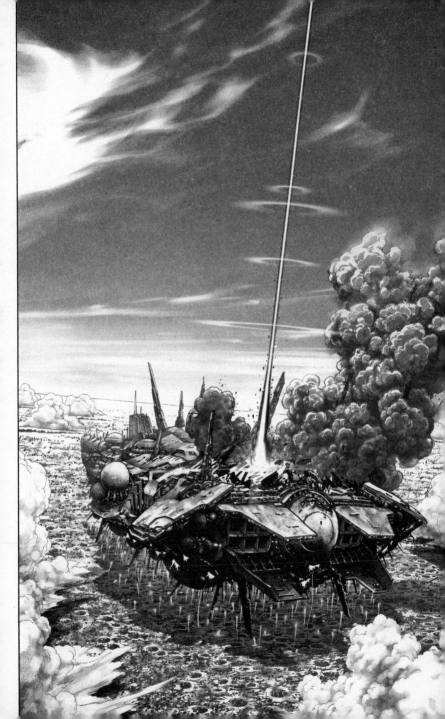

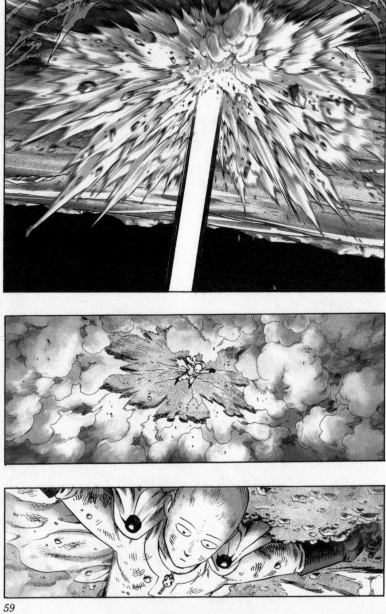

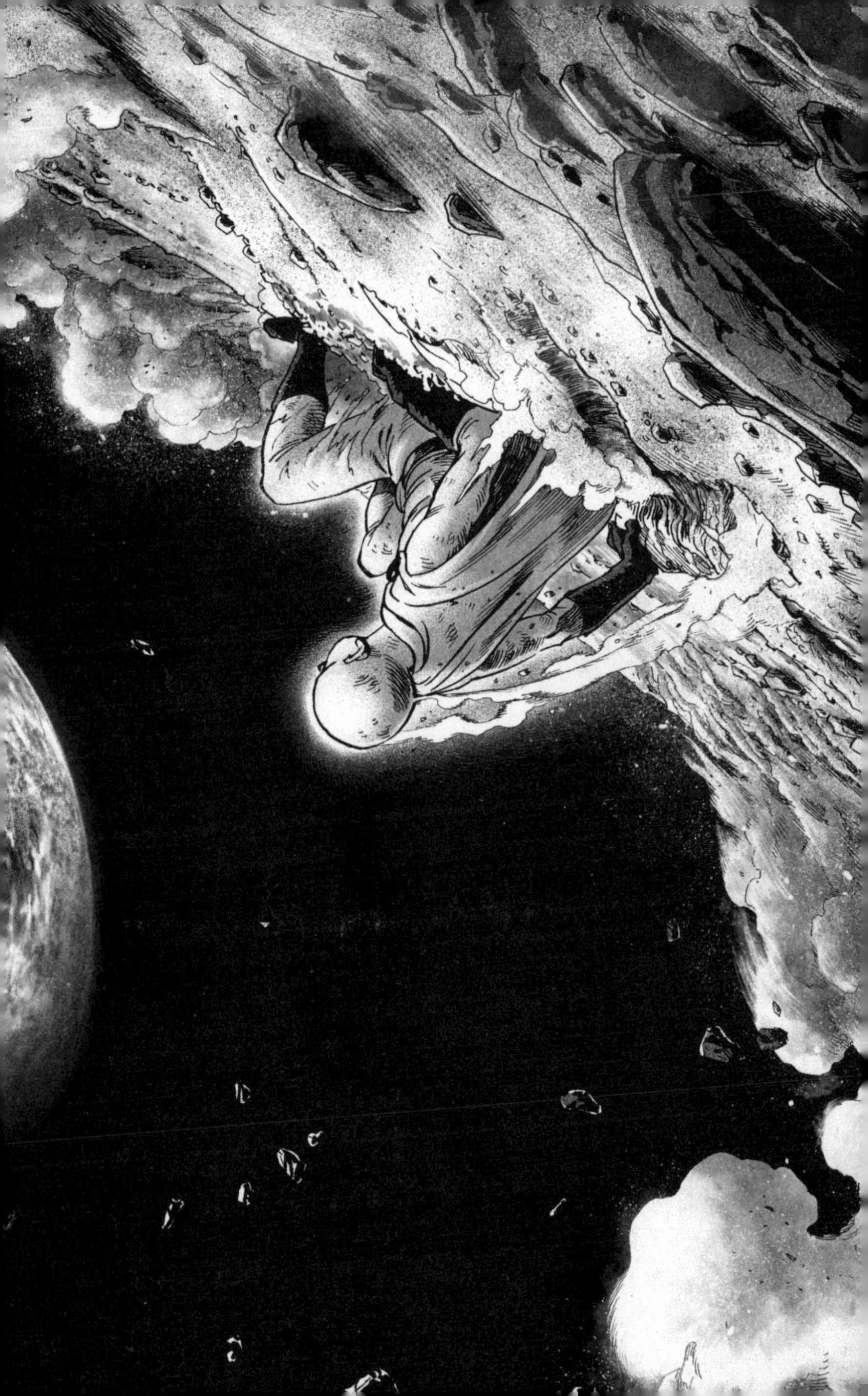

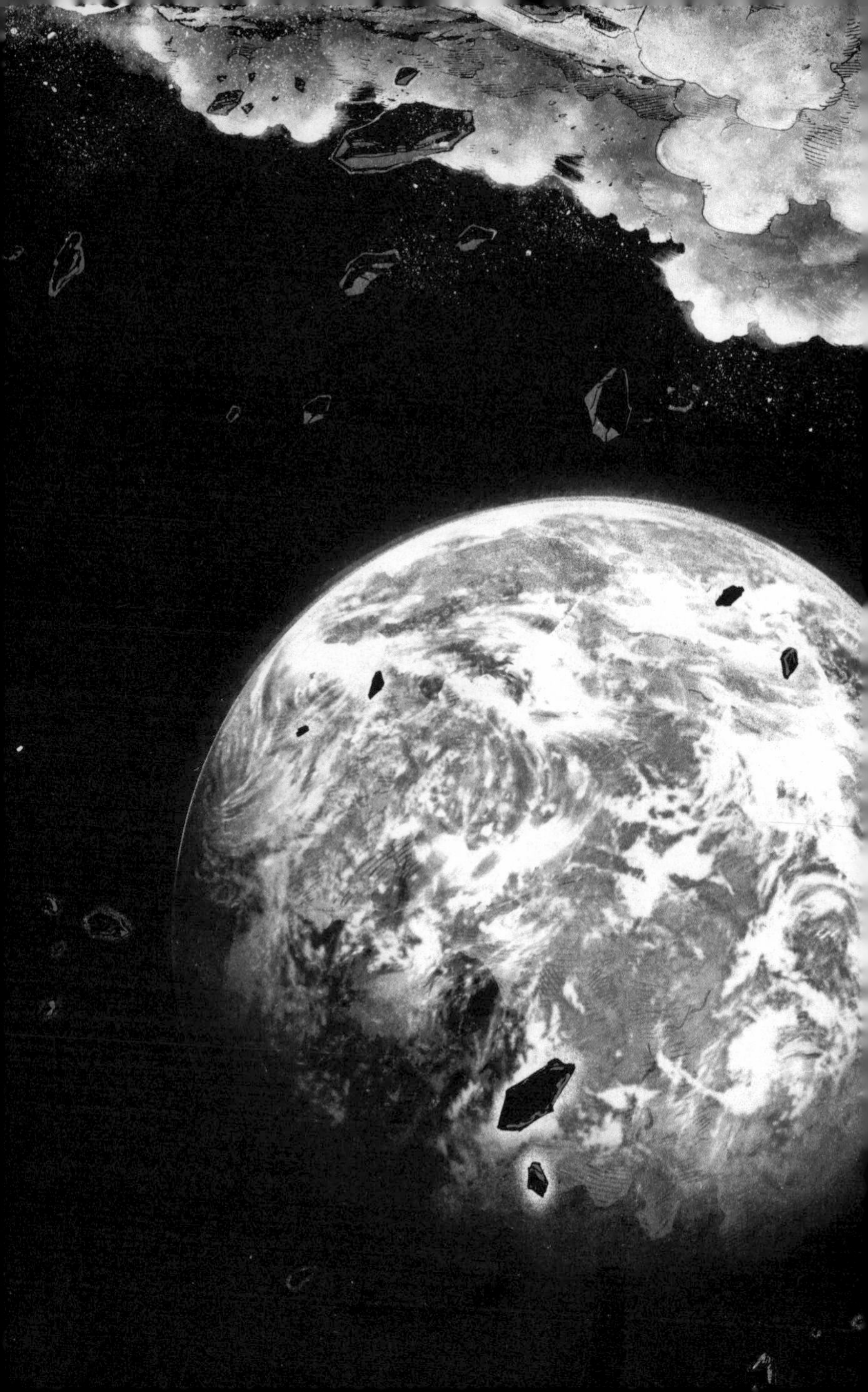

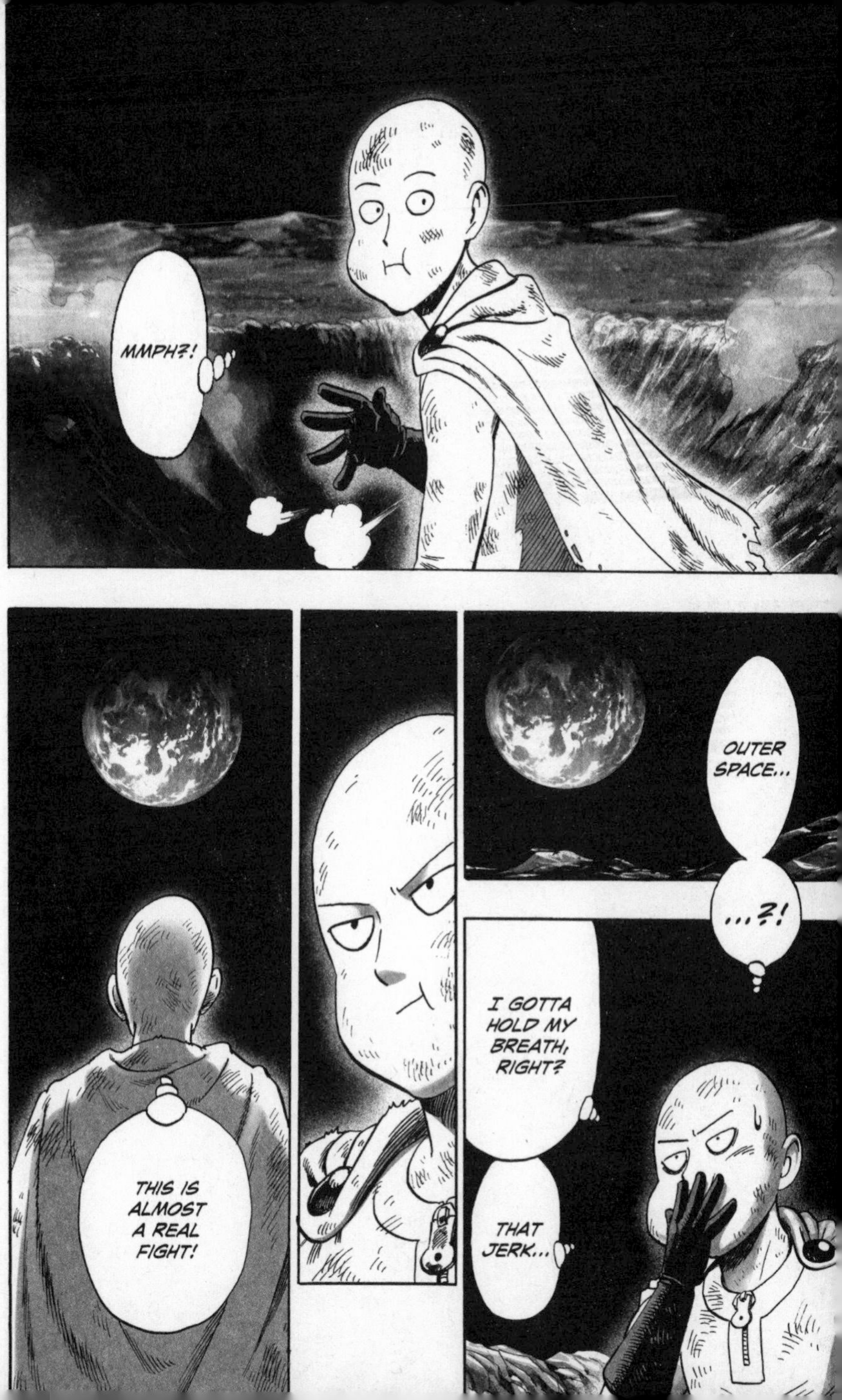
MMPH?!
OUTER SPACE...
...?!
I GOTTA HOLD MY BREATH, RIGHT?
THAT JERK...
THIS IS ALMOST A REAL FIGHT!

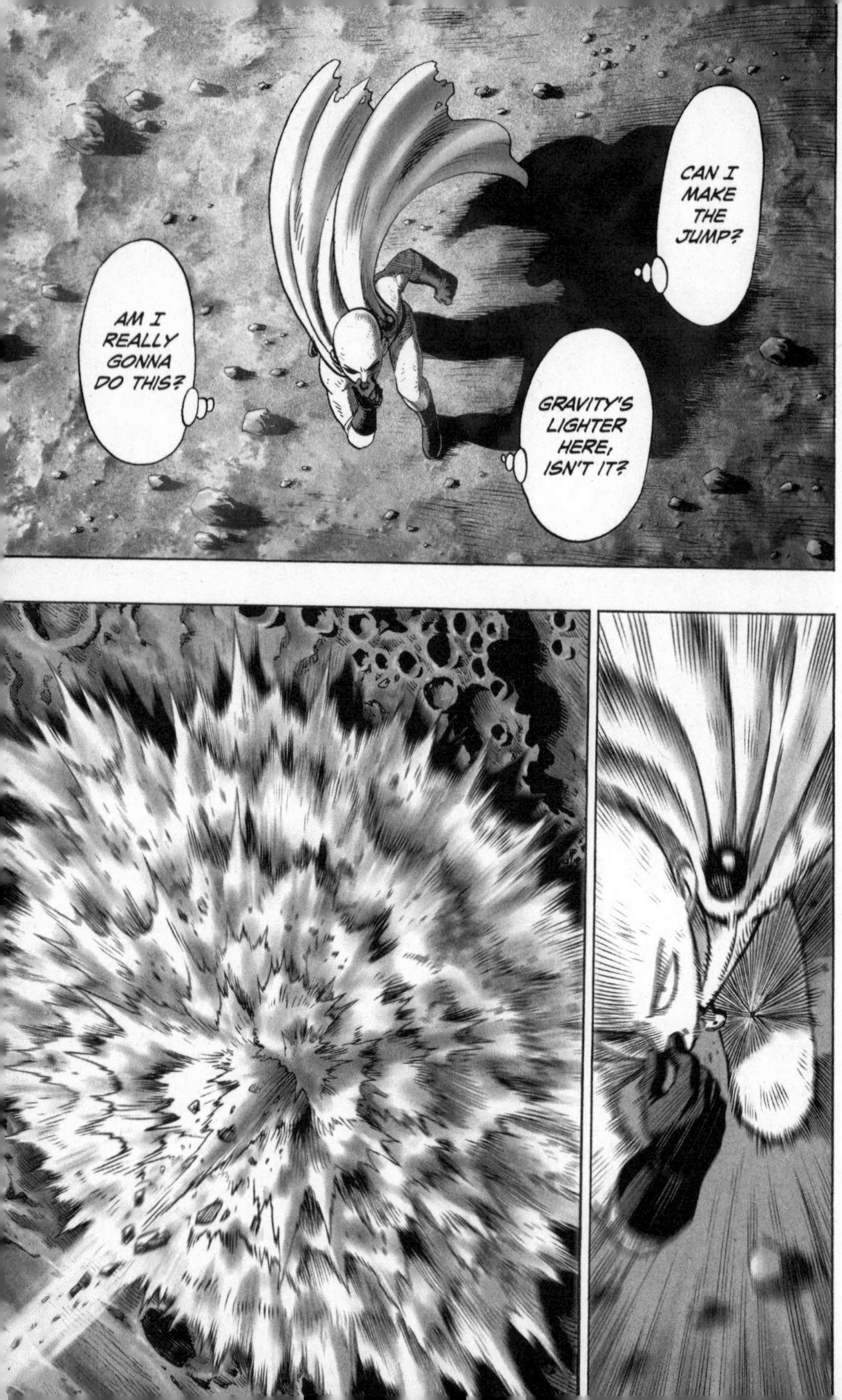
CAN I MAKE THE JUMP?
GRAVITY'S LIGHTER HERE, ISN'T IT?
AM I REALLY GONNA DO THIS?

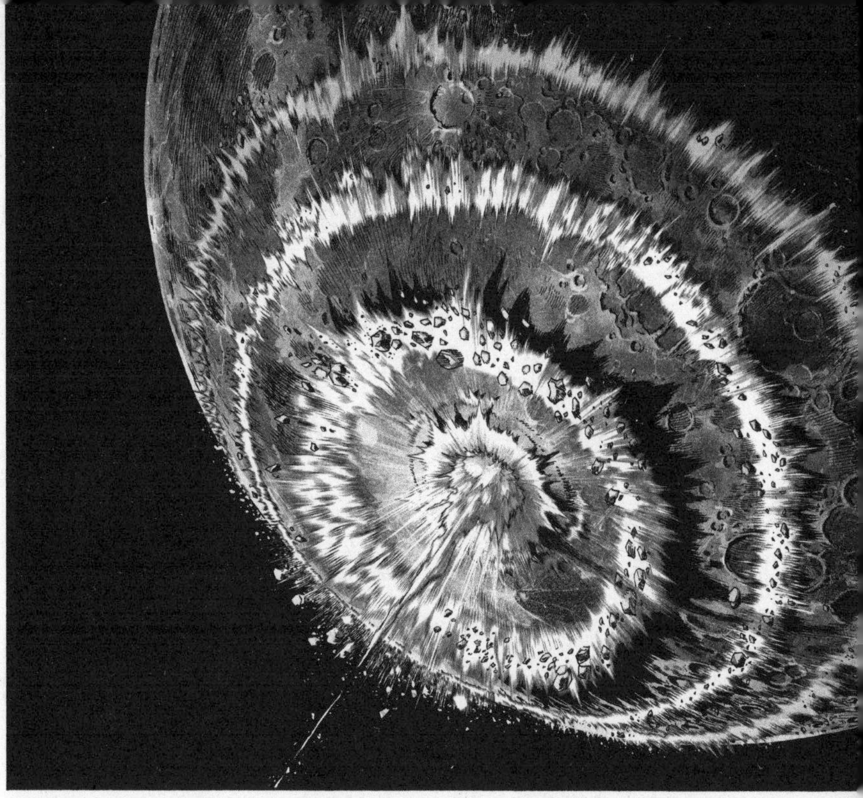

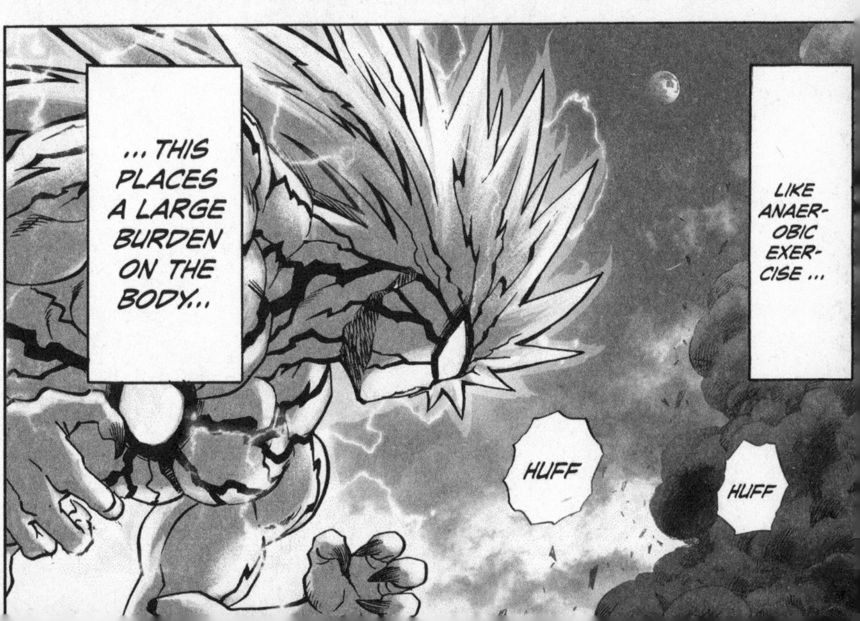
LIKE ANAER-OBIC EXER-CISE ...
... THIS PLACES A LARGE BURDEN ON THE BODY...
HUFF
HUFF

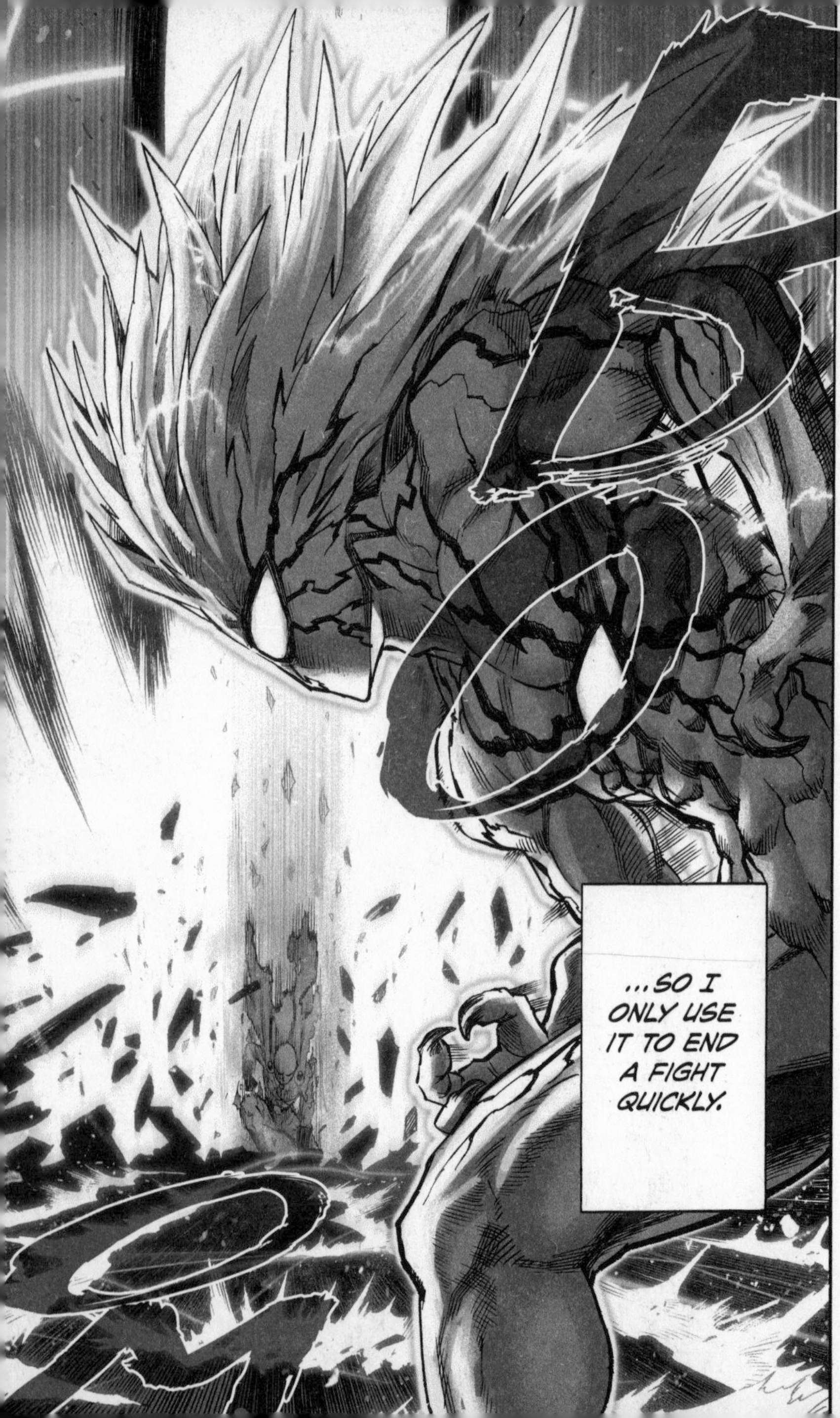
...SO I ONLY USE IT TO END A FIGHT QUICKLY.

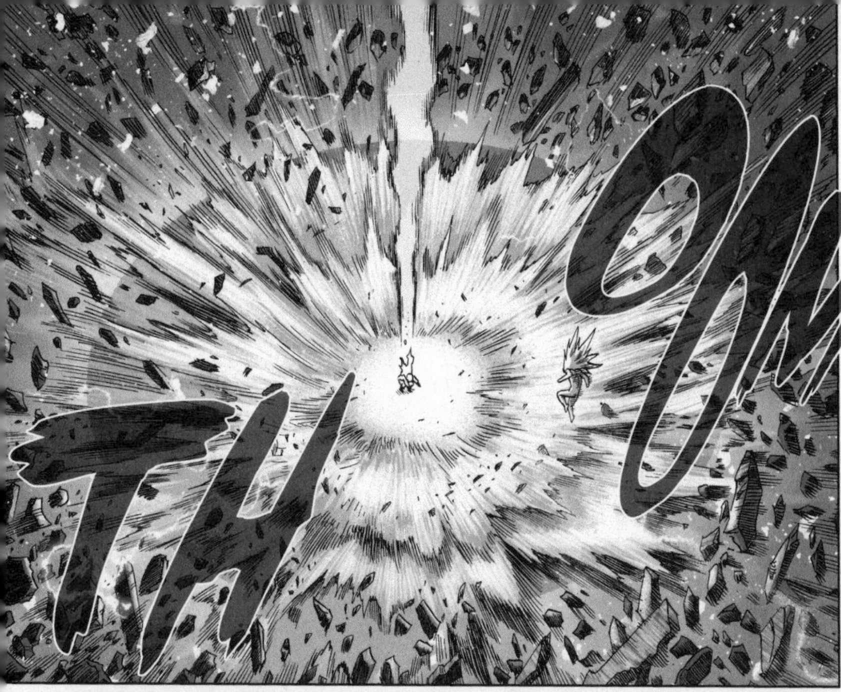

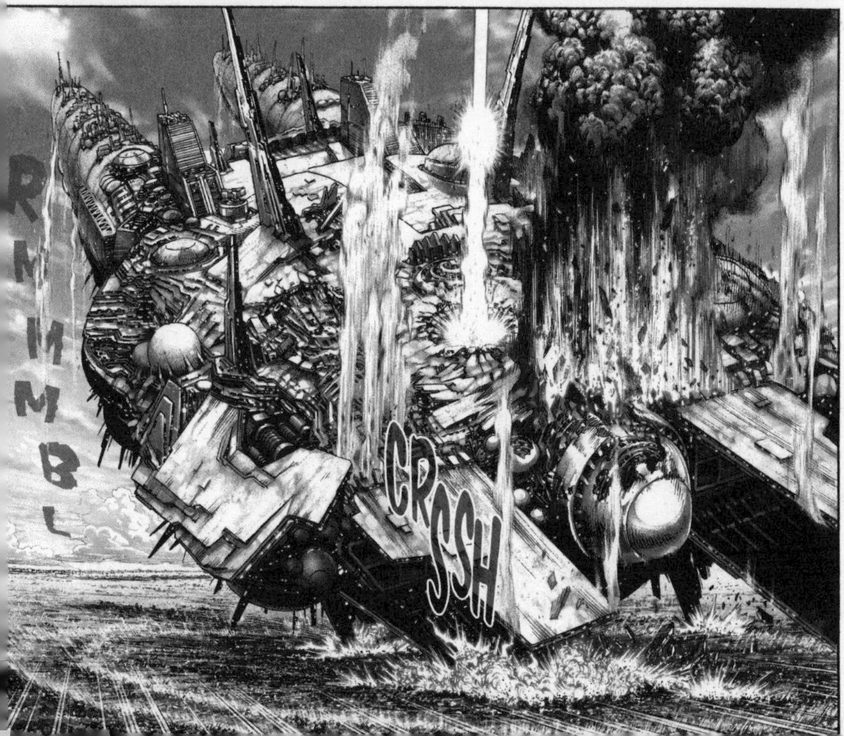
RMMMBL
CRSSH

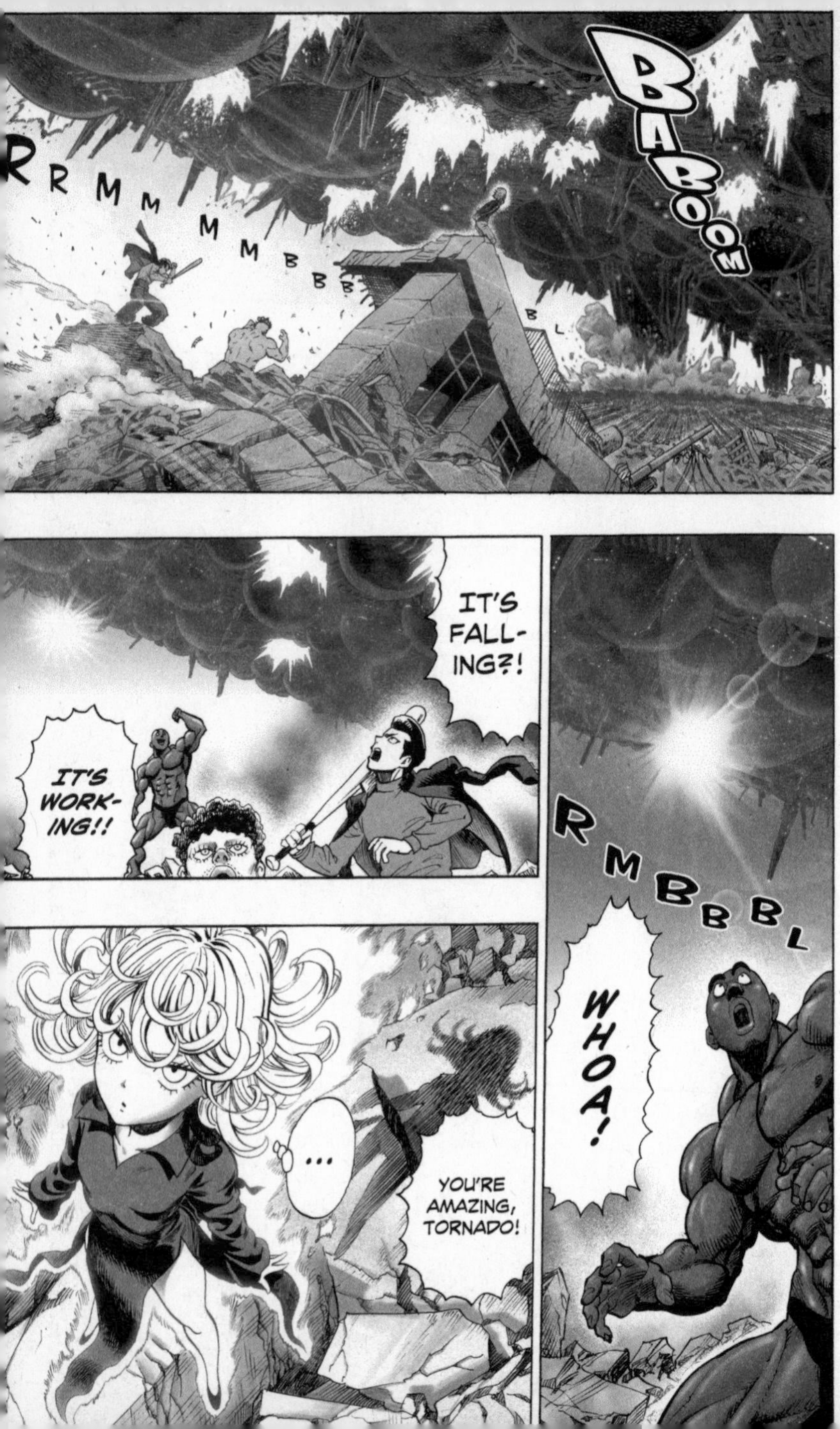
BABOOM
RRMMMMMBBBBL
RMBBBL
WHOA!
IT'S FALLING?!
IT'S WORKING!!
...
YOU'RE AMAZING, TORNADO!

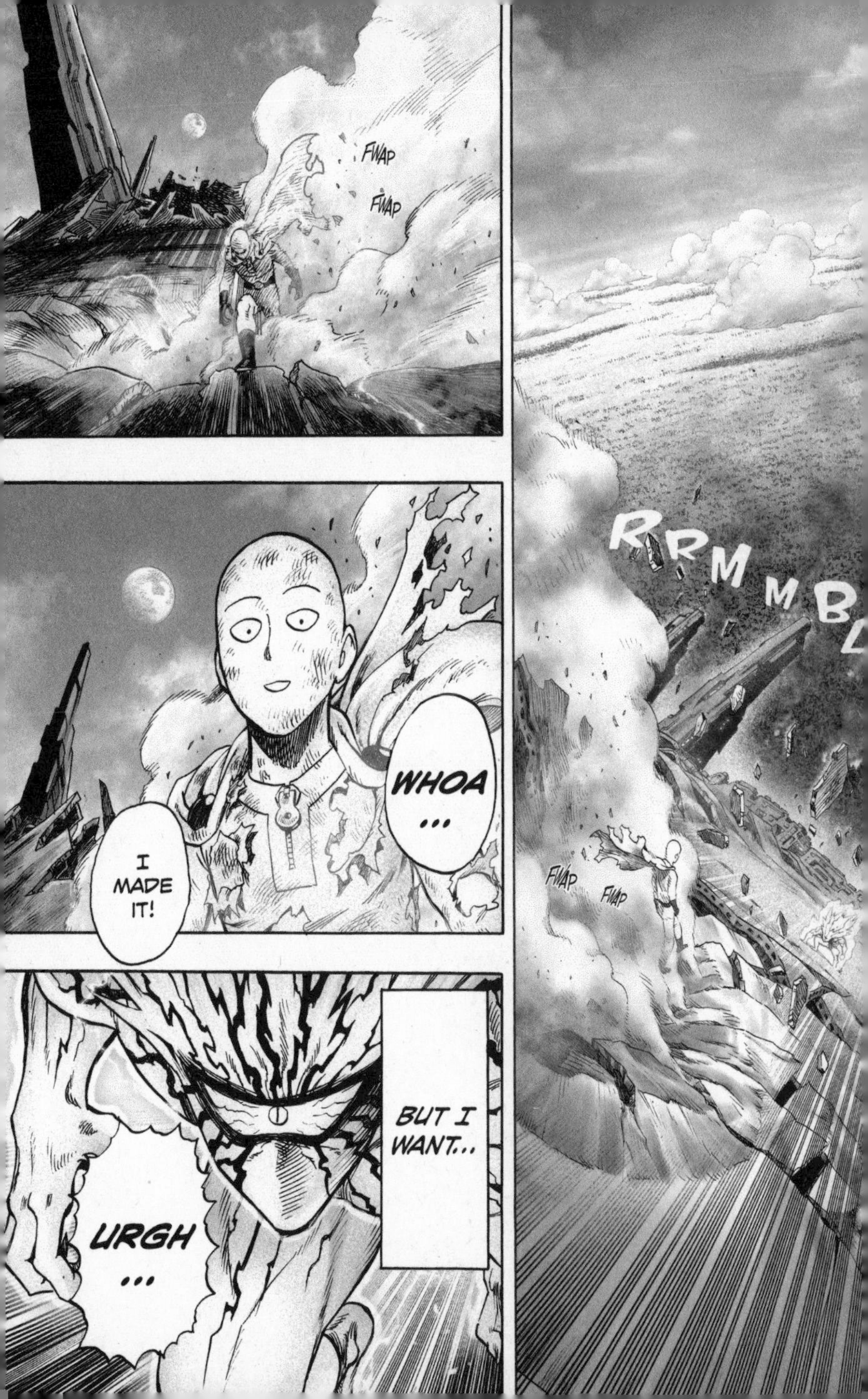
RRMMBL
FWAP
FWAP
FWAP
FWAP
WHOA...
I MADE IT!
BUT I WANT...
URGH...

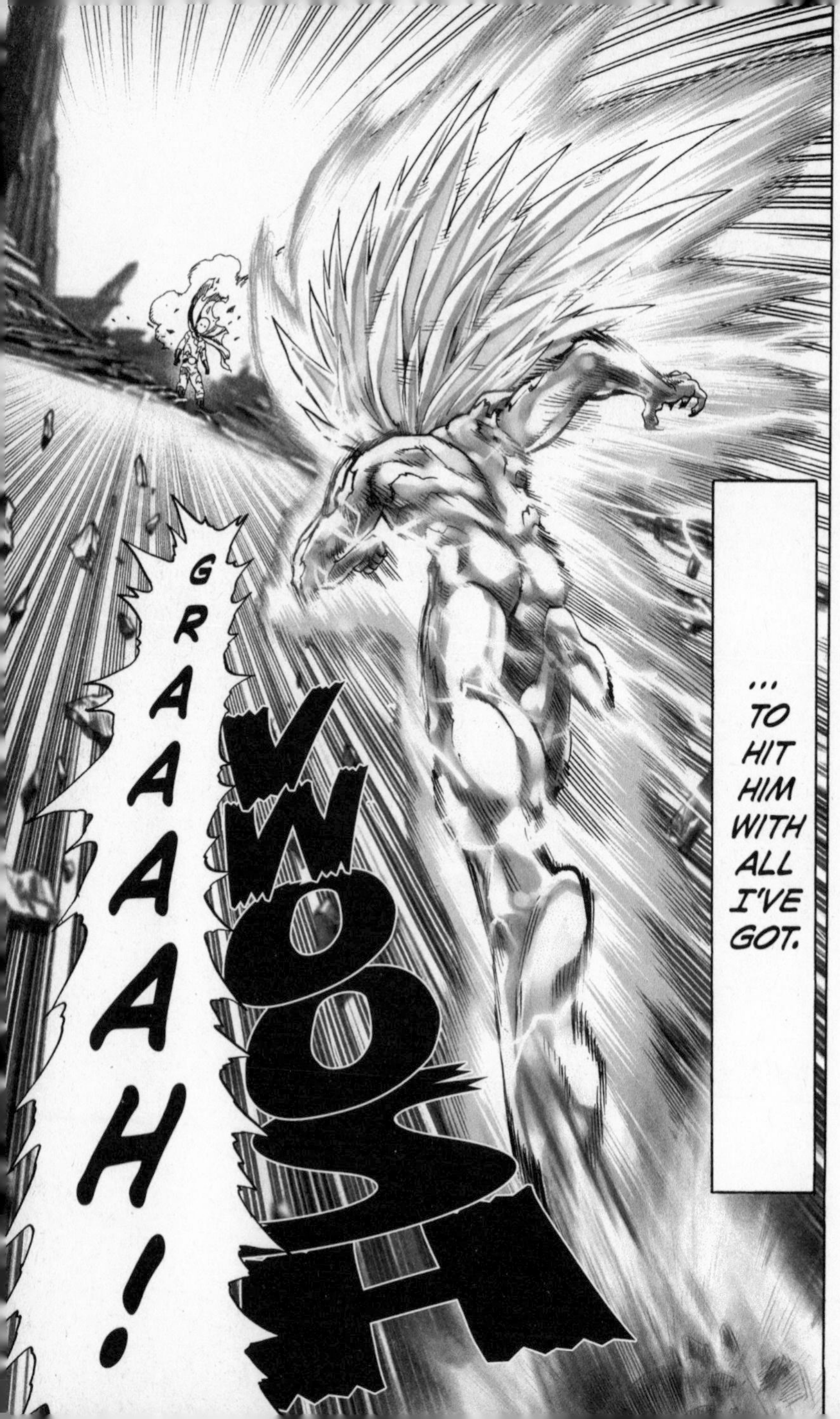
...TO HIT HIM WITH ALL I'VE GOT.
WOOSH
GRAAAAH!!

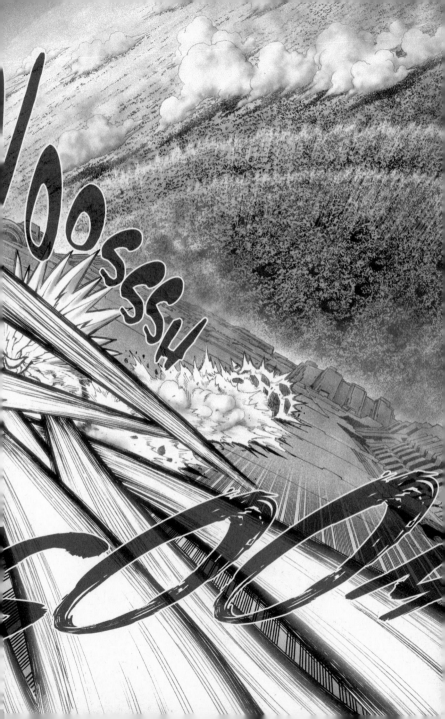

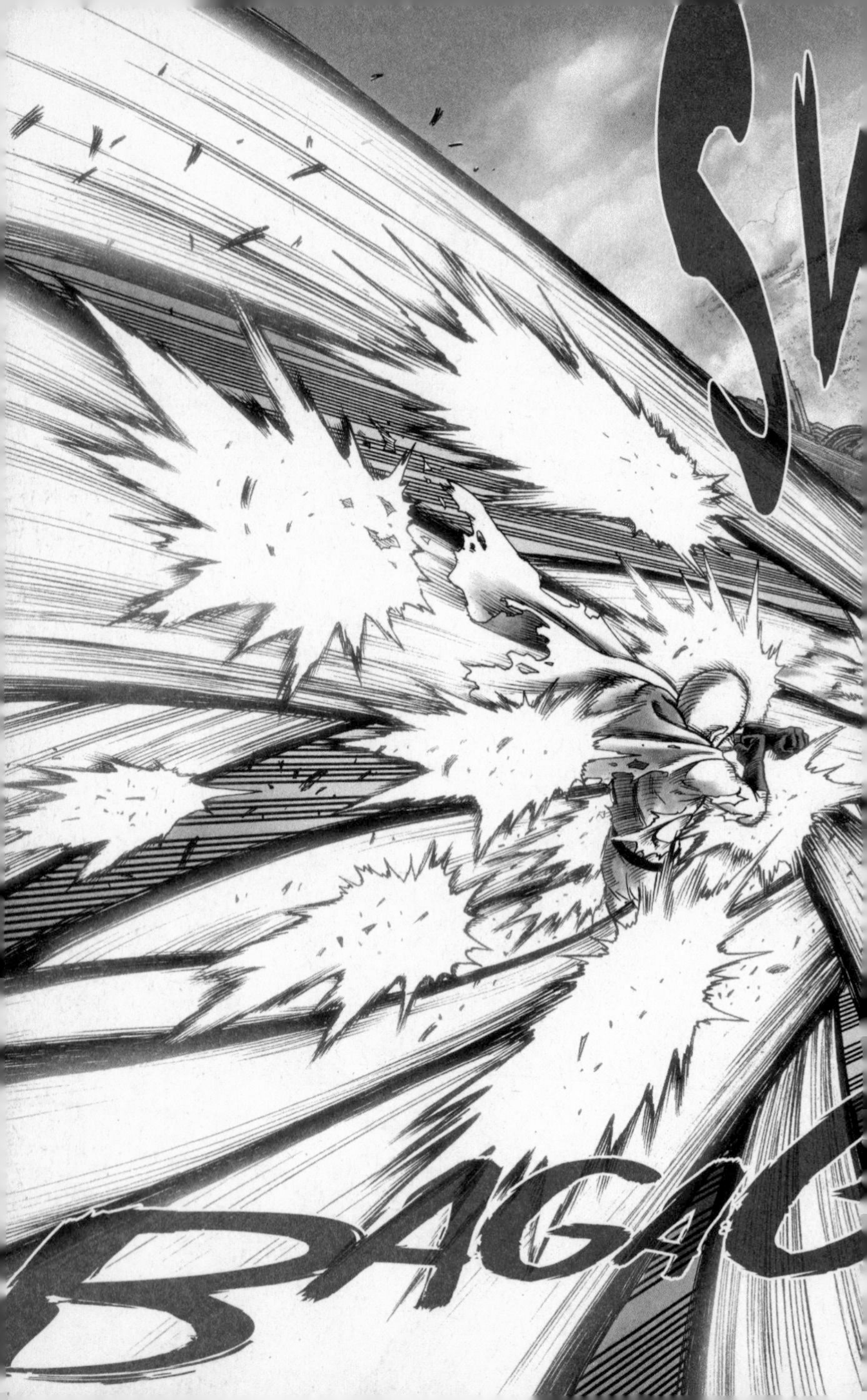
BAGA

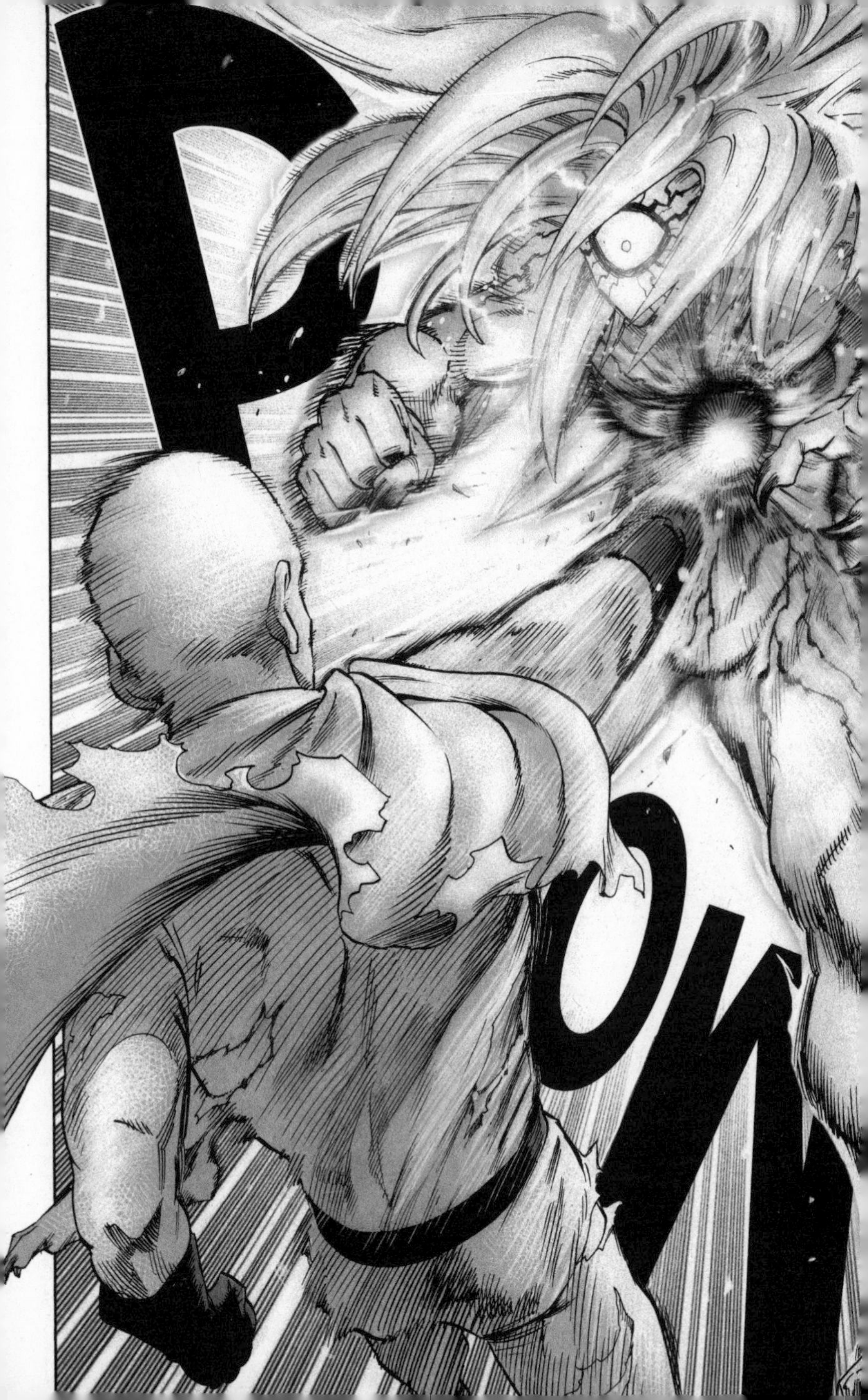
POW

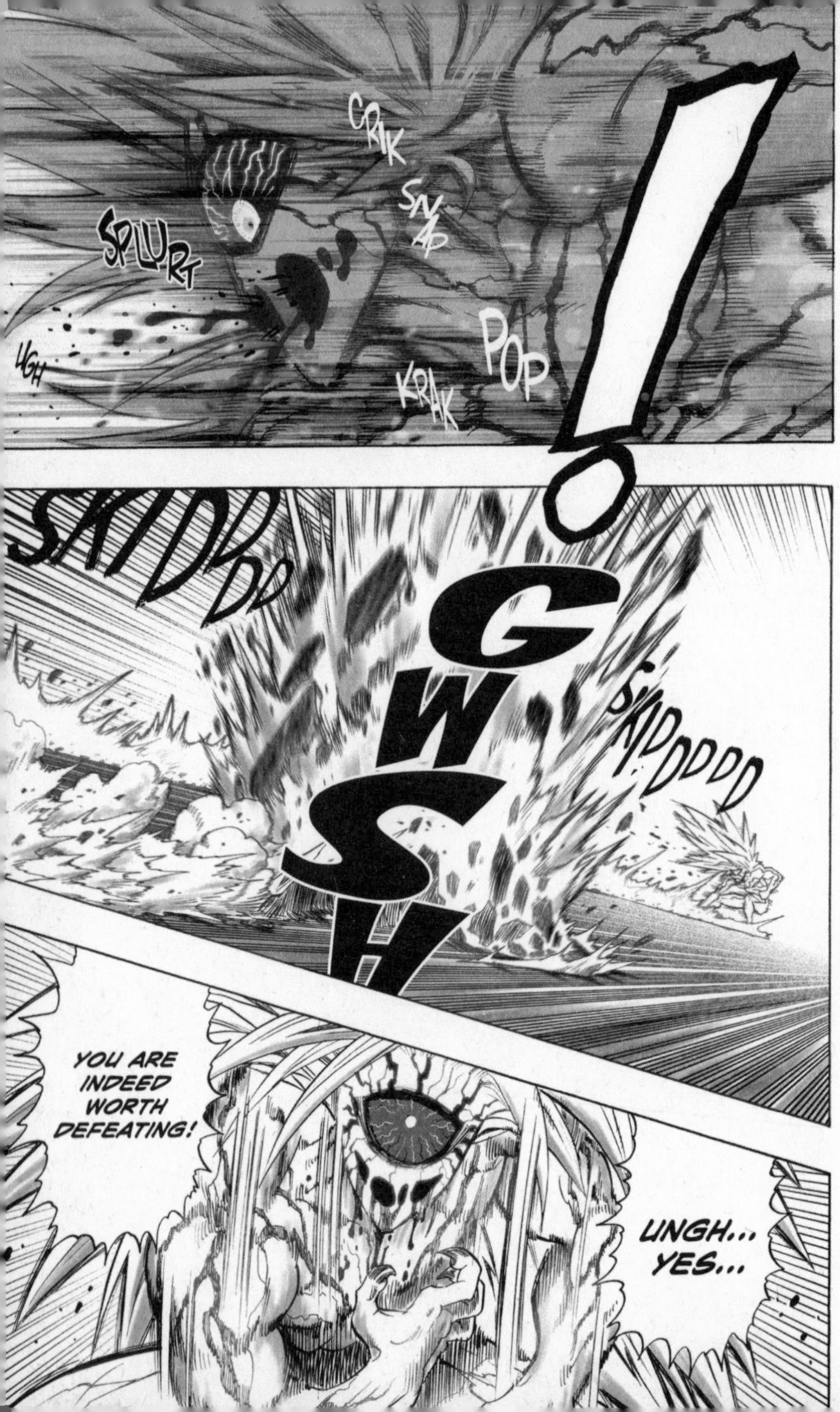
CRIK
SNAP
POP
KRAK
SPLURT
UGH
GWSH!
SKIDDDDD
SKIDDDDD
YOU ARE INDEED WORTH DEFEATING!
UNGH... YES...

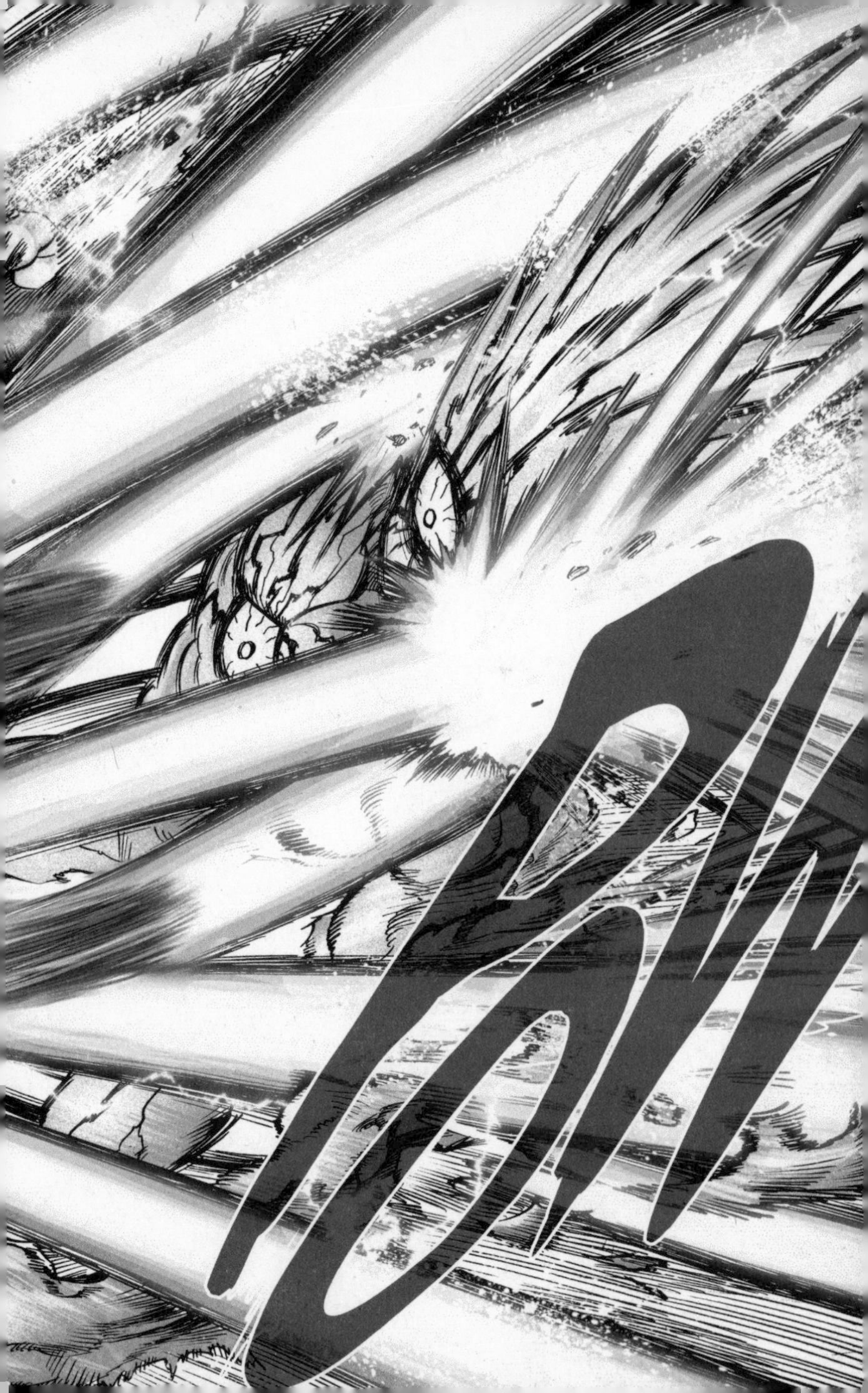

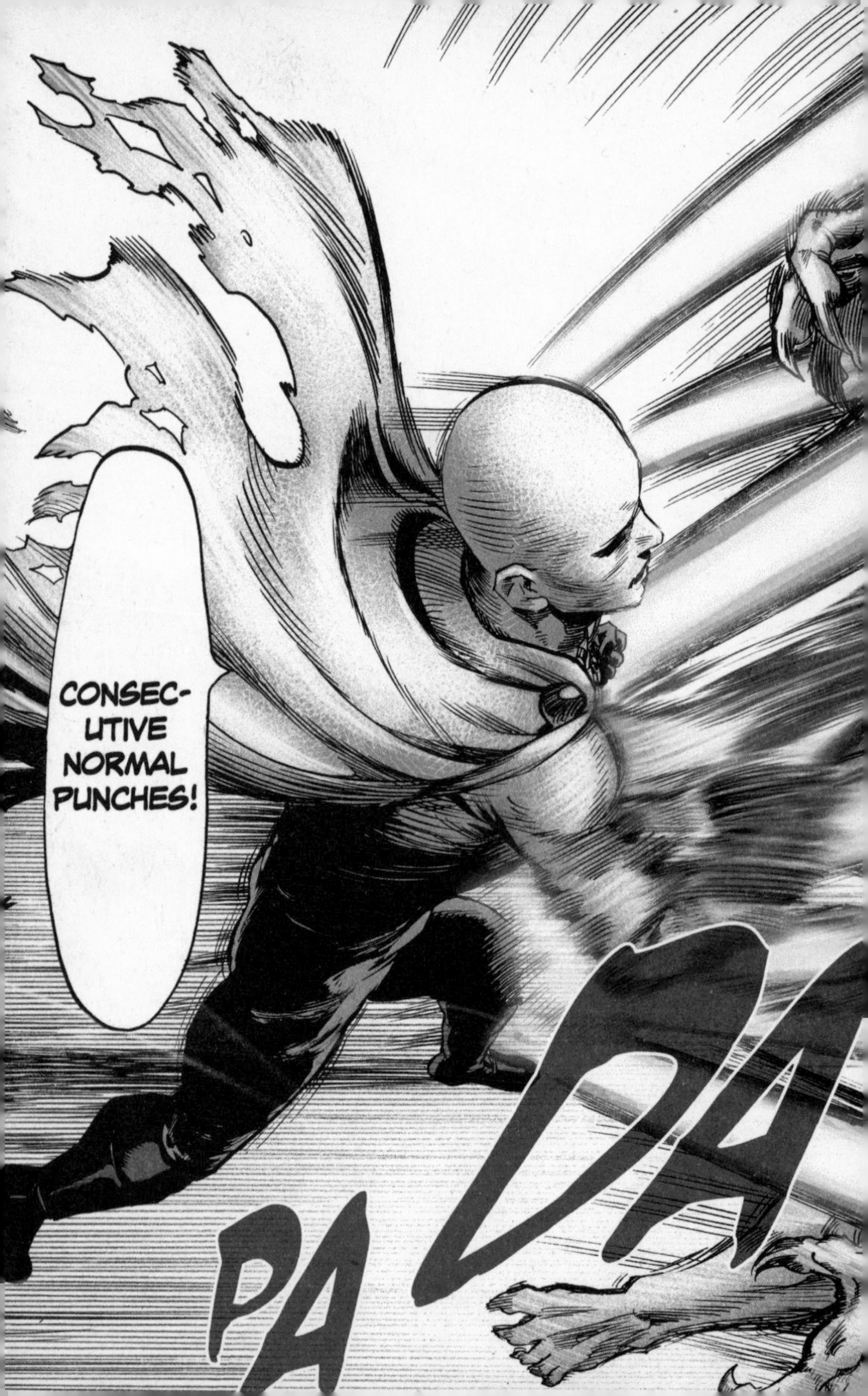
CONSEC-UTIVE NORMAL PUNCHES!
PA DA

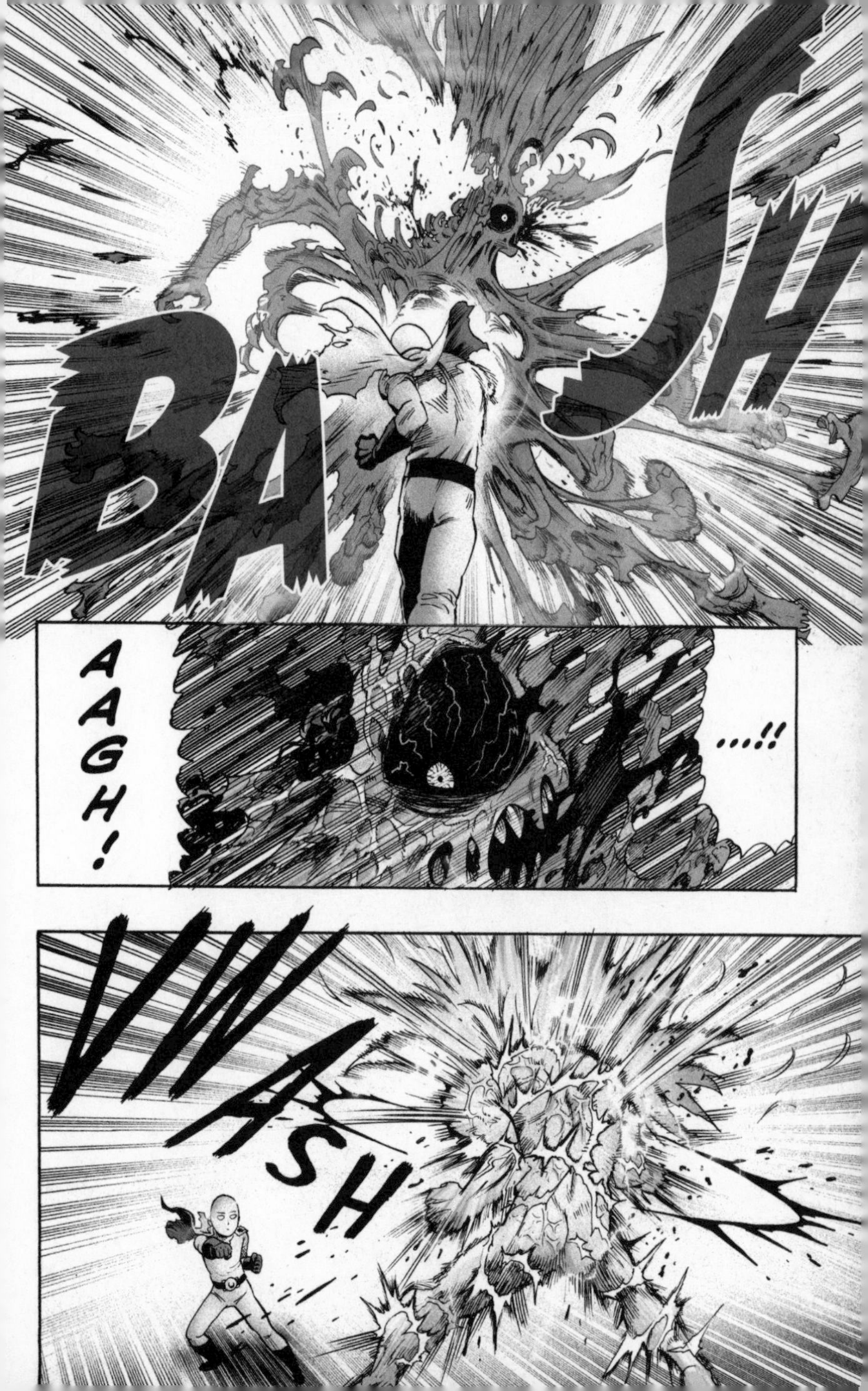
BASH
...!!
AAGH!
VWASH

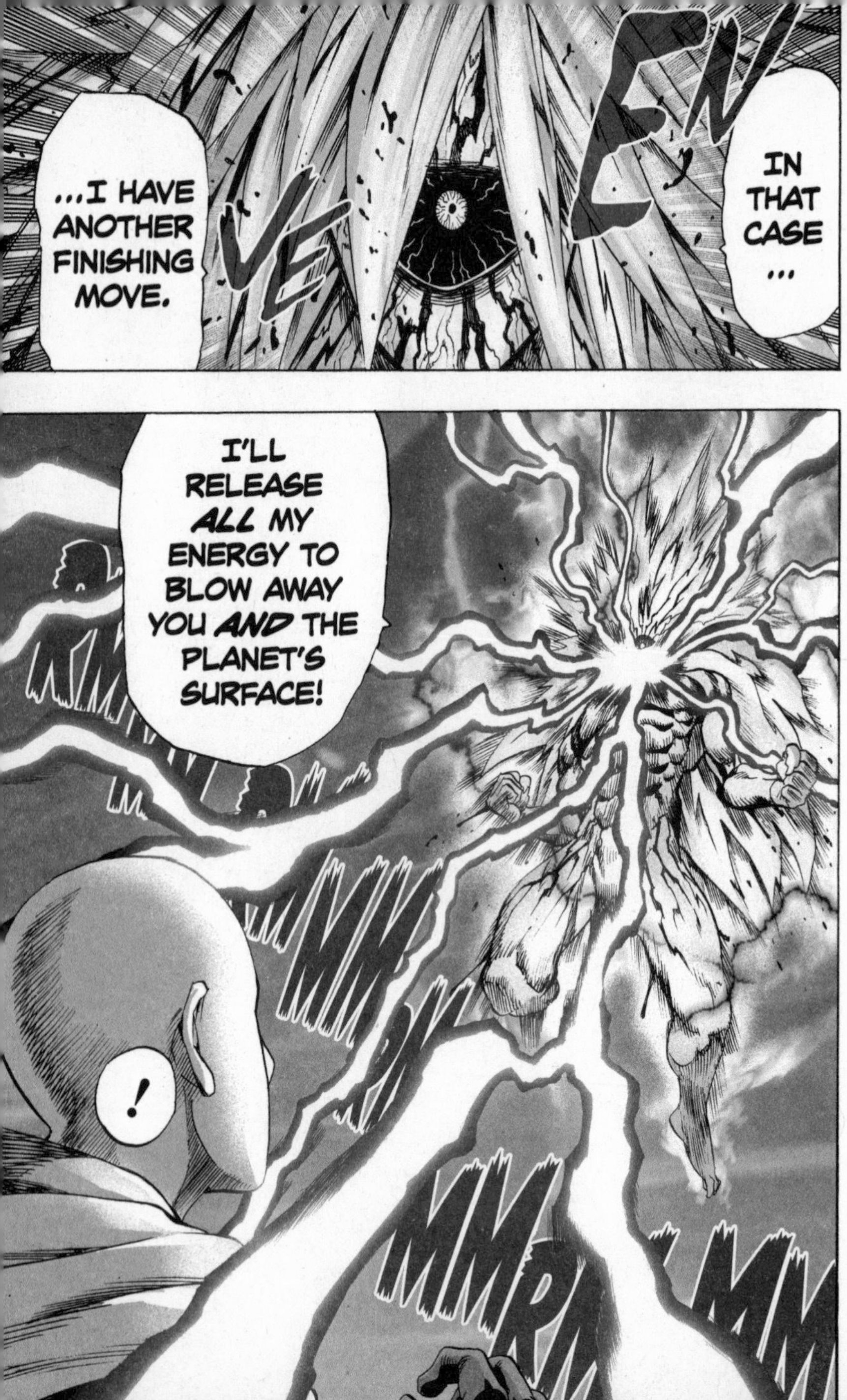
IN THAT CASE ...
...I HAVE ANOTHER FINISHING MOVE.
I'LL RELEASE ALL MY ENERGY TO BLOW AWAY YOU AND THE PLANET'S SURFACE!
!

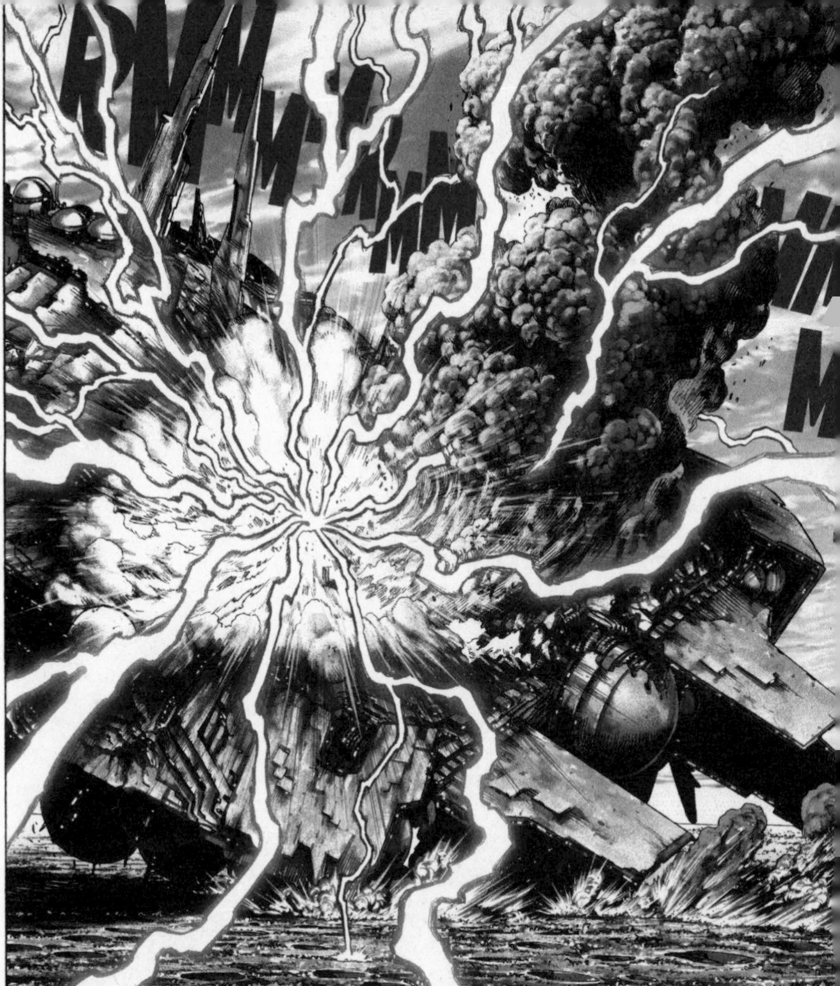

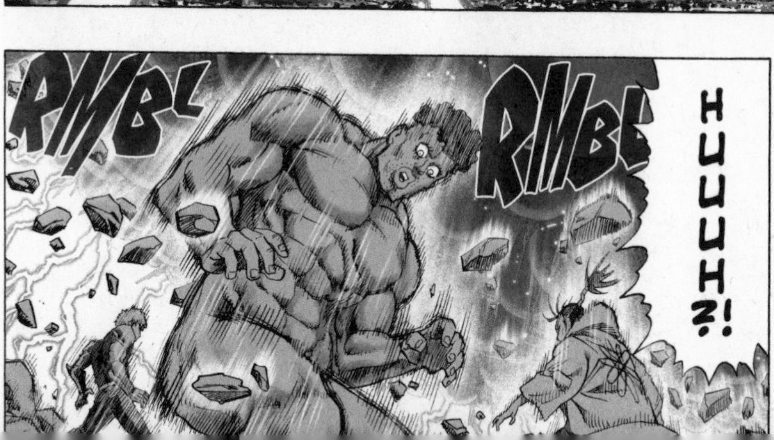
HUUUH?!

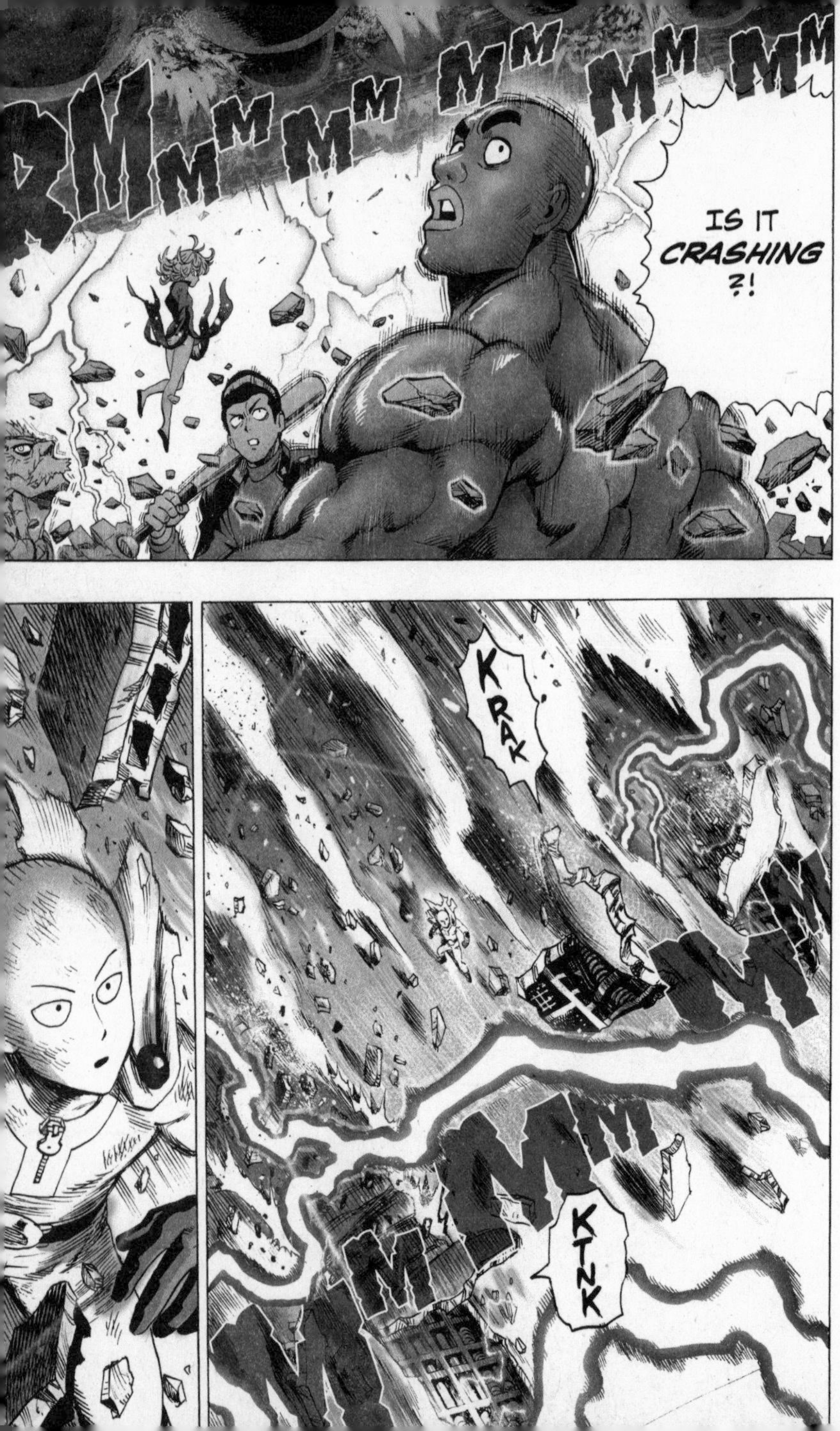
RMMMMMMMMMMMM
IS IT CRASHING ?!
KRAK
MMMM
MMMMM
KTNK

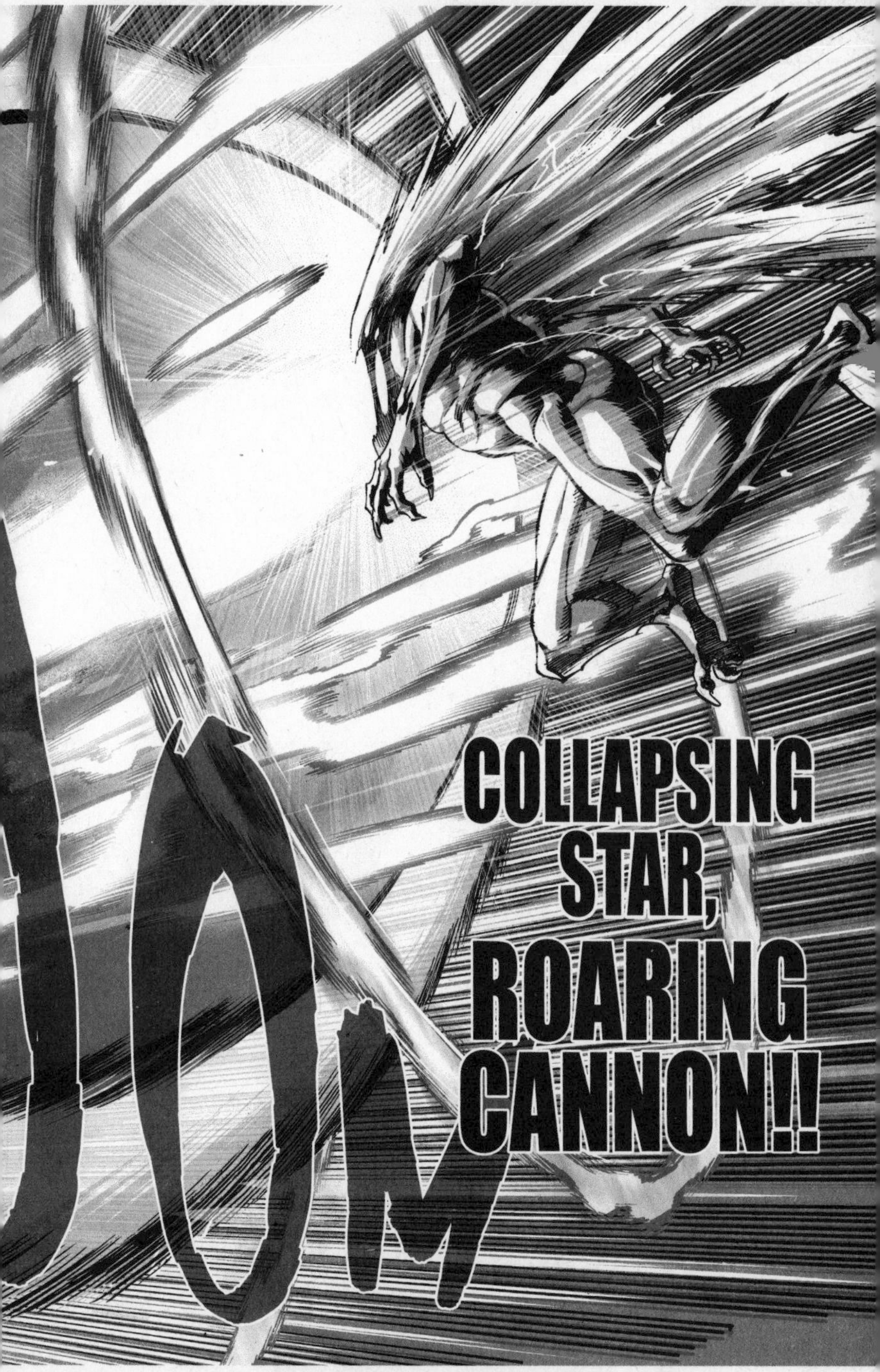
COLLAPSING STAR, ROARING CANNON!!

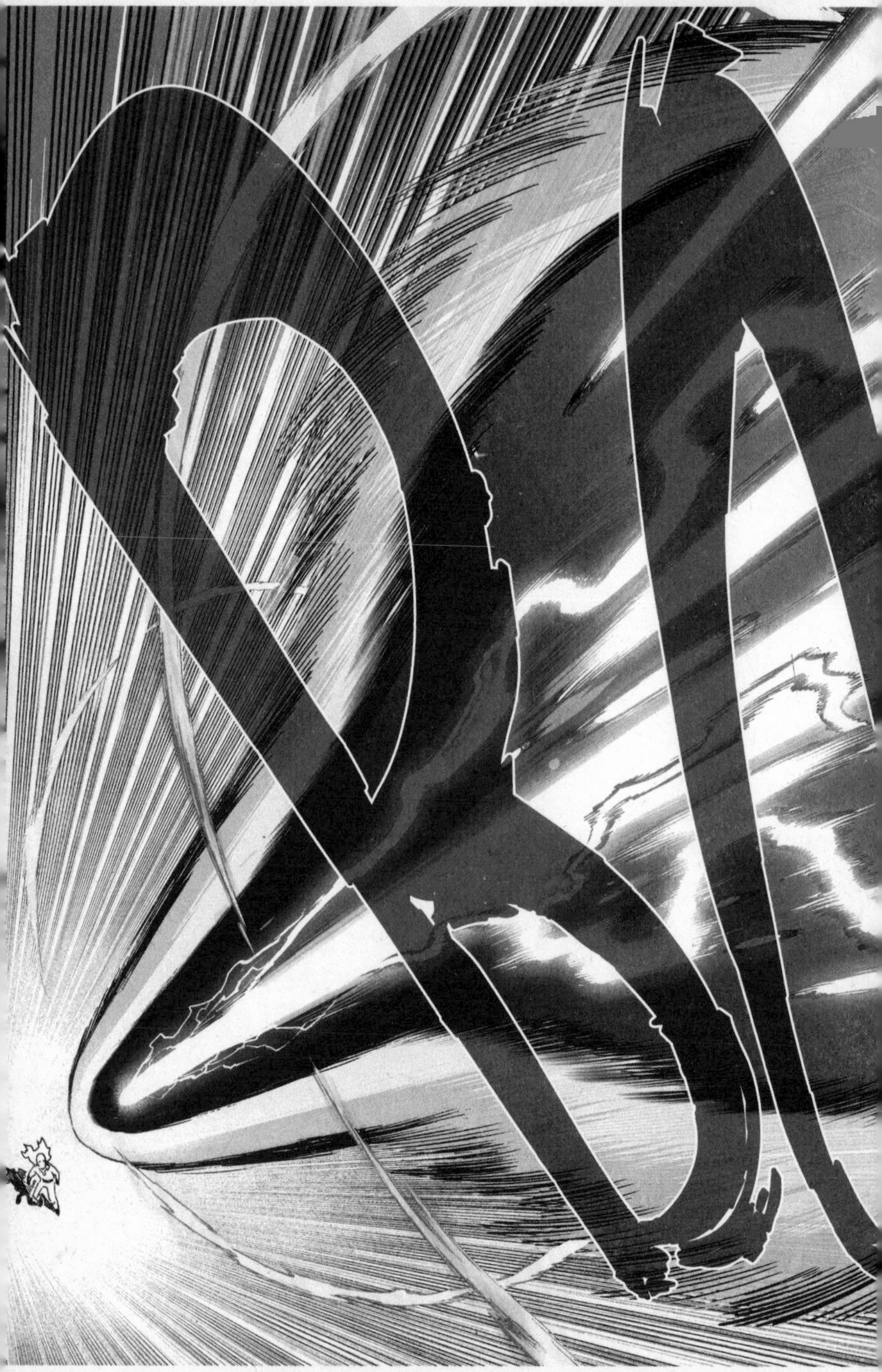

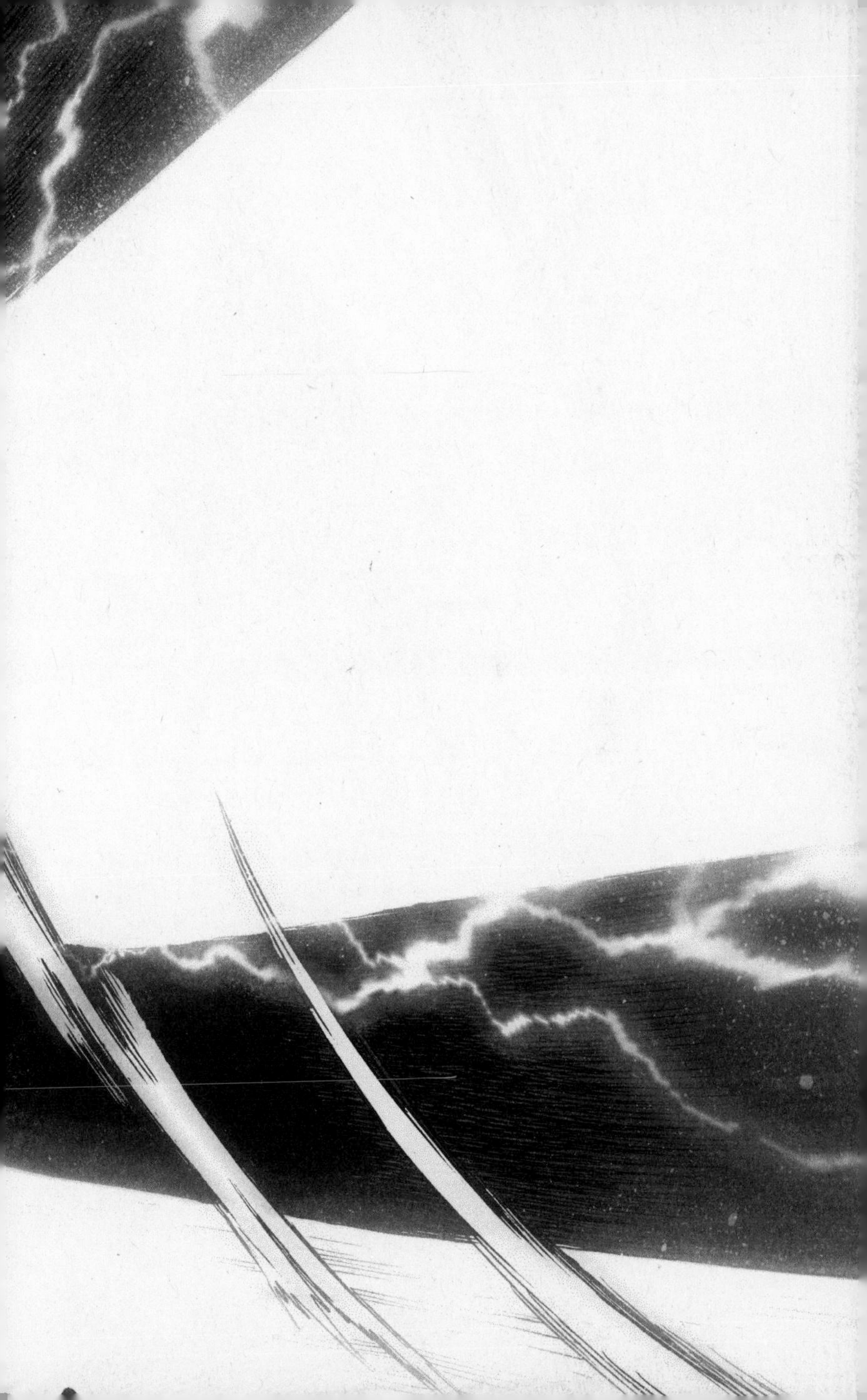

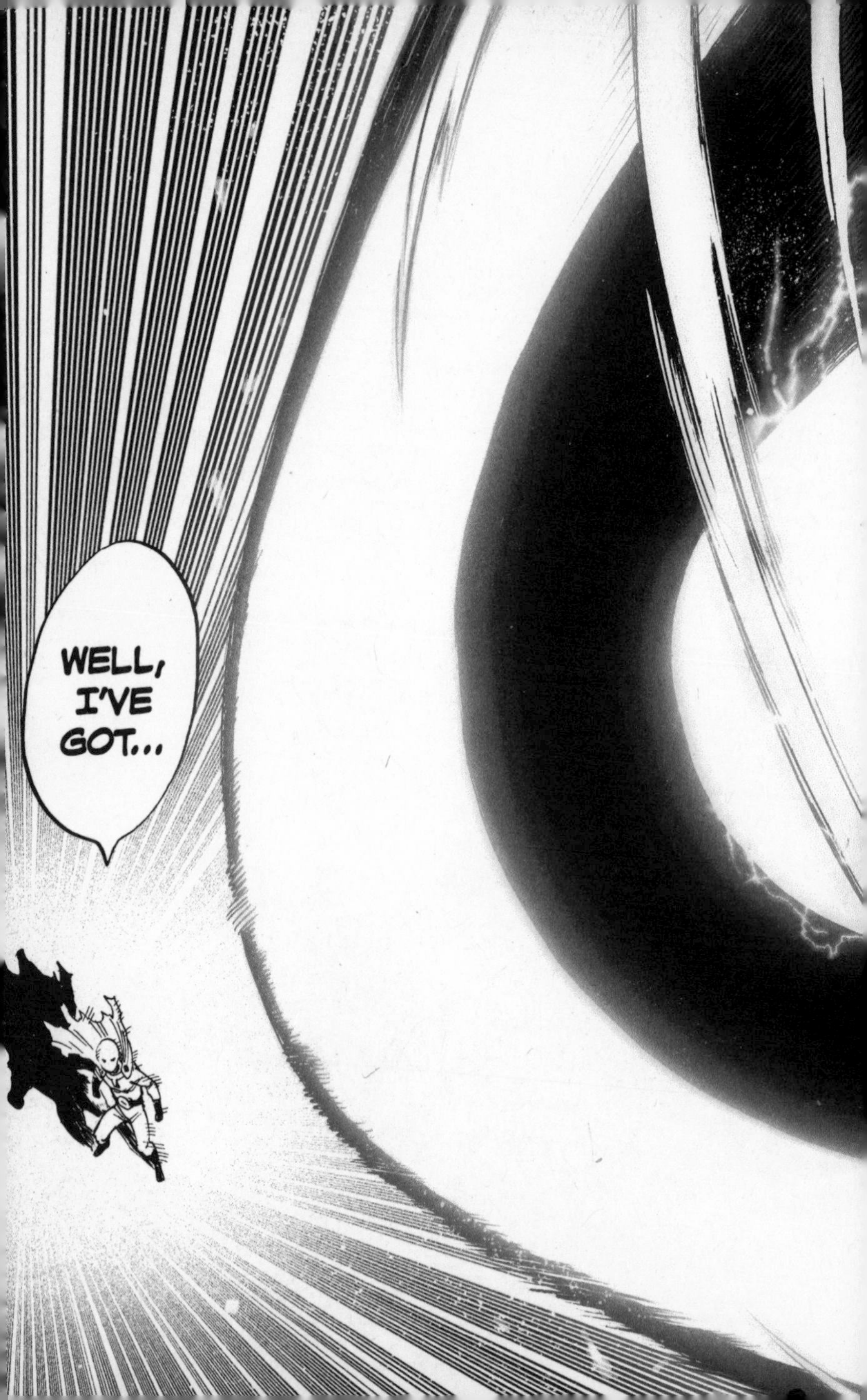
WELL, I'VE GOT...

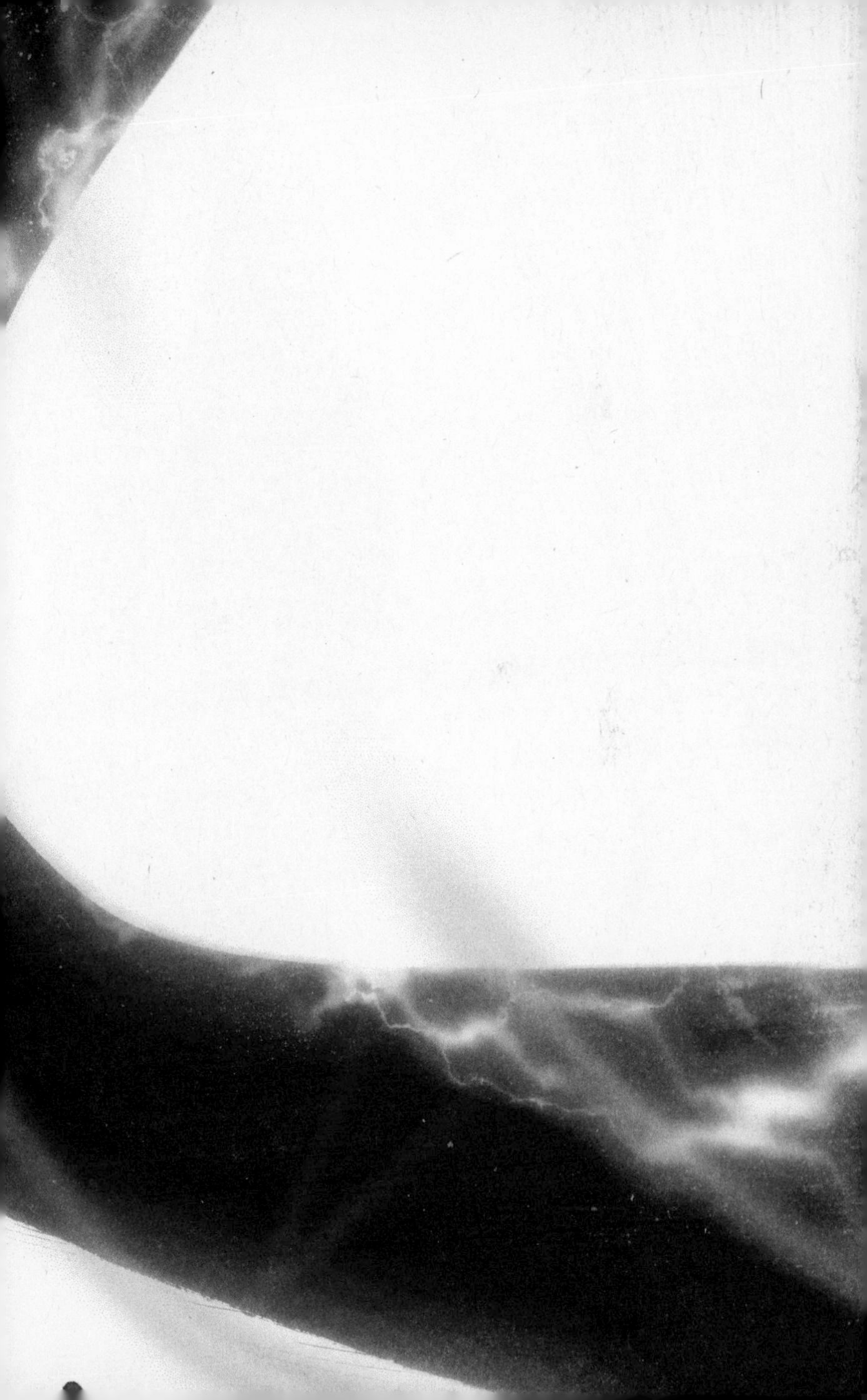

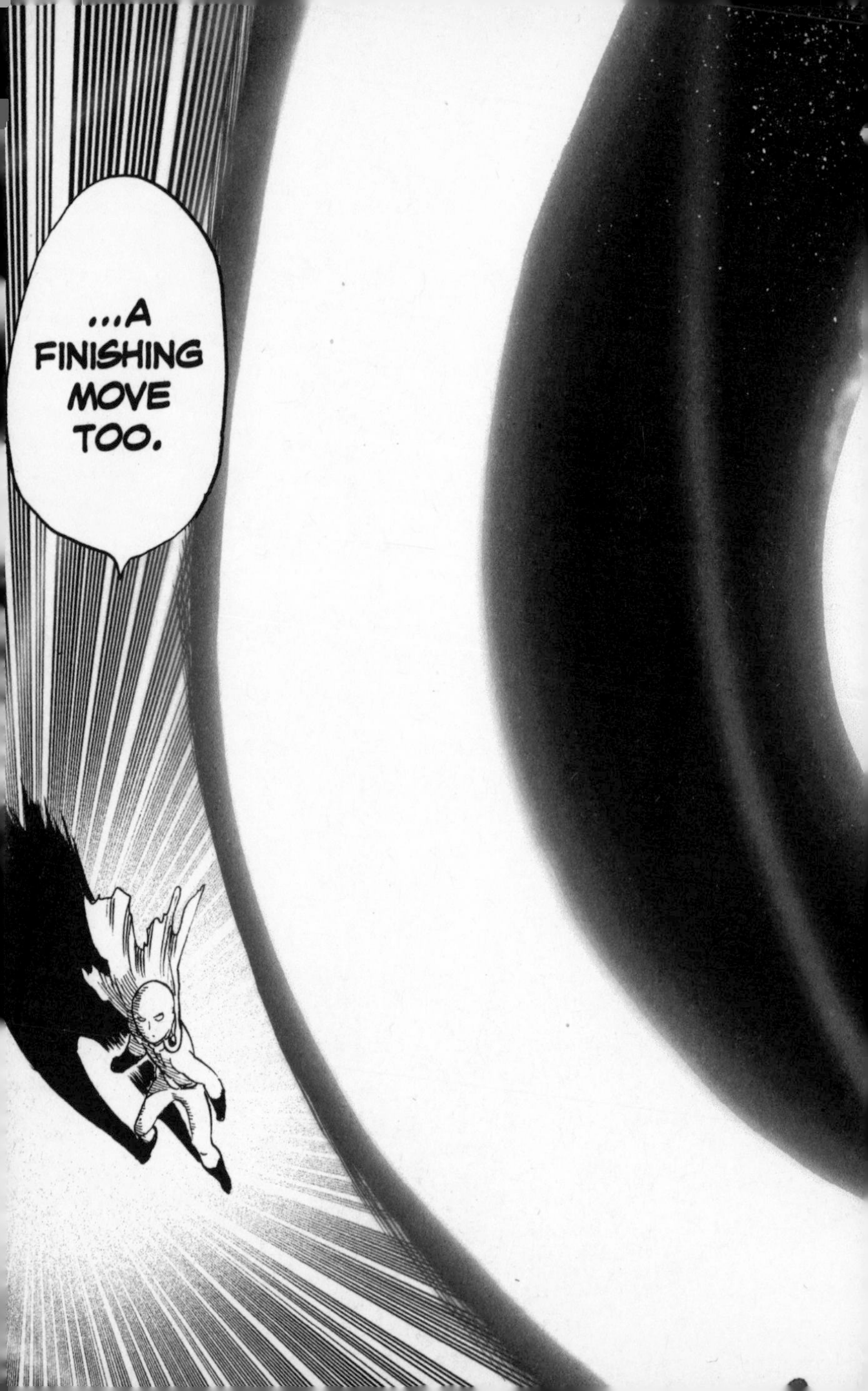
...A FINISHING MOVE TOO.

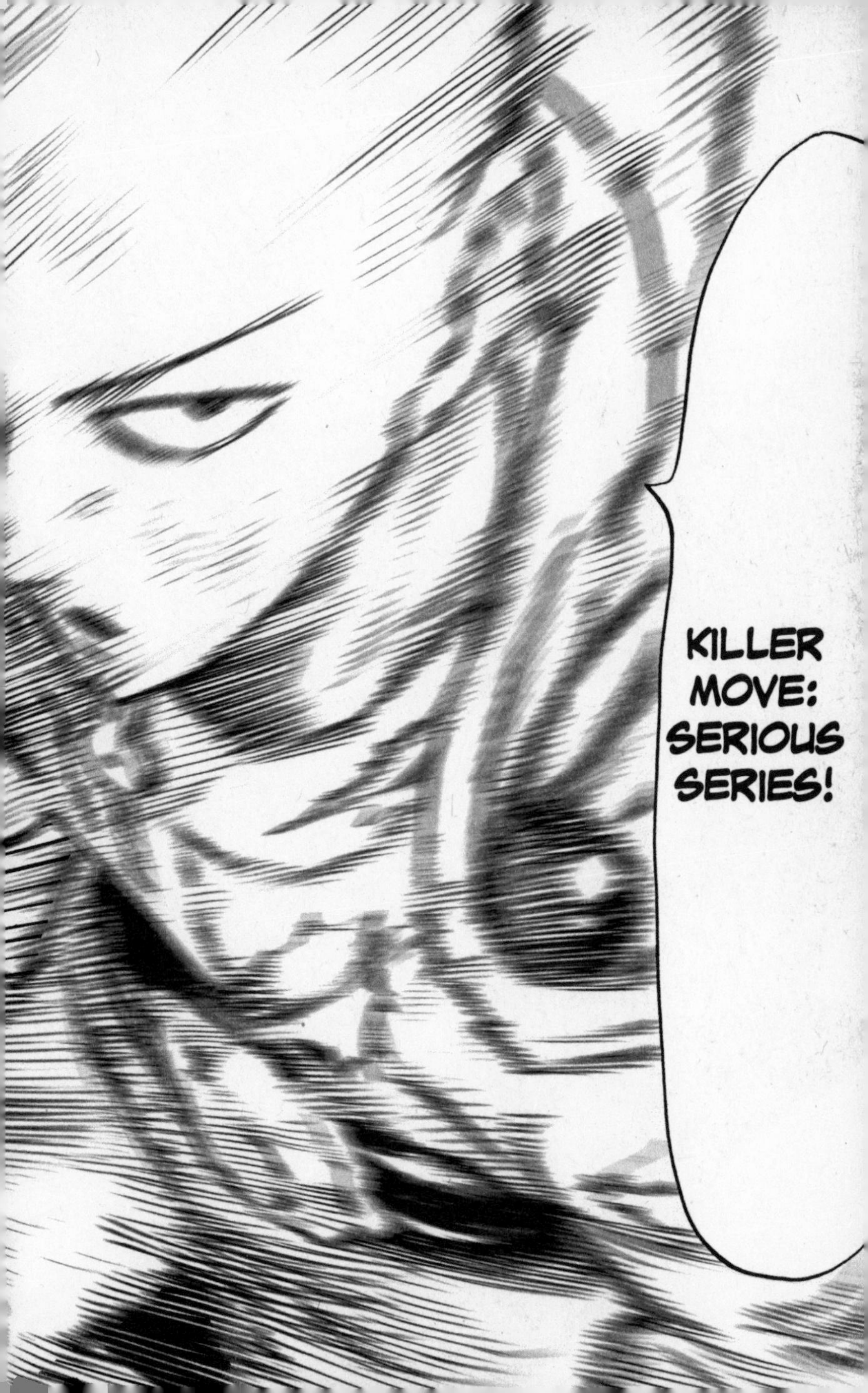
KILLER MOVE: SERIOUS SERIES!

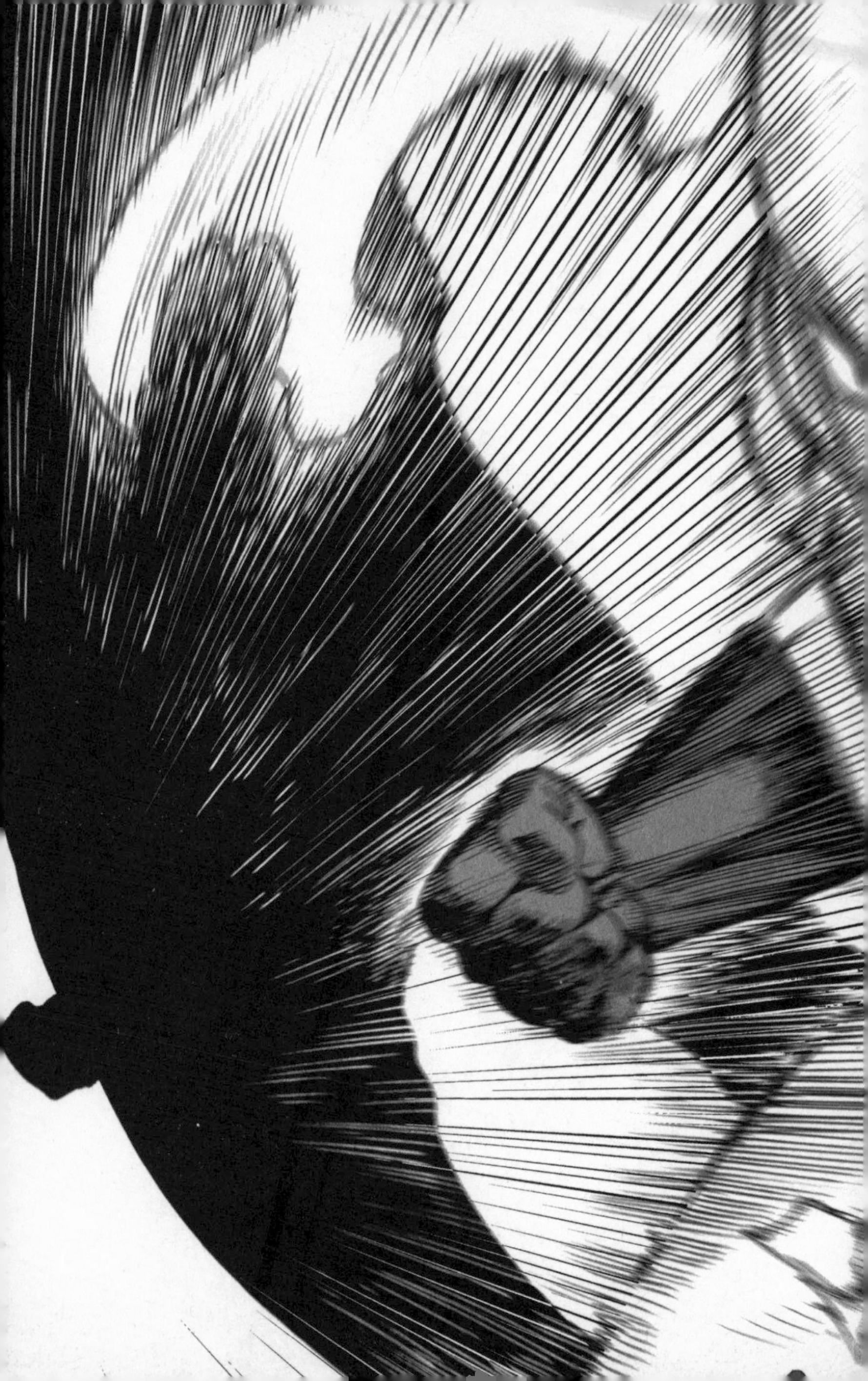

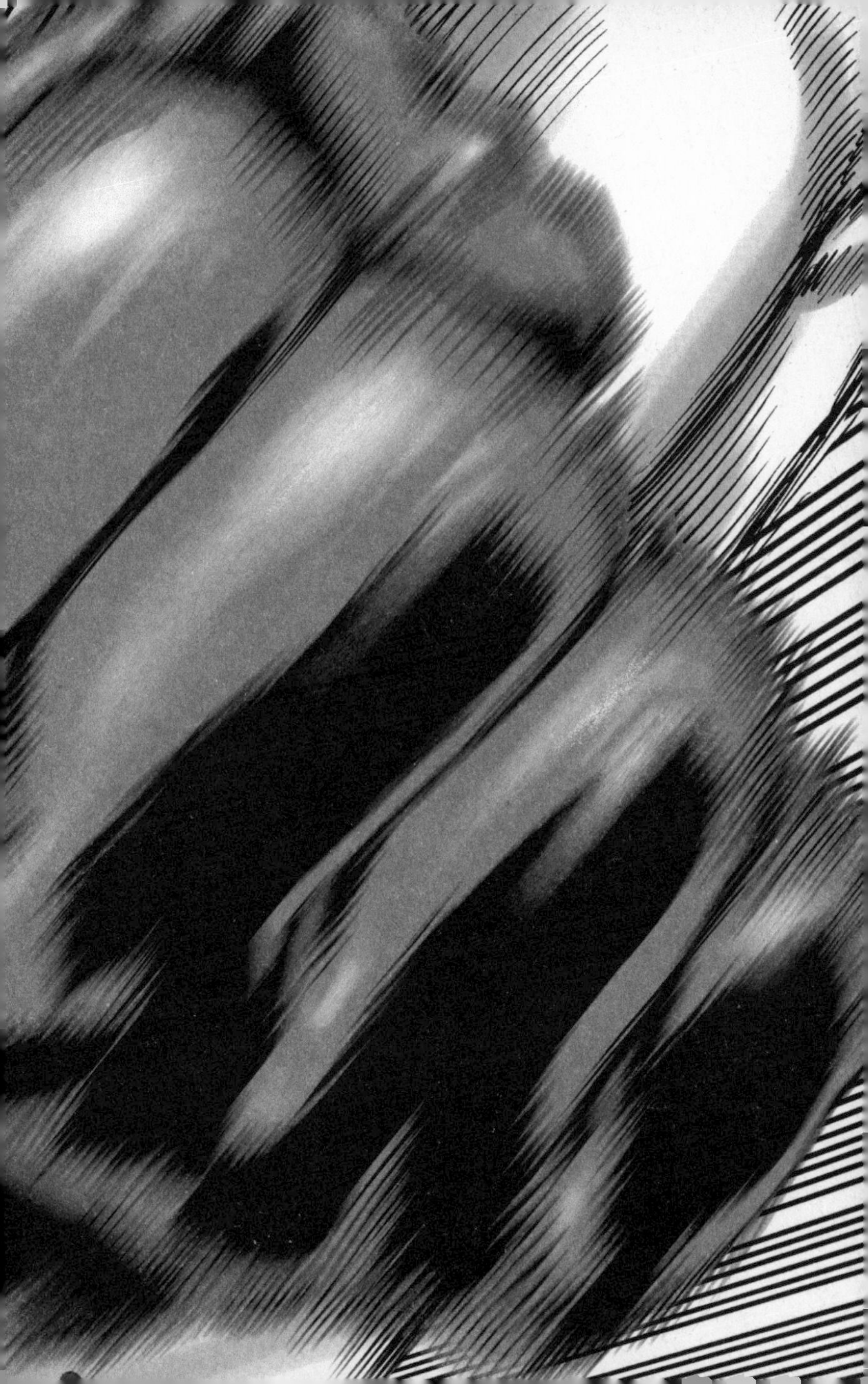

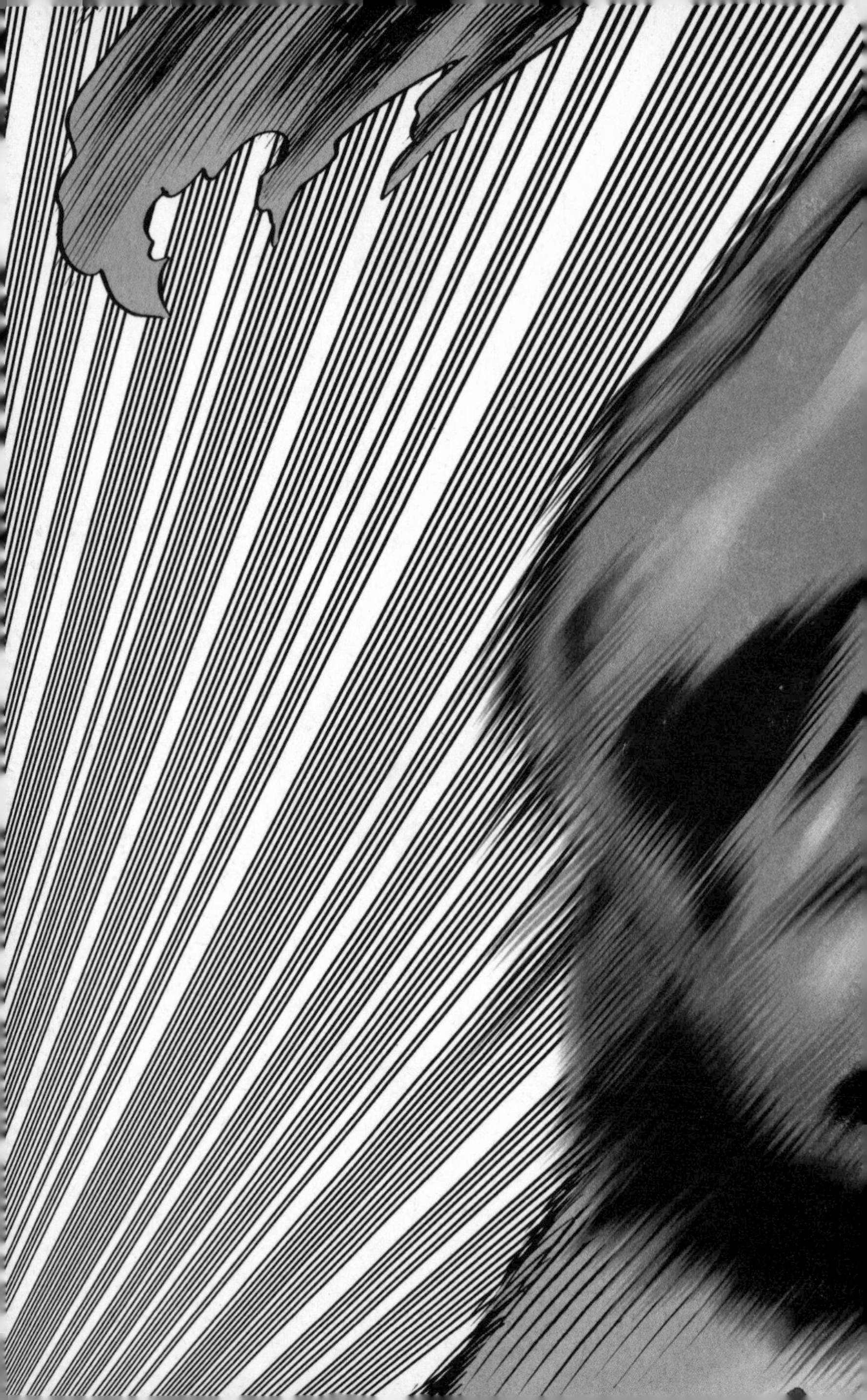

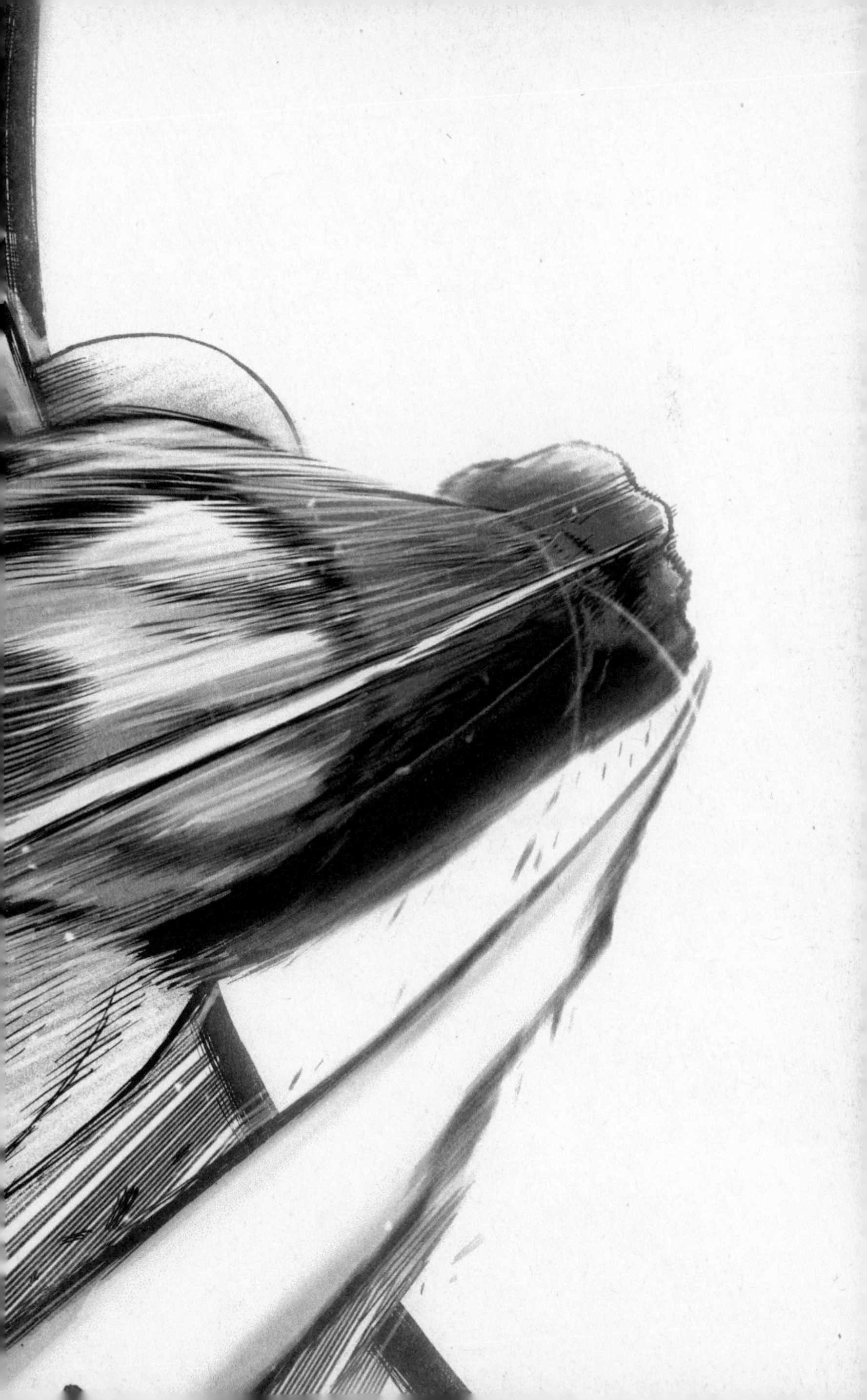

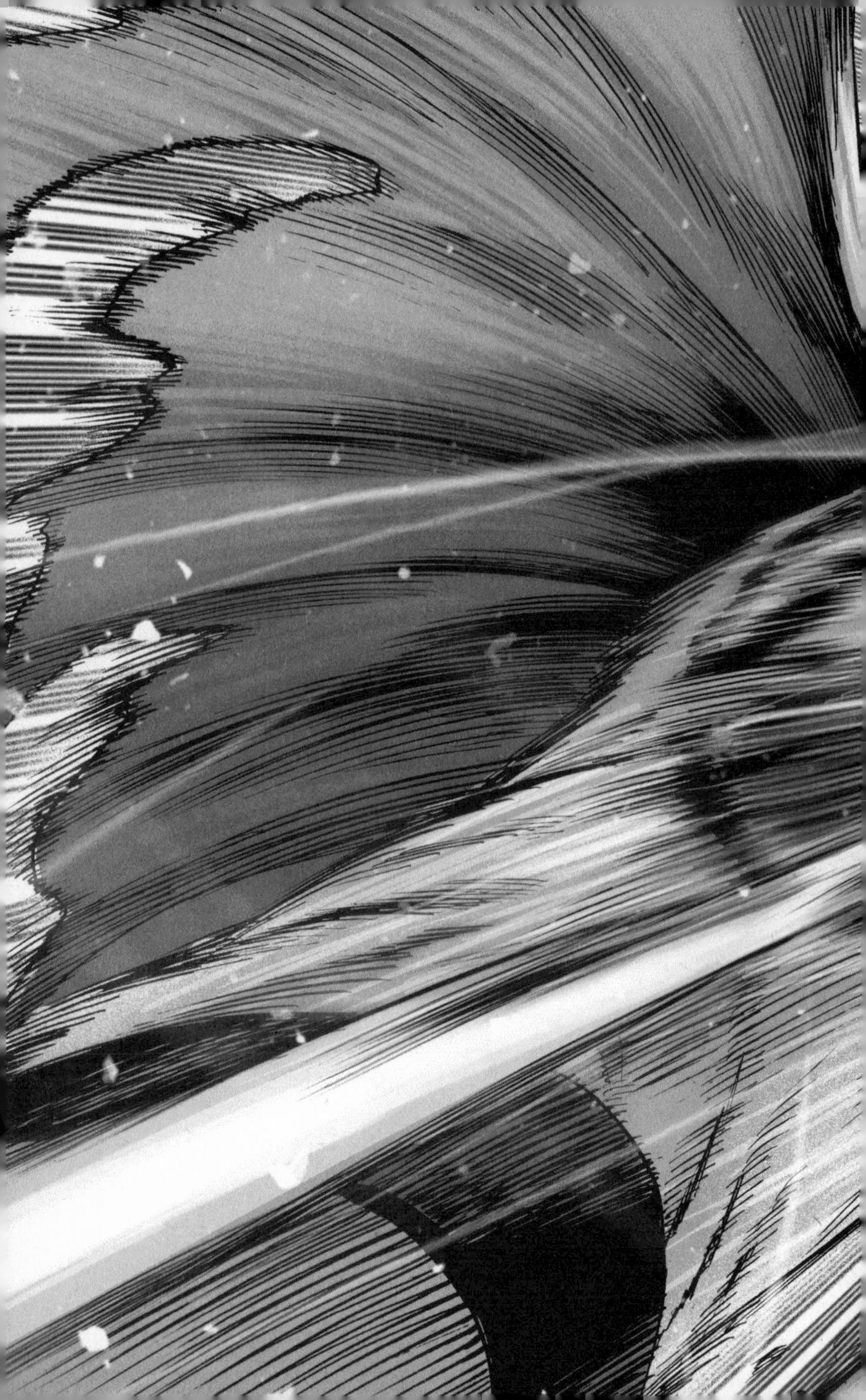

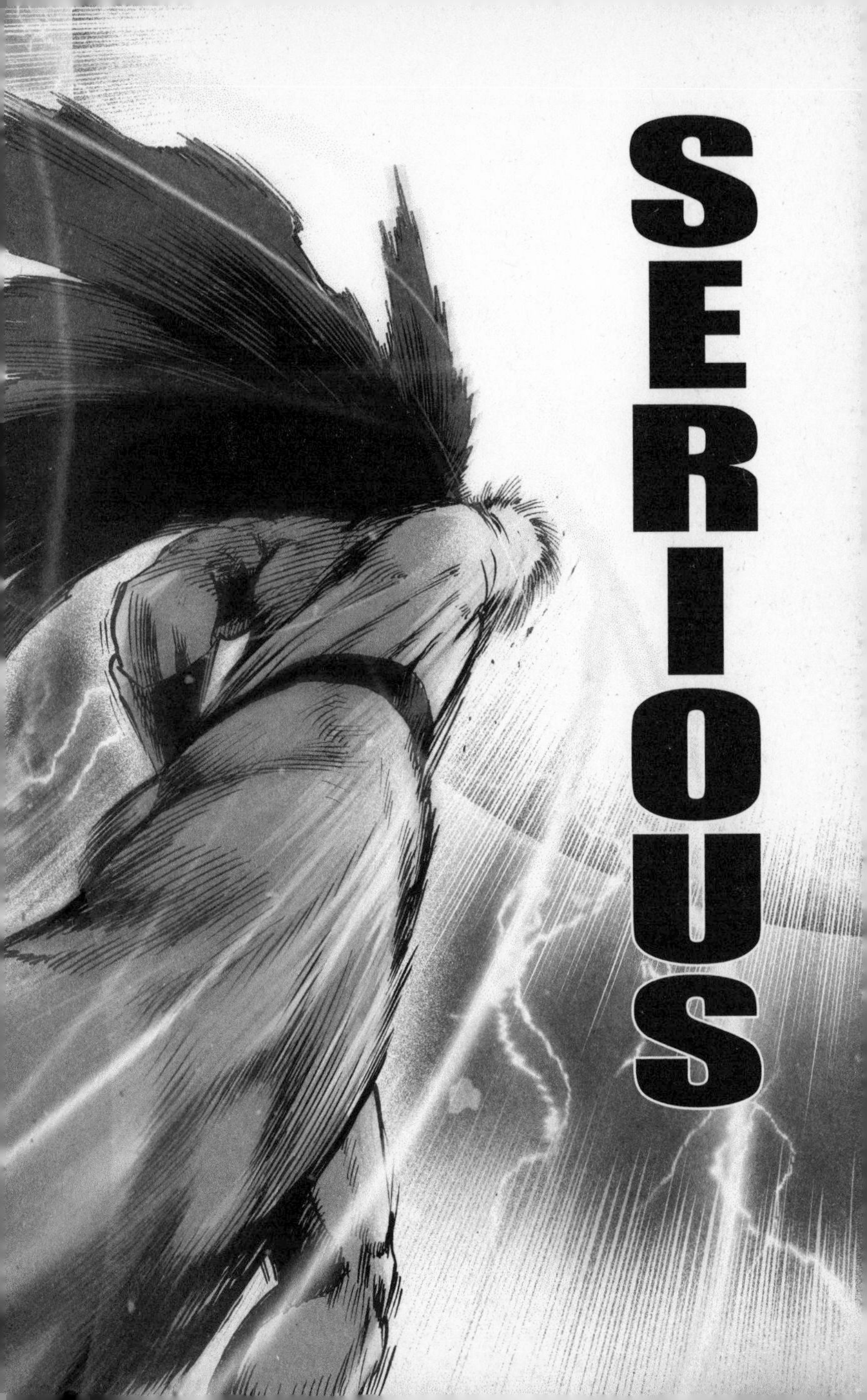
SERIOUS

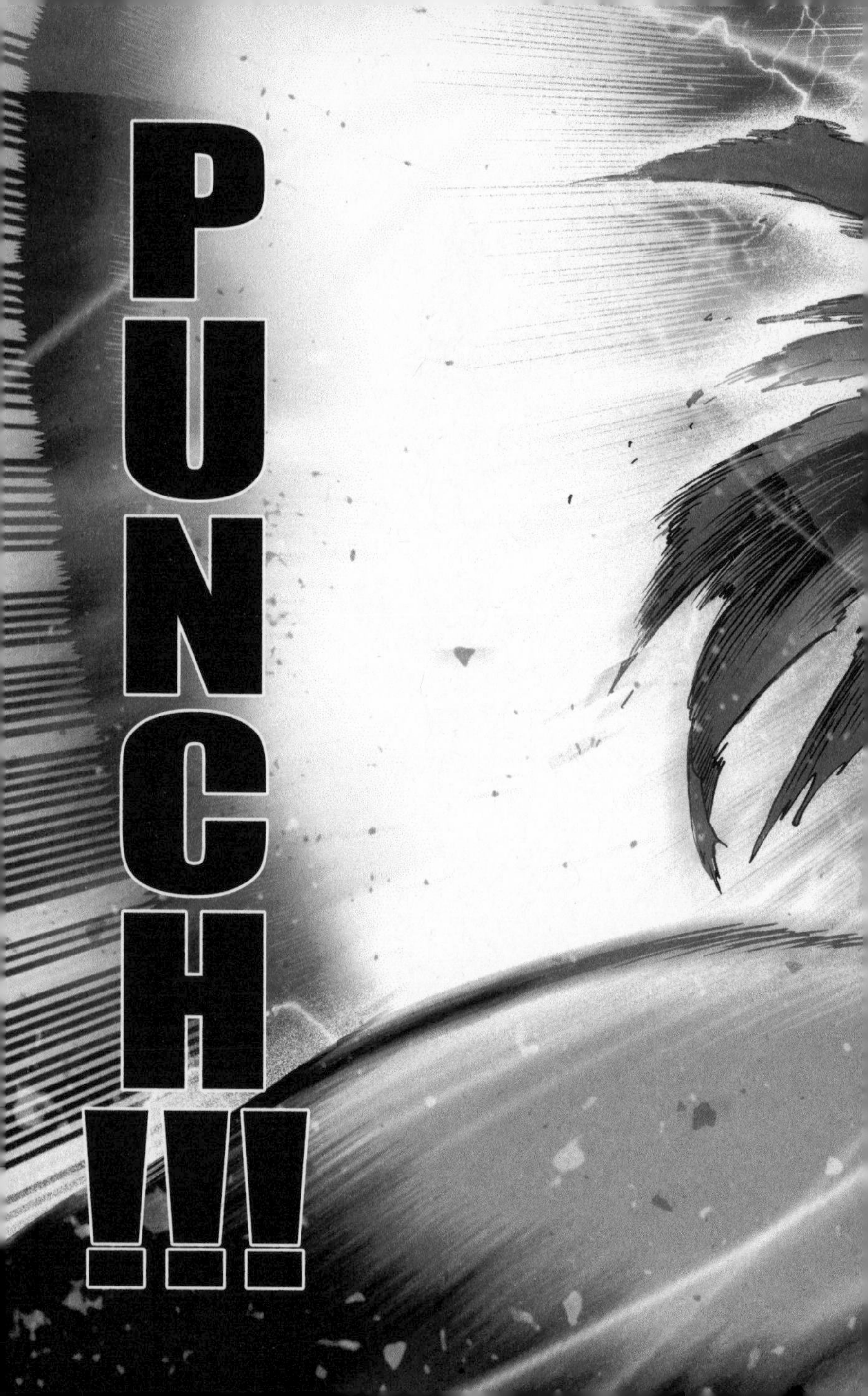
PUNCH!!!

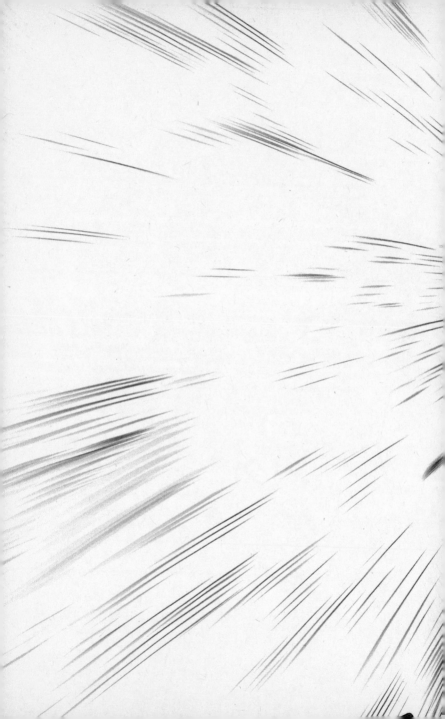

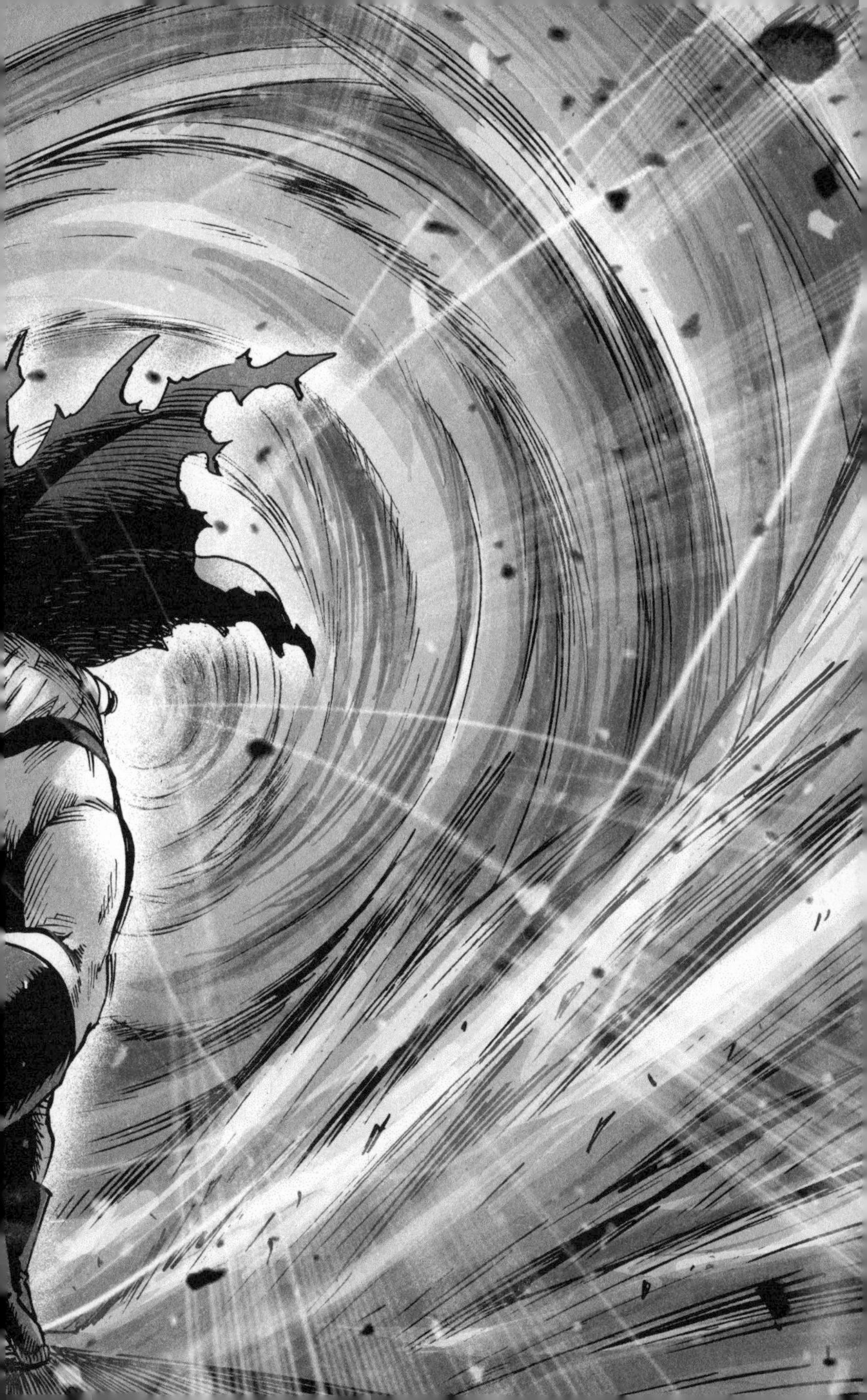

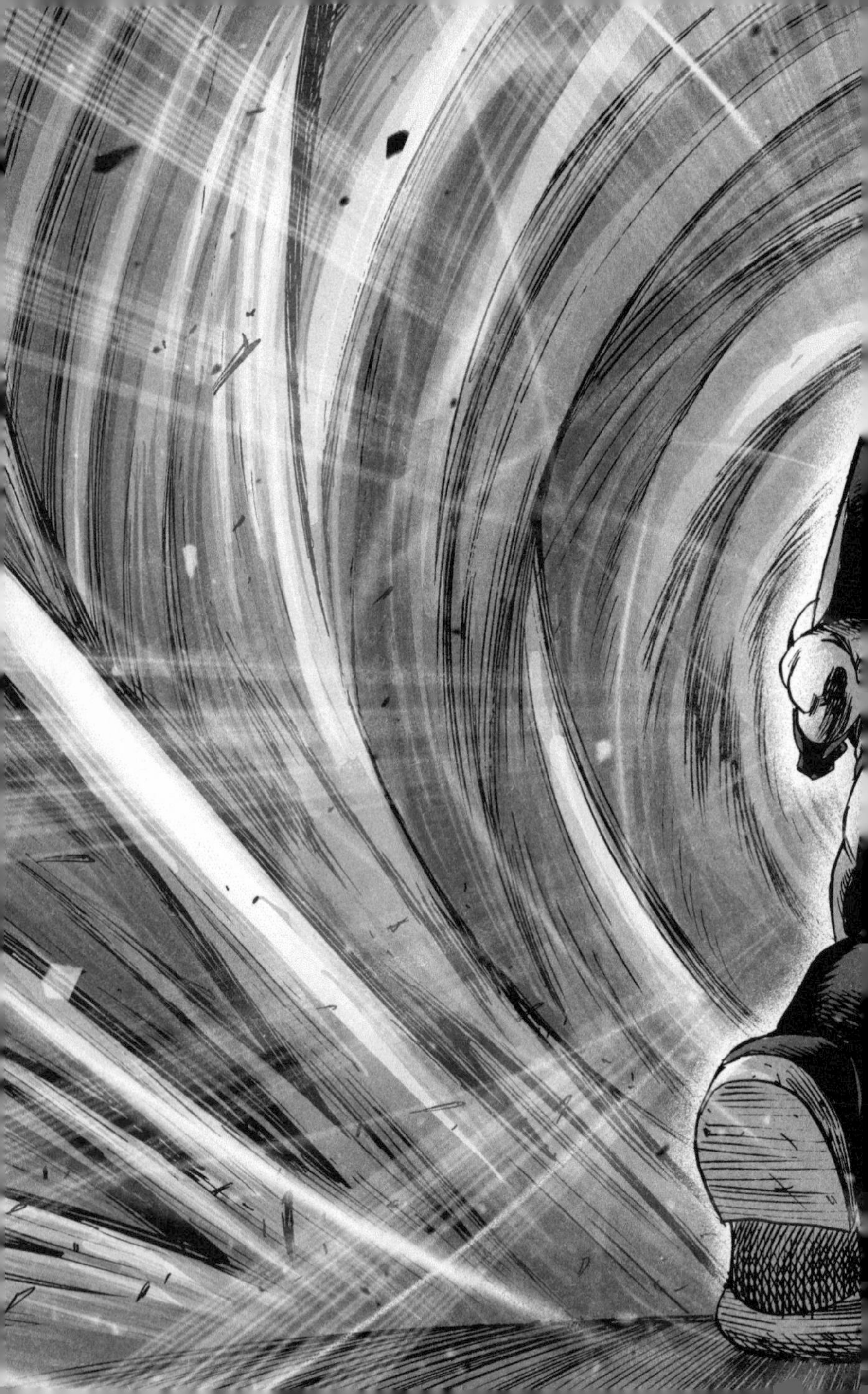

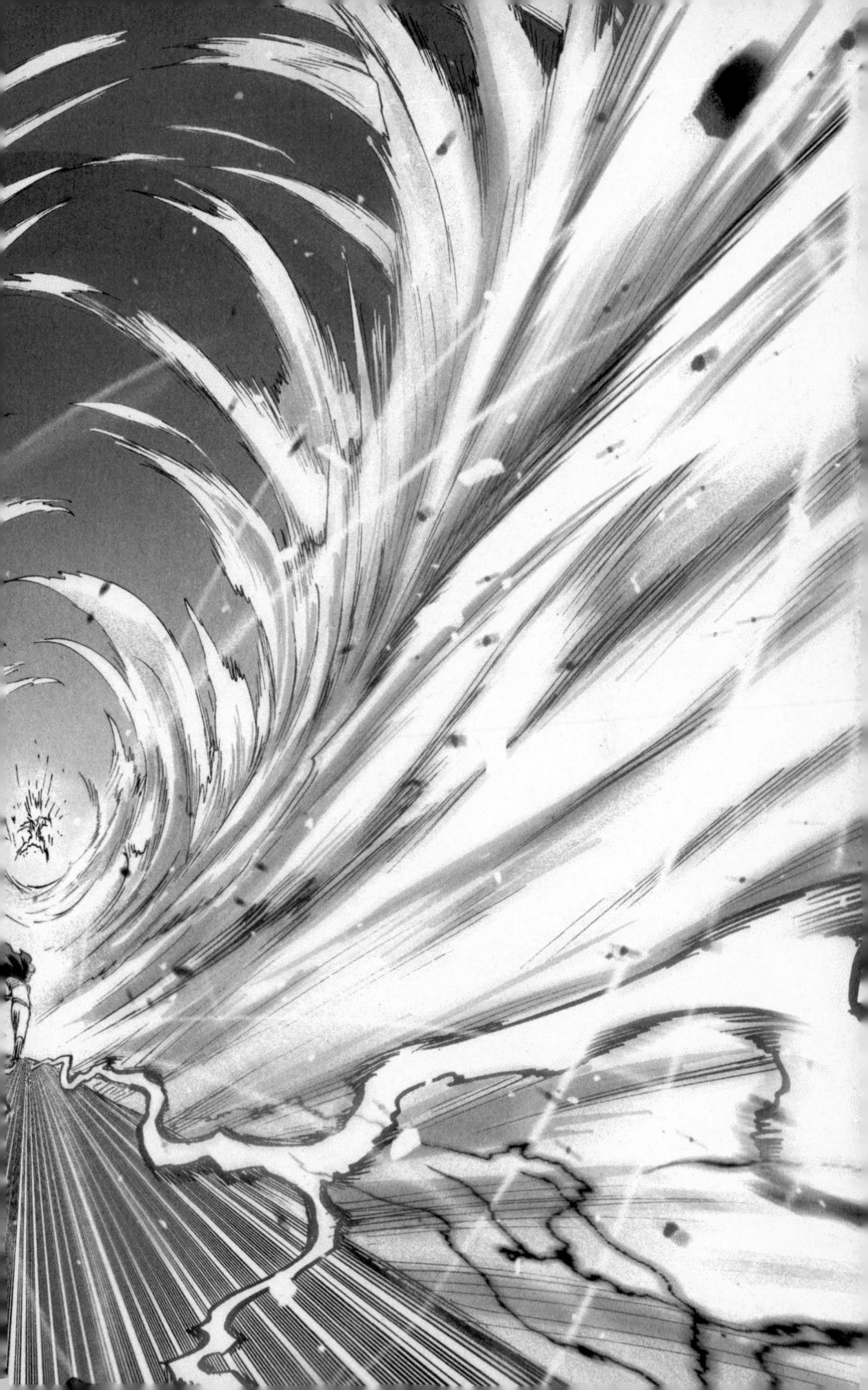

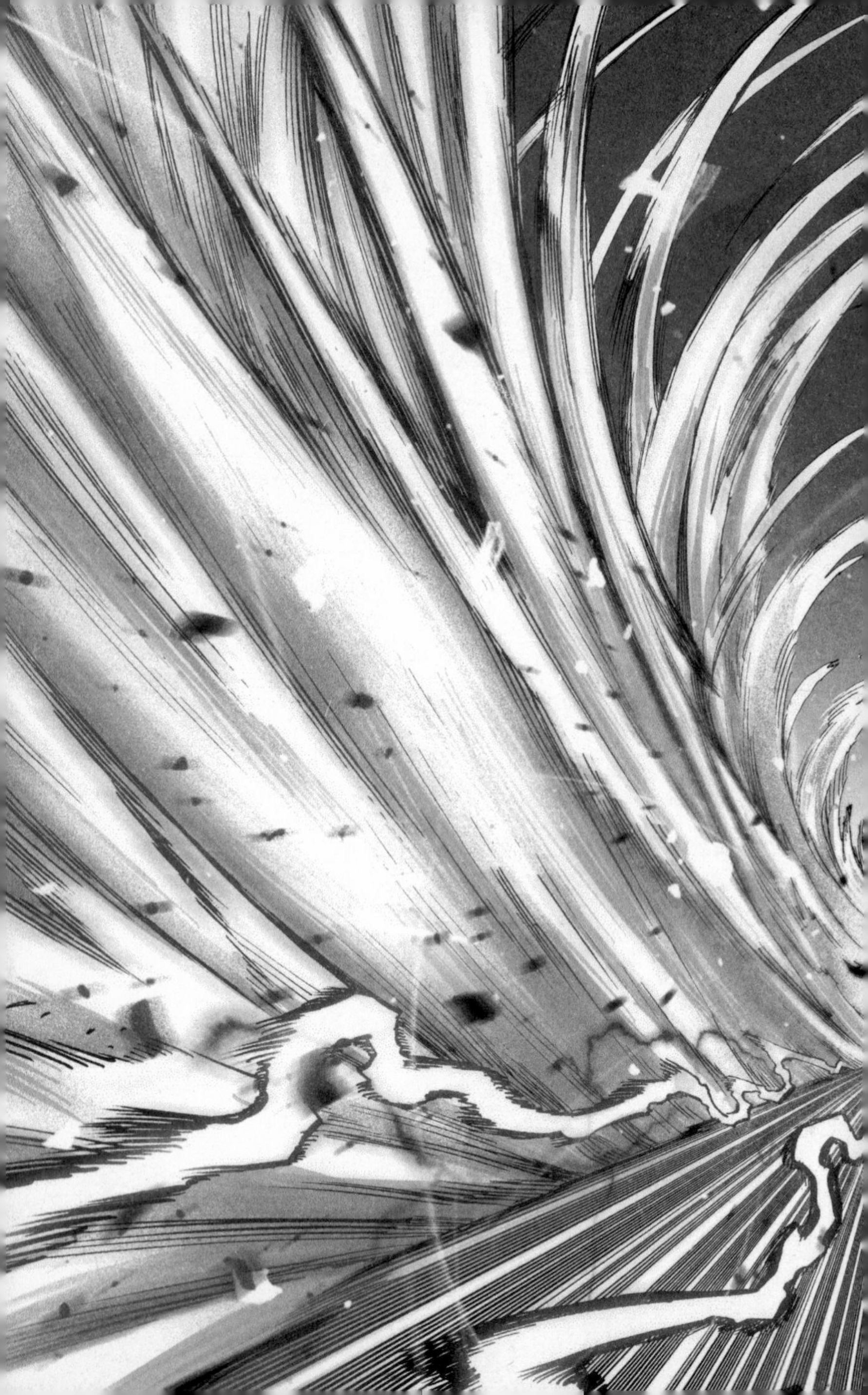

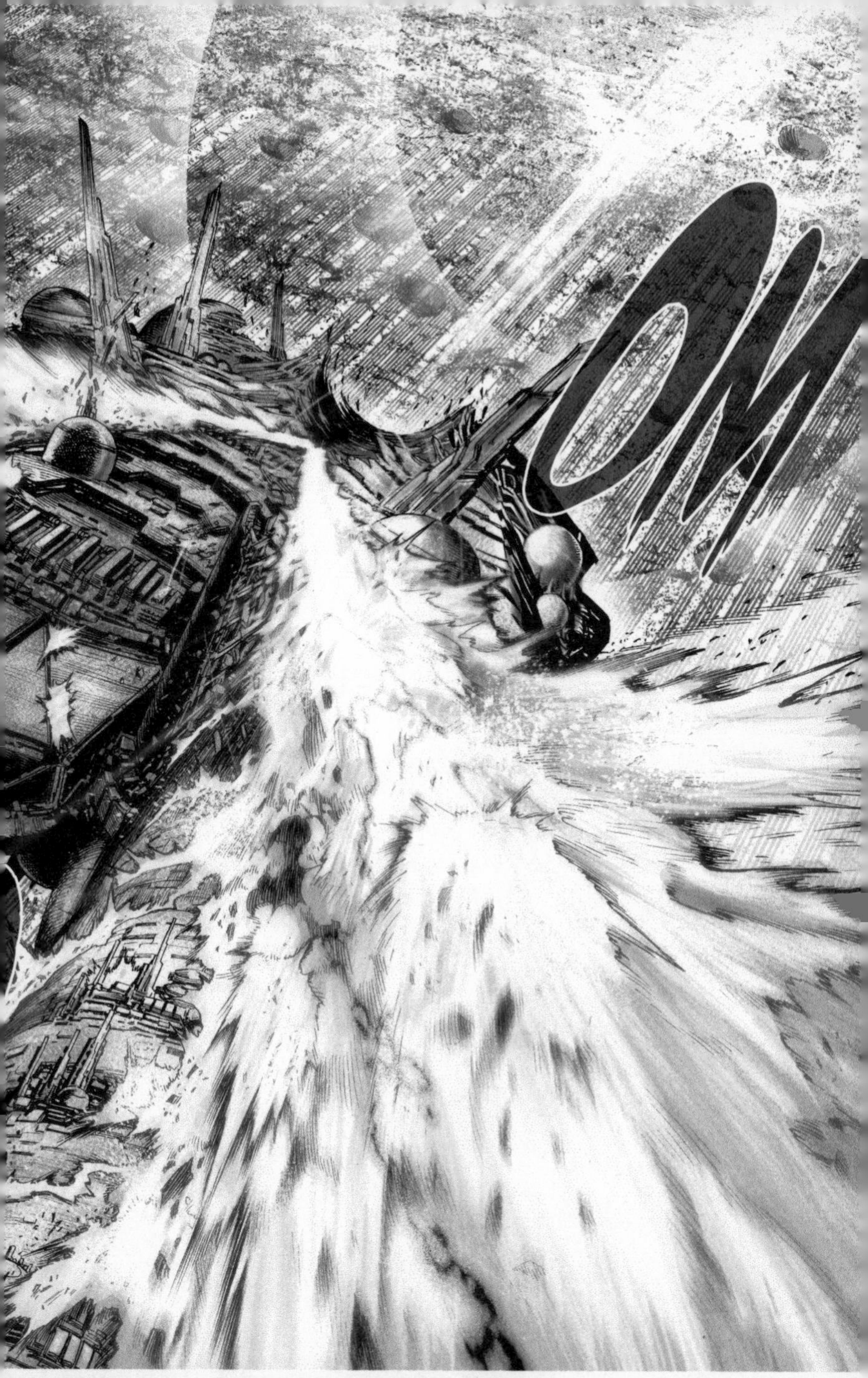
OM

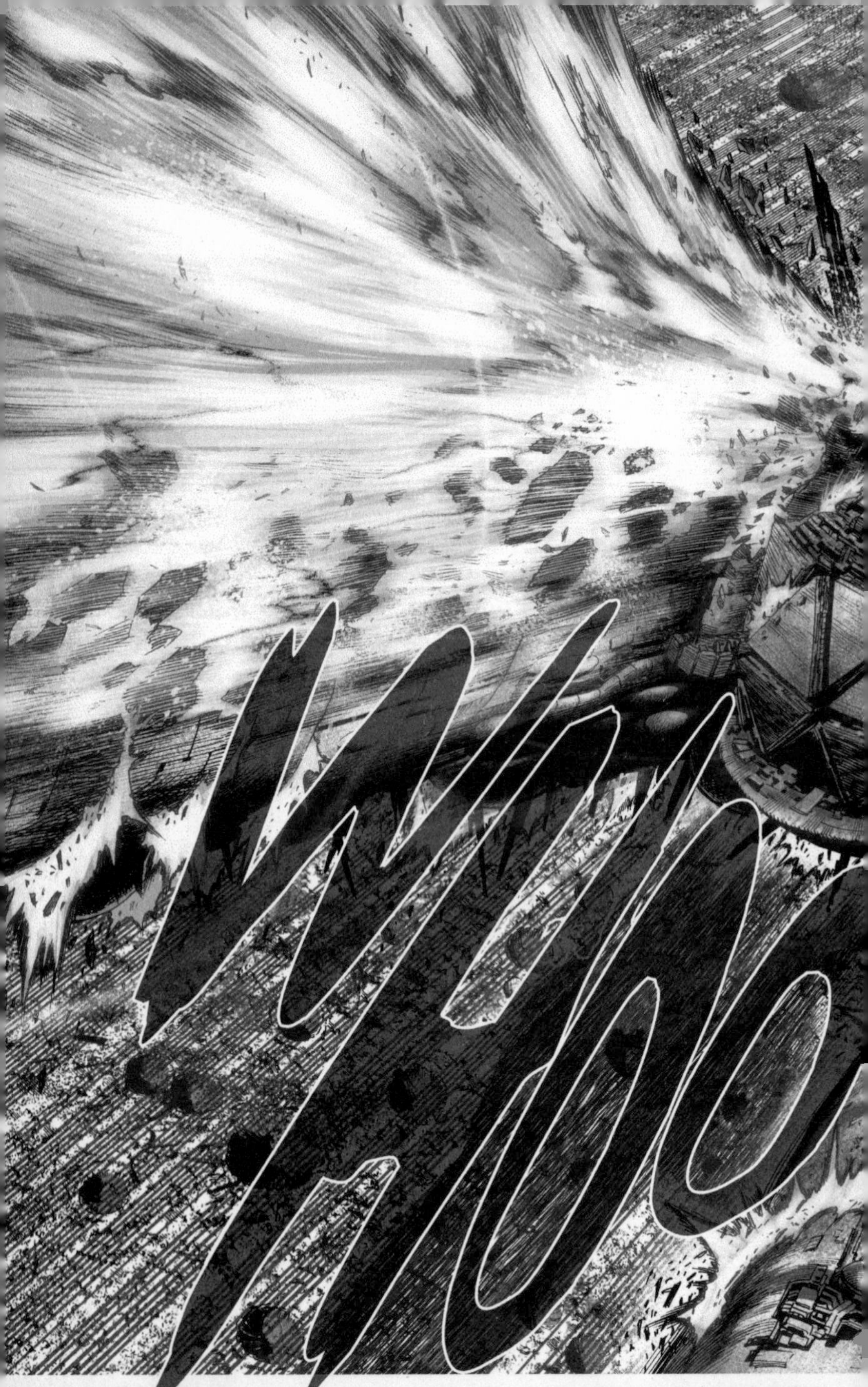

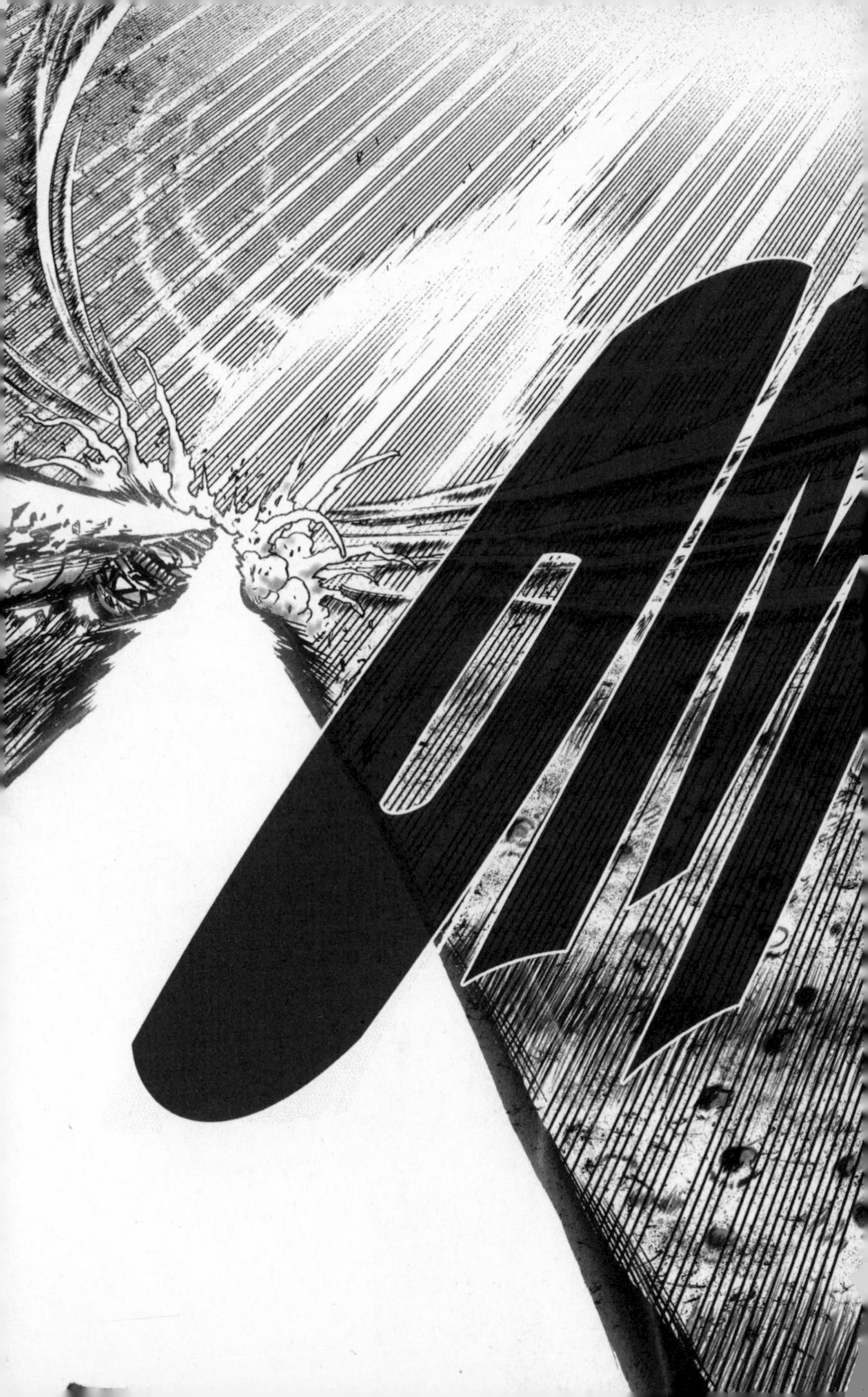

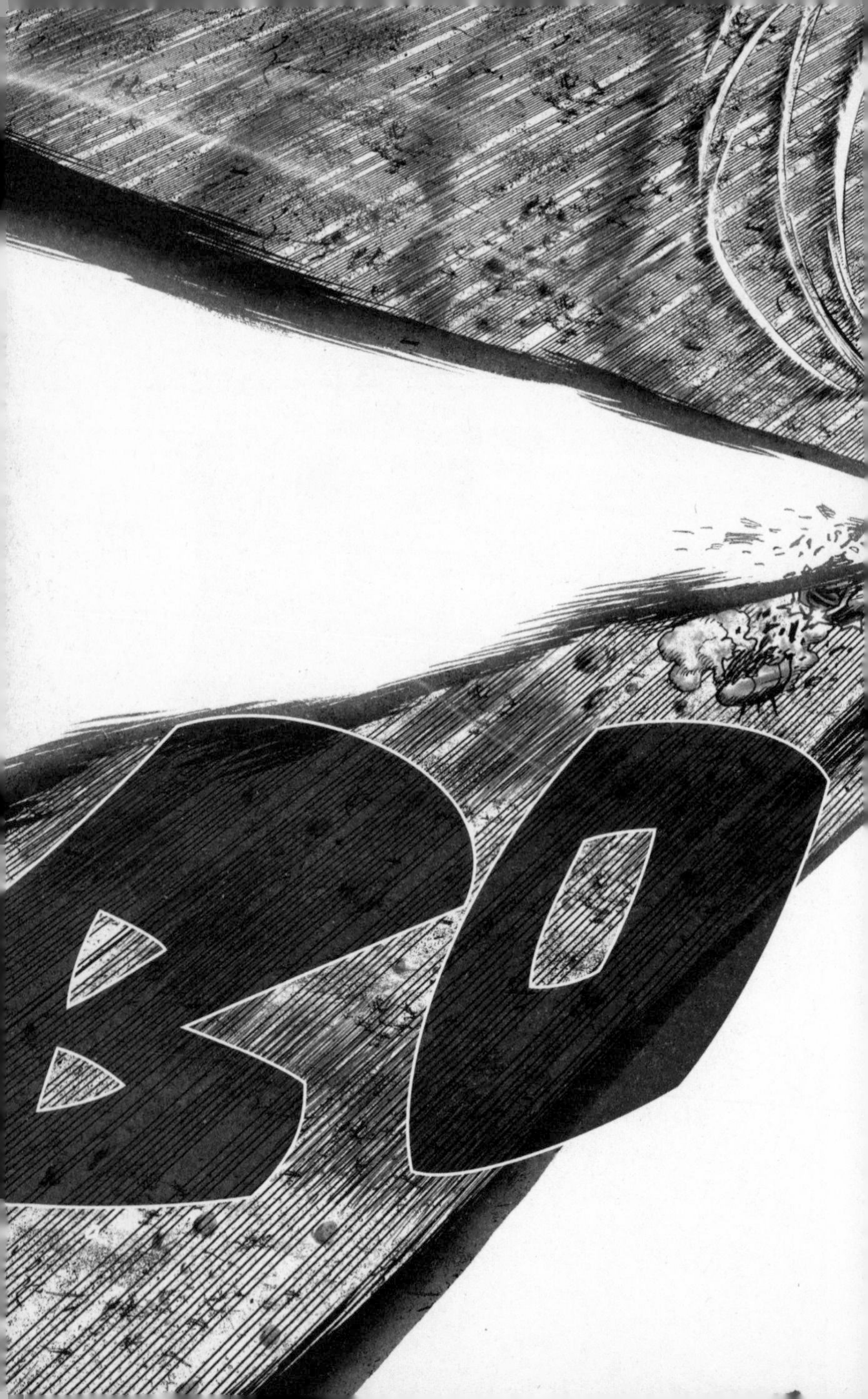

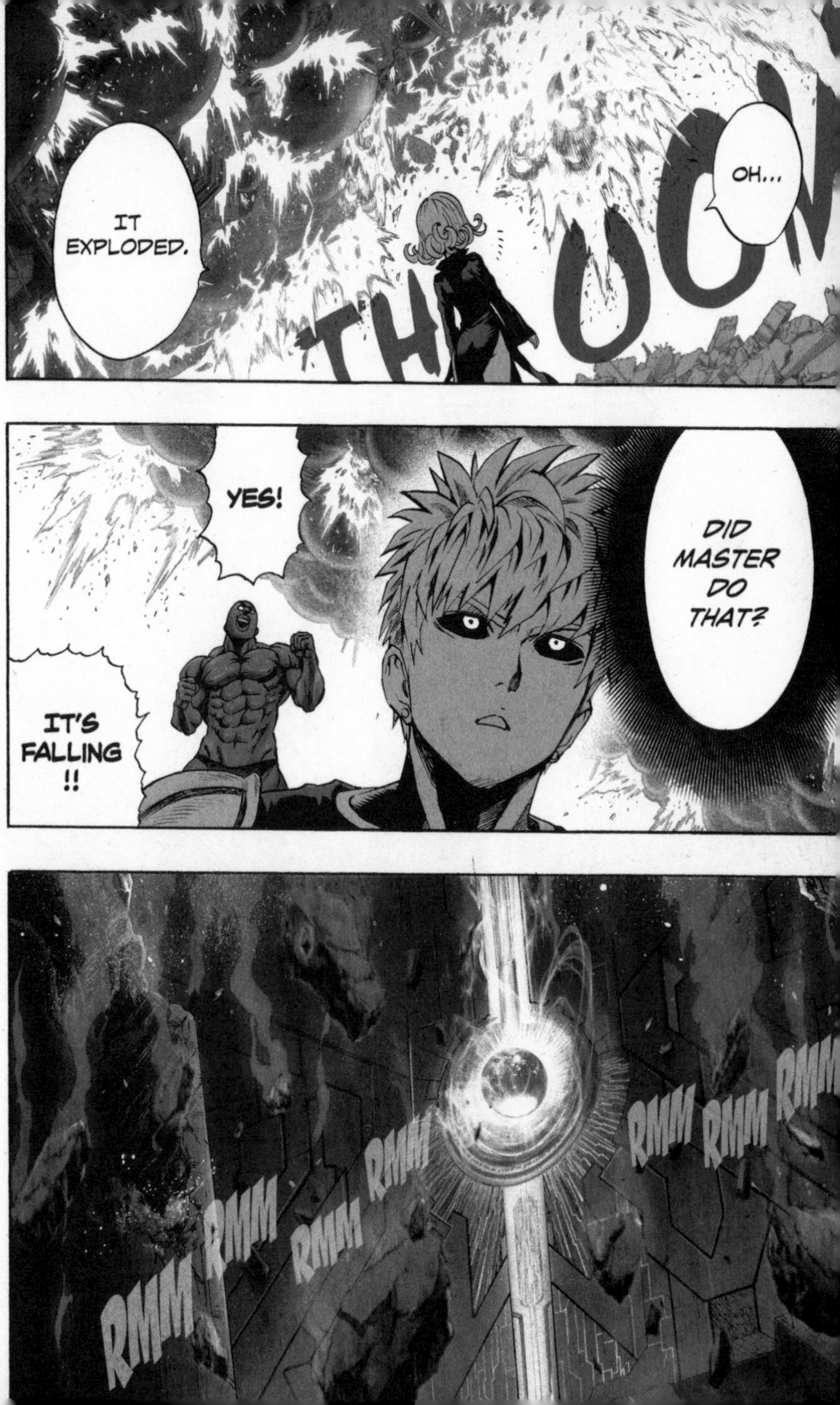
OH...
THOOM
IT EXPLODED.
DID MASTER DO THAT?
YES!
IT'S FALLING !!
RMM RMM RMM
RMM RMM RMM
RMM RMM RMM

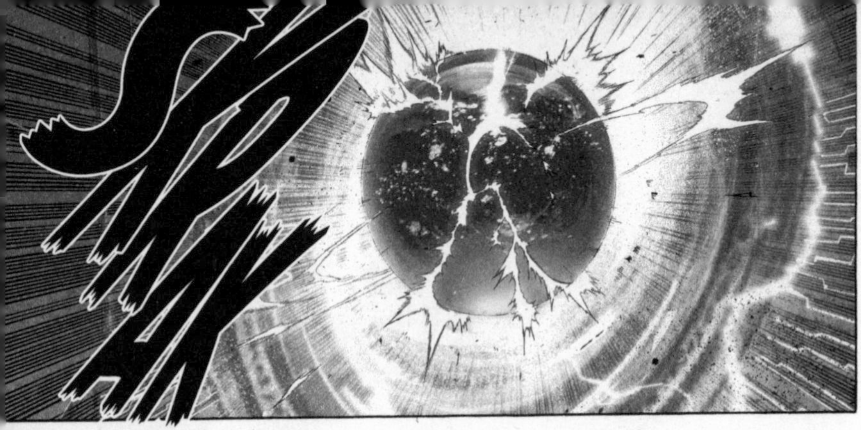

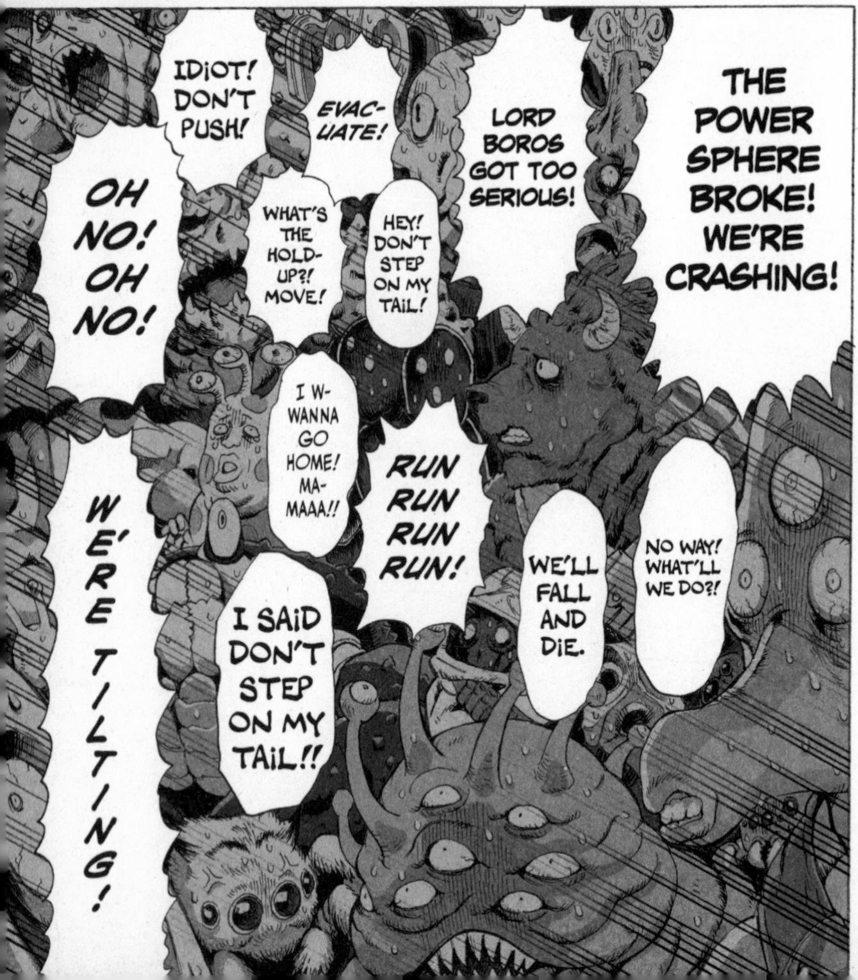
THE POWER SPHERE BROKE! WE'RE CRASHING!
LORD BOROS GOT TOO SERIOUS!
EVAC-UATE!
IDIOT! DON'T PUSH!
HEY! DON'T STEP ON MY TAIL!
WHAT'S THE HOLD-UP?! MOVE!
OH NO! OH NO!
NO WAY! WHAT'LL WE DO?!
WE'LL FALL AND DIE.
RUN RUN RUN RUN!
I W-WANNA GO HOME! MA-MAAA!!
I SAID DON'T STEP ON MY TAIL!!
WE'RE TILTING!

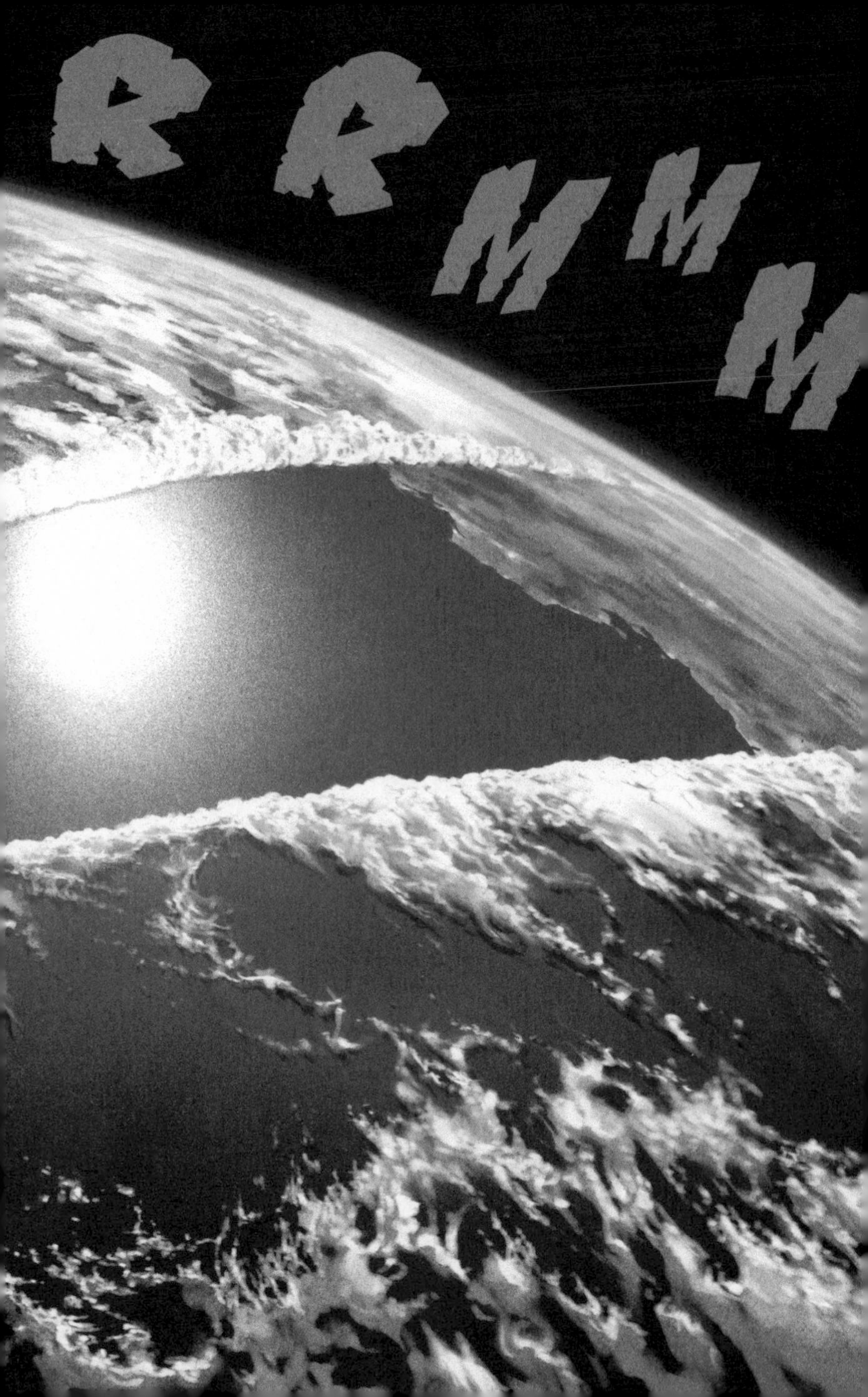
RRMMM

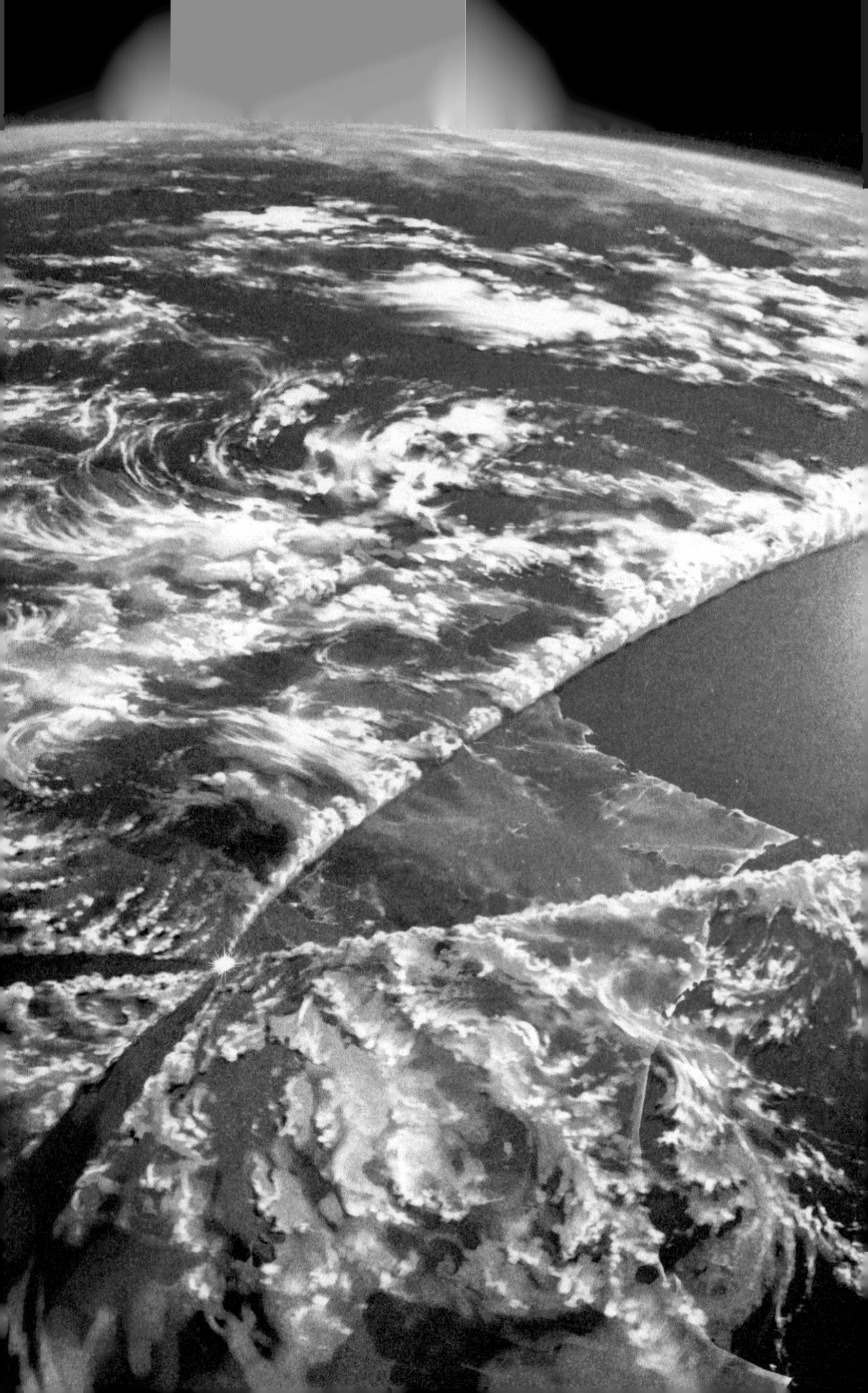

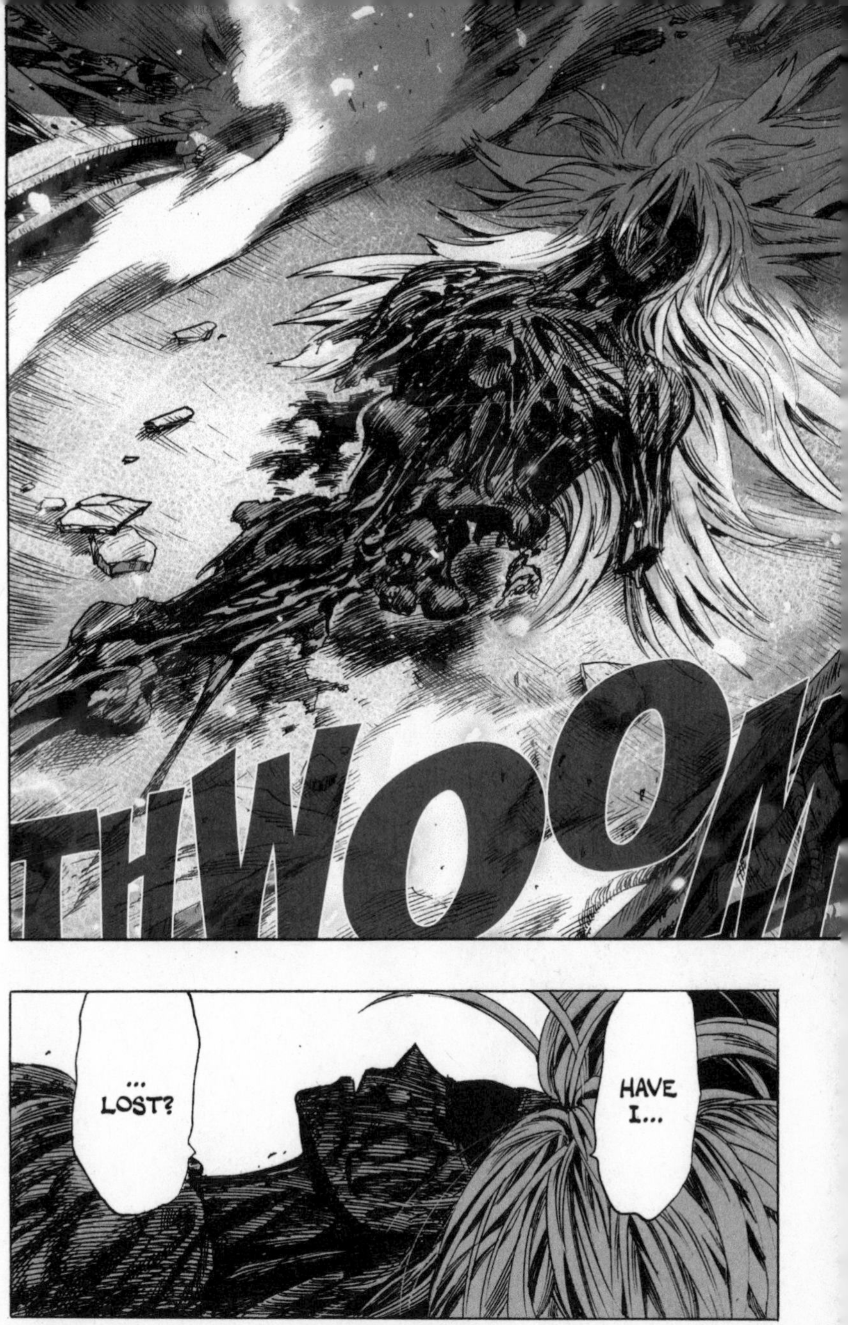
THWOOM
HAVE I...
... LOST?

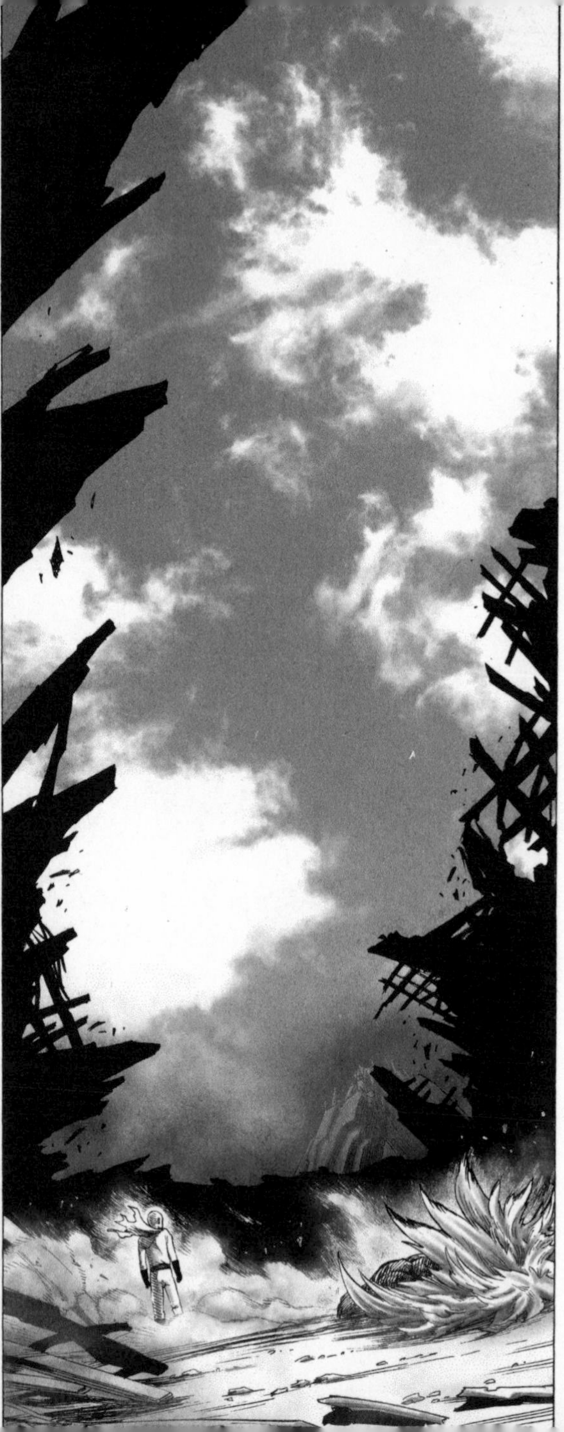

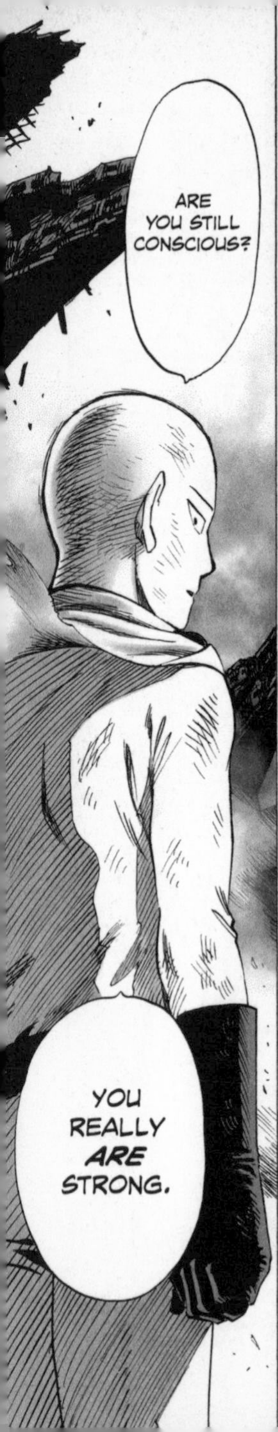
ARE YOU STILL CONSCIOUS?
YOU REALLY *ARE* STRONG.

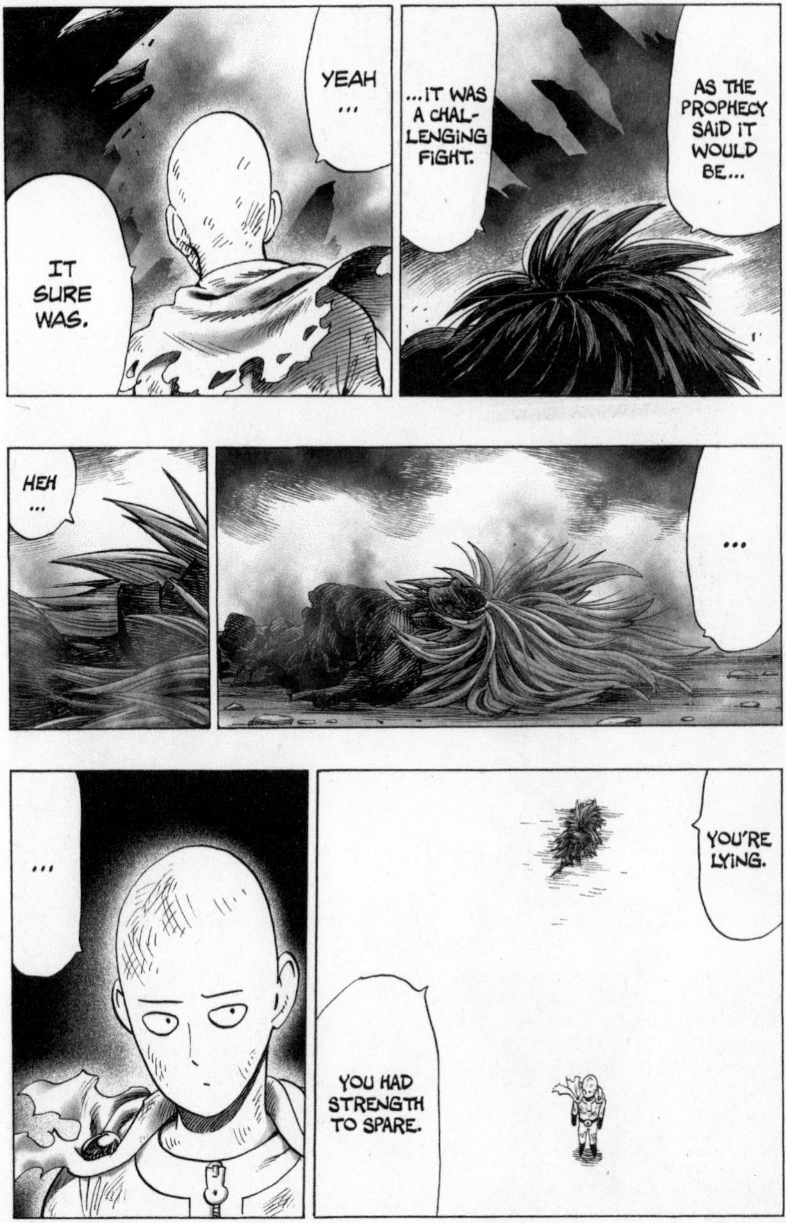
AS THE PROPHECY SAID IT WOULD BE...
...IT WAS A CHAL-LENGING FIGHT.
YEAH ...
IT SURE WAS.
...
HEH ...
YOU'RE LYING.
YOU HAD STRENGTH TO SPARE.
...

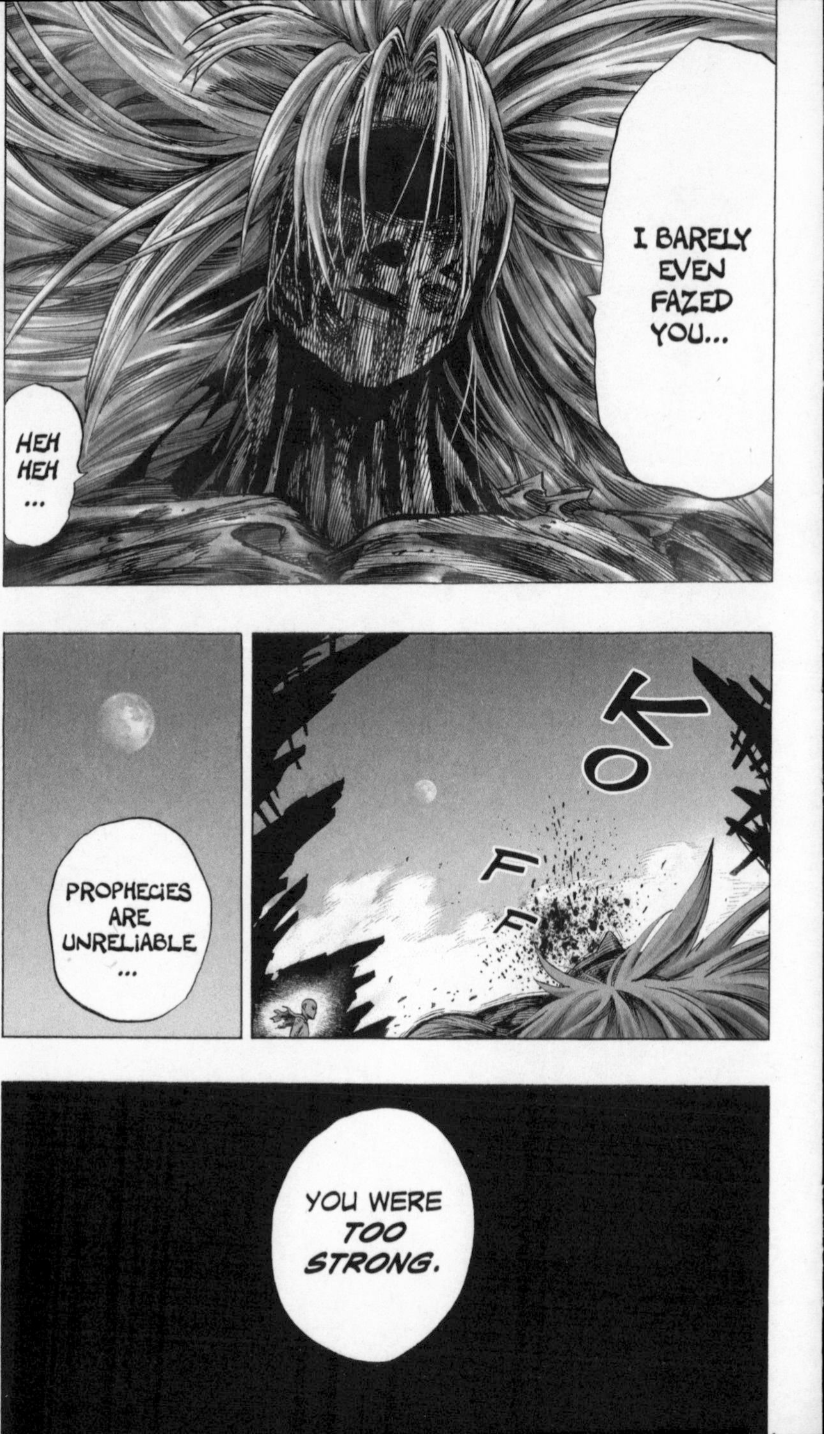
I BARELY EVEN FAZED YOU...
HEH HEH ...
KOFF
PROPHECIES ARE UNRELIABLE ...
YOU WERE *TOO STRONG*.

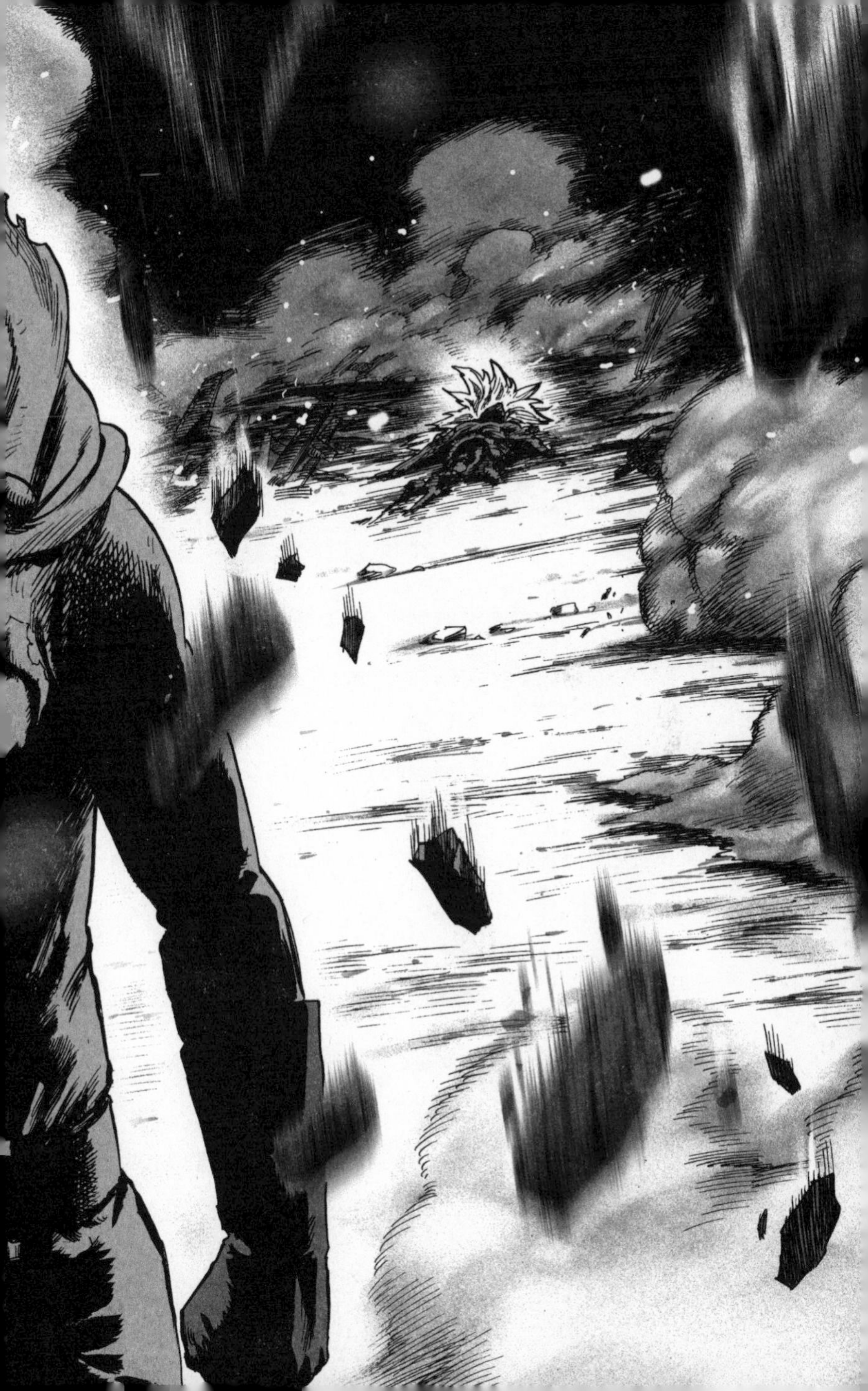

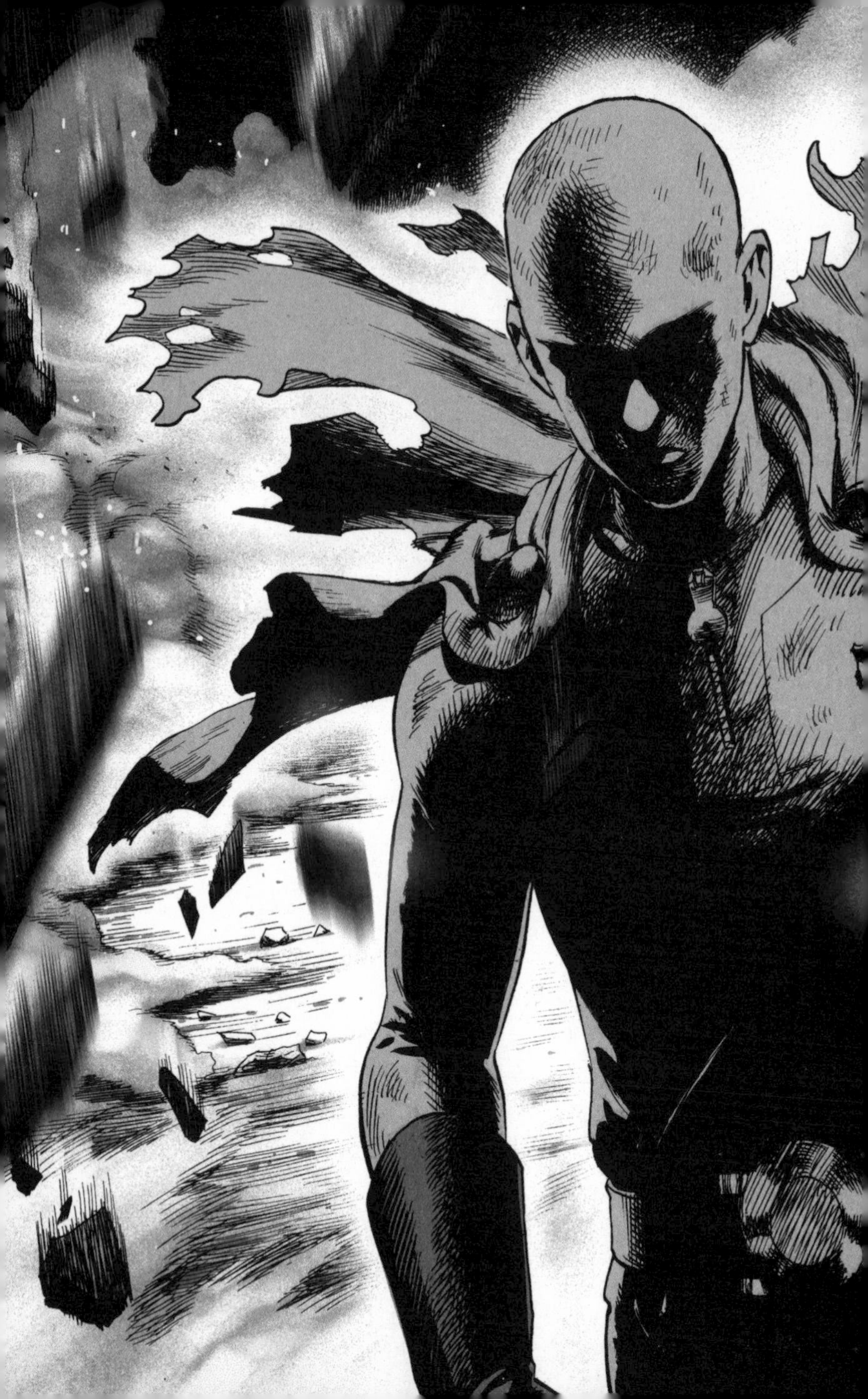

THE GIANT LABYRINTH IN THE SPACESHIP
APPEARS WITH THE CONSENT OF ITS
CREATOR, KAZUO NOMURA.

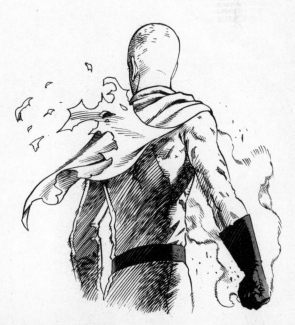

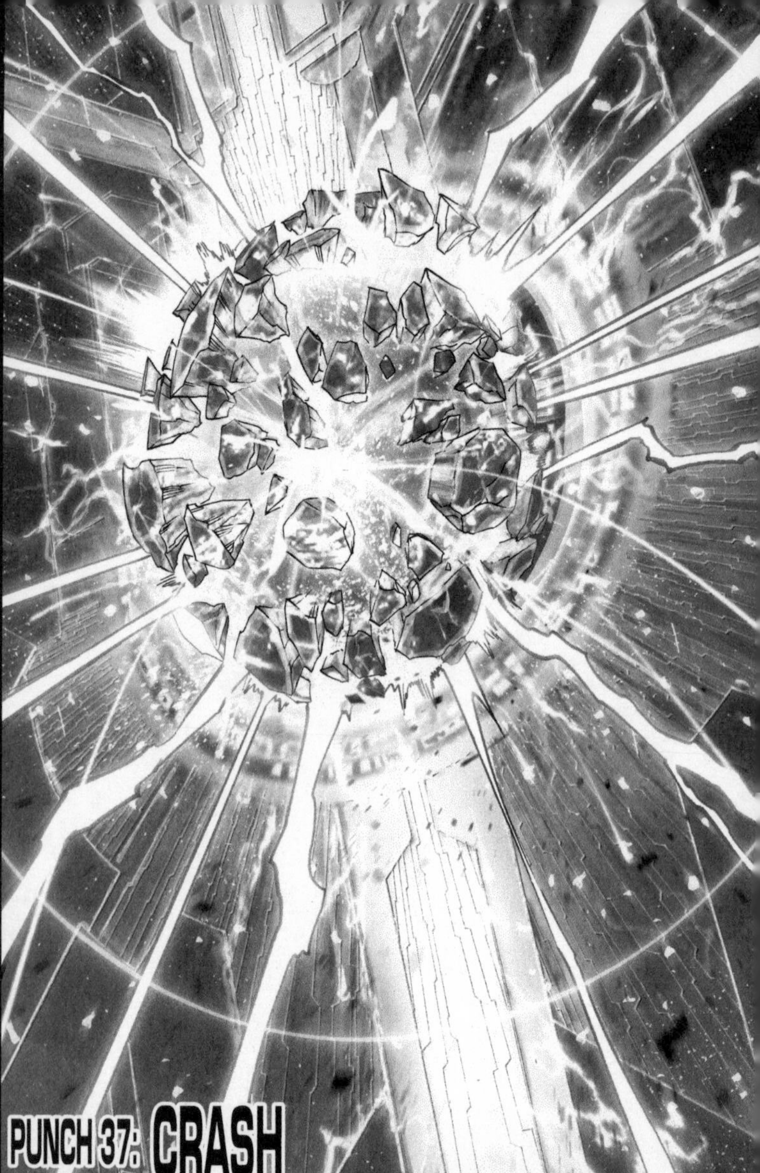

PUNCH 37: CRASH

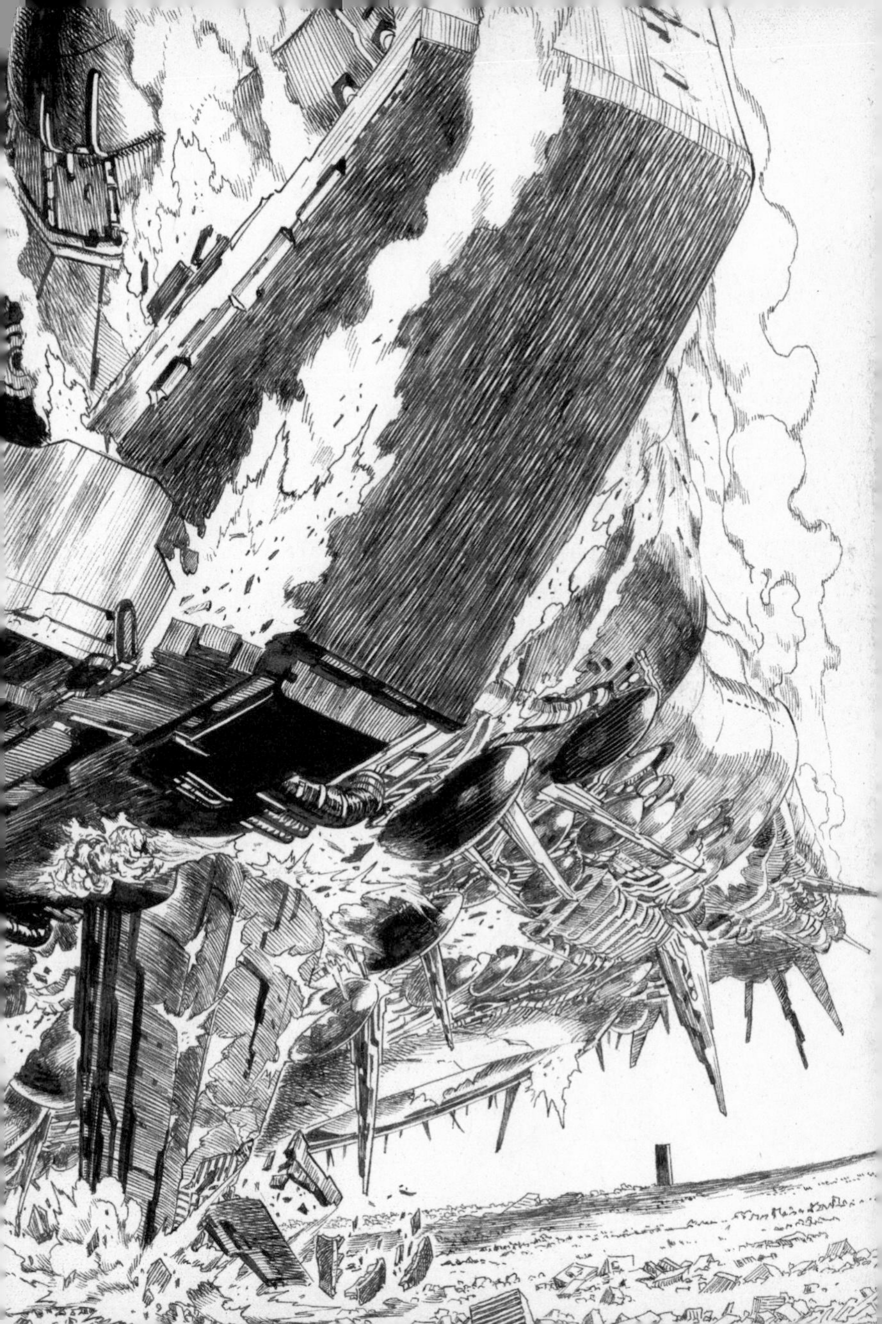

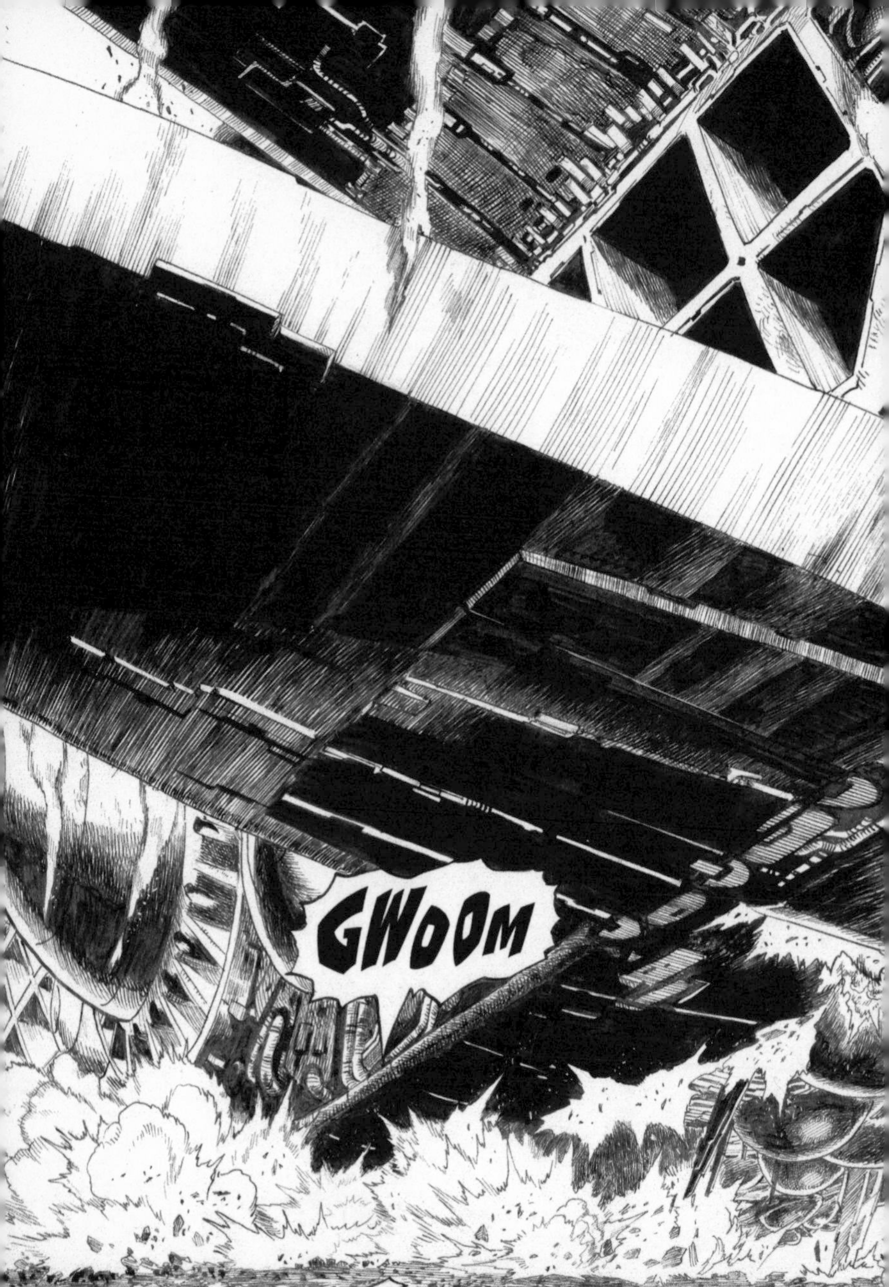
GWOOM

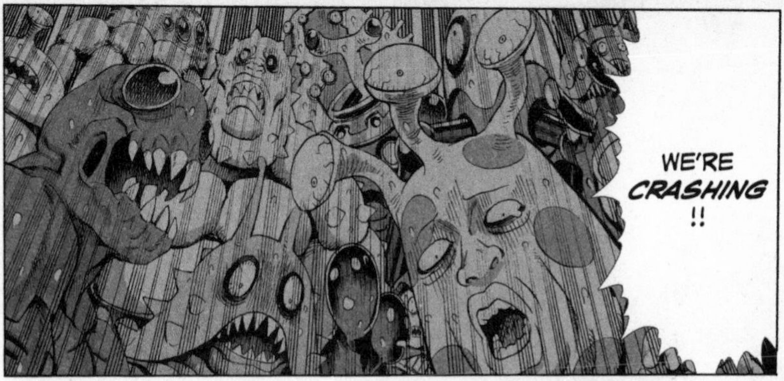
WE'RE CRASHING !!
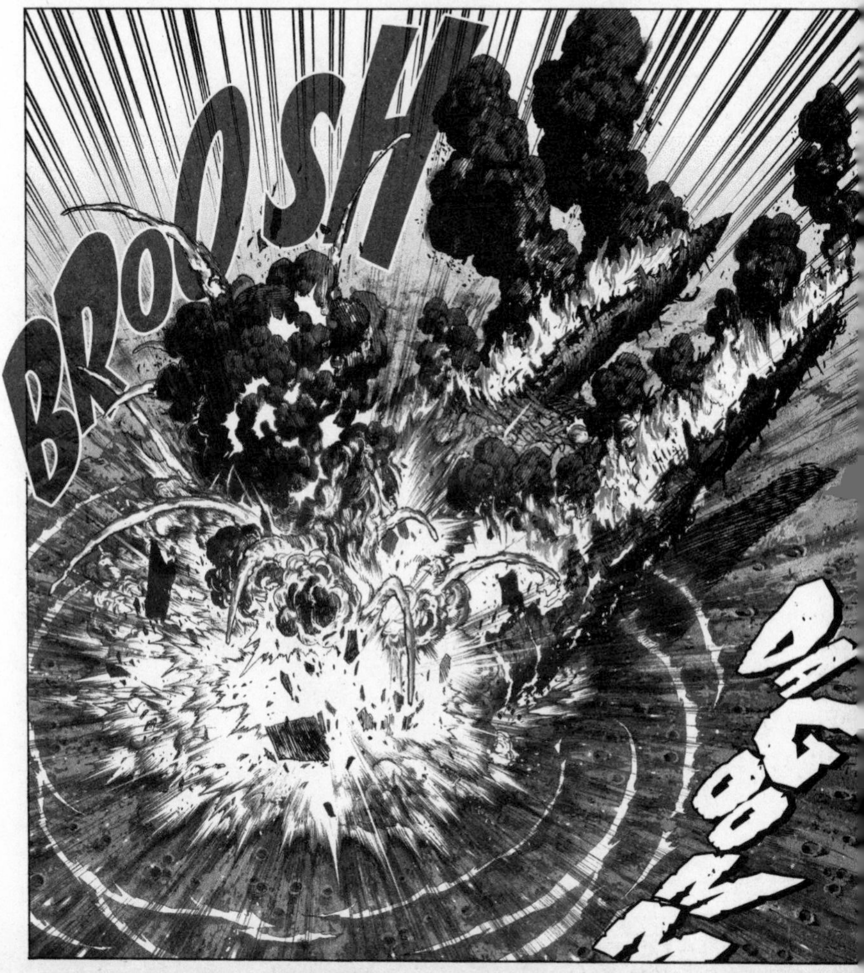
BROOOSH
DAGOOOMMM

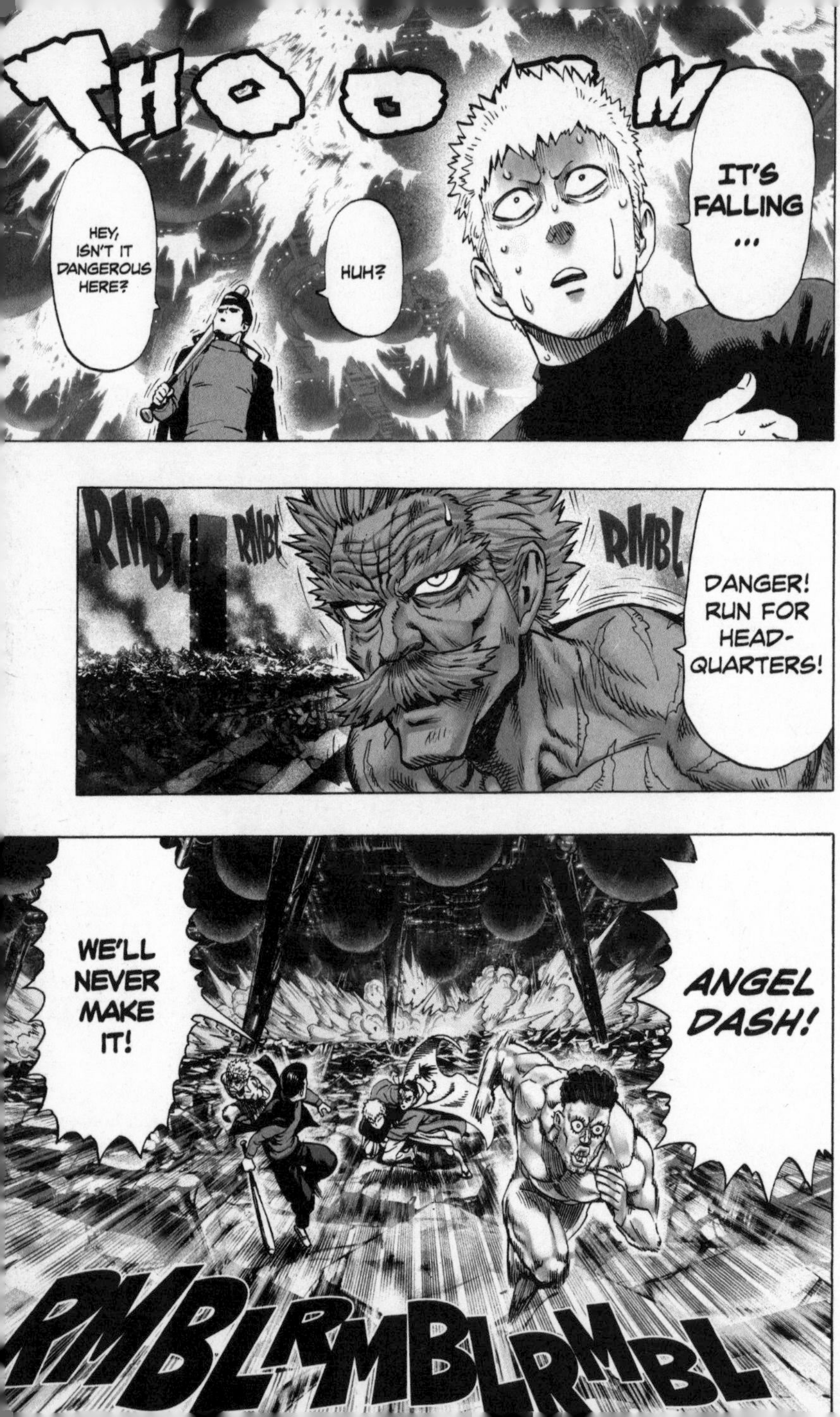
THOOM
IT'S FALLING ...
HUH?
HEY, ISN'T IT DANGEROUS HERE?
RMBL
DANGER! RUN FOR HEAD-QUARTERS!
RMBL
RMBL
ANGEL DASH!
WE'LL NEVER MAKE IT!
RMBLRMBLRMBL

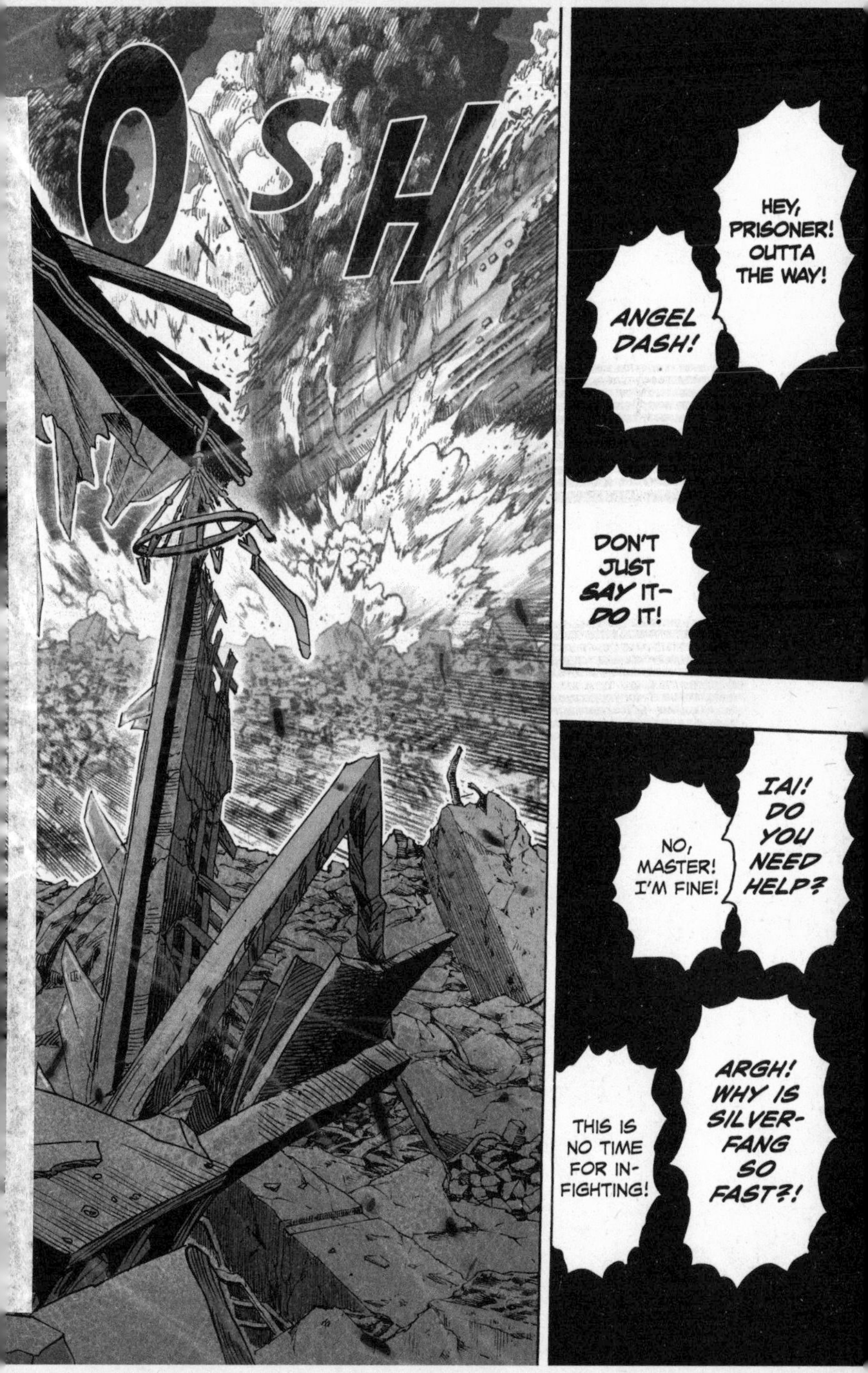
HEY, PRISONER! OUTTA THE WAY!
ANGEL DASH!
DON'T JUST SAY IT—DO IT!
IAI! DO YOU NEED HELP?
NO, MASTER! I'M FINE!
ARGH! WHY IS SILVER-FANG SO FAST?!
THIS IS NO TIME FOR IN-FIGHTING!
OSH

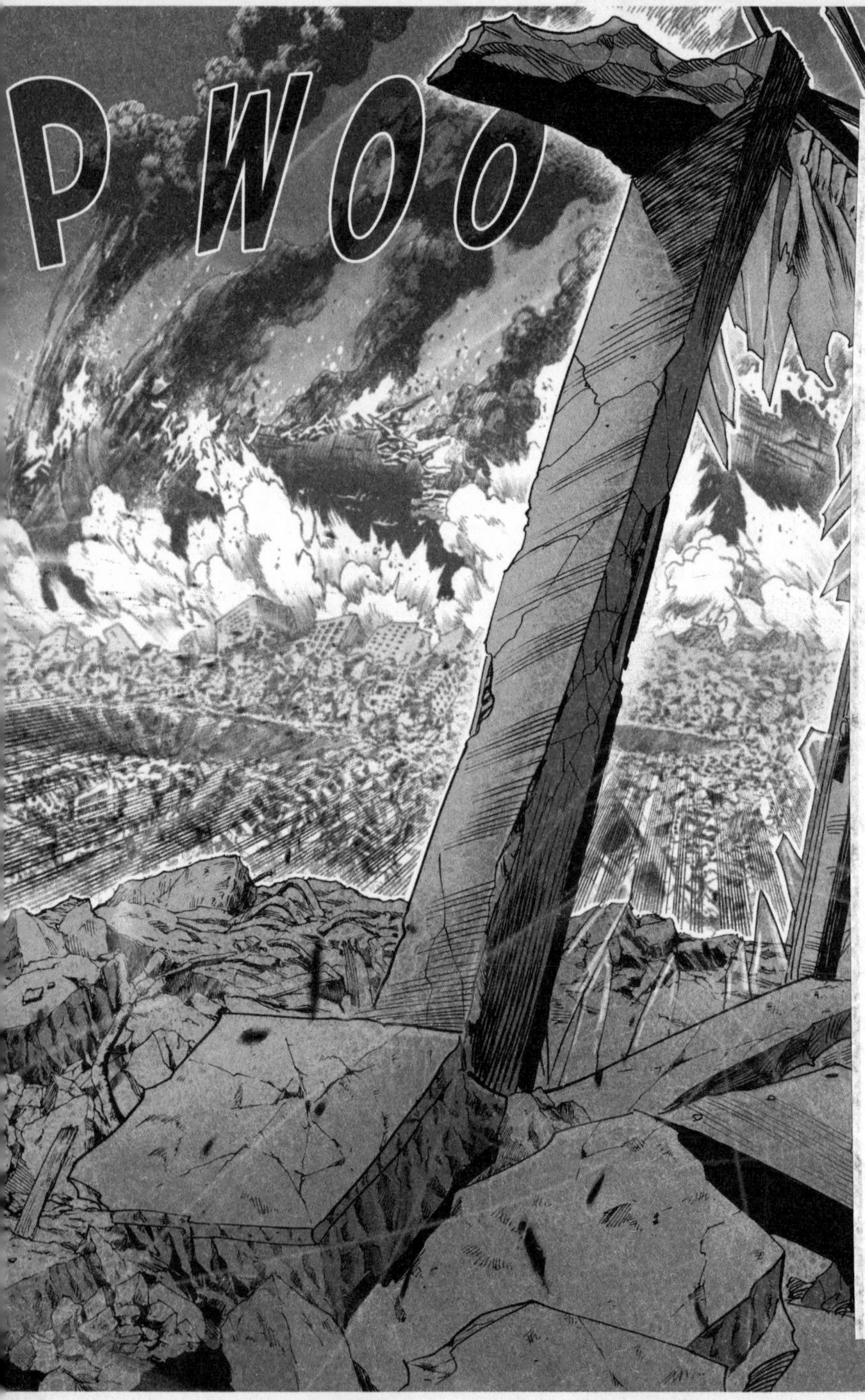
PWOO

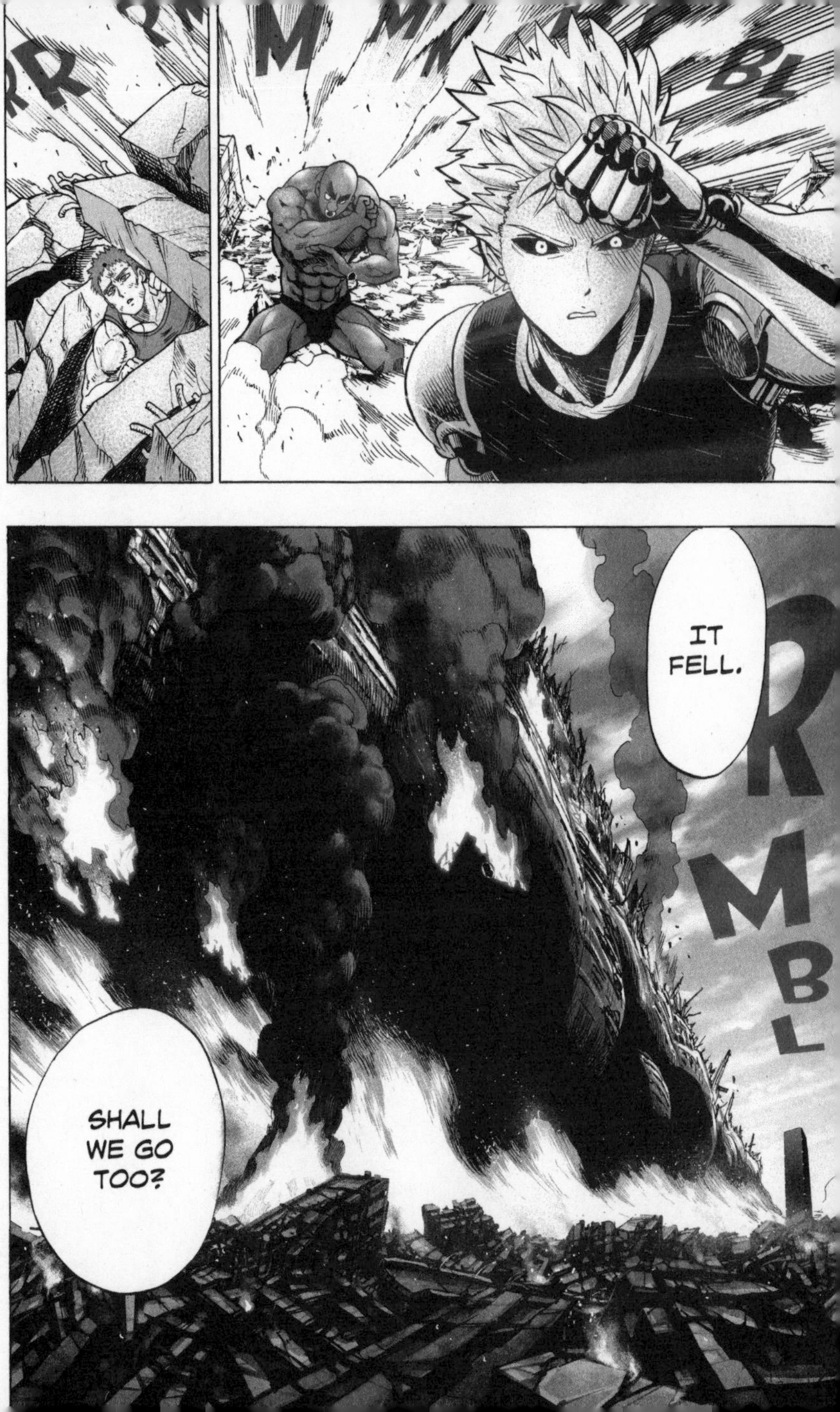
IT FELL.
RMBL
SHALL WE GO TOO?

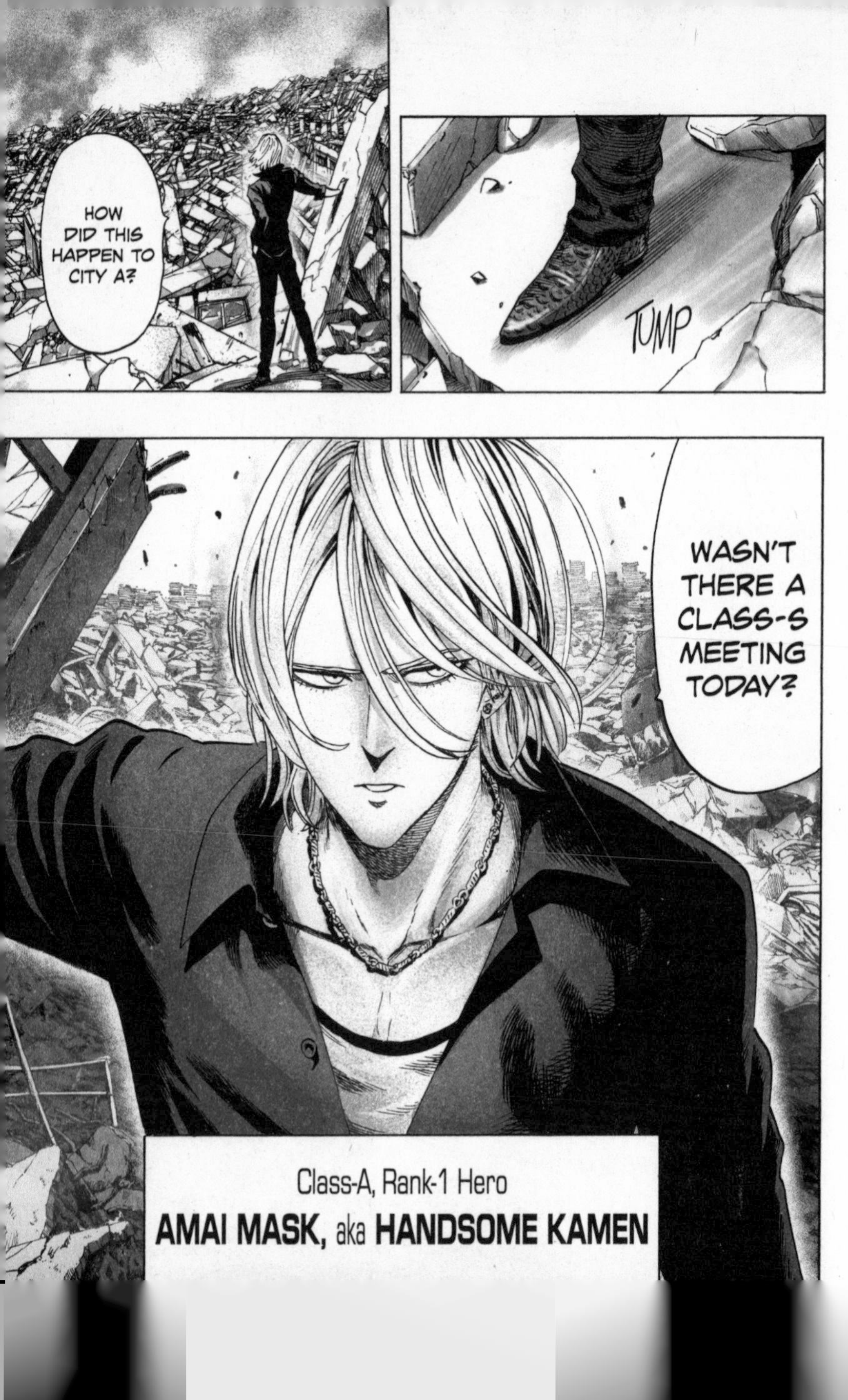
TUMP
HOW DID THIS HAPPEN TO CITY A?
WASN'T THERE A CLASS-S MEETING TODAY?
Class-A, Rank-1 Hero
AMAI MASK, aka HANDSOME KAMEN

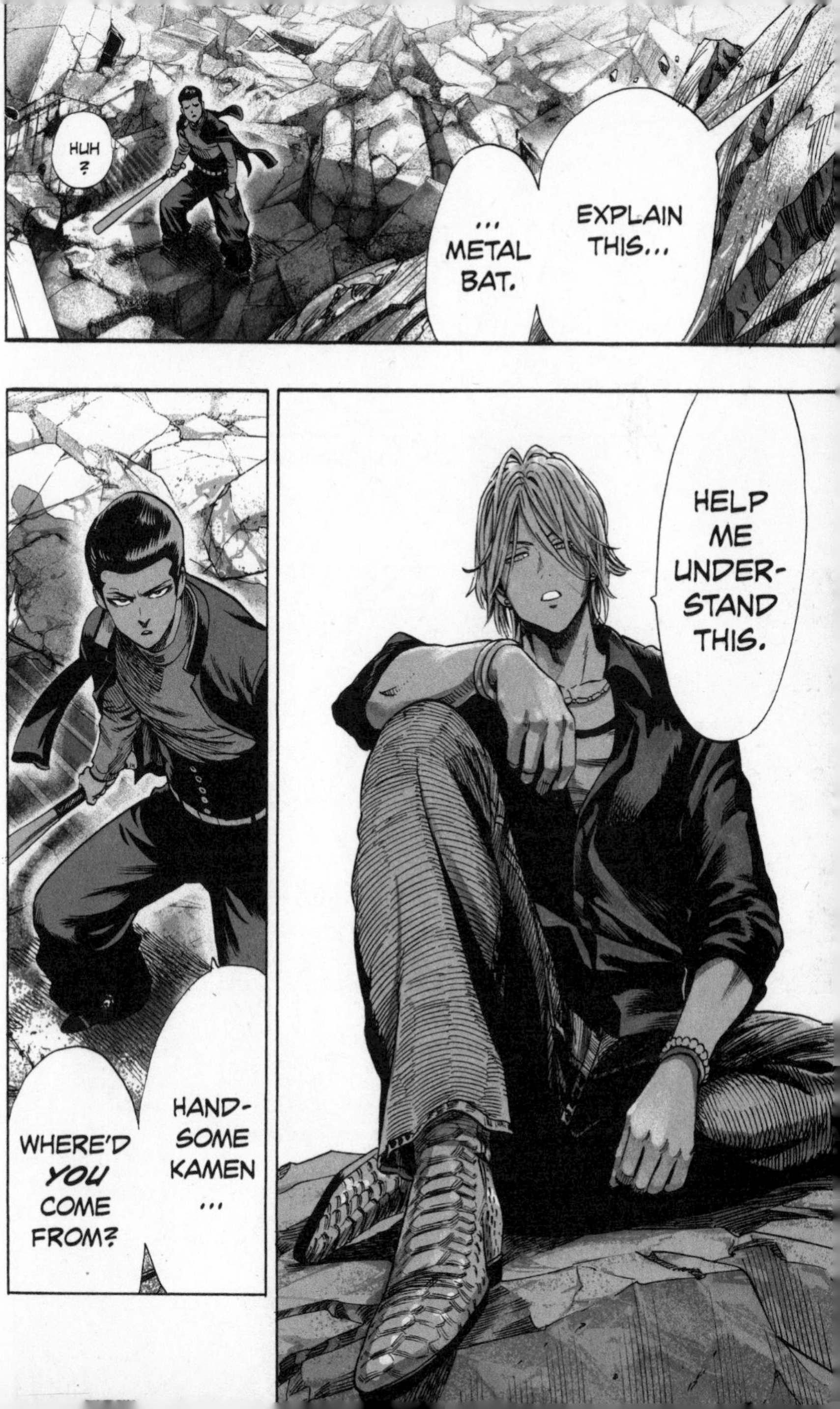
EXPLAIN THIS...
...METAL BAT.
HUH?
HELP ME UNDER-STAND THIS.
HAND-SOME KAMEN...
WHERE'D *YOU* COME FROM?

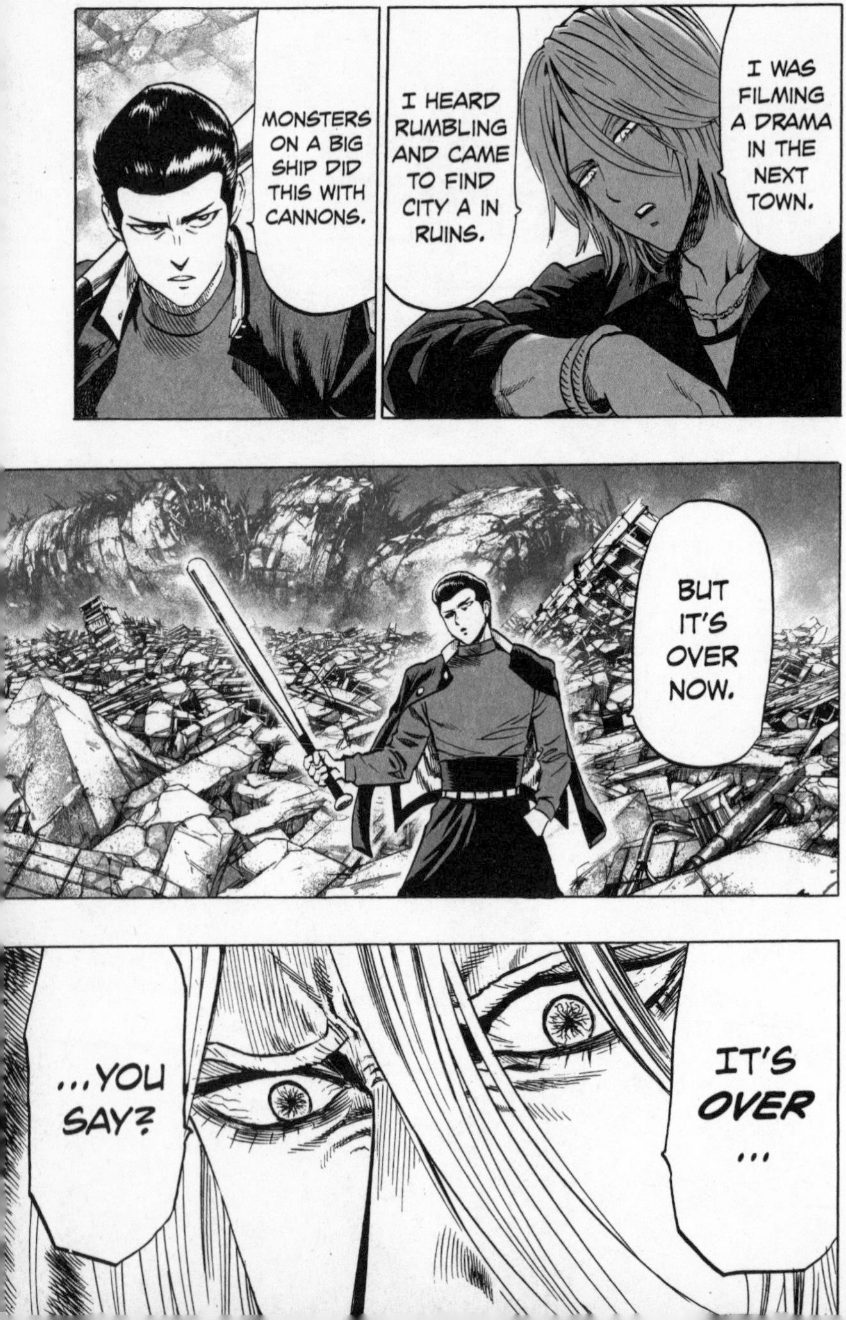
I WAS FILMING A DRAMA IN THE NEXT TOWN.
I HEARD RUMBLING AND CAME TO FIND CITY A IN RUINS.
MONSTERS ON A BIG SHIP DID THIS WITH CANNONS.
BUT IT'S OVER NOW.
IT'S *OVER* ...
...YOU SAY?

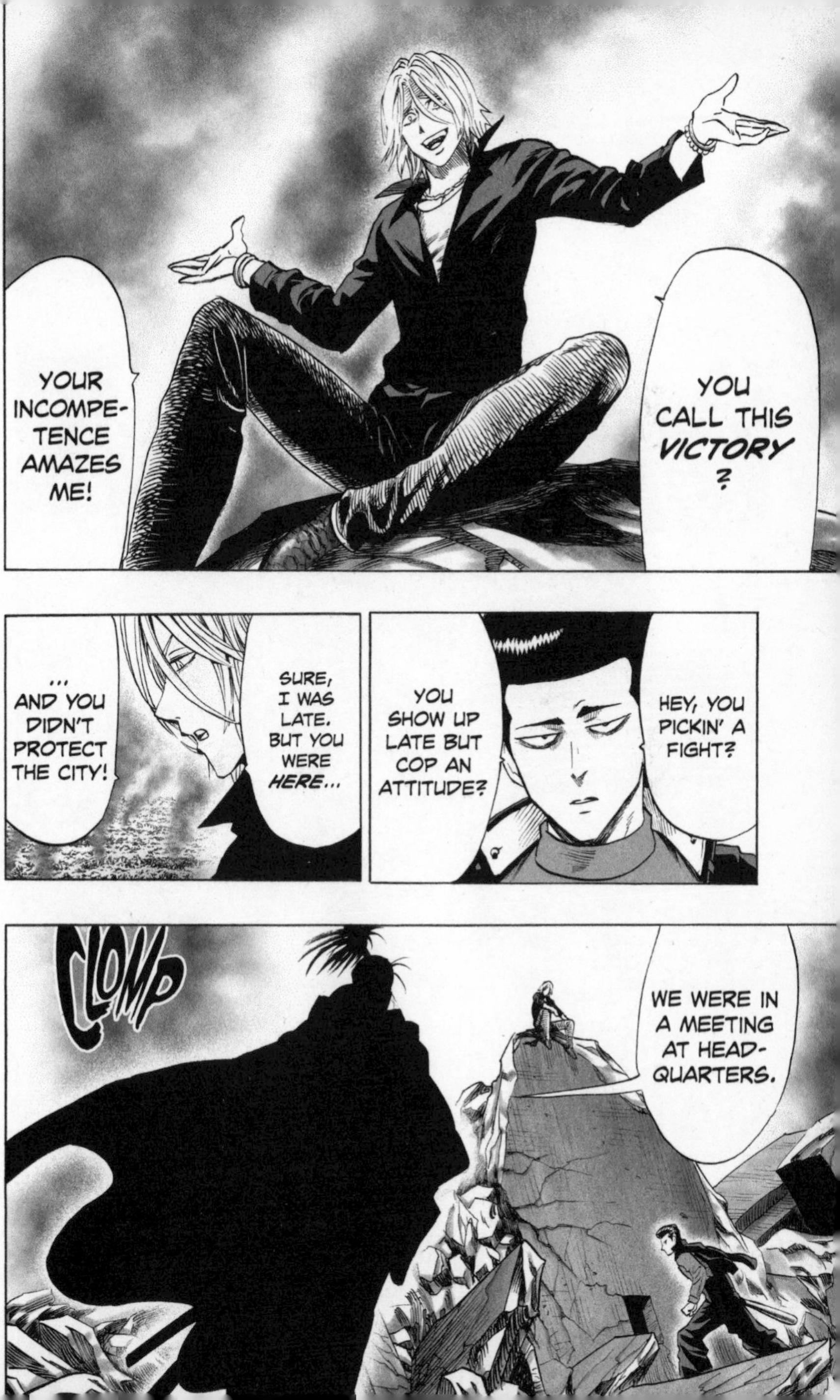
YOU CALL THIS VICTORY?
YOUR INCOMPE-TENCE AMAZES ME!
HEY, YOU PICKIN' A FIGHT?
YOU SHOW UP LATE BUT COP AN ATTITUDE?
SURE, I WAS LATE. BUT YOU WERE HERE...
... AND YOU DIDN'T PROTECT THE CITY!
WE WERE IN A MEETING AT HEAD-QUARTERS.
CLOMP

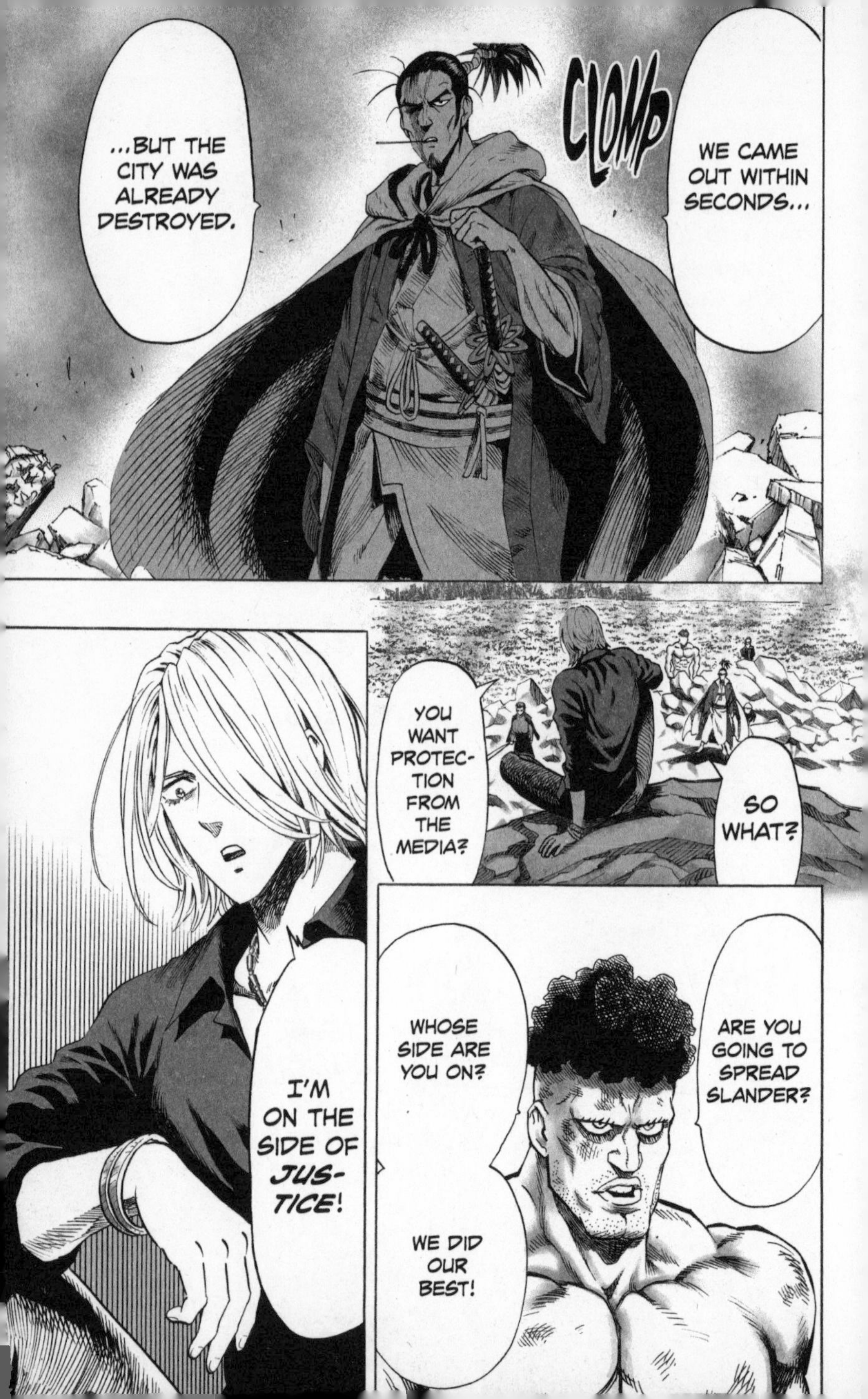
WE CAME OUT WITHIN SECONDS...
CLOMP
...BUT THE CITY WAS ALREADY DESTROYED.
SO WHAT?
YOU WANT PROTECTION FROM THE MEDIA?
ARE YOU GOING TO SPREAD SLANDER?
WHOSE SIDE ARE YOU ON?
WE DID OUR BEST!
I'M ON THE SIDE OF *JUSTICE*!

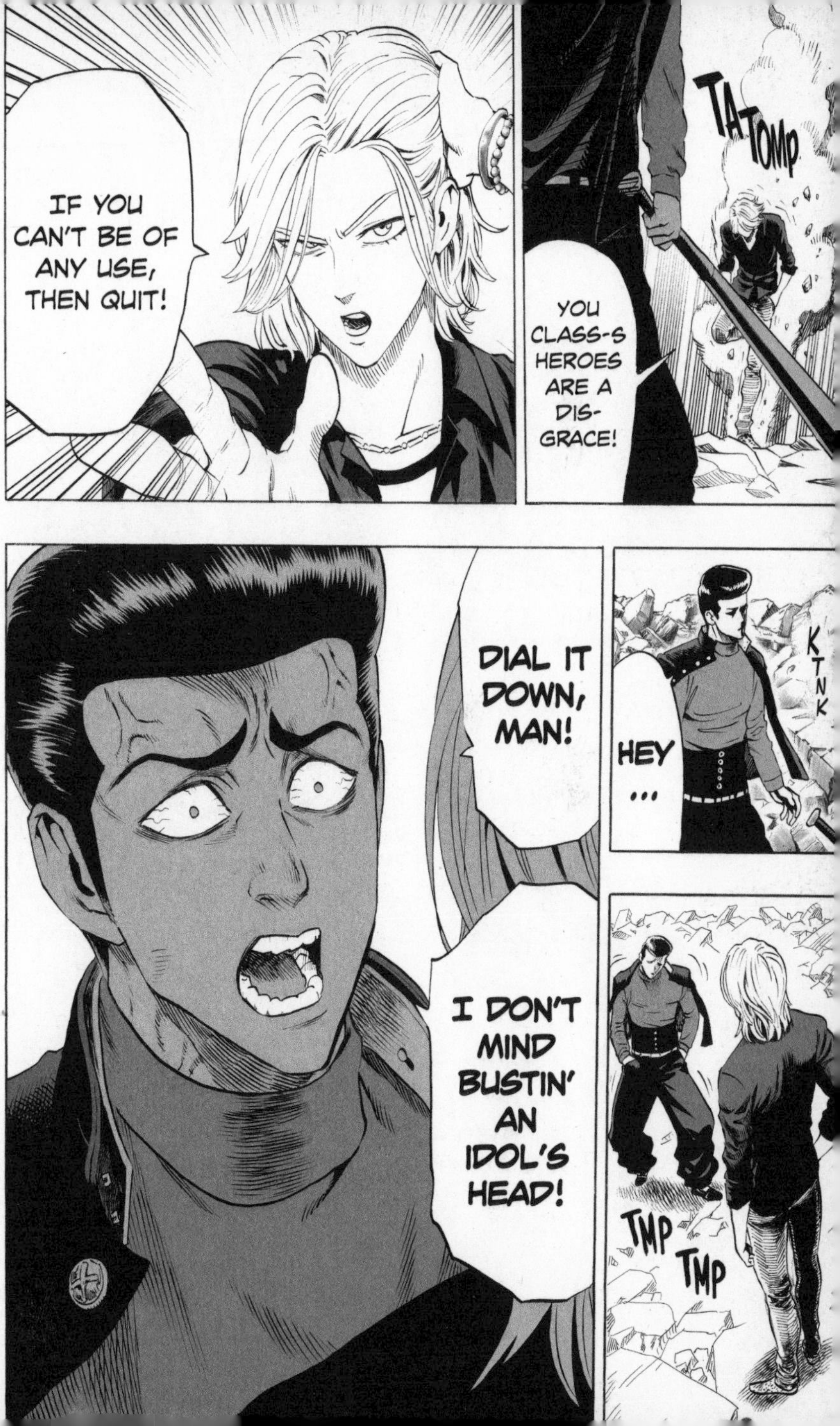
TATOMP
YOU CLASS-S HEROES ARE A DIS-GRACE!
IF YOU CAN'T BE OF ANY USE, THEN QUIT!
KTNK
HEY...
TMP TMP
DIAL IT DOWN, MAN!
I DON'T MIND BUSTIN' AN IDOL'S HEAD!

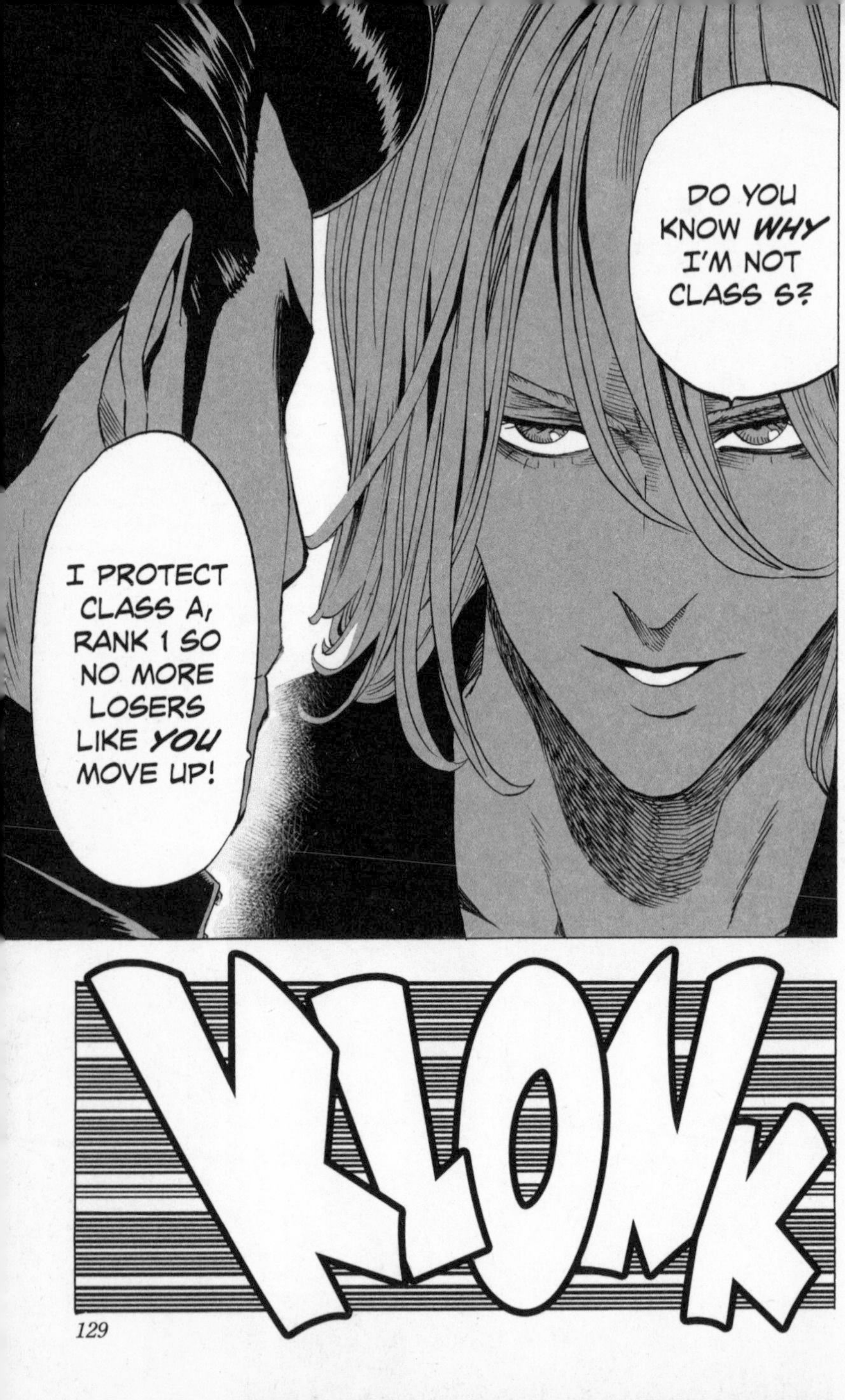
DO YOU KNOW *WHY* I'M NOT CLASS S?
I PROTECT CLASS A, RANK 1 SO NO MORE LOSERS LIKE *YOU* MOVE UP!
KLONK

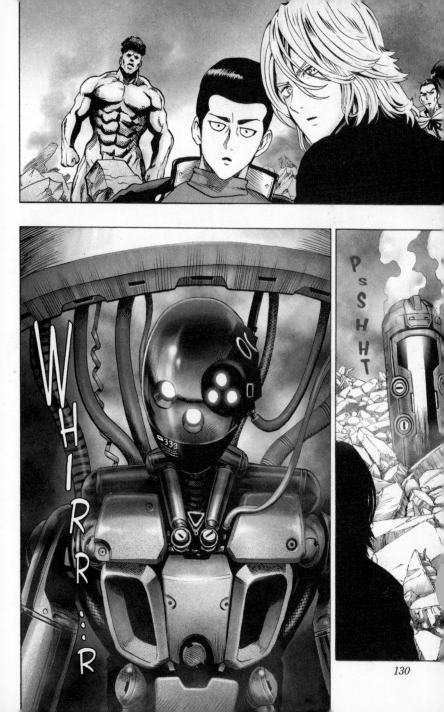

WHIRR...R

PSSHHT

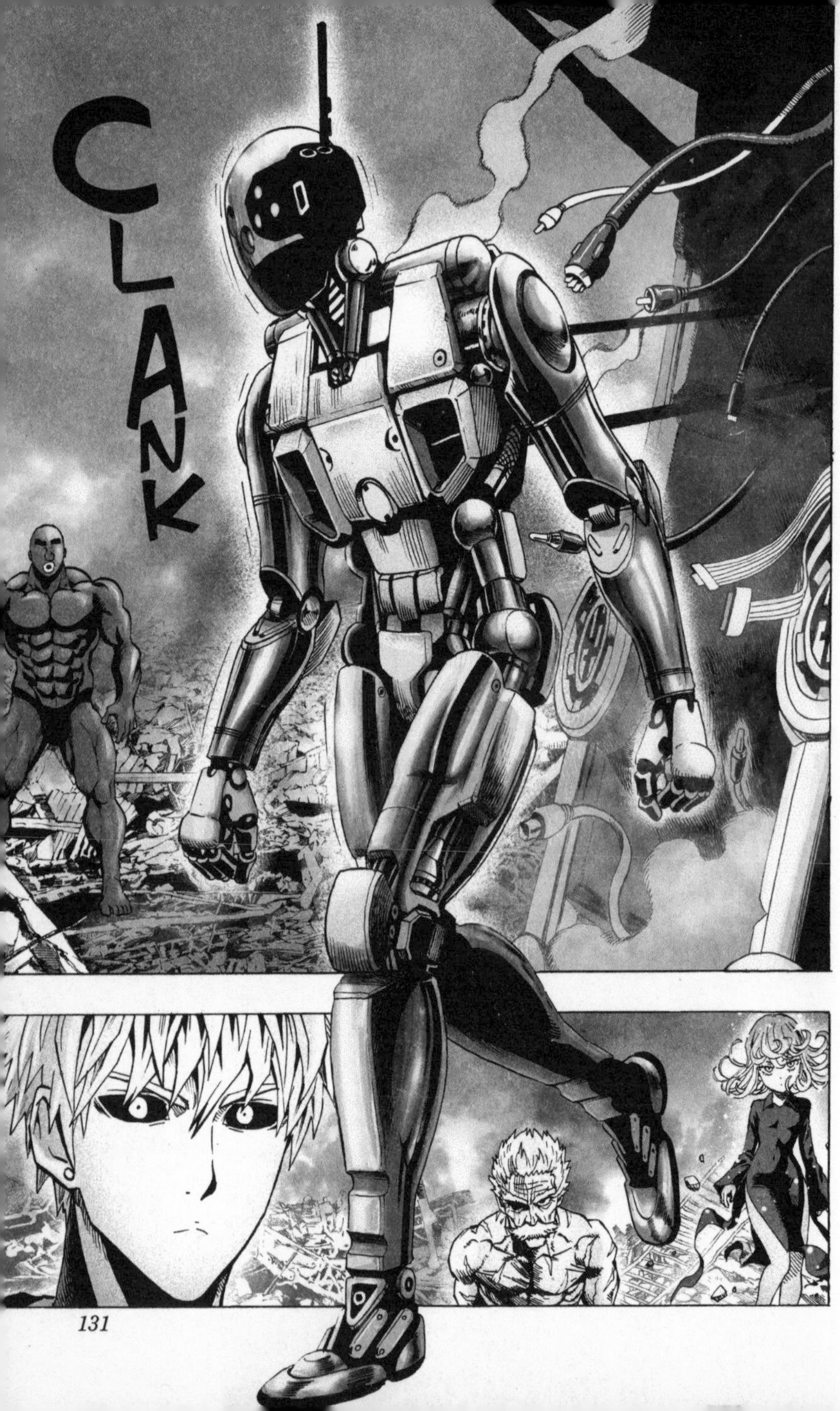
CLANK

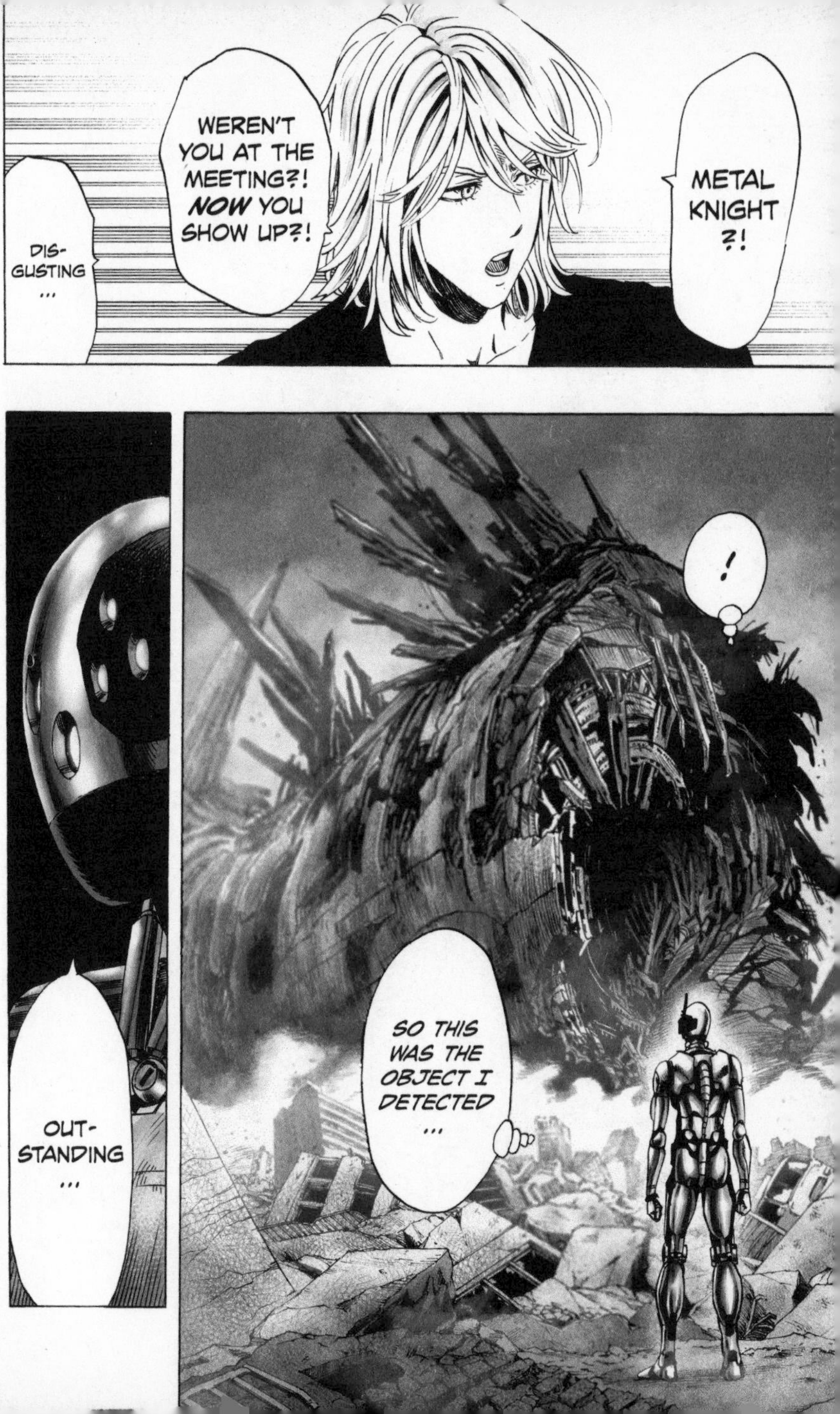
METAL KNIGHT ?!
WEREN'T YOU AT THE MEETING?! NOW YOU SHOW UP?!
DIS-GUSTING ...
!
SO THIS WAS THE OBJECT I DETECTED ...
OUT-STANDING ...

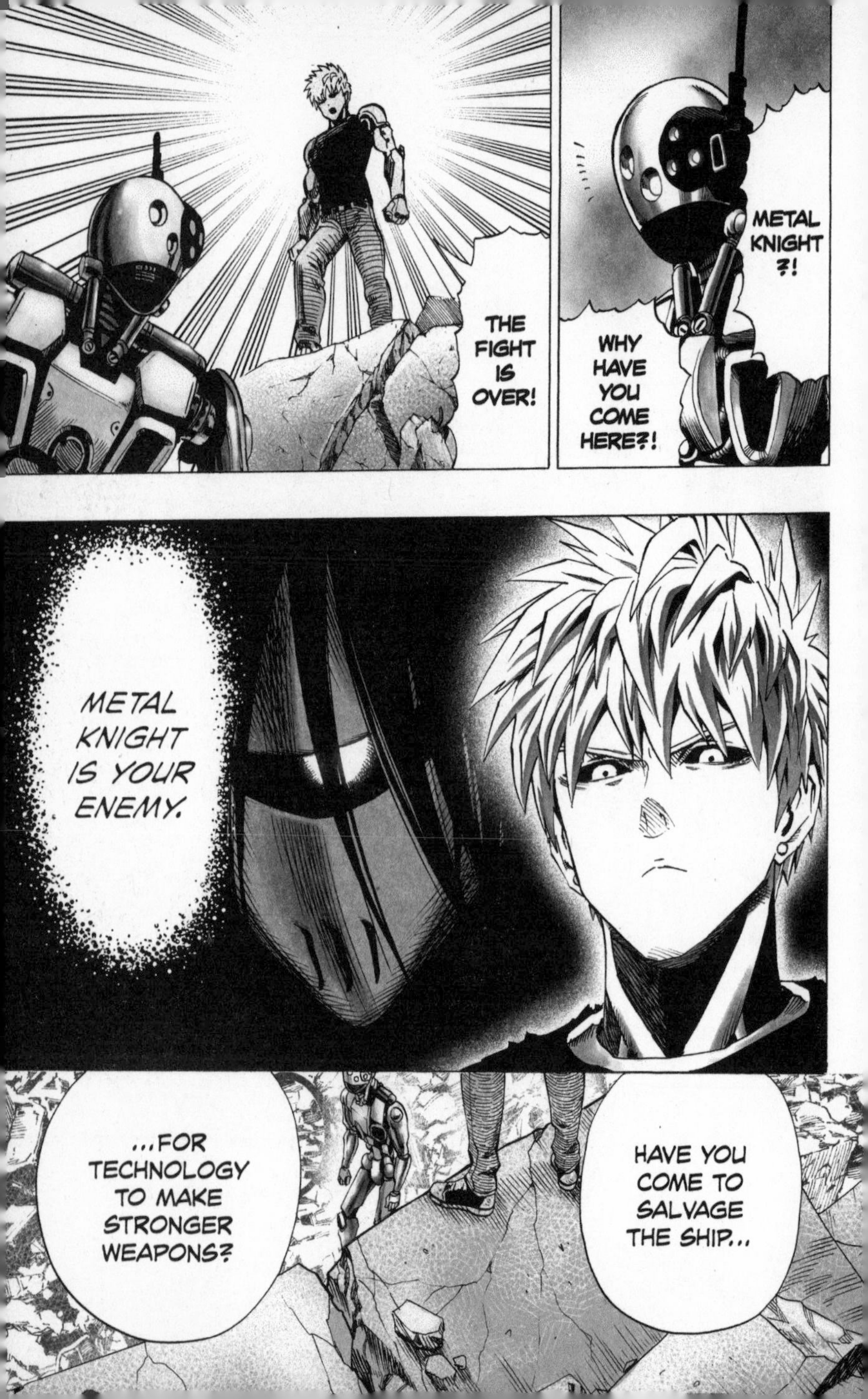
METAL KNIGHT ?!
WHY HAVE YOU COME HERE?!
THE FIGHT IS OVER!
METAL KNIGHT IS YOUR ENEMY.
HAVE YOU COME TO SALVAGE THE SHIP...
...FOR TECHNOLOGY TO MAKE STRONGER WEAPONS?

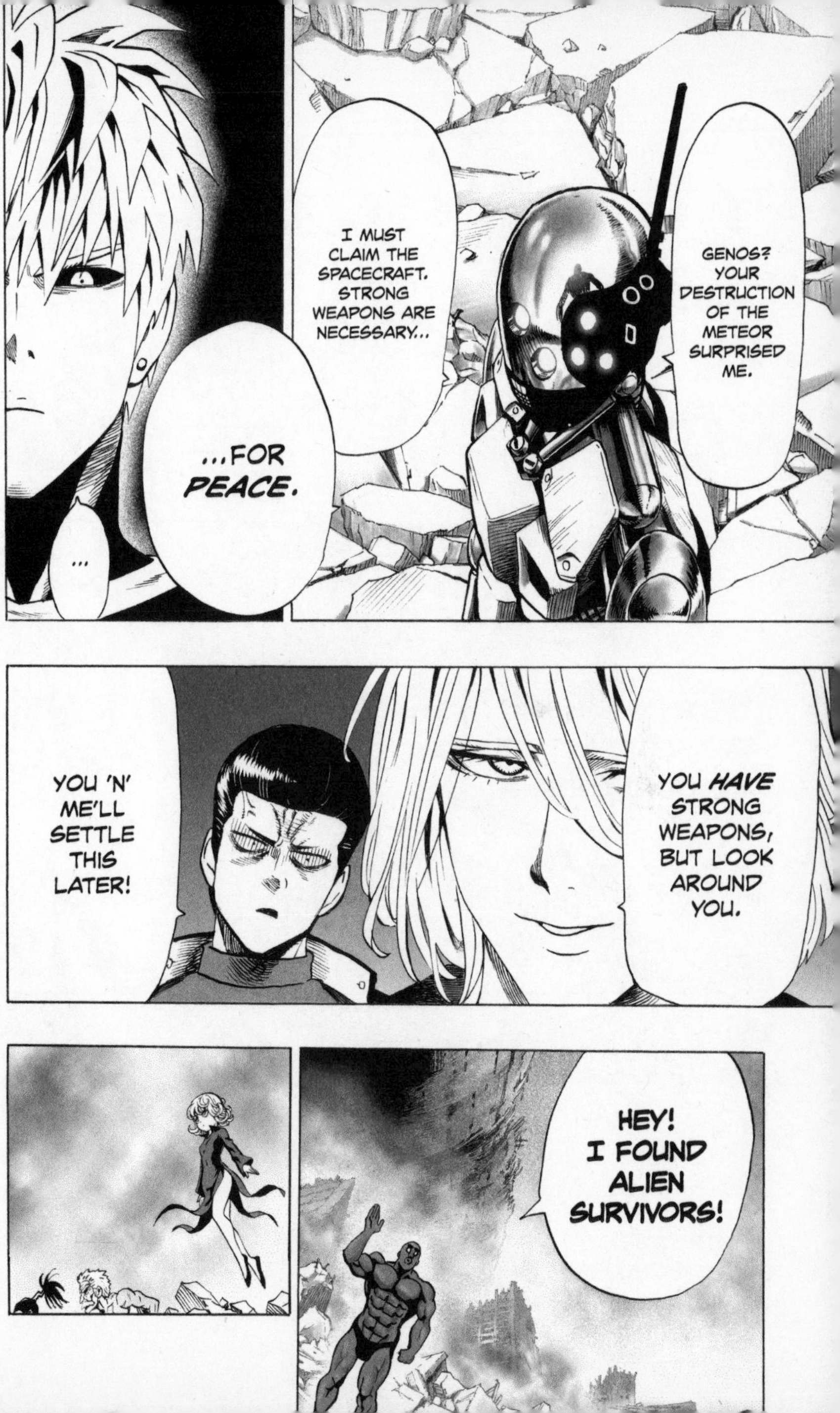
GENOS? YOUR DESTRUCTION OF THE METEOR SURPRISED ME.
I MUST CLAIM THE SPACECRAFT. STRONG WEAPONS ARE NECESSARY...
...FOR *PEACE*.
...
YOU *HAVE* STRONG WEAPONS, BUT LOOK AROUND YOU.
YOU 'N' ME'LL SETTLE THIS LATER!
HEY! I FOUND ALIEN SURVIVORS!

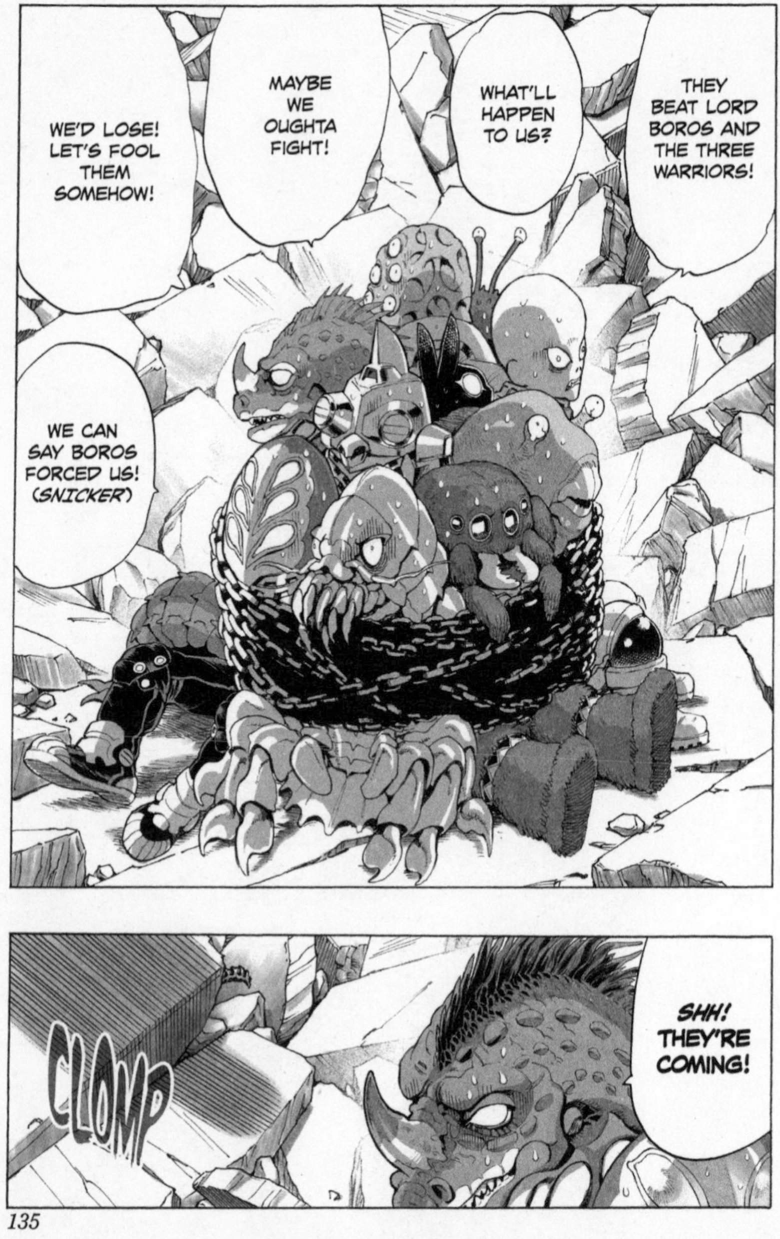
THEY BEAT LORD BOROS AND THE THREE WARRIORS!
WHAT'LL HAPPEN TO US?
MAYBE WE OUGHTA FIGHT!
WE'D LOSE! LET'S FOOL THEM SOMEHOW!
WE CAN SAY BOROS FORCED US! (*SNICKER*)
SHH! THEY'RE COMING!
CLOMP

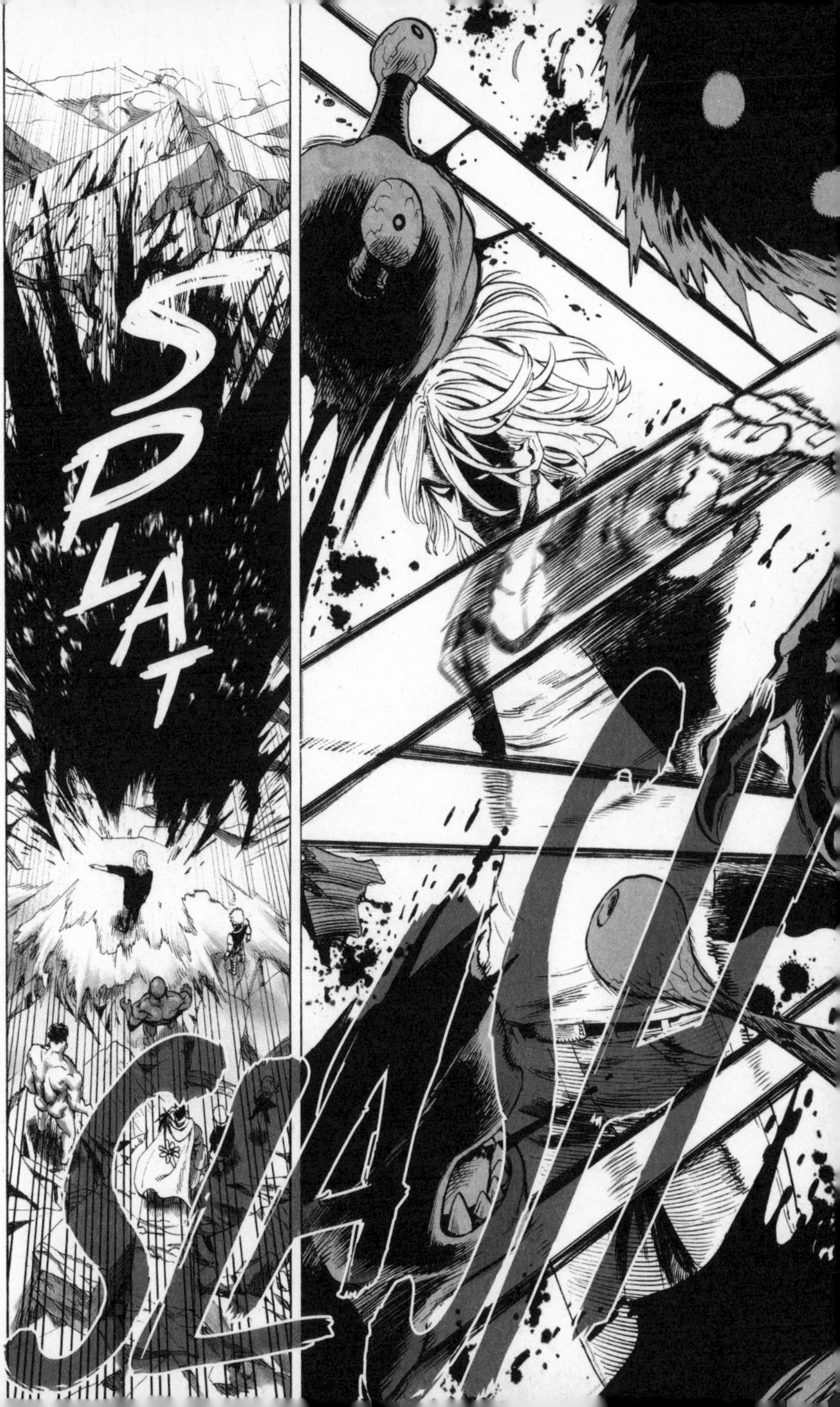
SLASH
SPLAT

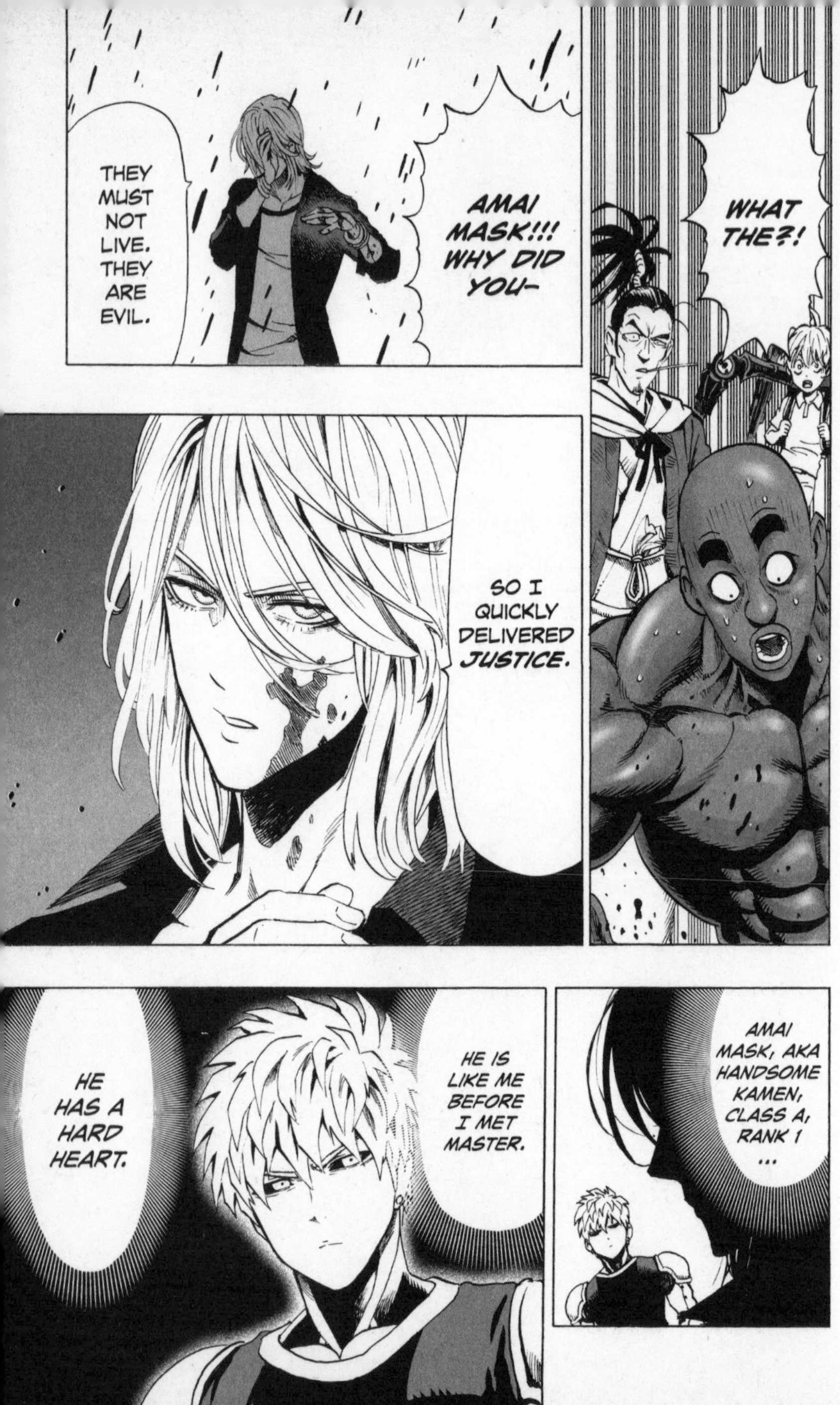
WHAT THE?!
AMAI MASK!!! WHY DID YOU-
THEY MUST NOT LIVE. THEY ARE EVIL.
SO I QUICKLY DELIVERED JUSTICE.
AMAI MASK, AKA HANDSOME KAMEN, CLASS A, RANK 1 ...
HE IS LIKE ME BEFORE I MET MASTER.
HE HAS A HARD HEART.

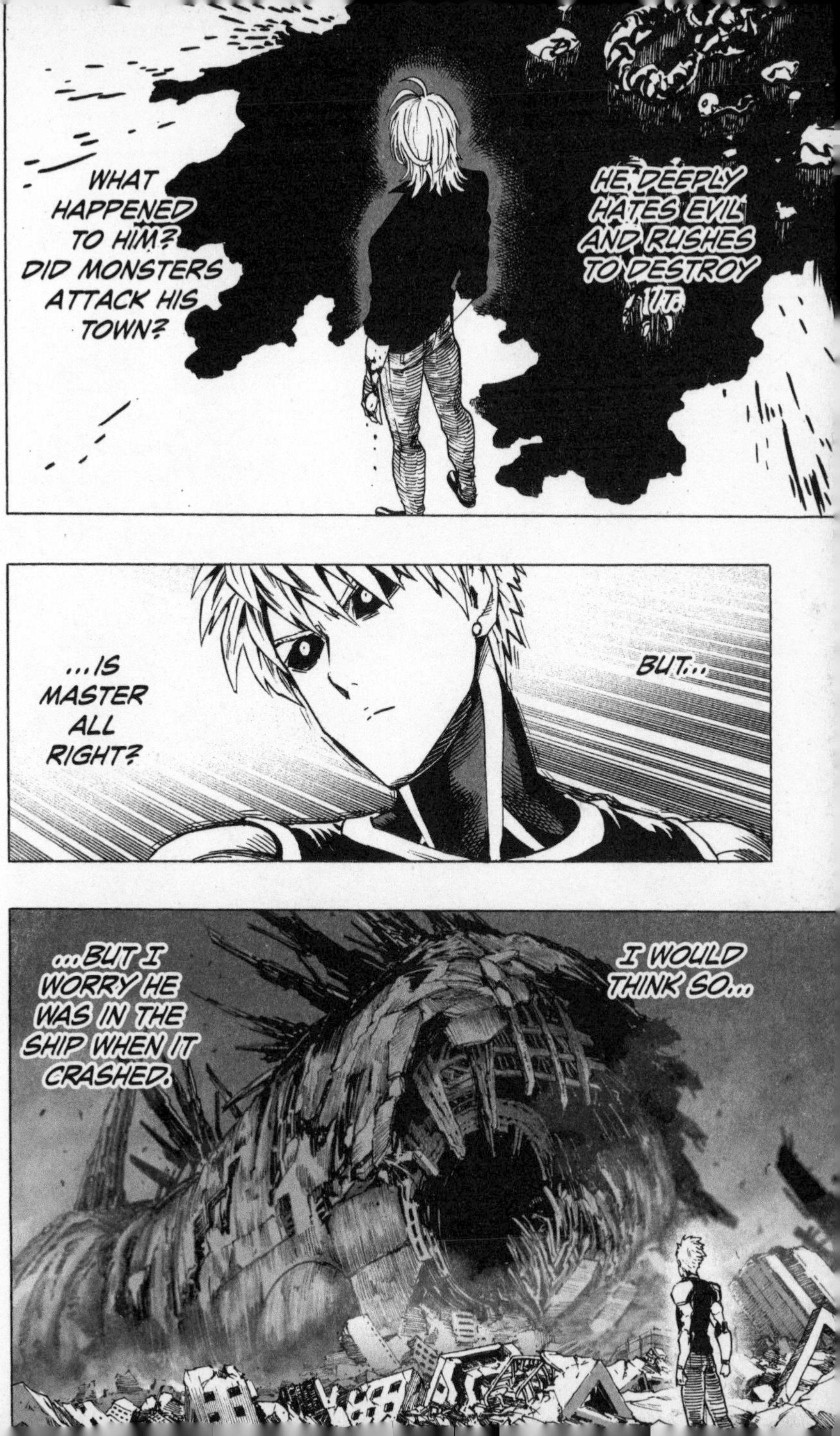
HE DEEPLY HATES EVIL AND RUSHES TO DESTROY IT.
WHAT HAPPENED TO HIM? DID MONSTERS ATTACK HIS TOWN?
BUT...
...IS MASTER ALL RIGHT?
I WOULD THINK SO...
...BUT I WORRY HE WAS IN THE SHIP WHEN IT CRASHED.

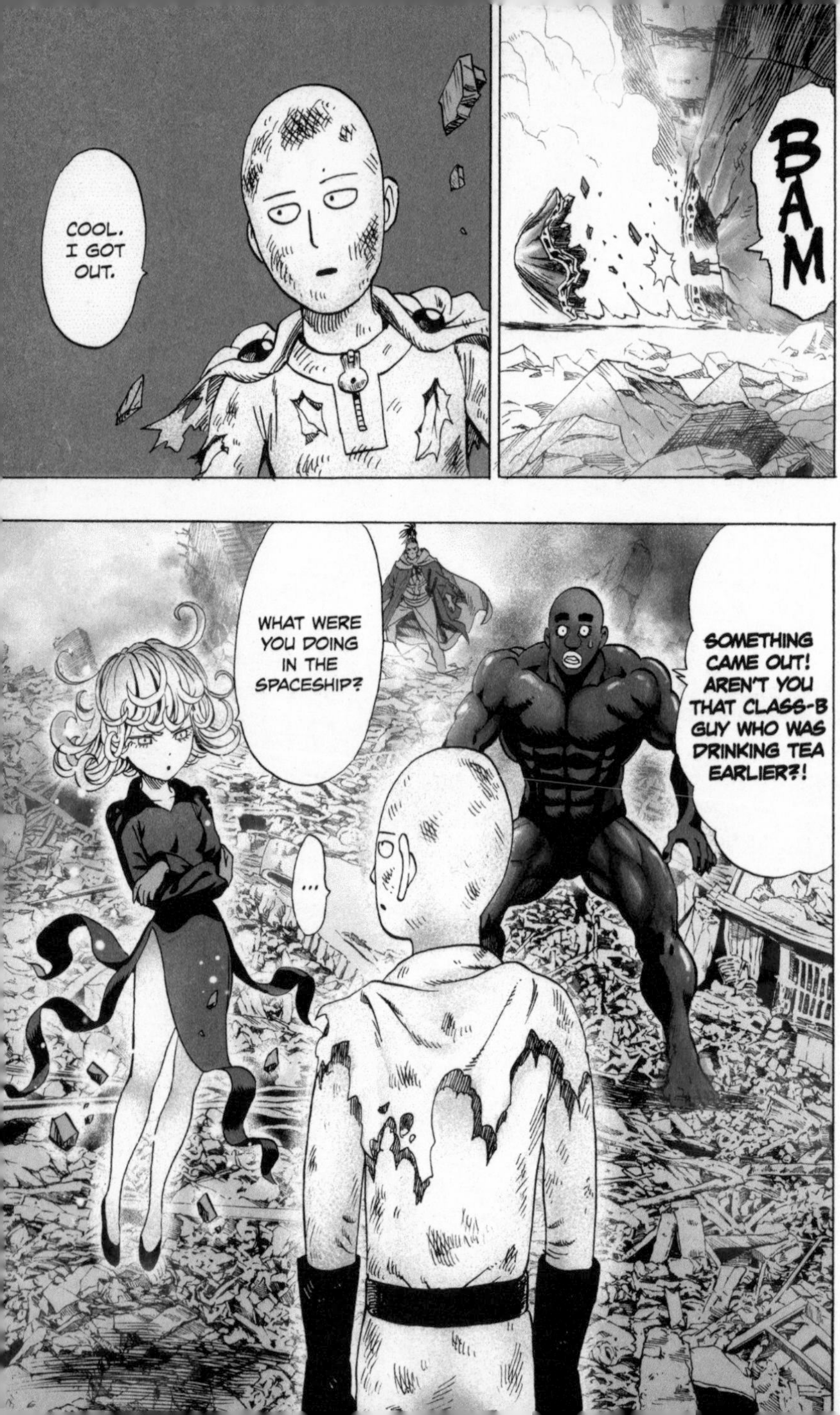
BAM
COOL. I GOT OUT.
SOMETHING CAME OUT! AREN'T YOU THAT CLASS-B GUY WHO WAS DRINKING TEA EARLIER?!
WHAT WERE YOU DOING IN THE SPACESHIP?
...

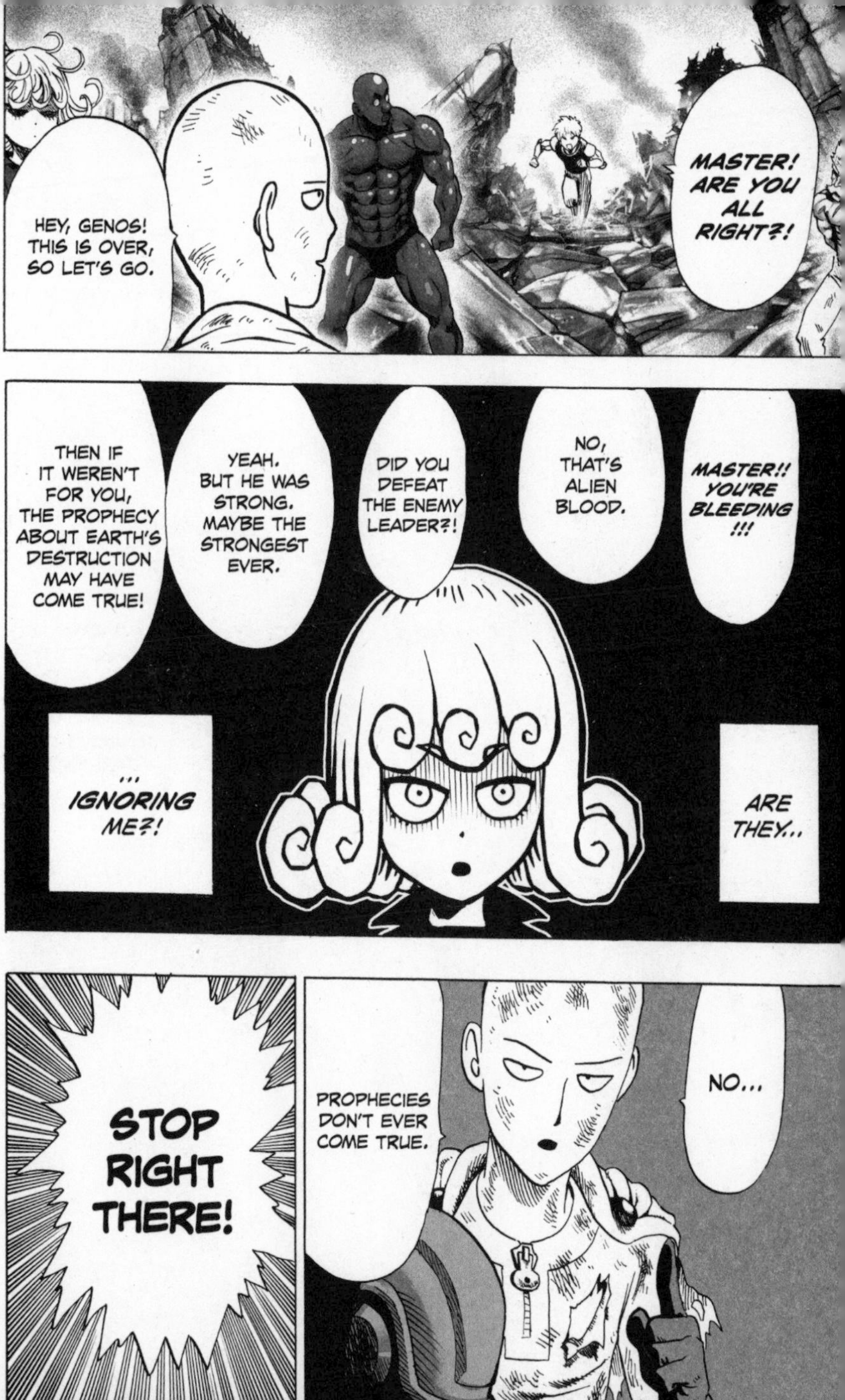
MASTER! ARE YOU ALL RIGHT?!
HEY, GENOS! THIS IS OVER, SO LET'S GO.
MASTER!! YOU'RE BLEEDING!!!
NO, THAT'S ALIEN BLOOD.
DID YOU DEFEAT THE ENEMY LEADER?!
YEAH. BUT HE WAS STRONG. MAYBE THE STRONGEST EVER.
THEN IF IT WEREN'T FOR YOU, THE PROPHECY ABOUT EARTH'S DESTRUCTION MAY HAVE COME TRUE!
ARE THEY...
... IGNORING ME?!
NO...
PROPHECIES DON'T EVER COME TRUE.
STOP RIGHT THERE!

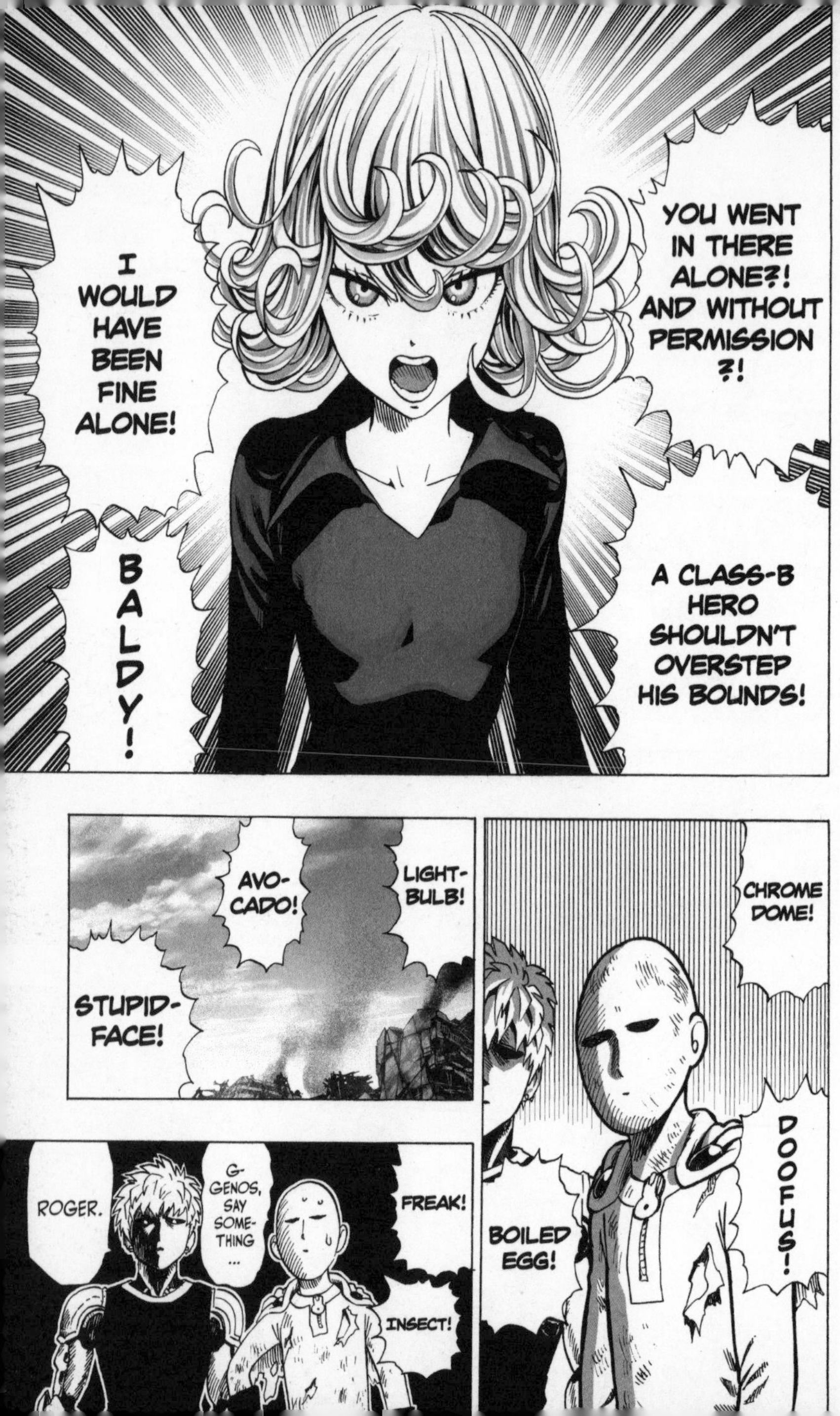
YOU WENT IN THERE ALONE?! AND WITHOUT PERMISSION?!
I WOULD HAVE BEEN FINE ALONE!
A CLASS-B HERO SHOULDN'T OVERSTEP HIS BOUNDS!
BALDY!
CHROME DOME!
DOOFUS!
BOILED EGG!
LIGHT-BULB!
AVOCADO!
STUPID-FACE!
FREAK!
G-GENOS, SAY SOMETHING...
ROGER.
INSECT!

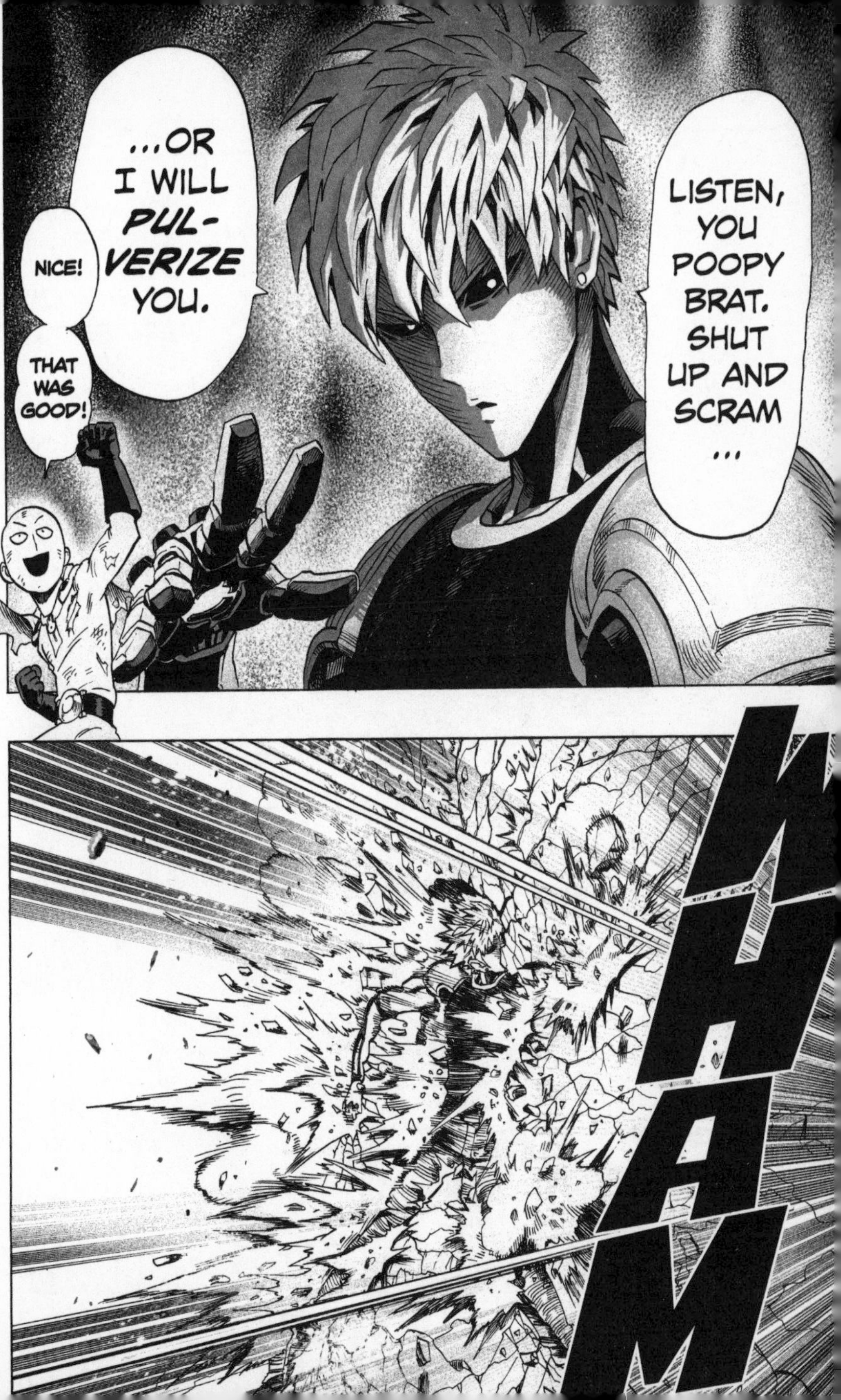
LISTEN, YOU POOPY BRAT. SHUT UP AND SCRAM ...
...OR I WILL *PUL-VERIZE* YOU.
NICE!
THAT WAS GOOD!
WHAM

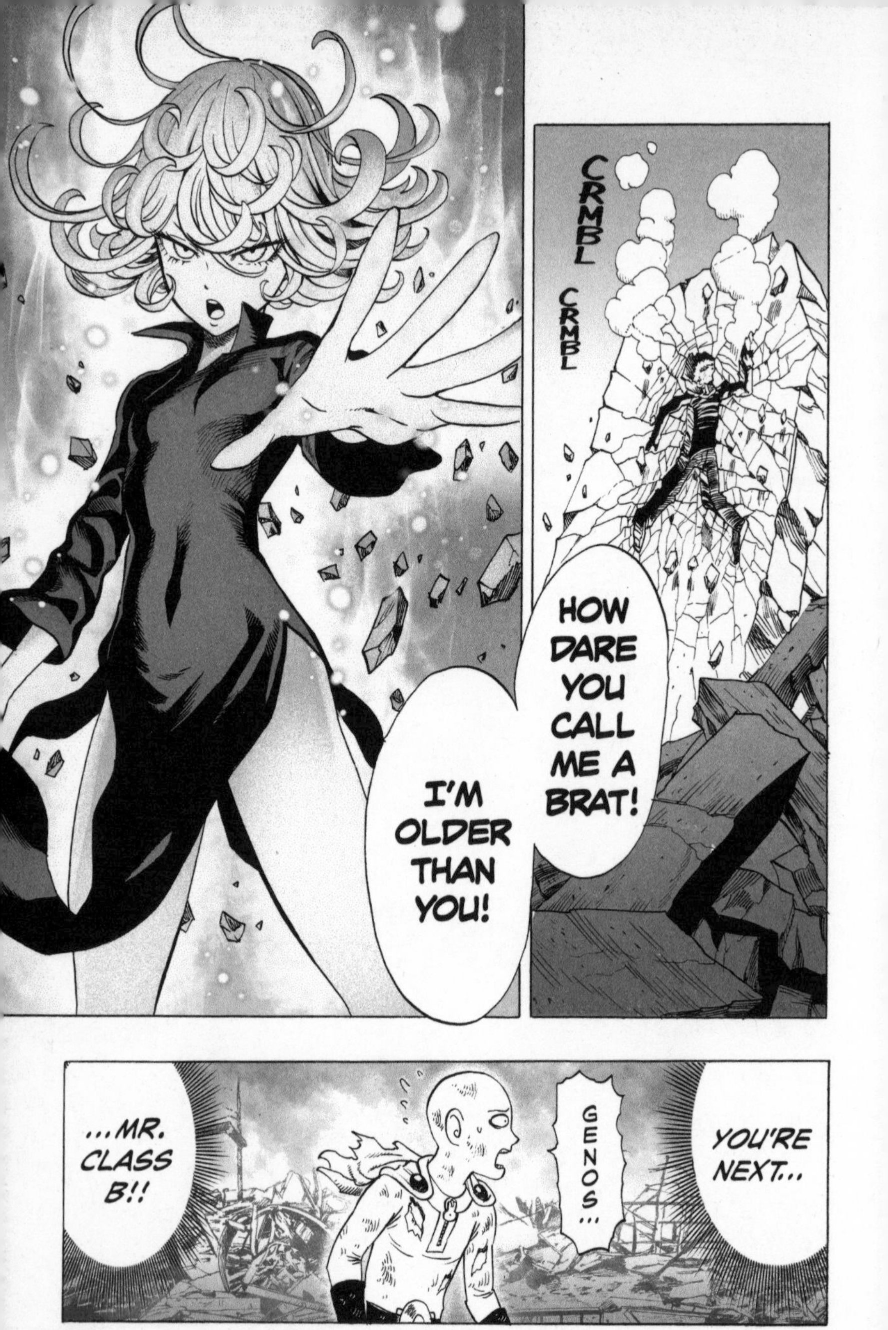
CRMBL CRMBL
HOW DARE YOU CALL ME A BRAT!
I'M OLDER THAN YOU!
YOU'RE NEXT...
GENOS...
...MR. CLASS B!!

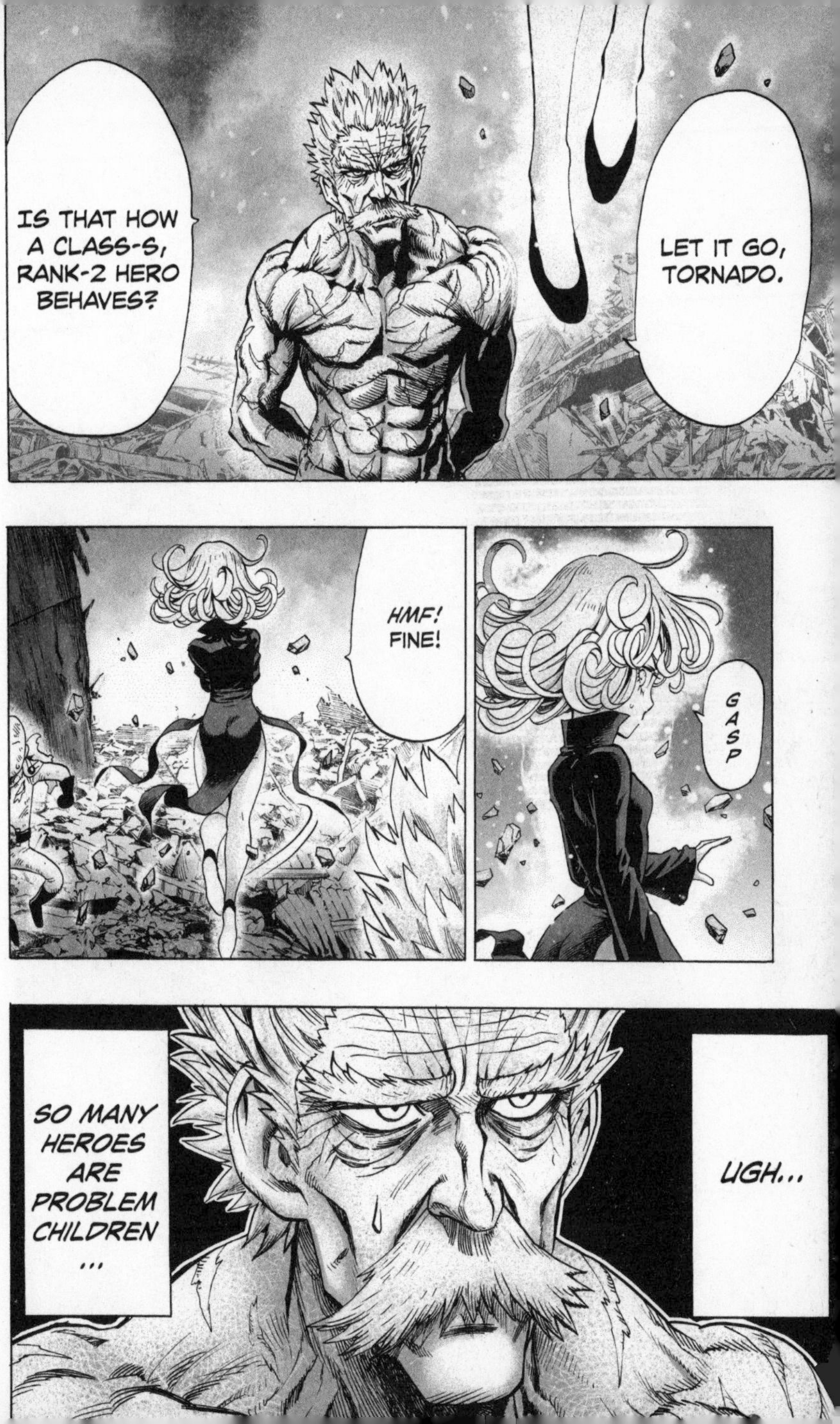
LET IT GO, TORNADO.
IS THAT HOW A CLASS-S, RANK-2 HERO BEHAVES?
GASP
HMF! FINE!
UGH...
SO MANY HEROES ARE PROBLEM CHILDREN...

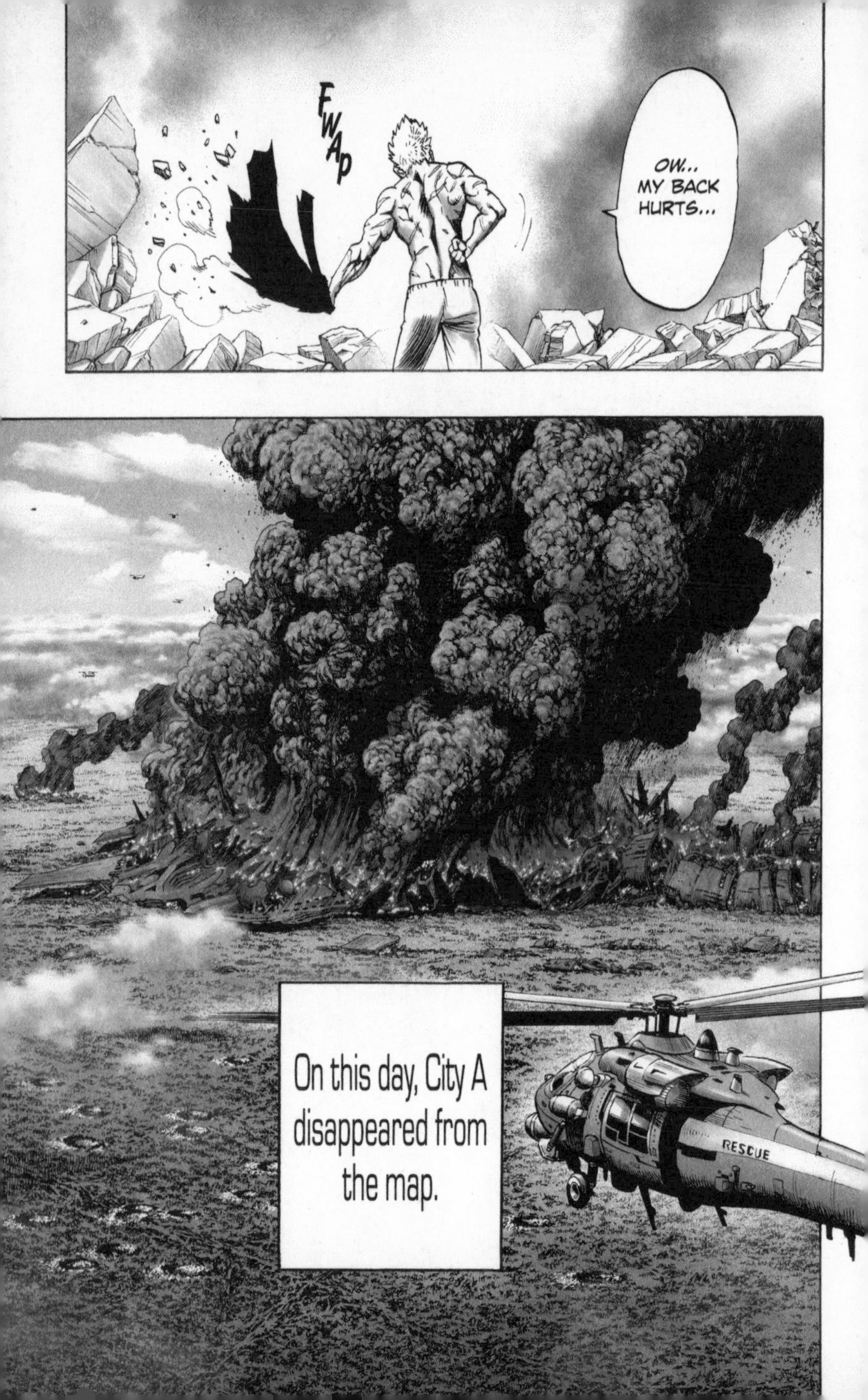
OW... MY BACK HURTS...
FWAP
On this day, City A disappeared from the map.
RESCUE

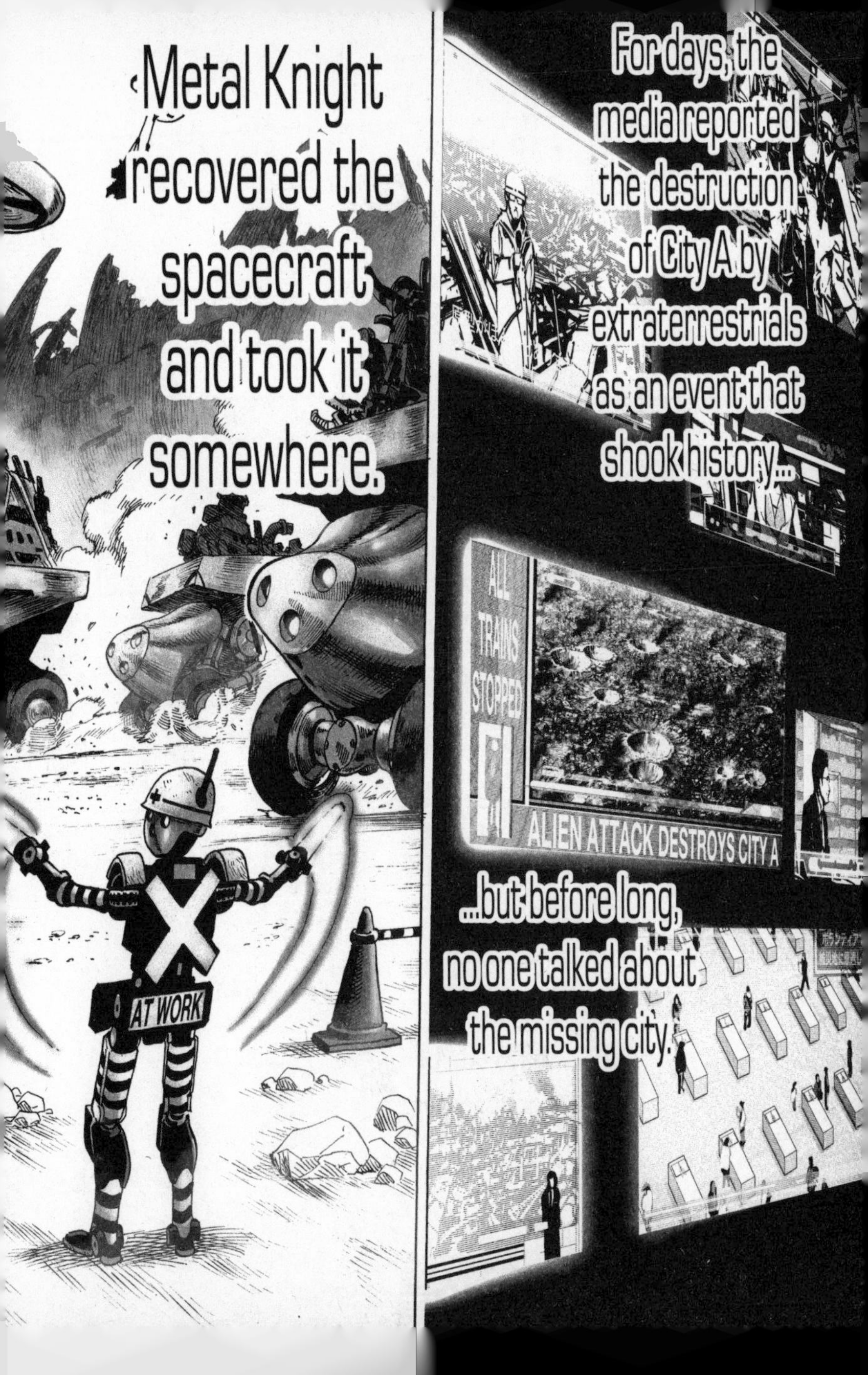
For days, the media reported the destruction of City A by extraterrestrials as an event that shook history...
ALL TRAINS STOPPED
ALIEN ATTACK DESTROYS CITY A
...but before long, no one talked about the missing city.
Metal Knight recovered the spacecraft and took it somewhere.
AT WORK

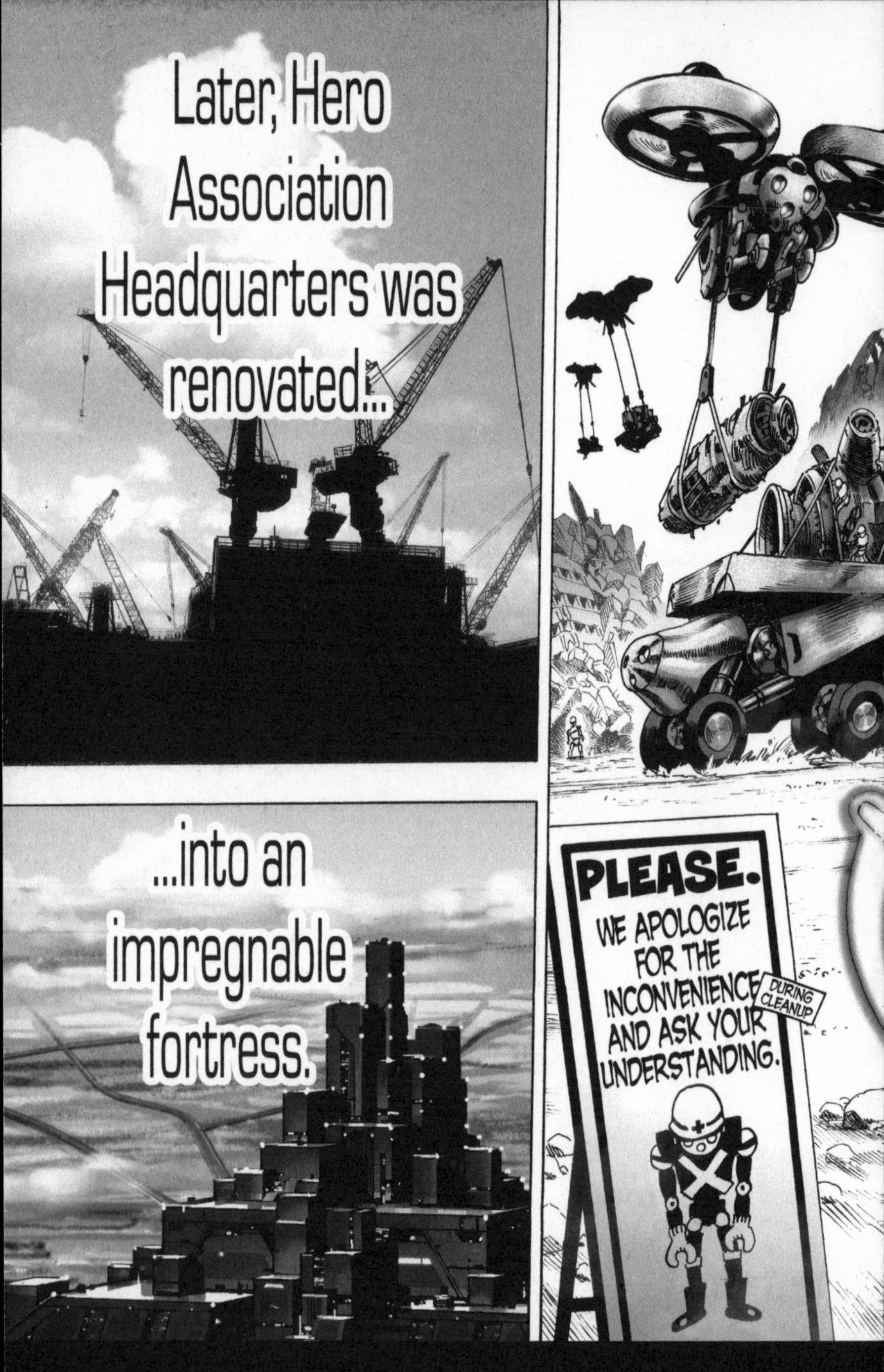
PLEASE.
WE APOLOGIZE FOR THE INCONVENIENCE DURING CLEANUP AND ASK YOUR UNDERSTANDING.
Later, Hero Association Headquarters was renovated...
...into an impregnable fortress.

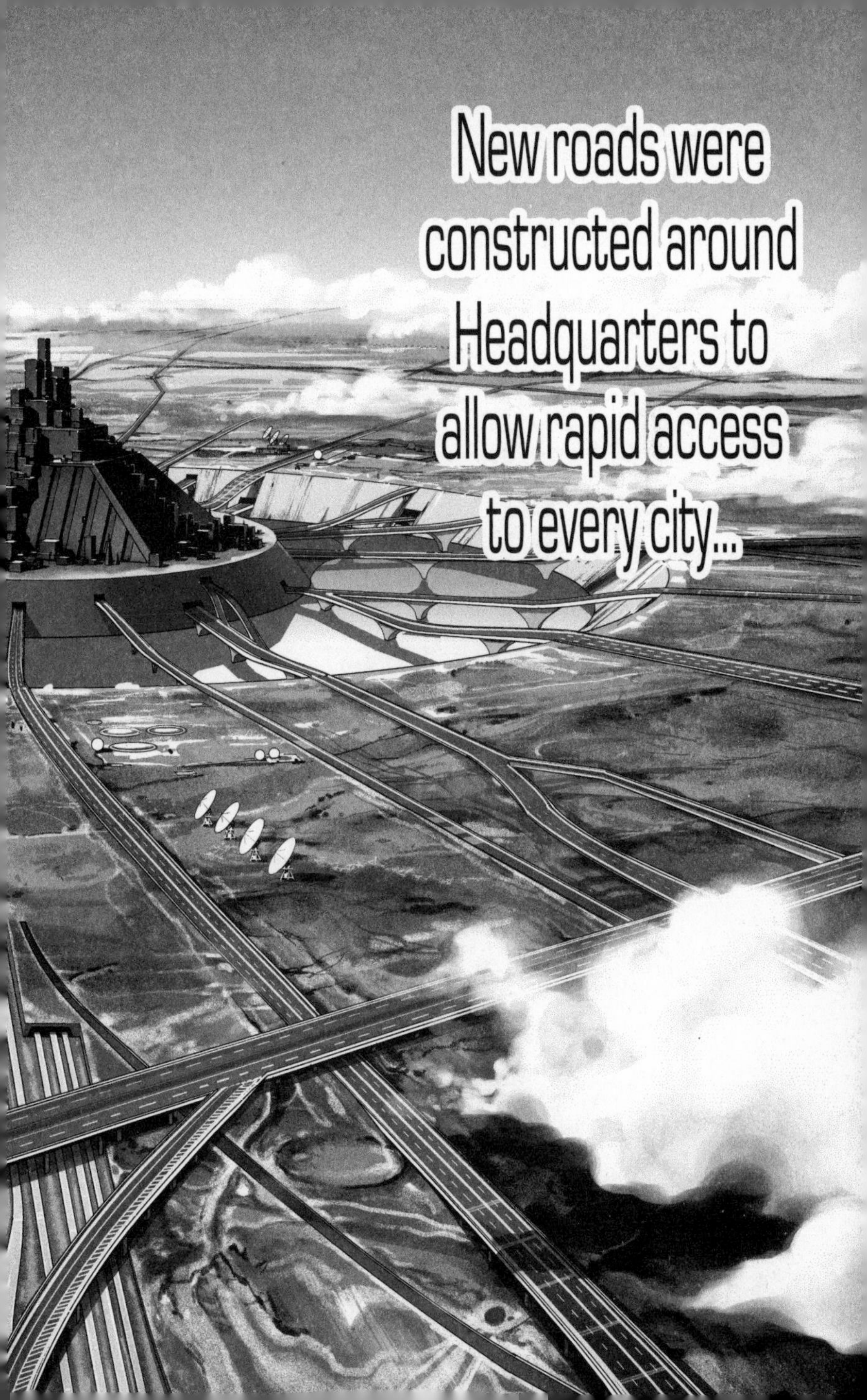
New roads were constructed around Headquarters to allow rapid access to every city...

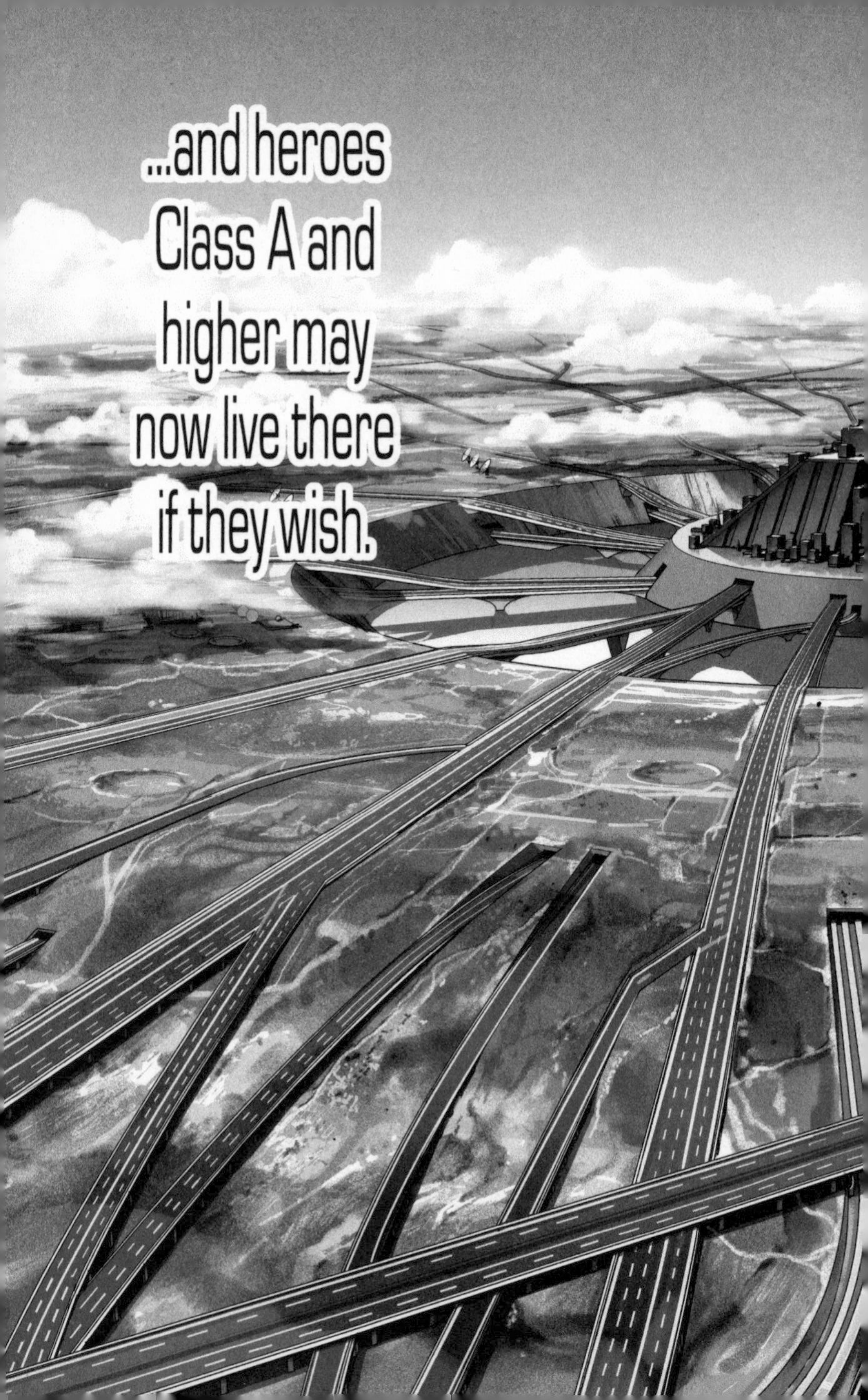
...and heroes Class A and higher may now live there if they wish.

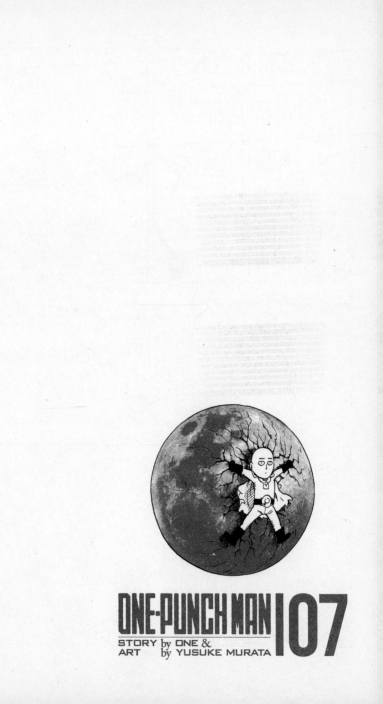

ONE-PUNCH MAN 07

STORY by ONE &
ART by YUSUKE MURATA

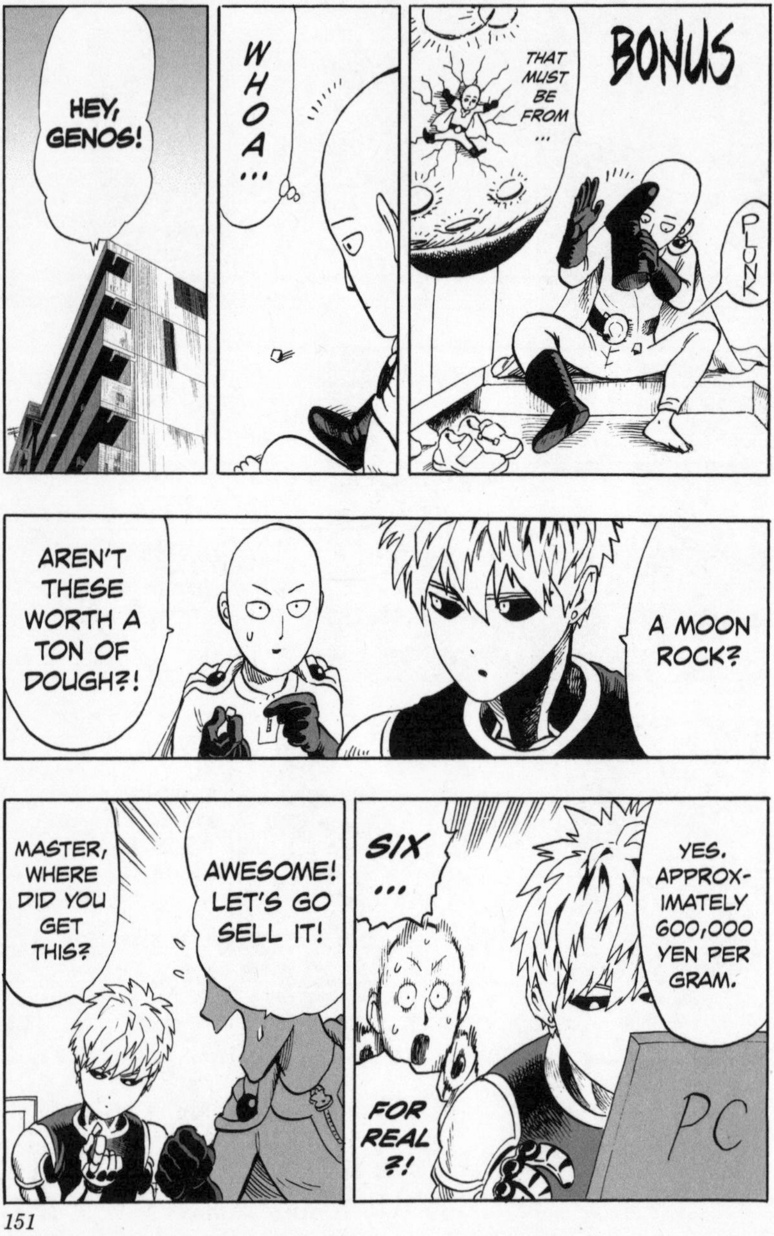
BONUS
THAT MUST BE FROM ...
PLUNK
WHOA...
HEY, GENOS!
A MOON ROCK?
AREN'T THESE WORTH A TON OF DOUGH?!
YES. APPROXIMATELY 600,000 YEN PER GRAM.
PC
SIX ...
FOR REAL ?!
AWESOME! LET'S GO SELL IT!
MASTER, WHERE DID YOU GET THIS?

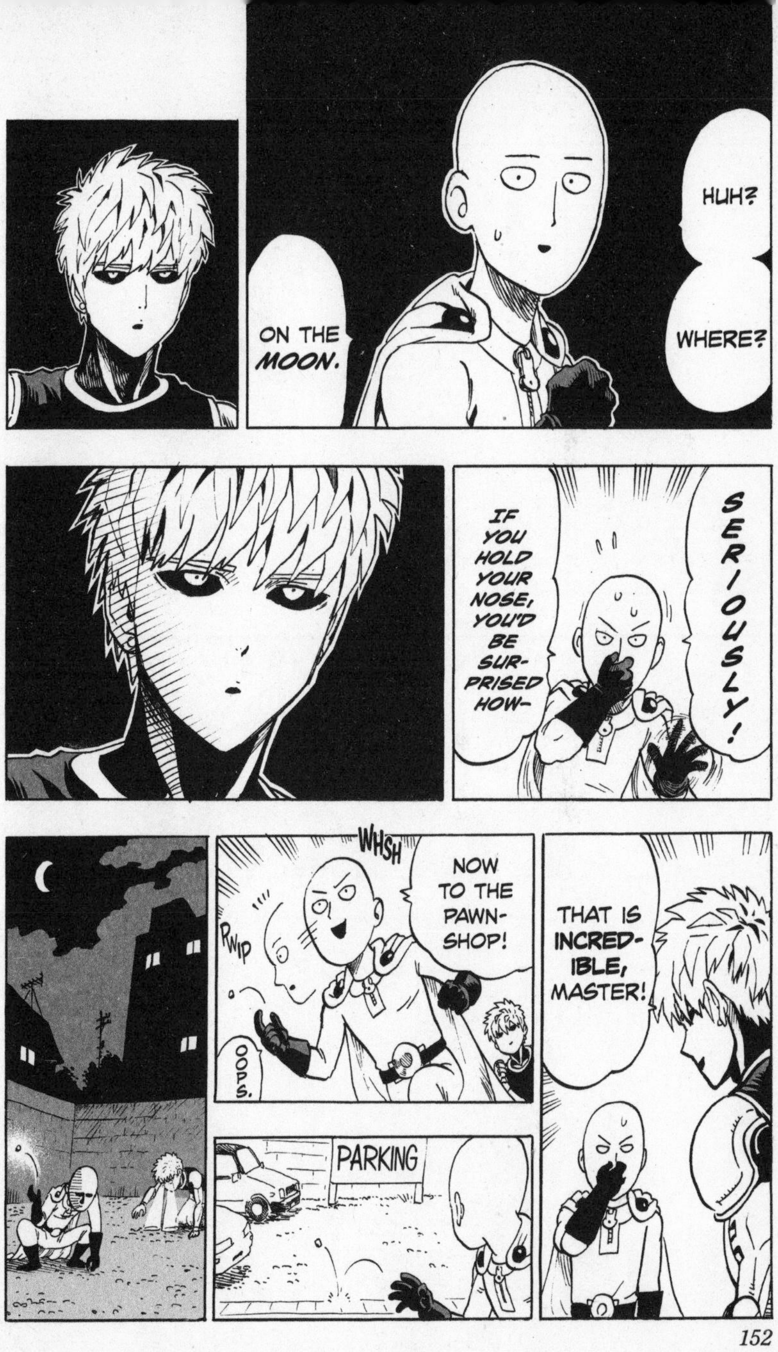
HUH?
WHERE?
ON THE MOON.
SERIOUSLY!
IF YOU HOLD YOUR NOSE, YOU'D BE SUR-PRISED HOW-
THAT IS INCRED-IBLE, MASTER!
WHSH
NOW TO THE PAWN-SHOP!
RWIP
OOPS.
PARKING

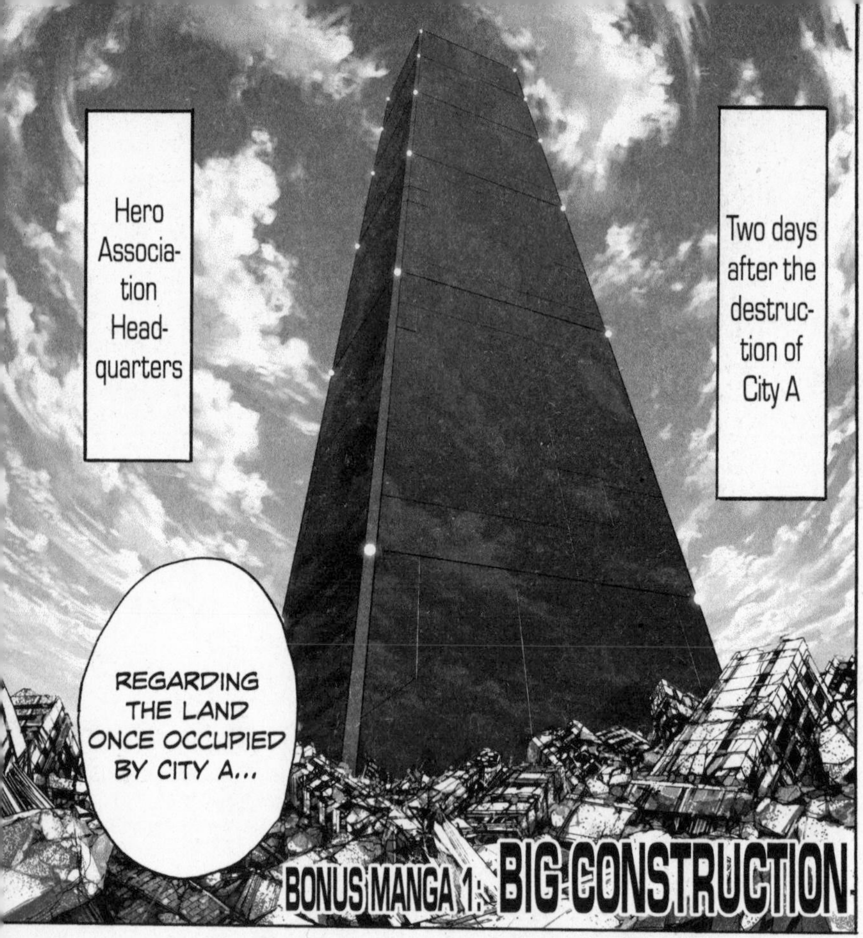
Two days after the destruction of City A
Hero Association Headquarters
REGARDING THE LAND ONCE OCCUPIED BY CITY A...
BONUS MANGA 1: BIG CONSTRUCTION

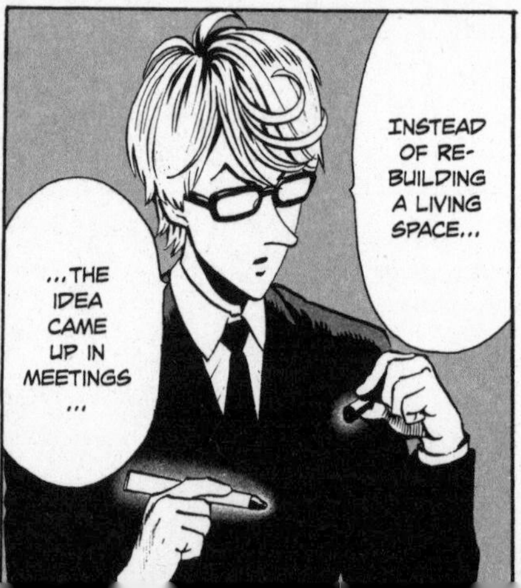
INSTEAD OF REBUILDING A LIVING SPACE...
...THE IDEA CAME UP IN MEETINGS...

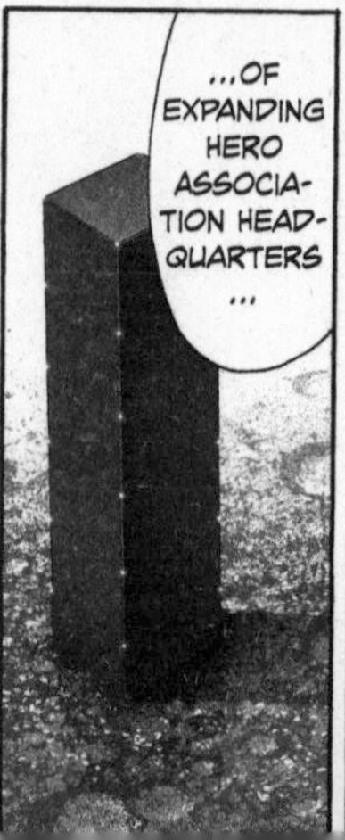
...OF EXPANDING HERO ASSOCIATION HEADQUARTERS...

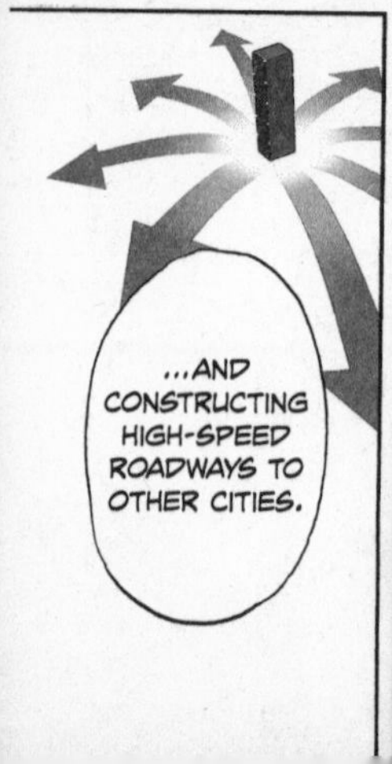
...AND CONSTRUCTING HIGH-SPEED ROADWAYS TO OTHER CITIES.

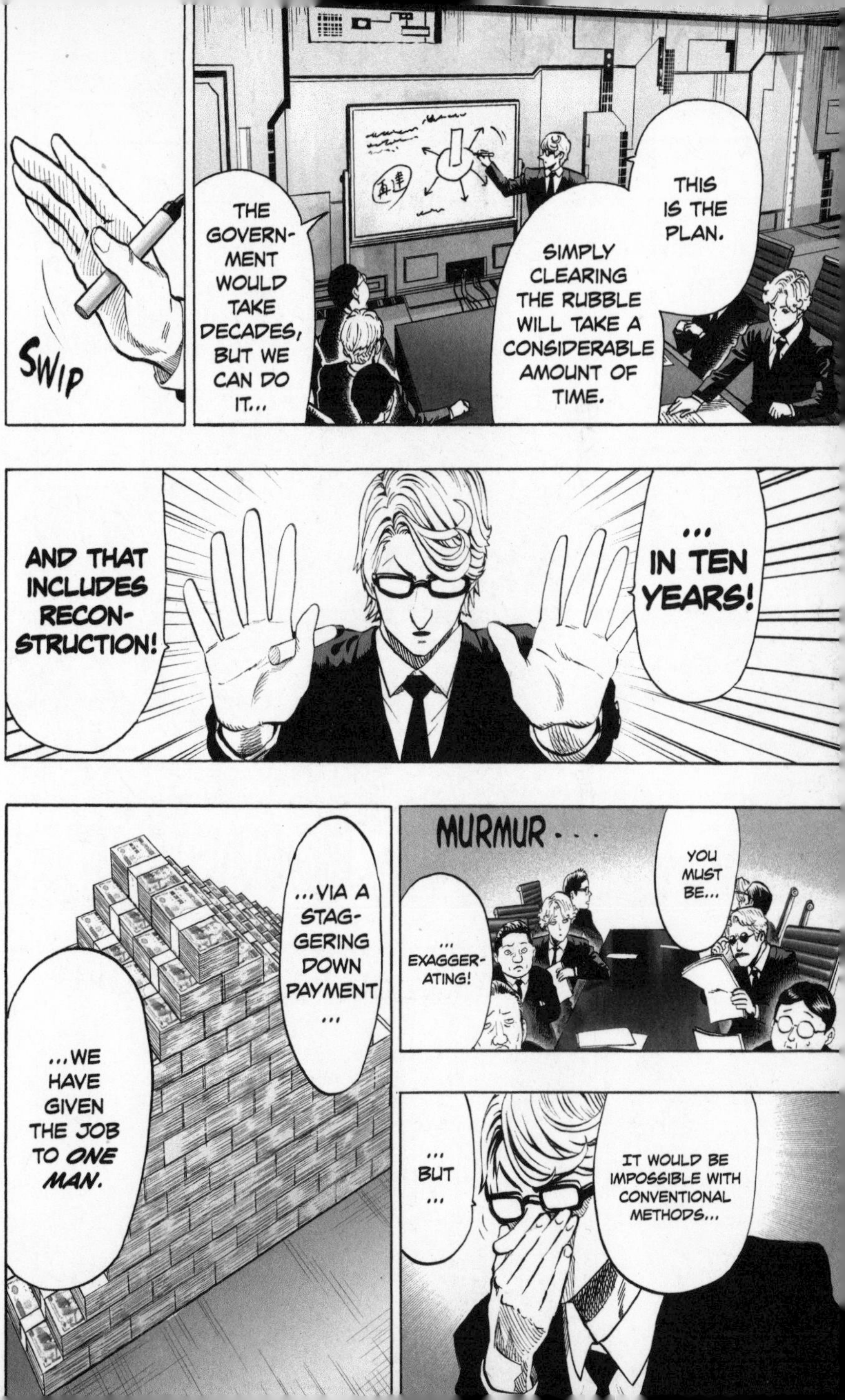
THIS IS THE PLAN.
SIMPLY CLEARING THE RUBBLE WILL TAKE A CONSIDERABLE AMOUNT OF TIME.
THE GOVERNMENT WOULD TAKE DECADES, BUT WE CAN DO IT...
SWIP
... IN TEN YEARS!
AND THAT INCLUDES RECONSTRUCTION!
MURMUR...
YOU MUST BE...
... EXAGGERATING!
IT WOULD BE IMPOSSIBLE WITH CONVENTIONAL METHODS...
... BUT ...
...VIA A STAGGERING DOWN PAYMENT ...
...WE HAVE GIVEN THE JOB TO *ONE MAN*.

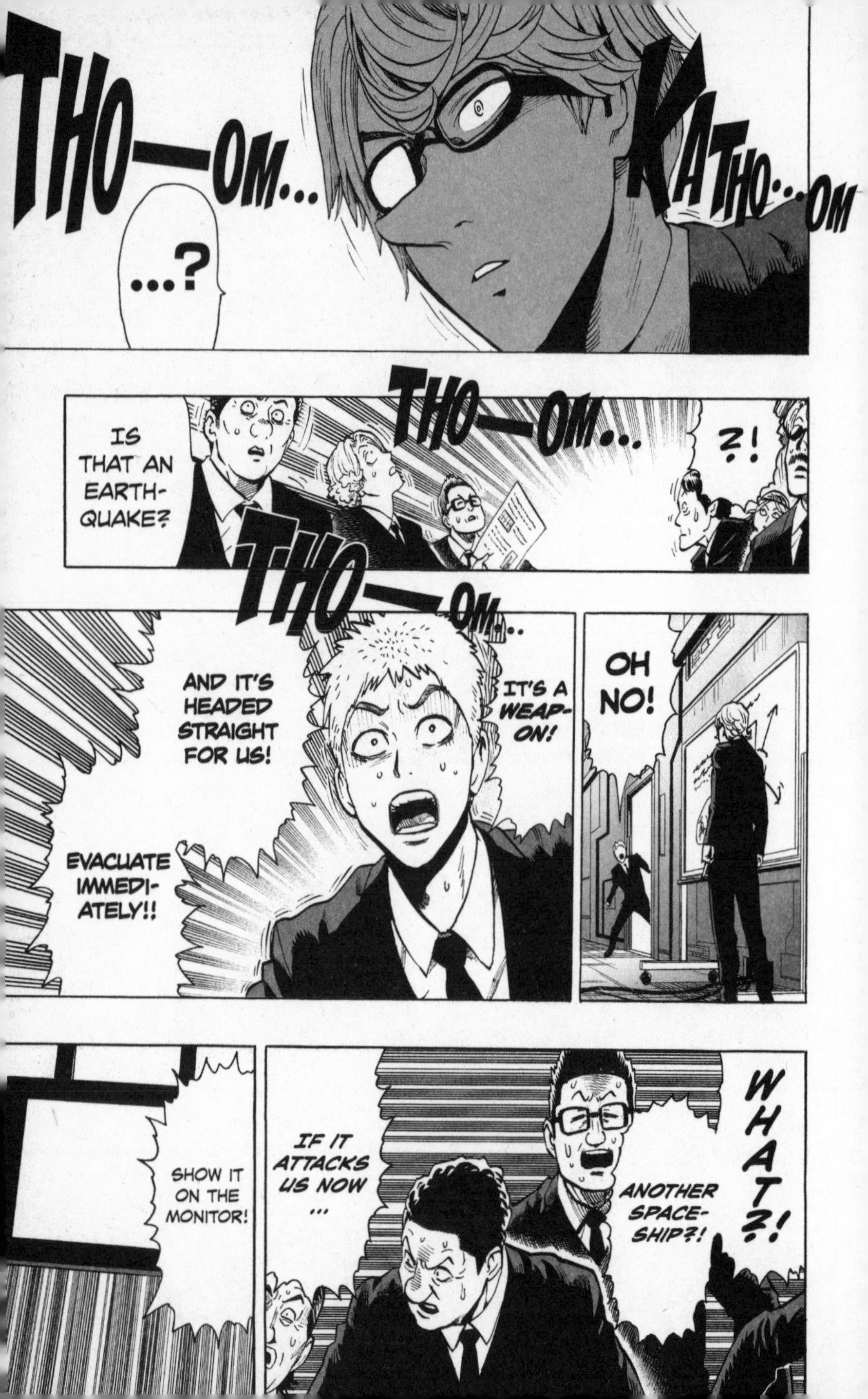
KATHO...OM
THO—OM...
...?
?!
THO—OM...
IS THAT AN EARTH-QUAKE?
THO—OM...
OH NO!
IT'S A WEAP-ON!
AND IT'S HEADED STRAIGHT FOR US!
EVACUATE IMMEDI-ATELY!!
WHAT?!
ANOTHER SPACE-SHIP?!
IF IT ATTACKS US NOW ...
SHOW IT ON THE MONITOR!

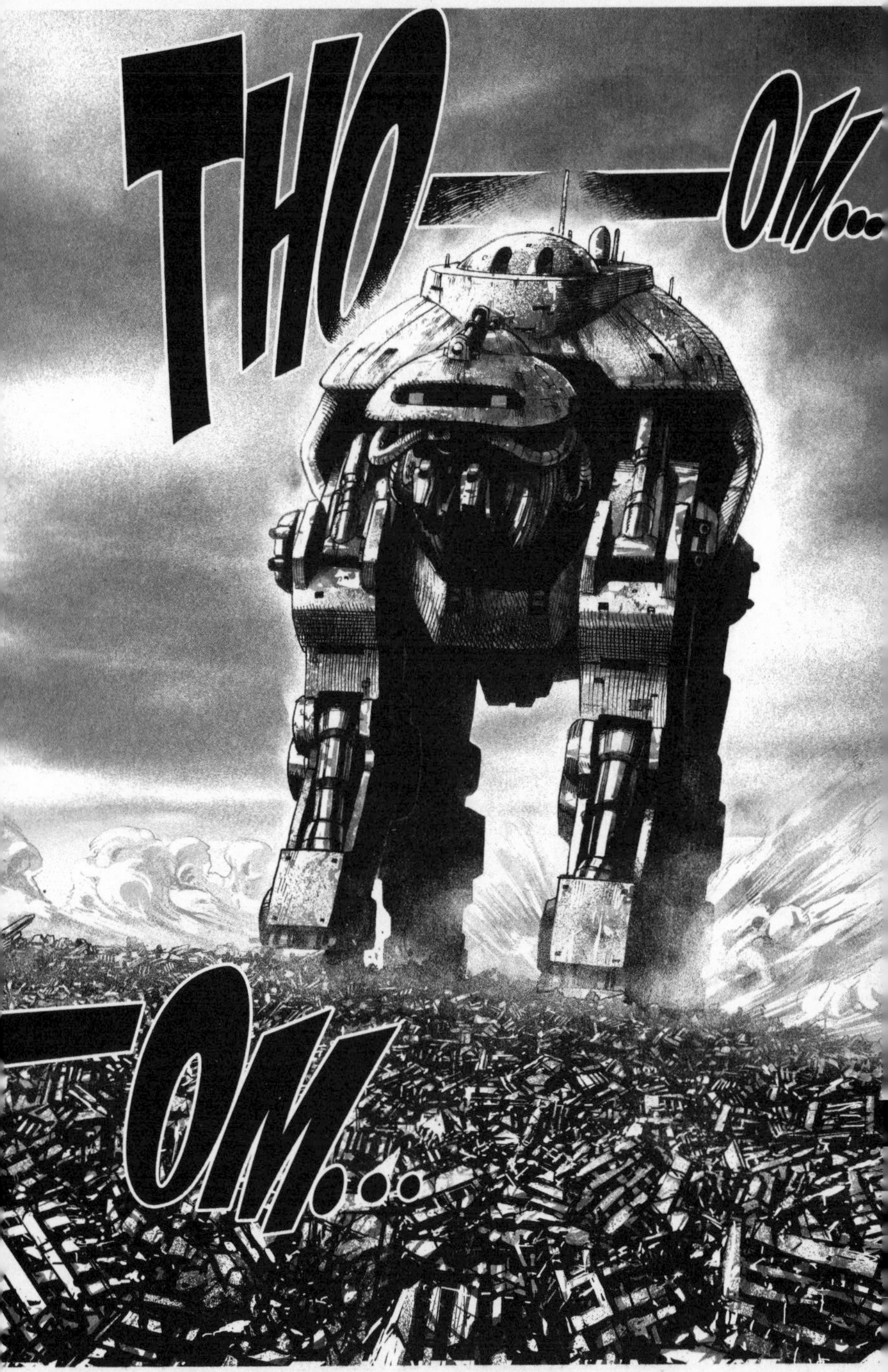
THO——OM...
—OM...

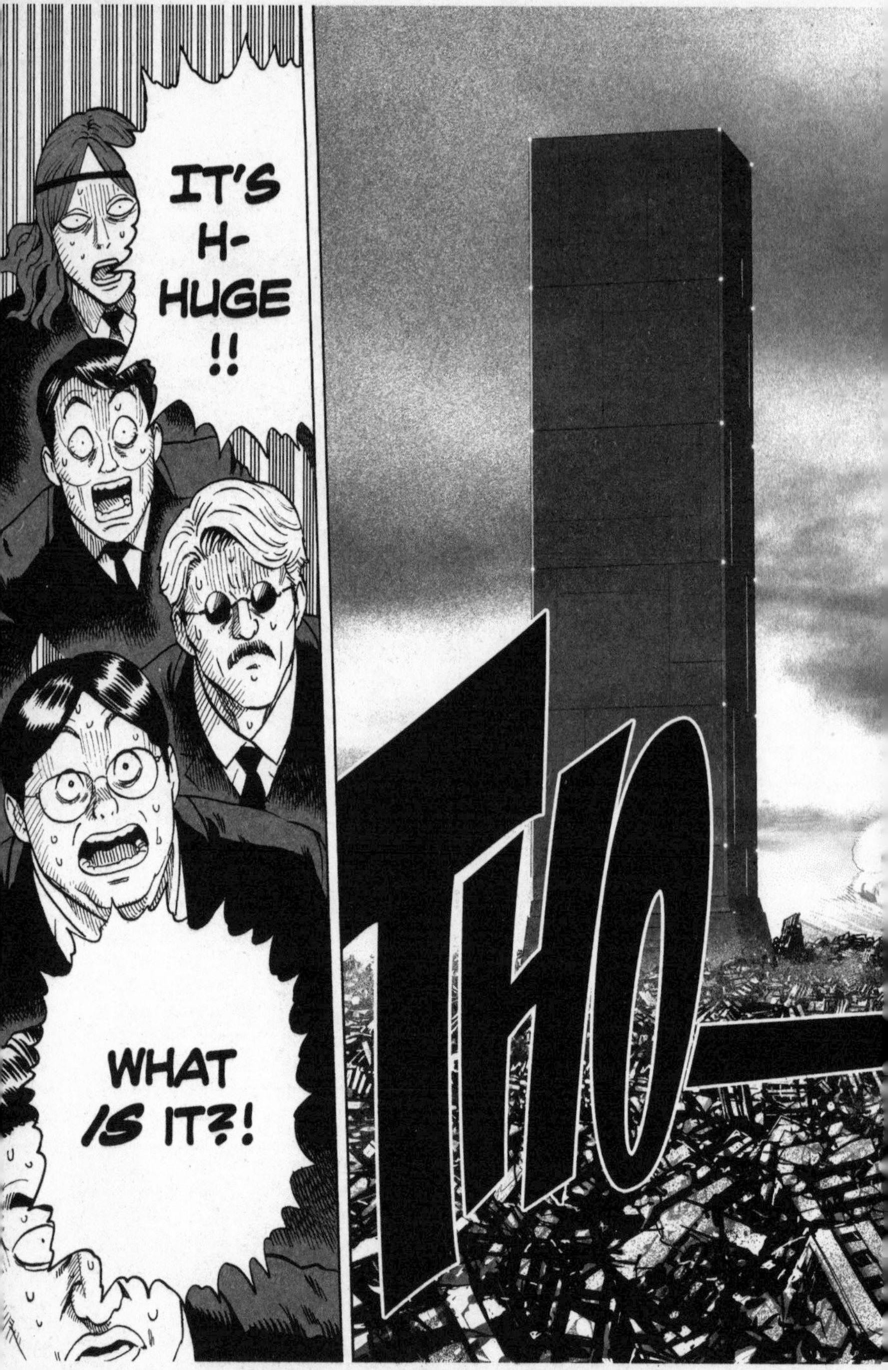
THO—
IT'S H-HUGE!!
WHAT IS IT?!

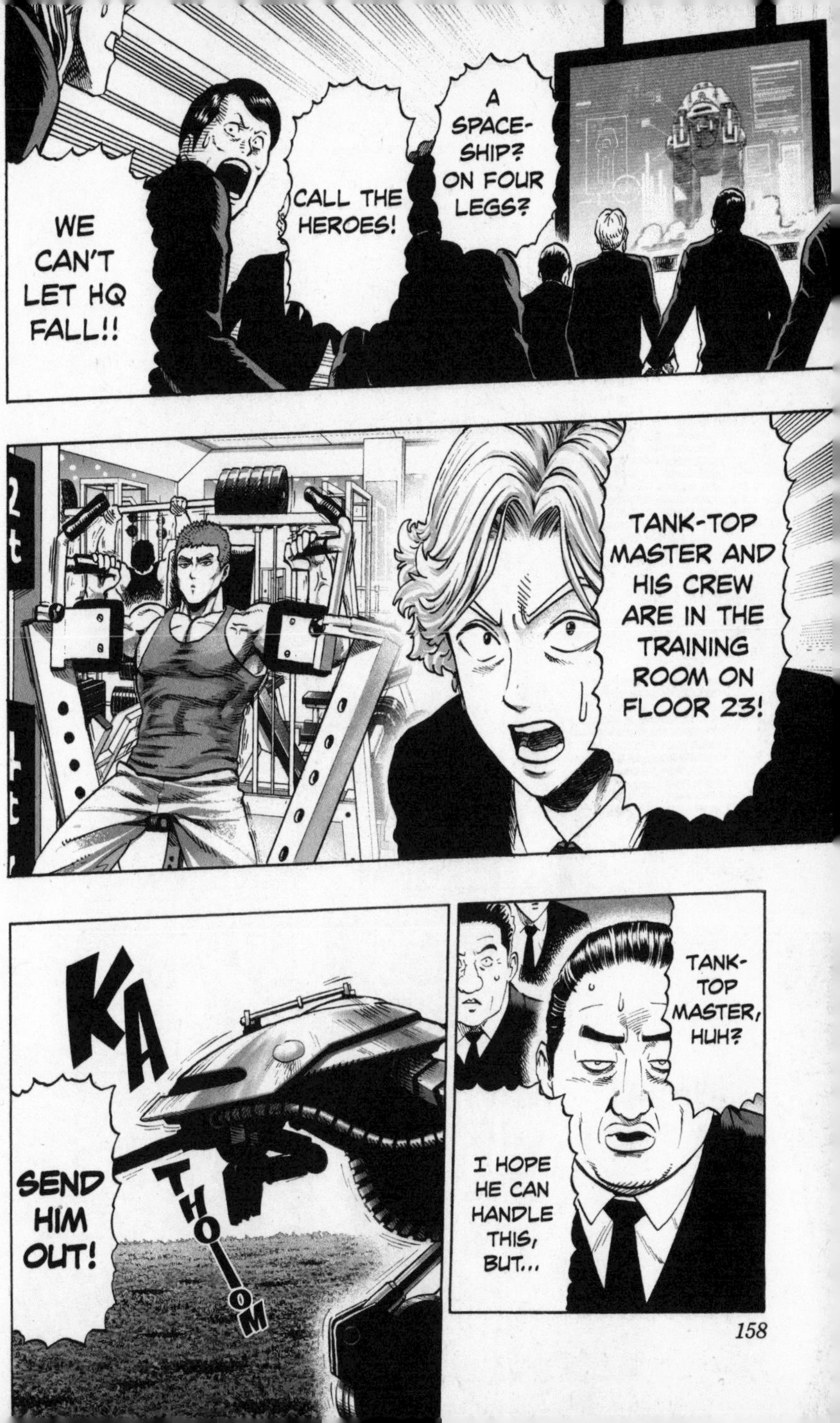
A SPACE-SHIP? ON FOUR LEGS?
CALL THE HEROES!
WE CAN'T LET HQ FALL!!
TANK-TOP MASTER AND HIS CREW ARE IN THE TRAINING ROOM ON FLOOR 23!
TANK-TOP MASTER, HUH?
I HOPE HE CAN HANDLE THIS, BUT...
KA
THOOOM
SEND HIM OUT!

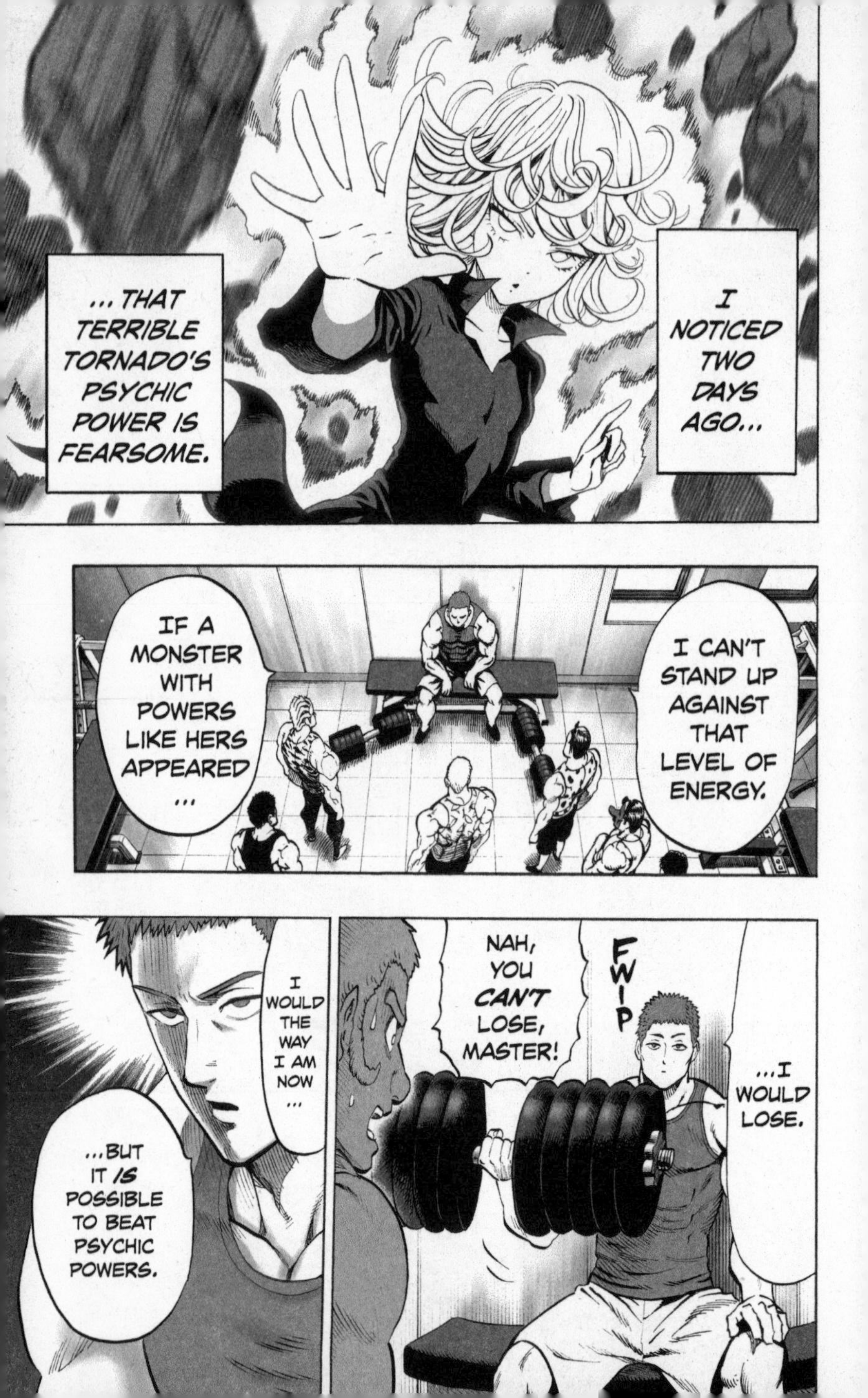
I NOTICED TWO DAYS AGO...
...THAT TERRIBLE TORNADO'S PSYCHIC POWER IS FEARSOME.
I CAN'T STAND UP AGAINST THAT LEVEL OF ENERGY.
IF A MONSTER WITH POWERS LIKE HERS APPEARED...
...I WOULD LOSE.
FWIP
NAH, YOU *CAN'T* LOSE, MASTER!
I WOULD THE WAY I AM NOW...
...BUT IT *IS* POSSIBLE TO BEAT PSYCHIC POWERS.

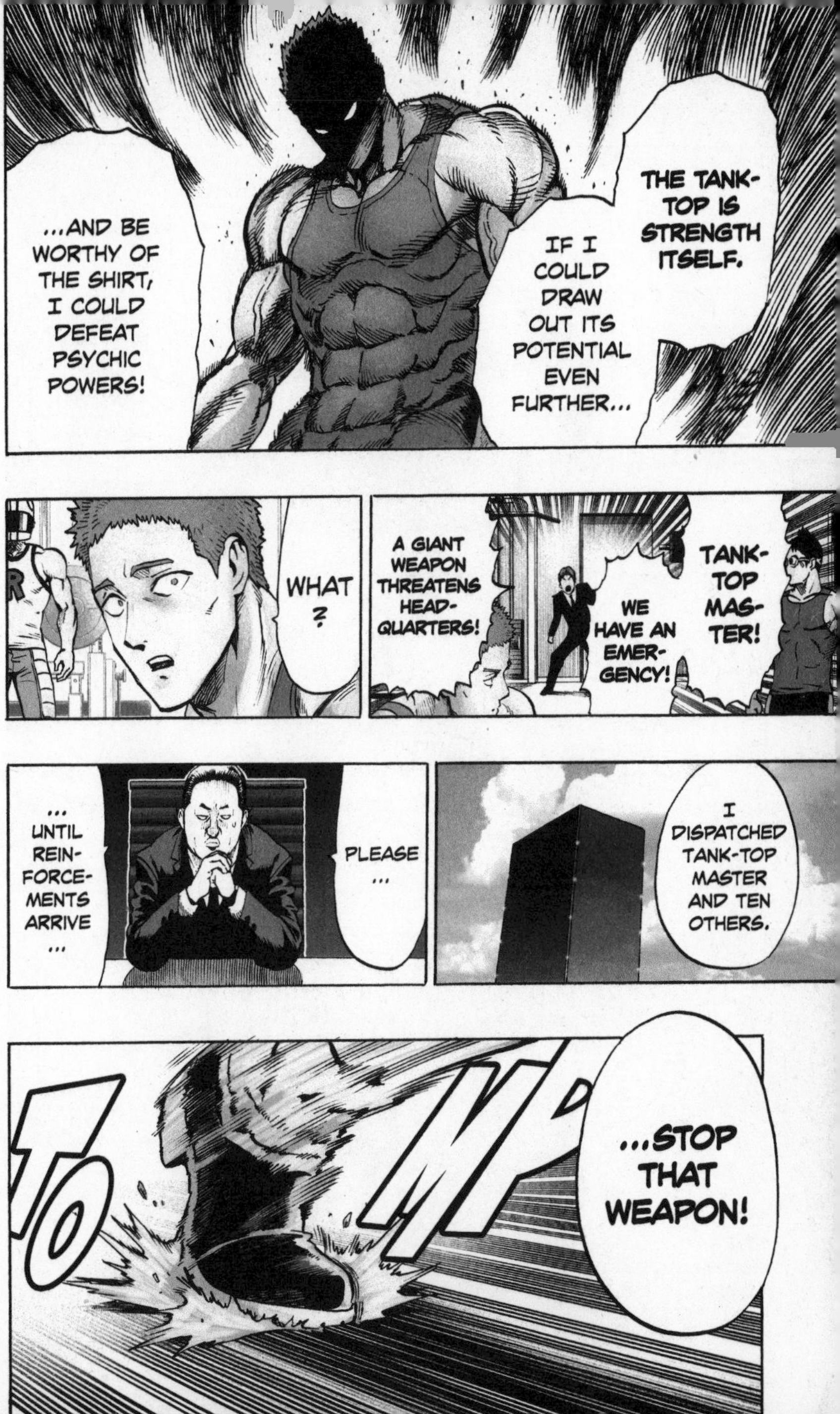
THE TANK-TOP IS STRENGTH ITSELF.
IF I COULD DRAW OUT ITS POTENTIAL EVEN FURTHER...
...AND BE WORTHY OF THE SHIRT, I COULD DEFEAT PSYCHIC POWERS!
TANK-TOP MASTER!
WE HAVE AN EMERGENCY!
A GIANT WEAPON THREATENS HEADQUARTERS!
WHAT?
I DISPATCHED TANK-TOP MASTER AND TEN OTHERS.
PLEASE...
...UNTIL REINFORCEMENTS ARRIVE...
...STOP THAT WEAPON!

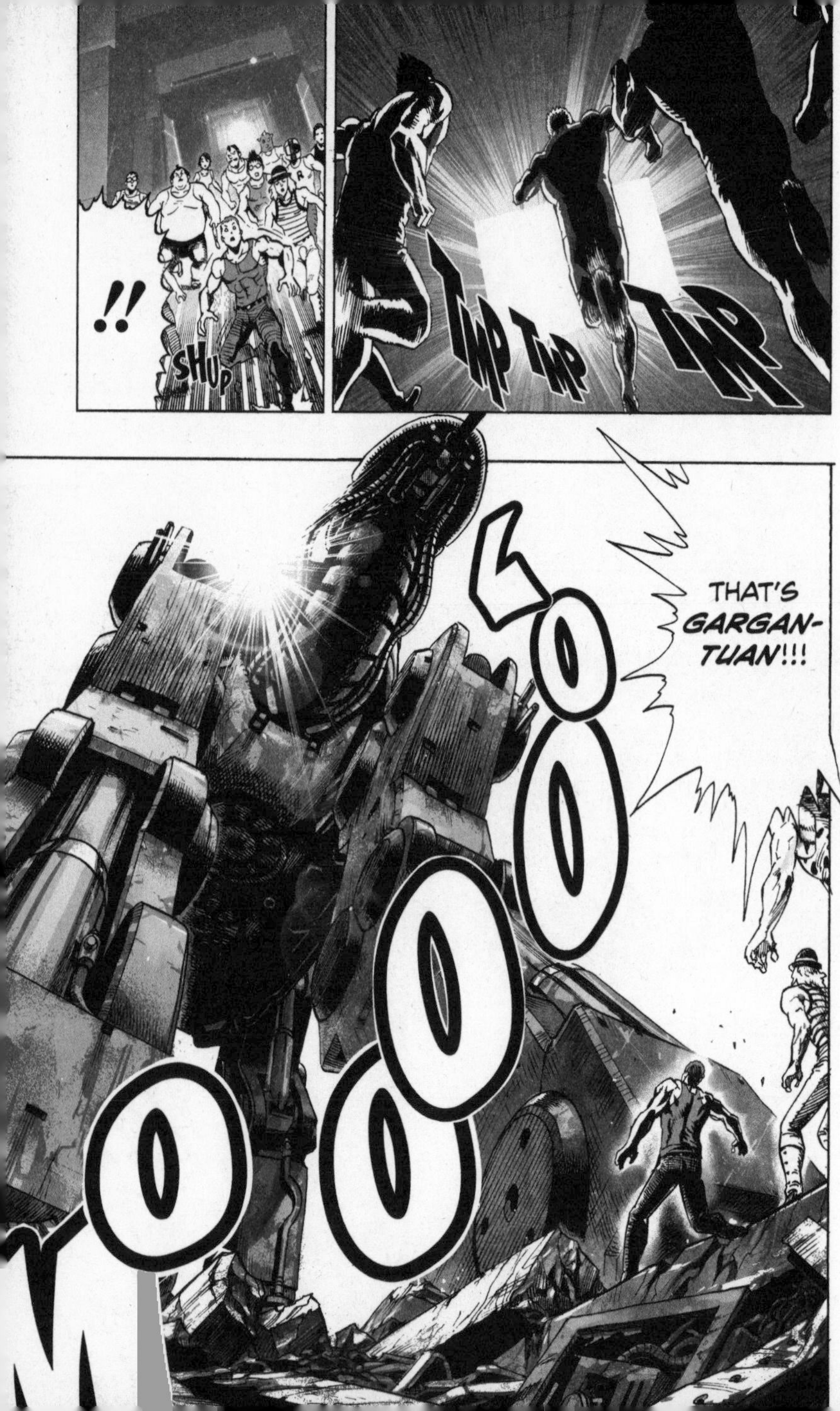
TMP TMP TMP
!!
SHUP
THAT'S GARGANTUAN!!!

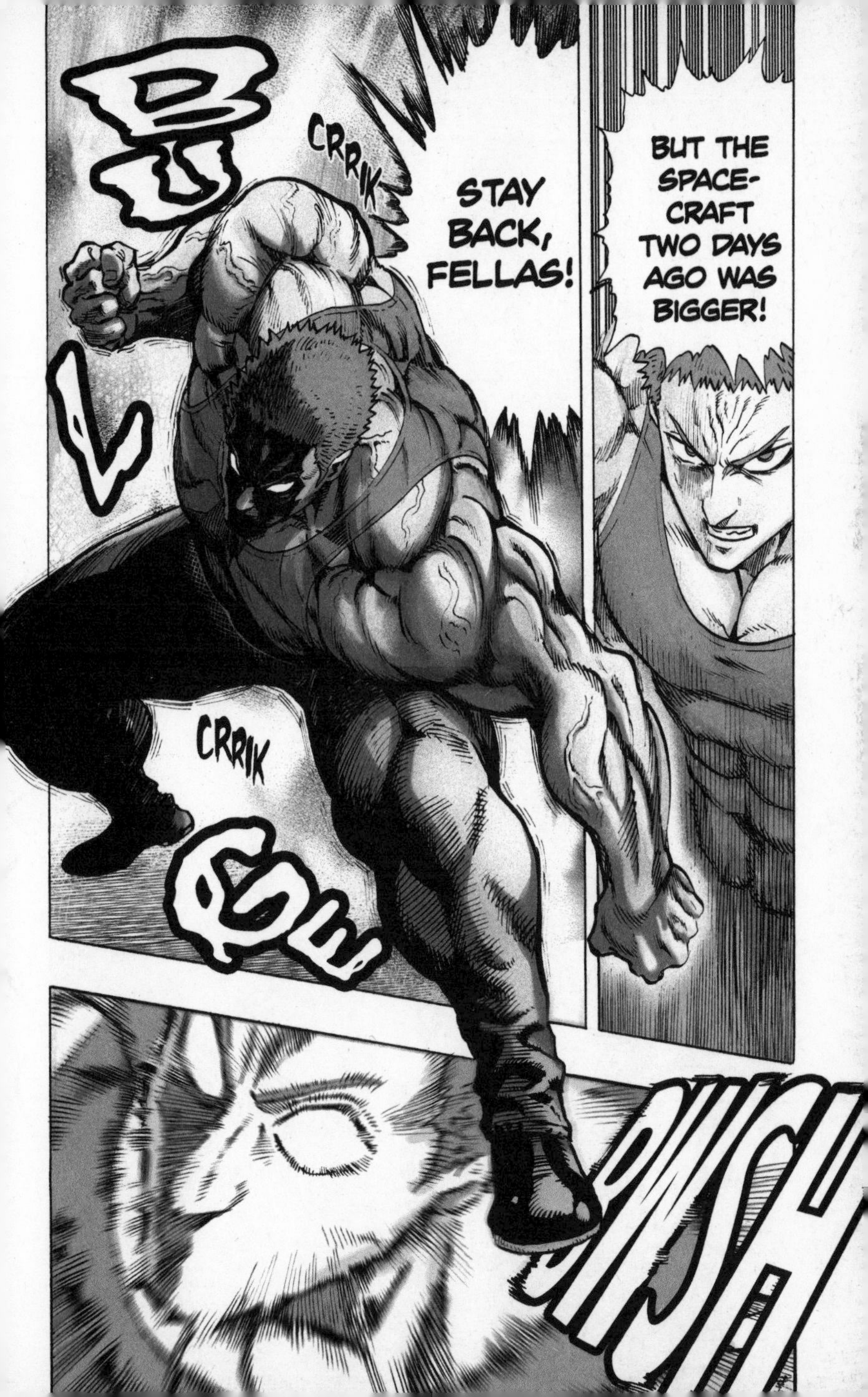
BUT THE SPACECRAFT TWO DAYS AGO WAS BIGGER!
STAY BACK, FELLAS!
CRRIK
CRRIK

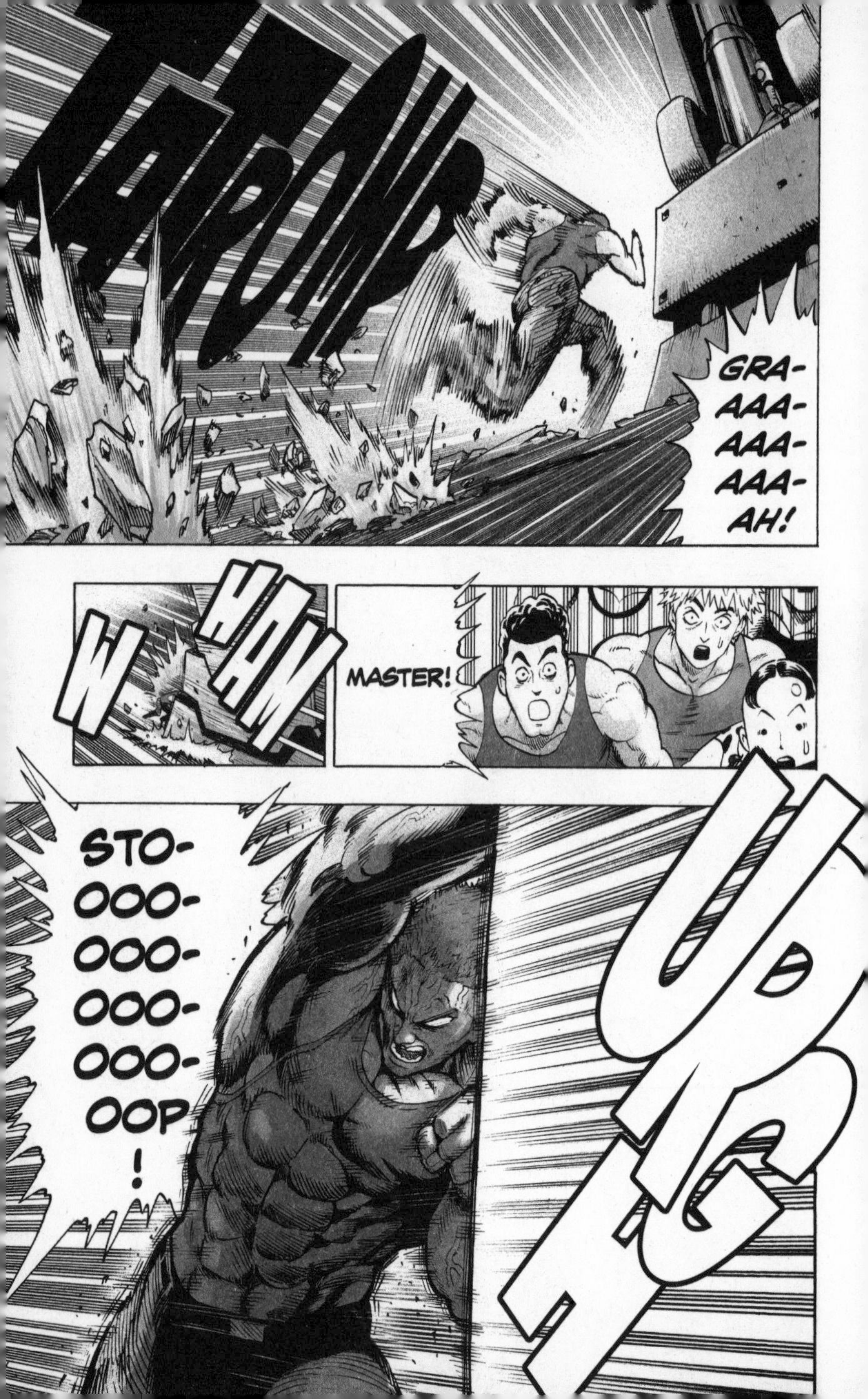
GRA-AAA-AAA-AAA-AH!
MASTER!
STO-OOO-OOO-OOO-OOO-OOP!

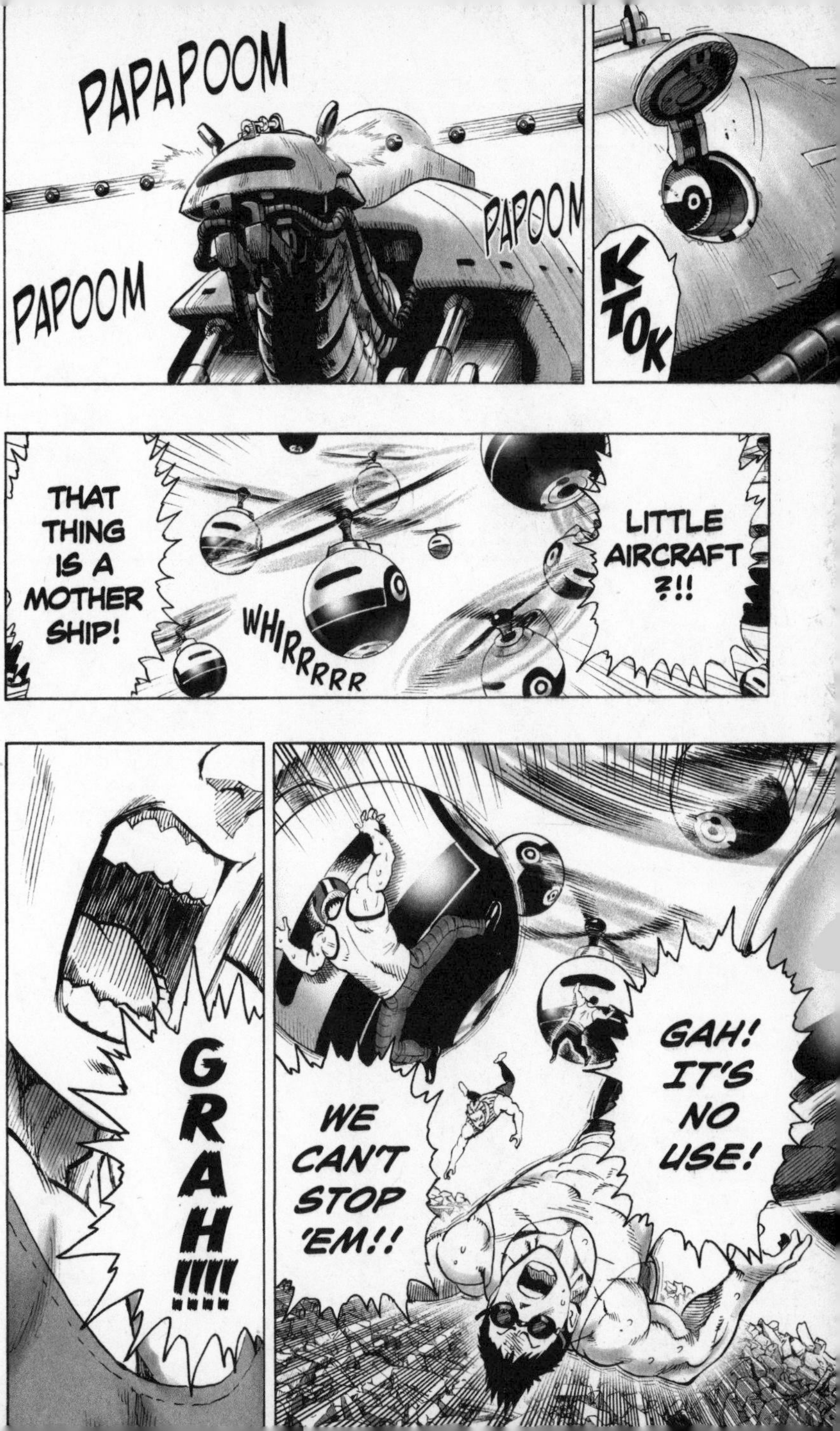
KTOK
PAPAPOOM
PAPOOM
PAPOOM
LITTLE AIRCRAFT ?!!
THAT THING IS A MOTHER SHIP!
WHIRRRRRR
GAH! IT'S NO USE!
WE CAN'T STOP 'EM!!
GRAH!!!!!

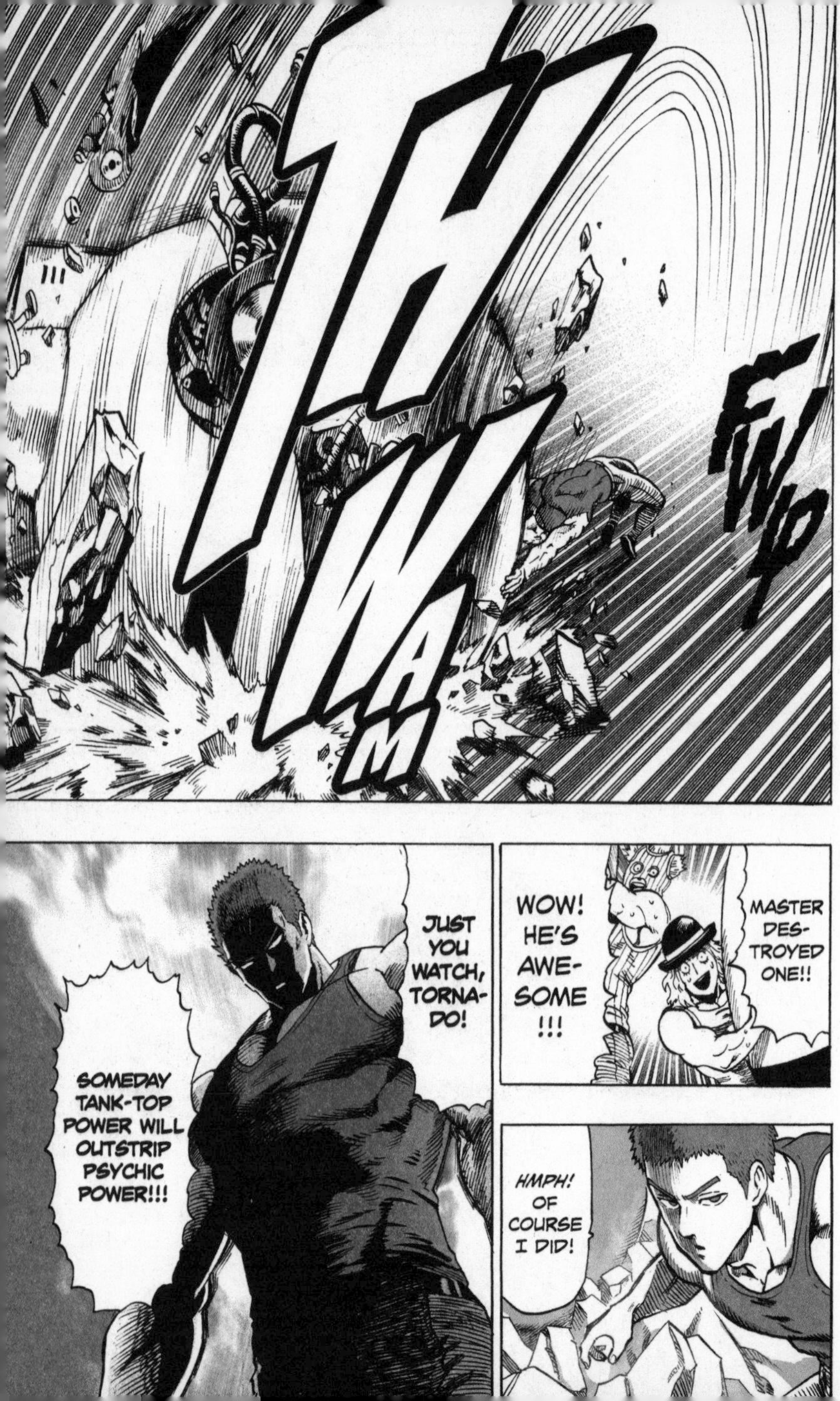
FWIP
WHAM
MASTER DES-TROYED ONE!!
WOW! HE'S AWE-SOME !!!
HMPH! OF COURSE I DID!
JUST YOU WATCH, TORNA-DO!
SOMEDAY TANK-TOP POWER WILL OUTSTRIP PSYCHIC POWER!!!

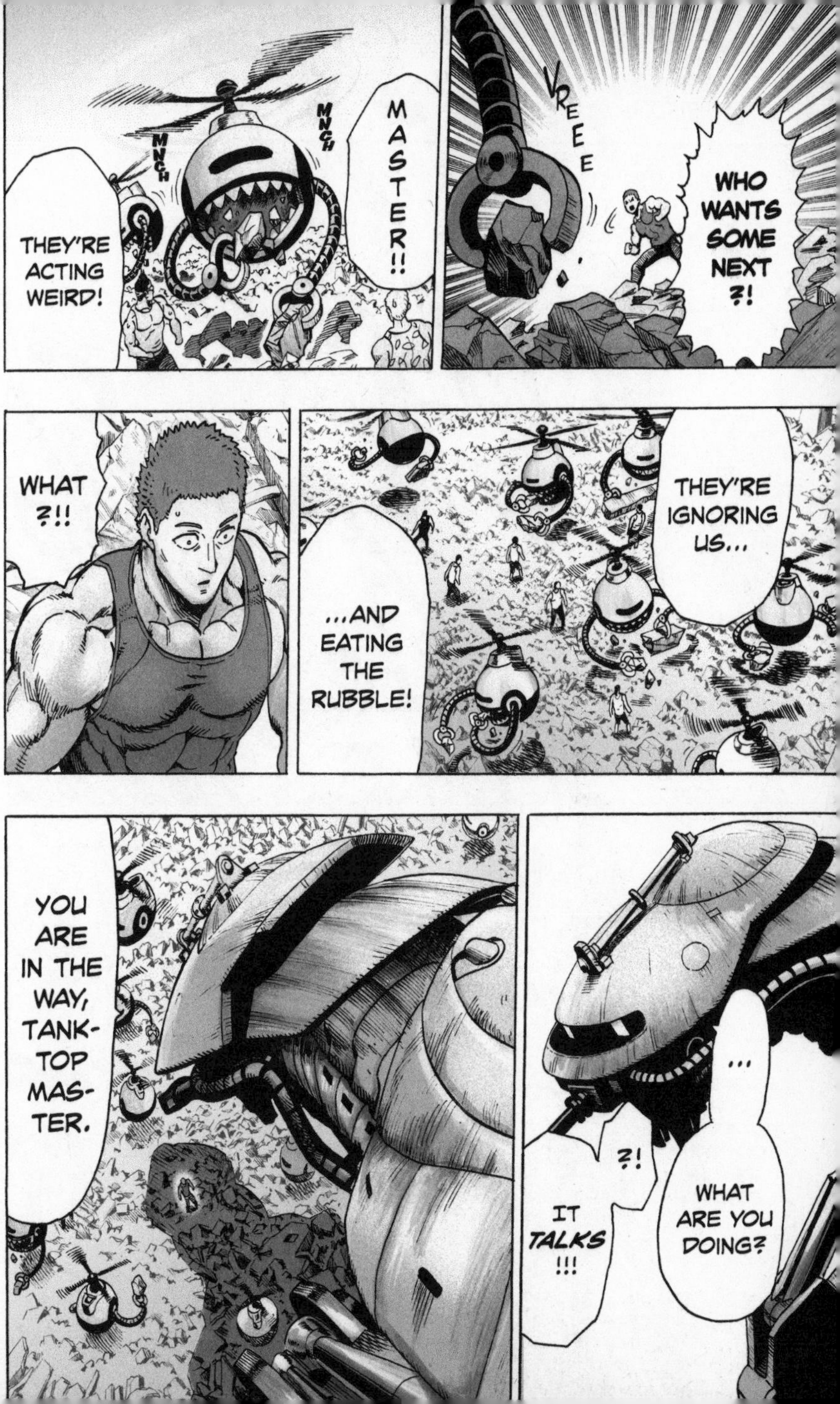
VREEEE
WHO WANTS SOME NEXT?!
MASTER!!
MNCH
MNCH
THEY'RE ACTING WEIRD!
THEY'RE IGNORING US...
...AND EATING THE RUBBLE!
WHAT?!!
...
WHAT ARE YOU DOING?
?!
IT TALKS!!!
YOU ARE IN THE WAY, TANK-TOP MASTER.

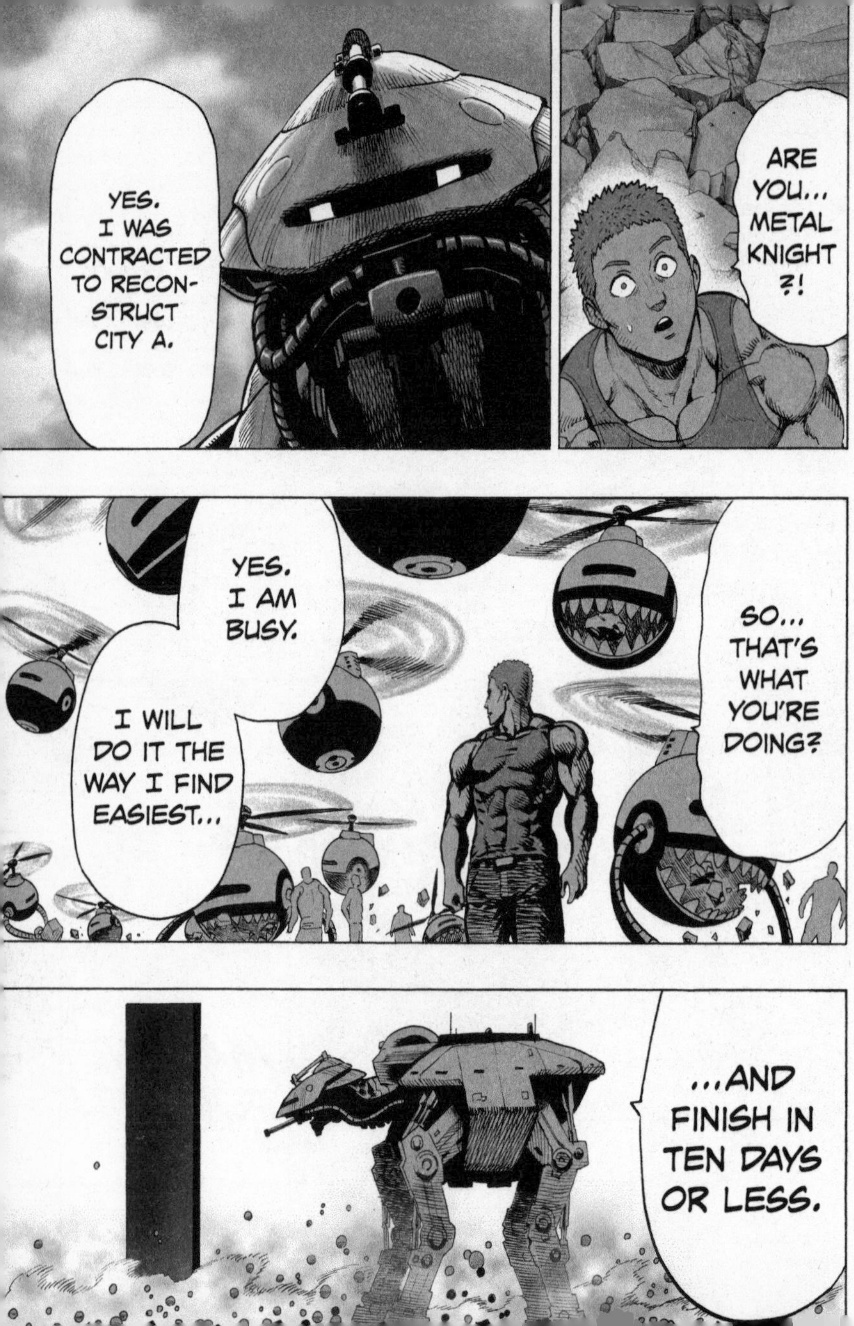
ARE YOU... METAL KNIGHT?!
YES. I WAS CONTRACTED TO RECON-STRUCT CITY A.
SO... THAT'S WHAT YOU'RE DOING?
YES. I AM BUSY.
I WILL DO IT THE WAY I FIND EASIEST...
...AND FINISH IN TEN DAYS OR LESS.

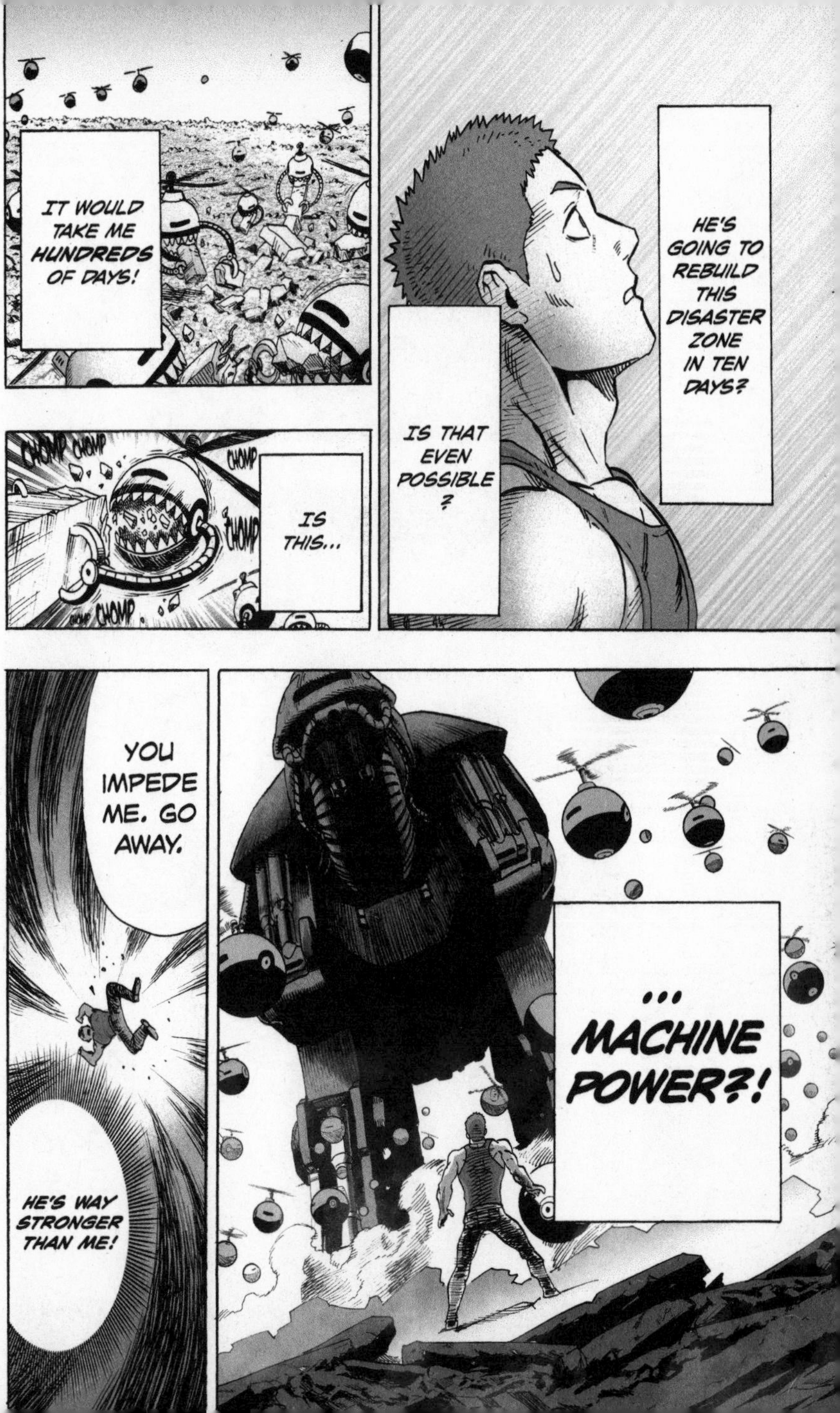
HE'S GOING TO REBUILD THIS DISASTER ZONE IN TEN DAYS?
IS THAT EVEN POSSIBLE?
IT WOULD TAKE ME HUNDREDS OF DAYS!
CHOMP CHOMP
CHOMP
CHOMP
CHOMP CHOMP
IS THIS...
... MACHINE POWER?!
YOU IMPEDE ME. GO AWAY.
HE'S WAY STRONGER THAN ME!

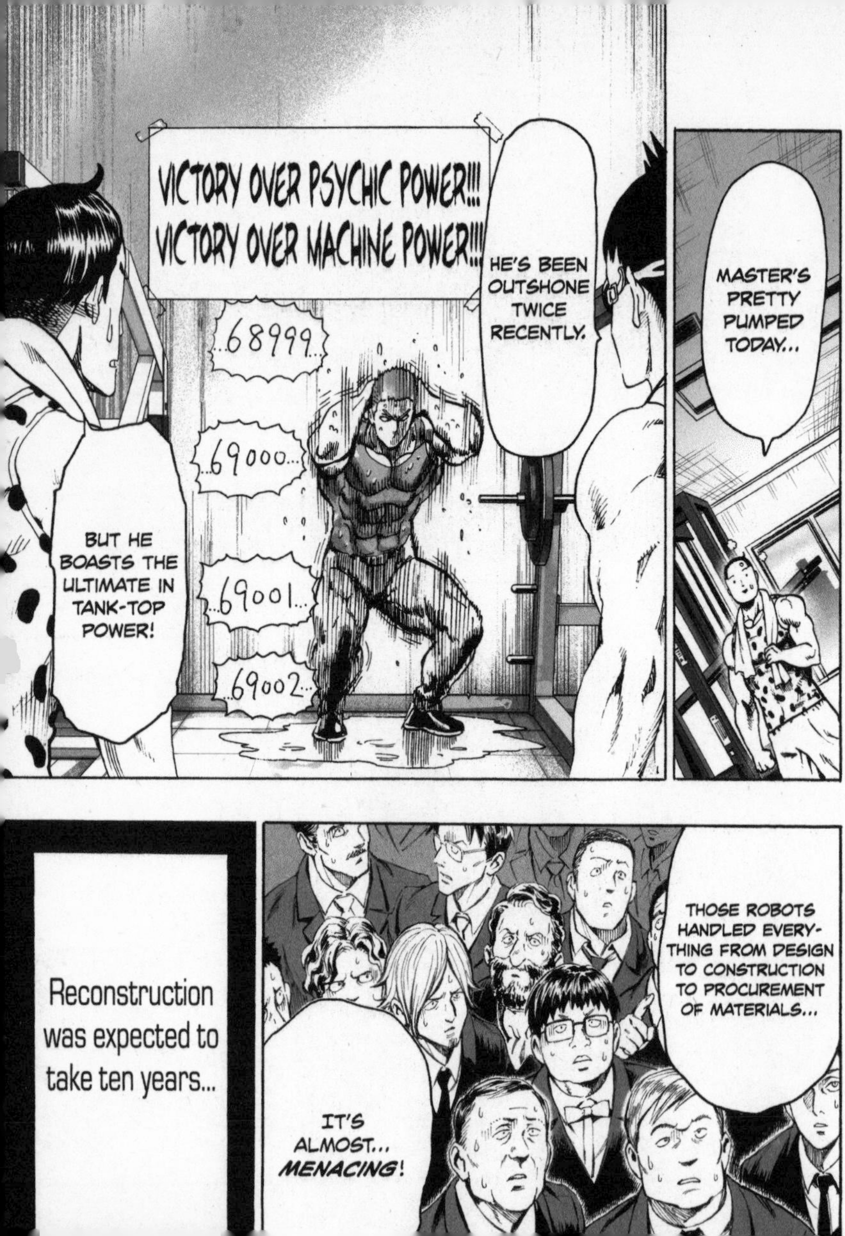
MASTER'S PRETTY PUMPED TODAY...
HE'S BEEN OUTSHONE TWICE RECENTLY.
VICTORY OVER PSYCHIC POWER!!!
VICTORY OVER MACHINE POWER!!!
...68999...
...69000...
...69001...
...69002...
BUT HE BOASTS THE ULTIMATE IN TANK-TOP POWER!
THOSE ROBOTS HANDLED EVERYTHING FROM DESIGN TO CONSTRUCTION TO PROCUREMENT OF MATERIALS...
IT'S ALMOST... *MENACING*!
Reconstruction was expected to take ten years...

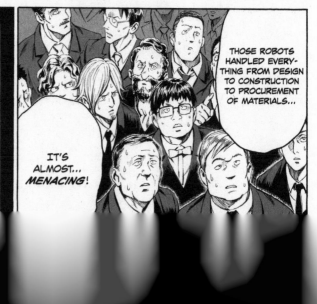

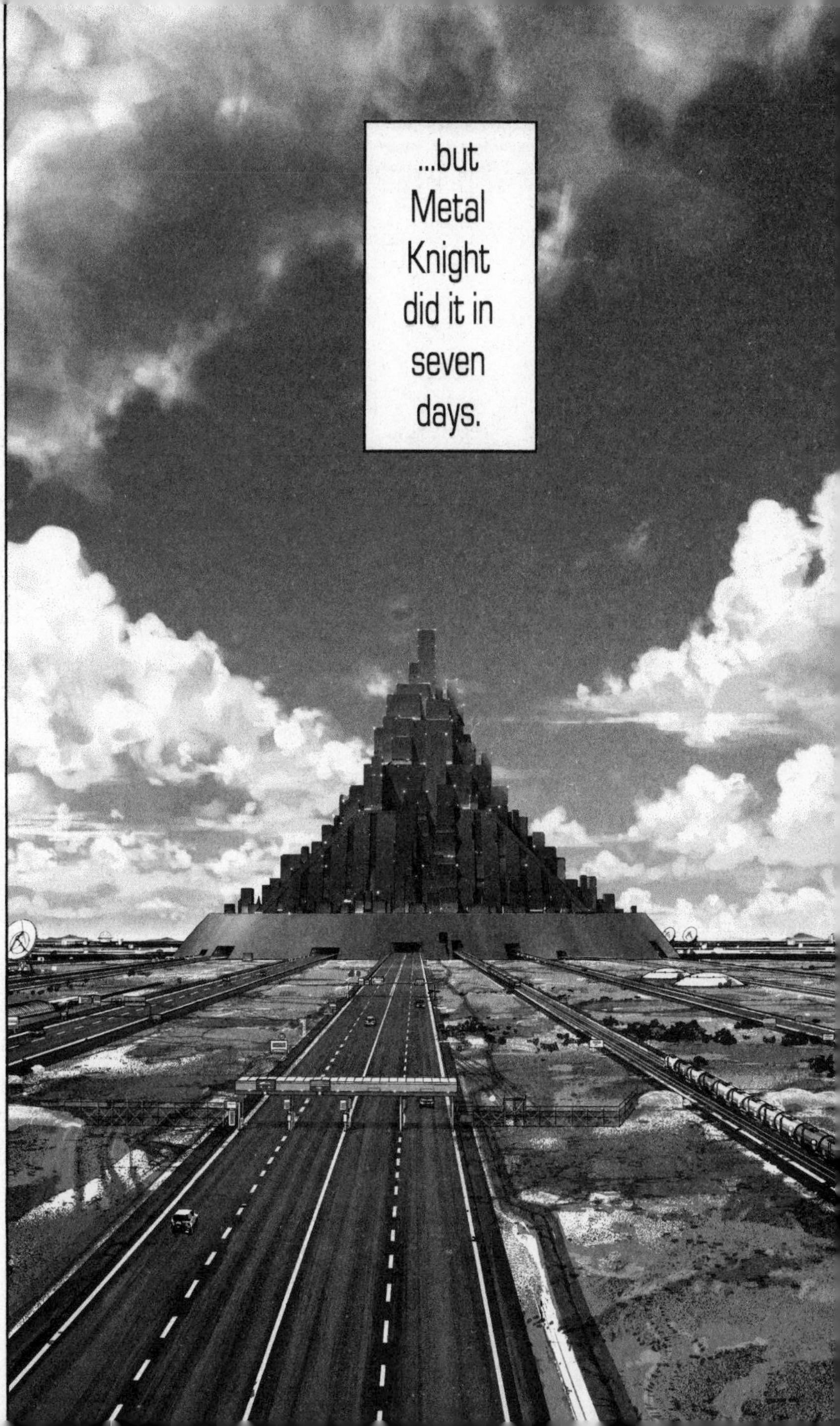
...but Metal Knight did it in seven days.

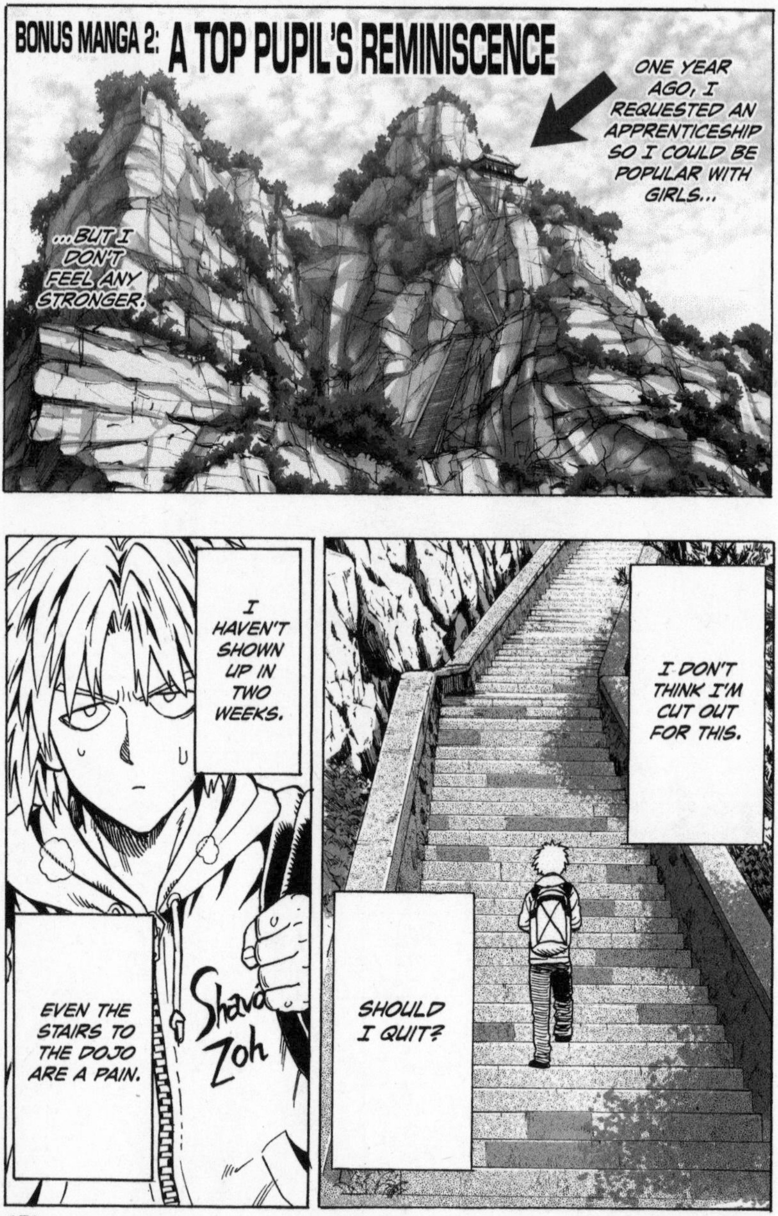
BONUS MANGA 2: A TOP PUPIL'S REMINISCENCE
ONE YEAR AGO, I REQUESTED AN APPRENTICESHIP SO I COULD BE POPULAR WITH GIRLS...
...BUT I DON'T FEEL ANY STRONGER.
I DON'T THINK I'M CUT OUT FOR THIS.
SHOULD I QUIT?
I HAVEN'T SHOWN UP IN TWO WEEKS.
Shava Zoh
EVEN THE STAIRS TO THE DOJO ARE A PAIN.

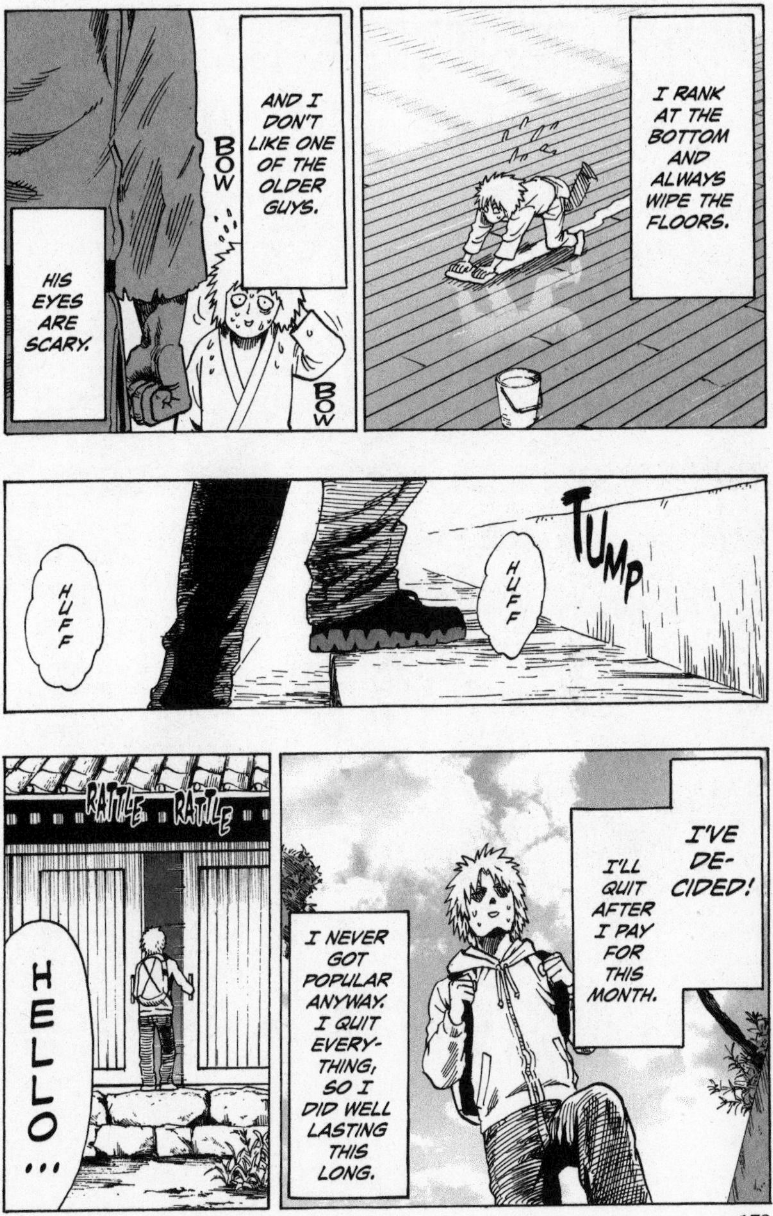
I RANK AT THE BOTTOM AND ALWAYS WIPE THE FLOORS.
AND I DON'T LIKE ONE OF THE OLDER GUYS.
BOW
BOW
HIS EYES ARE SCARY.
TUMP
HUFF
HUFF
I'VE DE-CIDED!
I'LL QUIT AFTER I PAY FOR THIS MONTH.
I NEVER GOT POPULAR ANYWAY. I QUIT EVERY-THING, SO I DID WELL LASTING THIS LONG.
RATTLE RATTLE
HELLO...

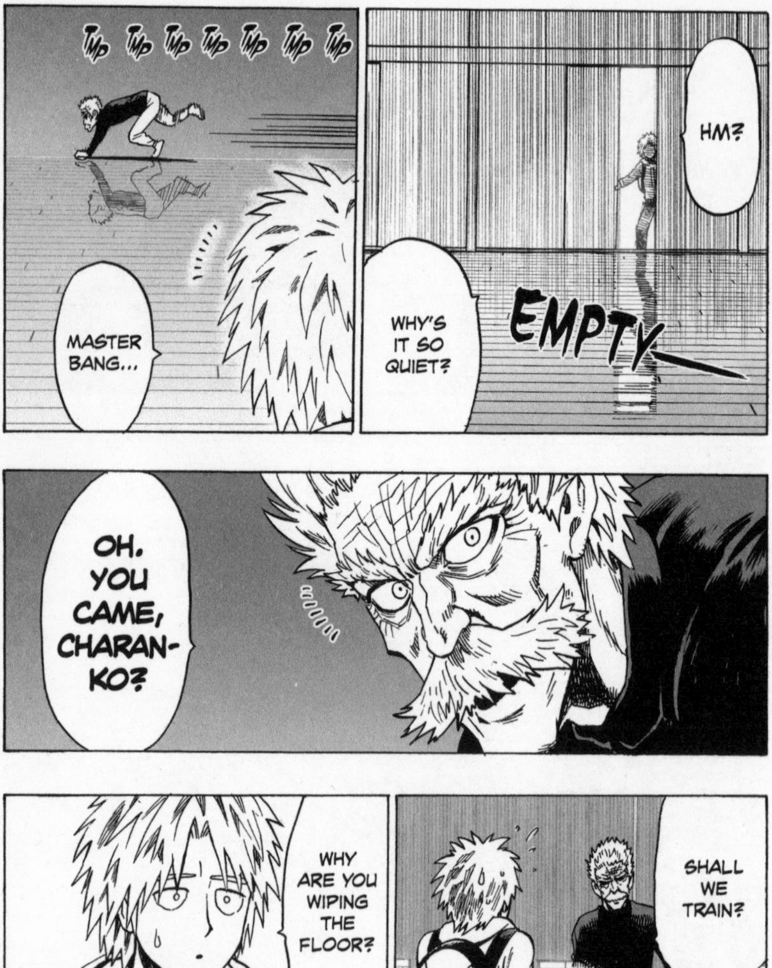
TMP TMP TMP TMP TMP TMP TMP
MASTER BANG...
HM?
WHY'S IT SO QUIET?
EMPTY
OH. YOU CAME, CHARAN-KO?
WHY ARE YOU WIPING THE FLOOR?
WHERE ARE THE OTHER GUYS?
SHALL WE TRAIN?
NO... WAIT!

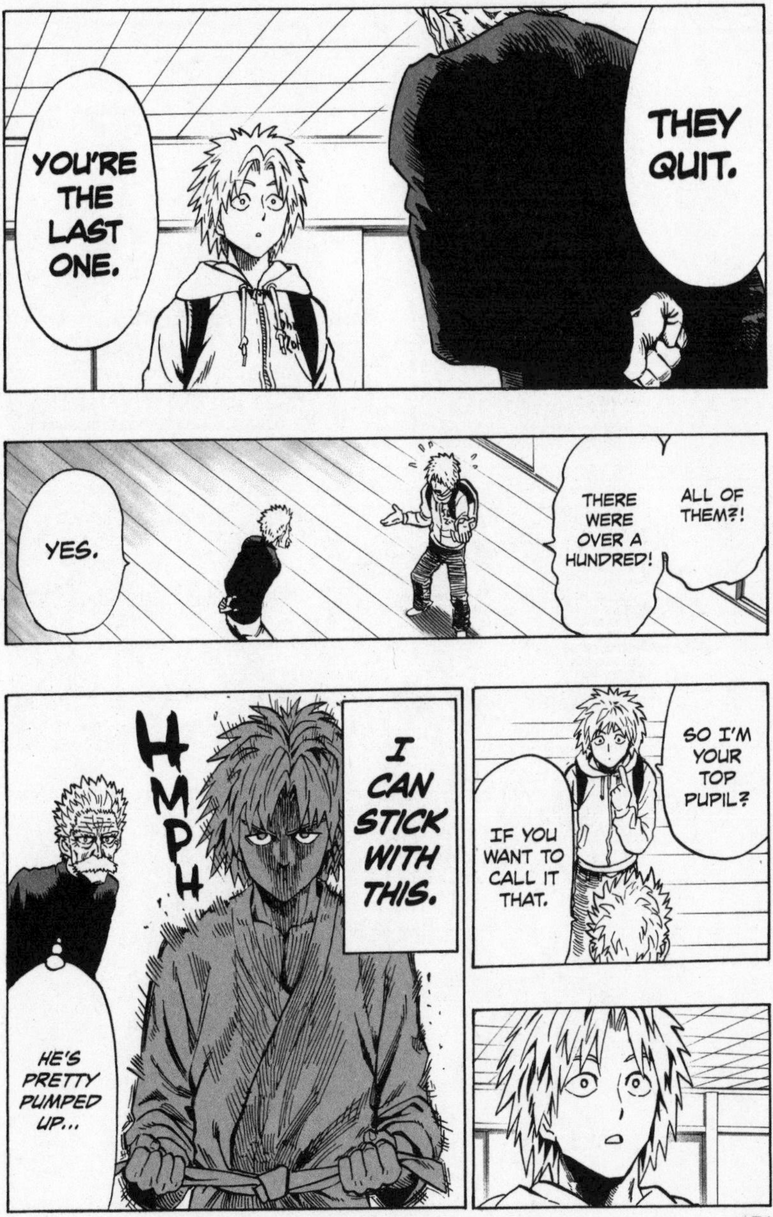
THEY QUIT.
YOU'RE THE LAST ONE.
ALL OF THEM?!
THERE WERE OVER A HUNDRED!
YES.
SO I'M YOUR TOP PUPIL?
IF YOU WANT TO CALL IT THAT.
I CAN STICK WITH THIS.
HMPH
HE'S PRETTY PUMPED UP...

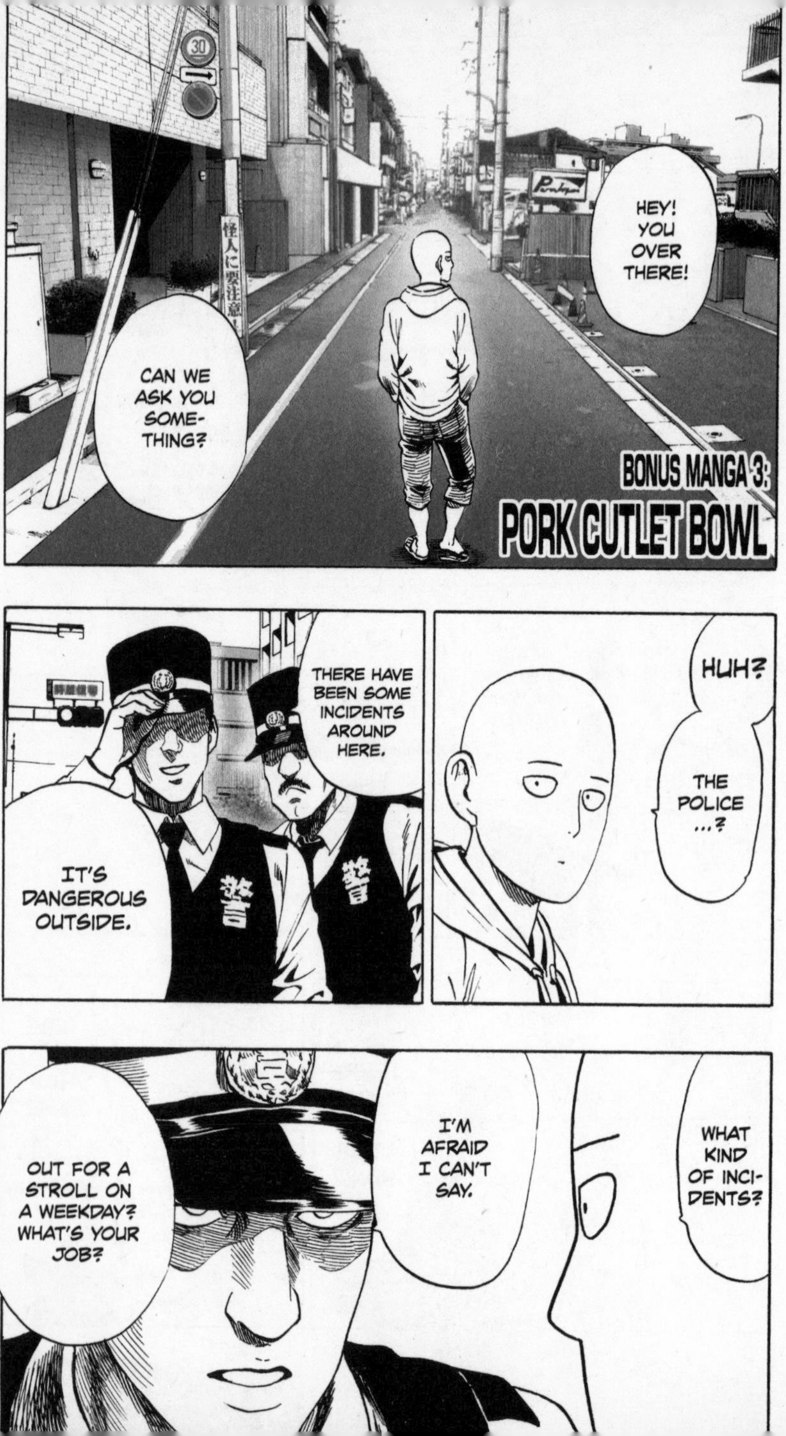
HEY! YOU OVER THERE!
CAN WE ASK YOU SOME-THING?
BONUS MANGA 3: PORK CUTLET BOWL
HUH?
THE POLICE ...?
THERE HAVE BEEN SOME INCIDENTS AROUND HERE.
IT'S DANGEROUS OUTSIDE.
WHAT KIND OF INCI-DENTS?
I'M AFRAID I CAN'T SAY.
OUT FOR A STROLL ON A WEEKDAY? WHAT'S YOUR JOB?

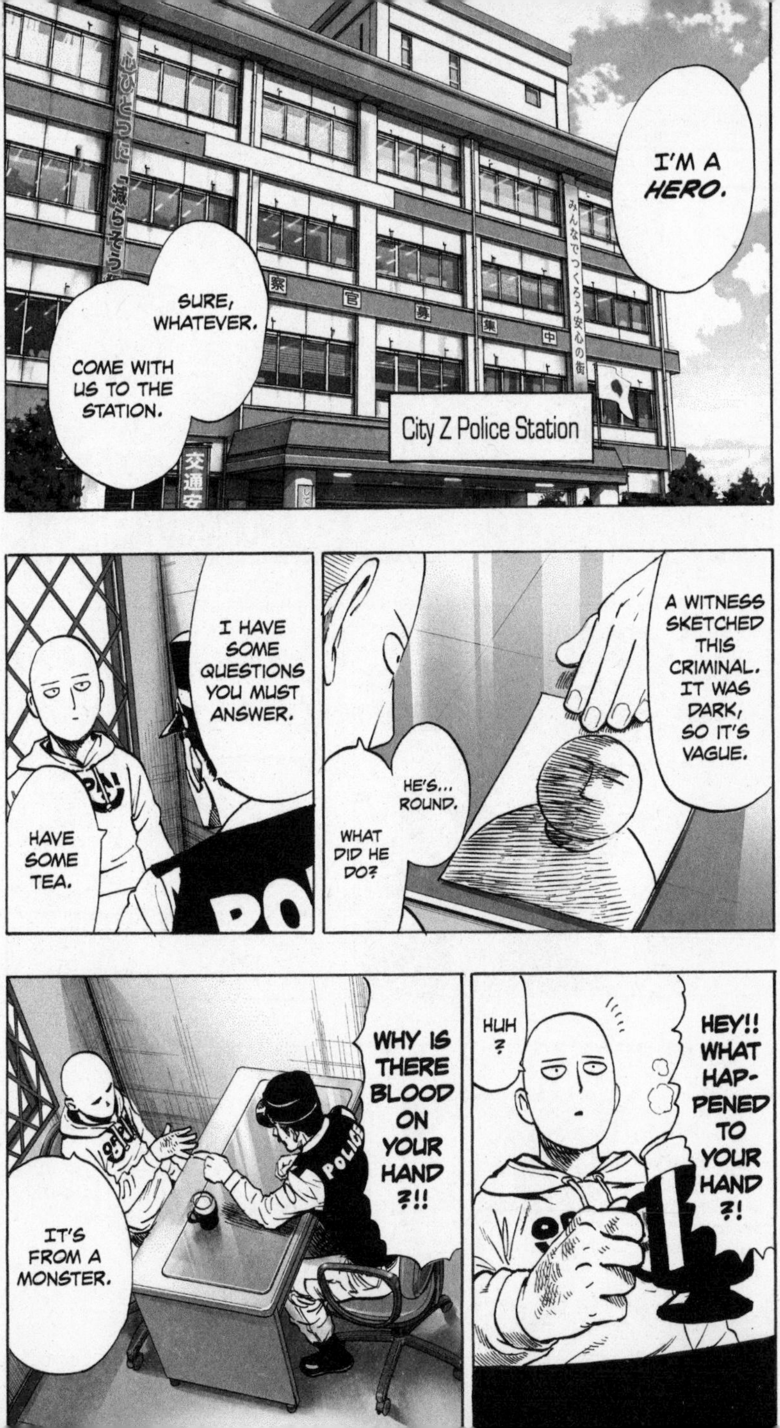
I'M A *HERO.*
みんなでつくろう安心の街
City Z Police Station
SURE, WHATEVER.
COME WITH US TO THE STATION.
A WITNESS SKETCHED THIS CRIMINAL. IT WAS DARK, SO IT'S VAGUE.
HE'S... ROUND.
WHAT DID HE DO?
I HAVE SOME QUESTIONS YOU MUST ANSWER.
HAVE SOME TEA.
HEY!! WHAT HAP-PENED TO YOUR HAND?!
HUH?
WHY IS THERE BLOOD ON YOUR HAND?!!
POLICE
IT'S FROM A MONSTER.

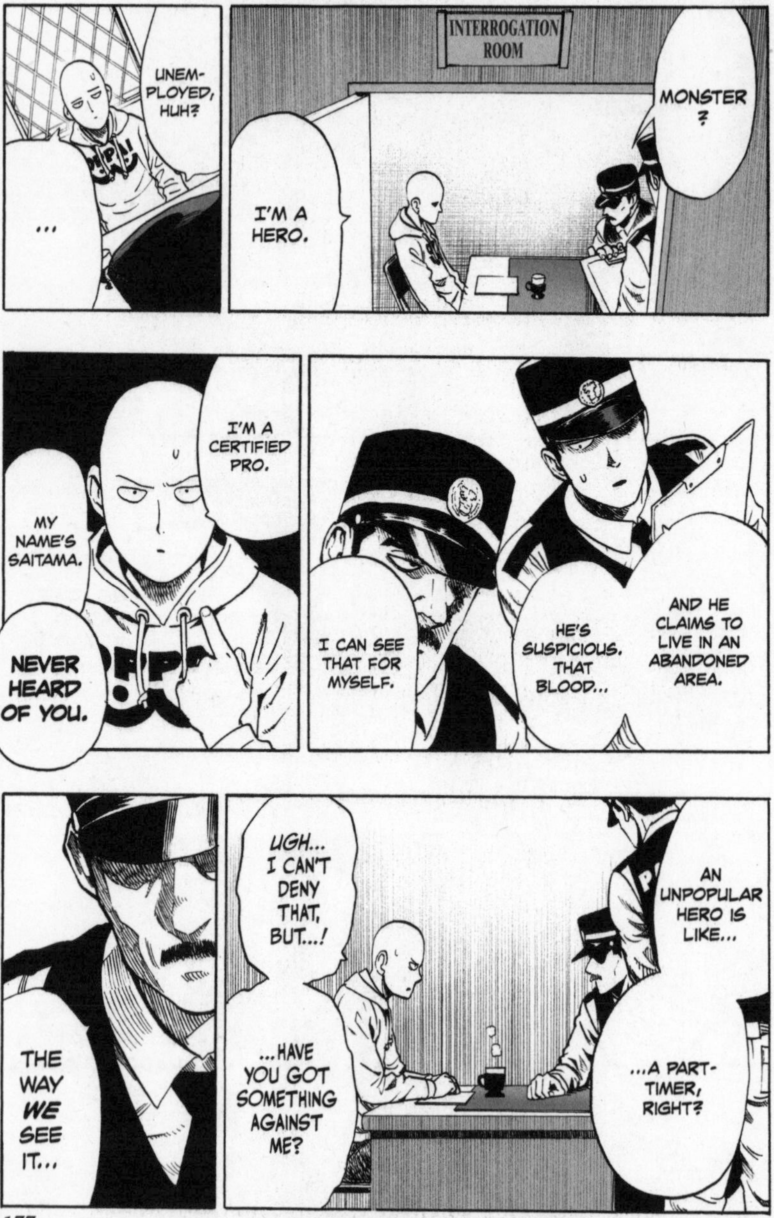
INTERROGATION ROOM
MONSTER?
I'M A HERO.
UNEMPLOYED, HUH?
...
AND HE CLAIMS TO LIVE IN AN ABANDONED AREA.
HE'S SUSPICIOUS. THAT BLOOD...
I CAN SEE THAT FOR MYSELF.
I'M A CERTIFIED PRO.
MY NAME'S SAITAMA.
NEVER HEARD OF YOU.
AN UNPOPULAR HERO IS LIKE...
...A PART-TIMER, RIGHT?
UGH... I CAN'T DENY THAT, BUT...!
...HAVE YOU GOT SOMETHING AGAINST ME?
THE WAY *WE* SEE IT...

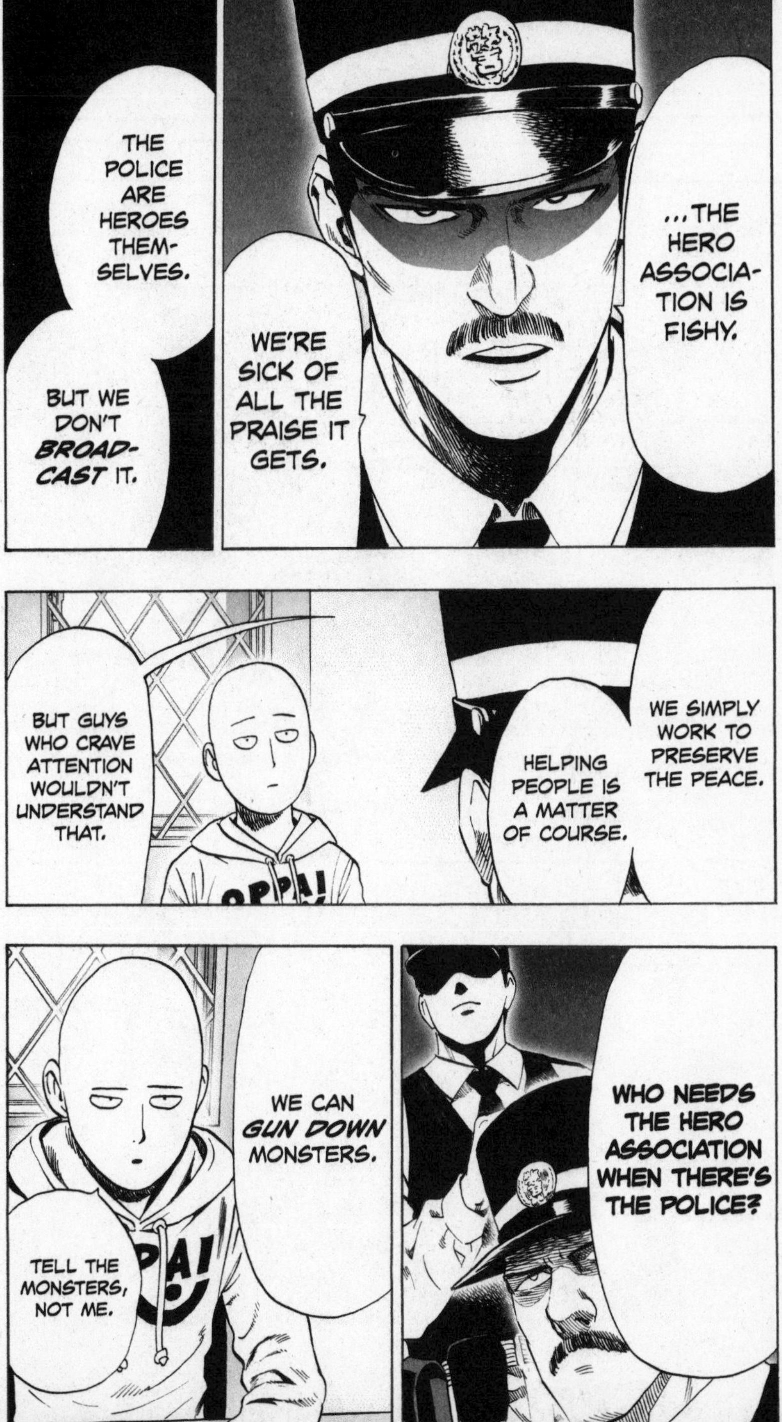
...THE HERO ASSOCIA-TION IS FISHY.
WE'RE SICK OF ALL THE PRAISE IT GETS.
THE POLICE ARE HEROES THEM-SELVES.
BUT WE DON'T *BROAD-CAST* IT.
WE SIMPLY WORK TO PRESERVE THE PEACE.
HELPING PEOPLE IS A MATTER OF COURSE.
BUT GUYS WHO CRAVE ATTENTION WOULDN'T UNDERSTAND THAT.
WHO NEEDS THE HERO ASSOCIATION WHEN THERE'S THE POLICE?
WE CAN *GUN DOWN* MONSTERS.
TELL THE MONSTERS, NOT ME.

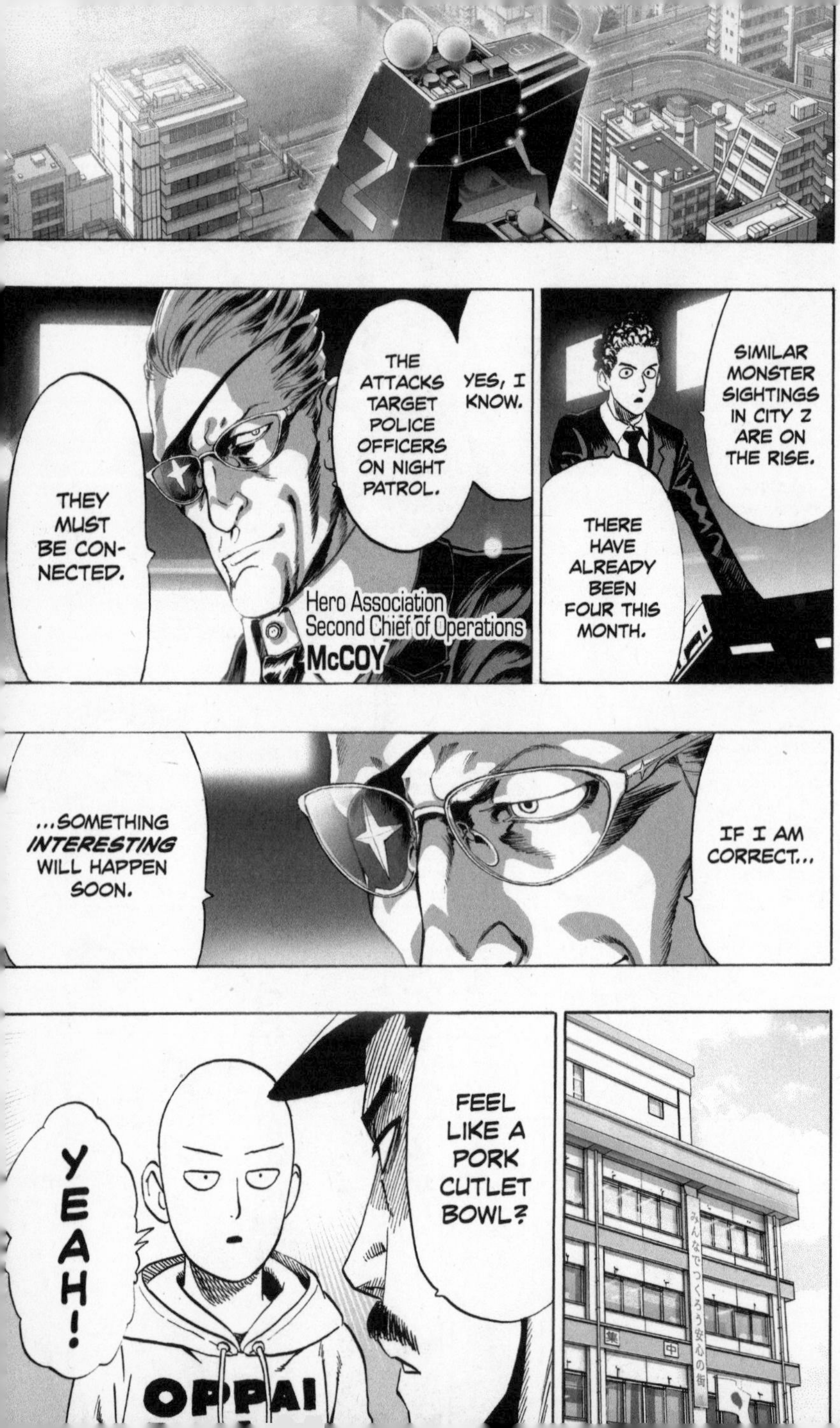
SIMILAR MONSTER SIGHTINGS IN CITY Z ARE ON THE RISE.
THERE HAVE ALREADY BEEN FOUR THIS MONTH.
YES, I KNOW.
THE ATTACKS TARGET POLICE OFFICERS ON NIGHT PATROL.
THEY MUST BE CON-NECTED.
Hero Association Second Chief of Operations McCOY
IF I AM CORRECT...
...SOMETHING *INTERESTING* WILL HAPPEN SOON.
みんなでつくろう安心の街
FEEL LIKE A PORK CUTLET BOWL?
YEAH!
OPPAI

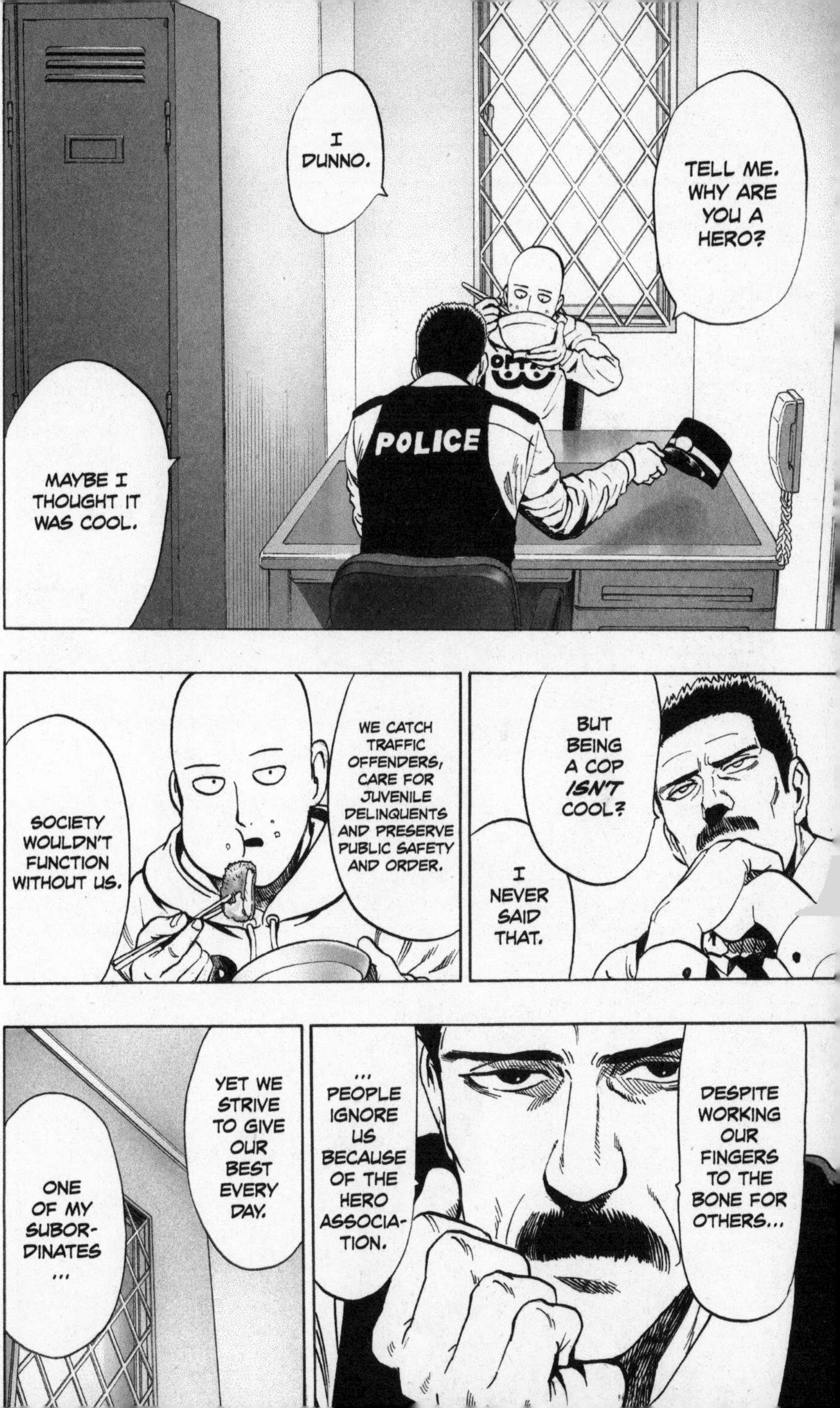
TELL ME. WHY ARE YOU A HERO?
I DUNNO.
MAYBE I THOUGHT IT WAS COOL.
BUT BEING A COP *ISN'T* COOL?
I NEVER SAID THAT.
WE CATCH TRAFFIC OFFENDERS, CARE FOR JUVENILE DELINQUENTS AND PRESERVE PUBLIC SAFETY AND ORDER.
SOCIETY WOULDN'T FUNCTION WITHOUT US.
DESPITE WORKING OUR FINGERS TO THE BONE FOR OTHERS...
... PEOPLE IGNORE US BECAUSE OF THE HERO ASSOCIATION.
YET WE STRIVE TO GIVE OUR BEST EVERY DAY.
ONE OF MY SUBORDINATES ...
POLICE

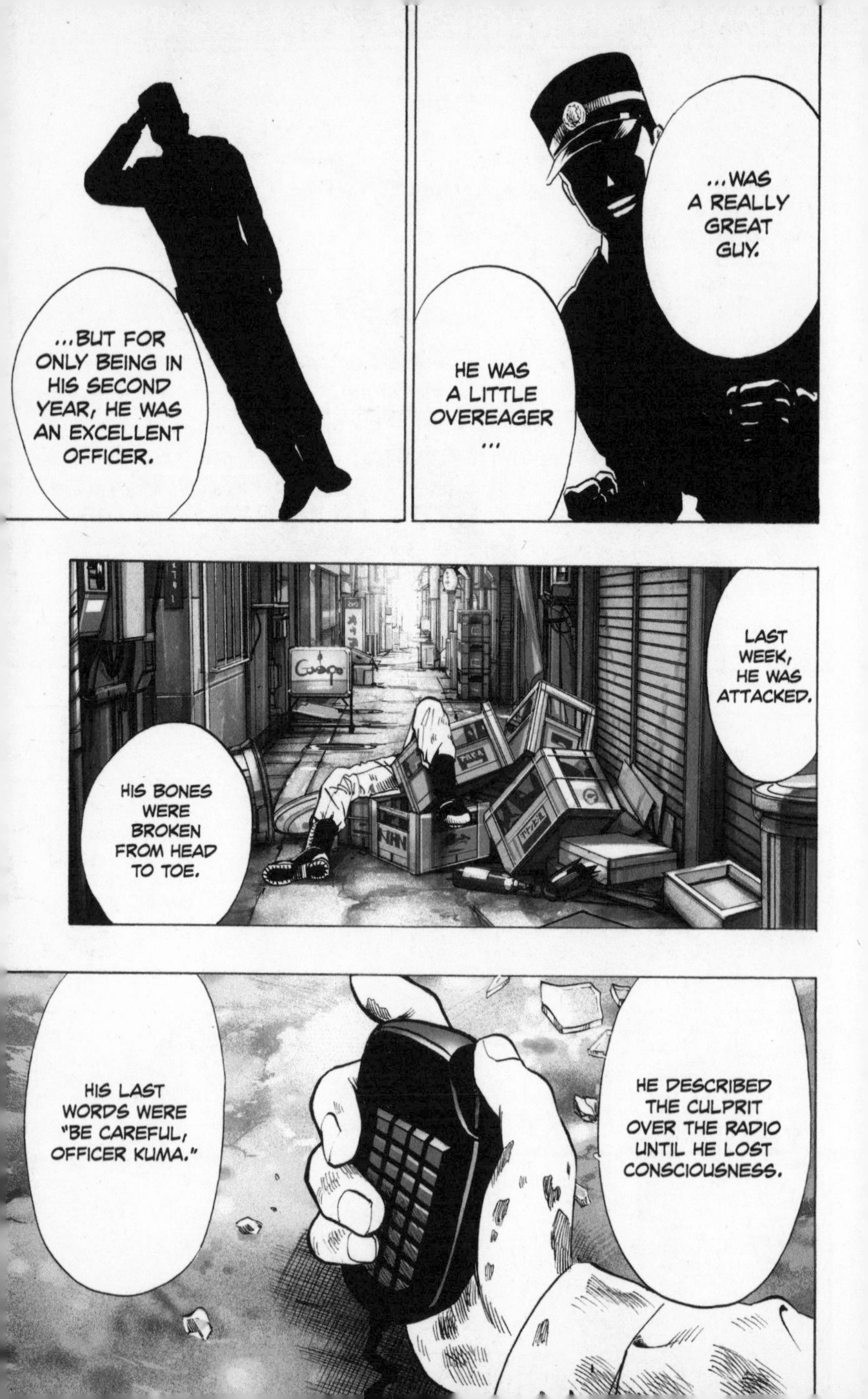
...WAS A REALLY GREAT GUY.
HE WAS A LITTLE OVEREAGER ...
...BUT FOR ONLY BEING IN HIS SECOND YEAR, HE WAS AN EXCELLENT OFFICER.
LAST WEEK, HE WAS ATTACKED.
HIS BONES WERE BROKEN FROM HEAD TO TOE.
HE DESCRIBED THE CULPRIT OVER THE RADIO UNTIL HE LOST CONSCIOUSNESS.
HIS LAST WORDS WERE "BE CAREFUL, OFFICER KUMA."

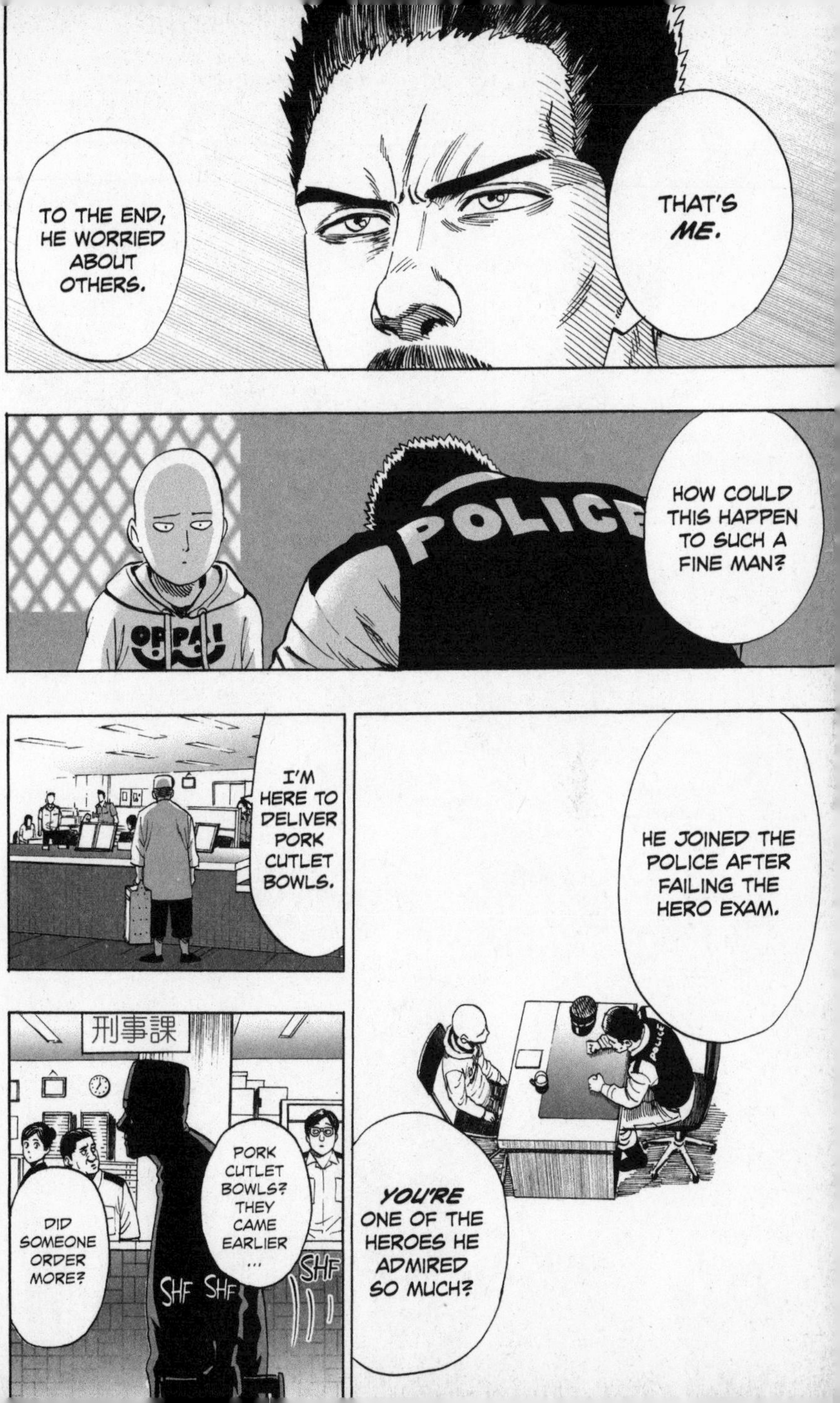
THAT'S *ME.*
TO THE END, HE WORRIED ABOUT OTHERS.
HOW COULD THIS HAPPEN TO SUCH A FINE MAN?
HE JOINED THE POLICE AFTER FAILING THE HERO EXAM.
YOU'RE ONE OF THE HEROES HE ADMIRED SO MUCH?
I'M HERE TO DELIVER PORK CUTLET BOWLS.
刑事課
PORK CUTLET BOWLS? THEY CAME EARLIER ...
SHF
DID SOMEONE ORDER MORE?
SHF SHF

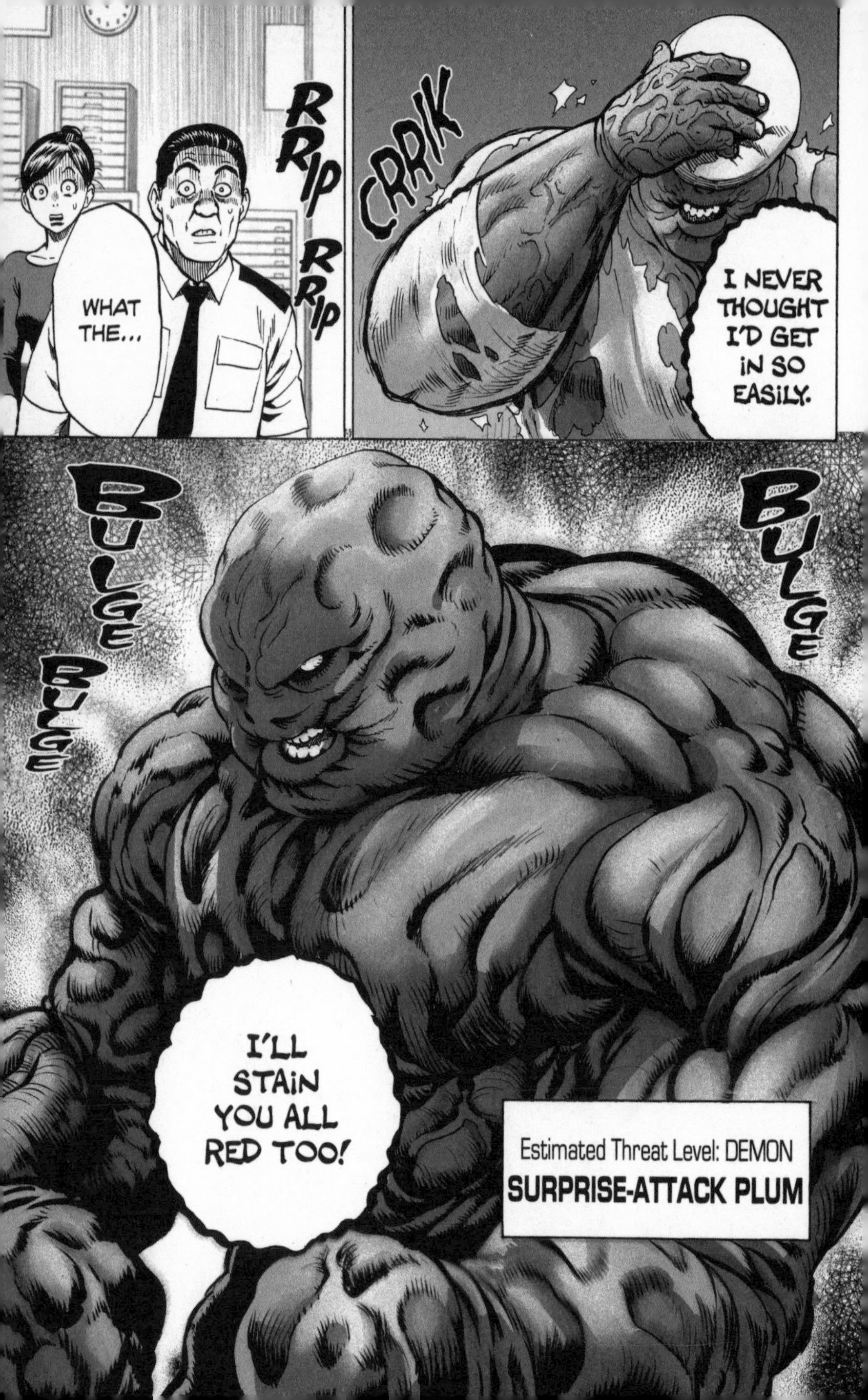
CRRIK
I NEVER THOUGHT I'D GET IN SO EASILY.
RRIP RRIP
WHAT THE...
BULGE
BULGE BULGE
I'LL STAIN YOU ALL RED TOO!
Estimated Threat Level: DEMON
SURPRISE-ATTACK PLUM

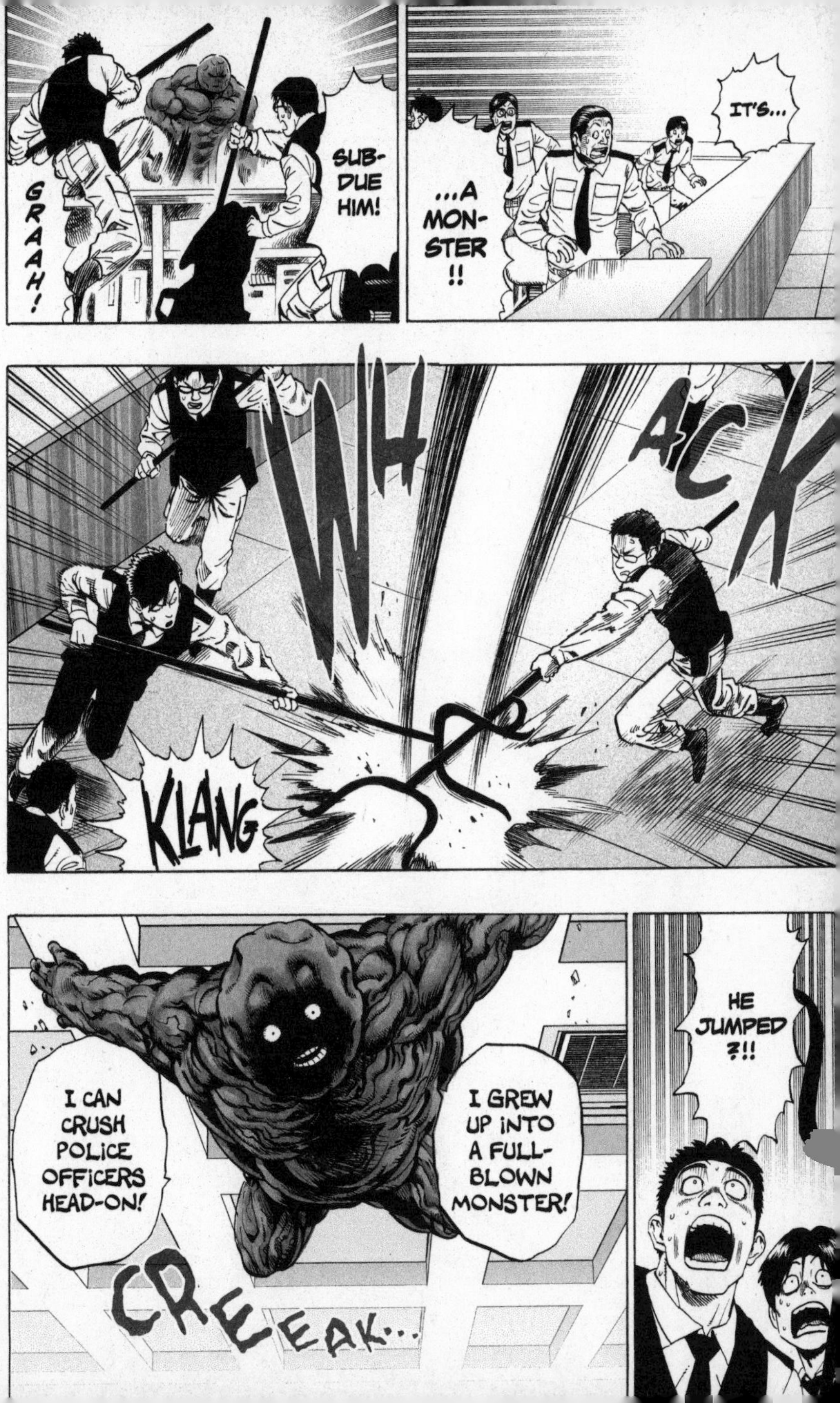
IT'S...
...A MONSTER!!
SUBDUE HIM!
GRAAH!
WHACK
KLANG
HE JUMPED?!!
I GREW UP INTO A FULL-BLOWN MONSTER!
I CAN CRUSH POLICE OFFICERS HEAD-ON!
CREEAK...

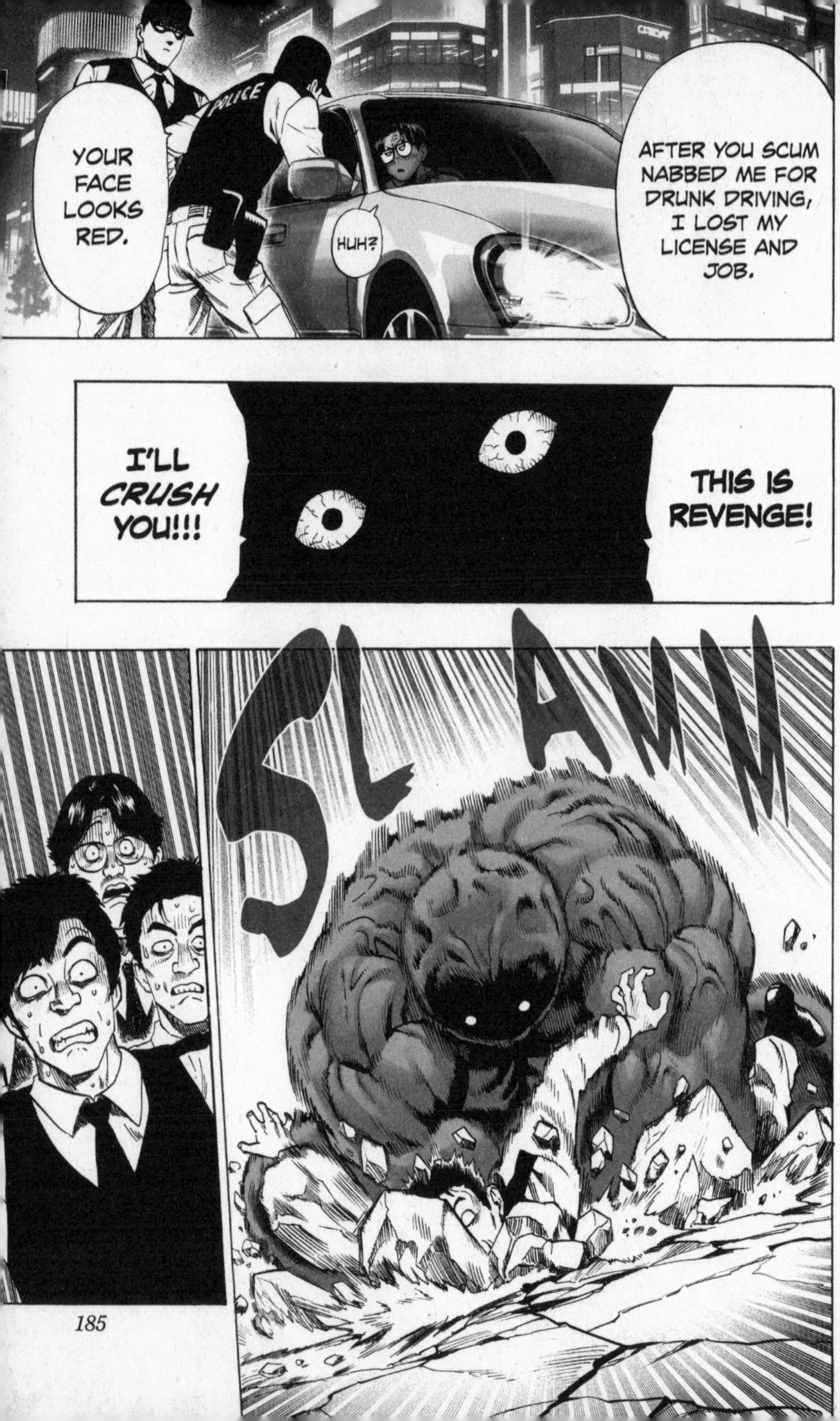
AFTER YOU SCUM NABBED ME FOR DRUNK DRIVING, I LOST MY LICENSE AND JOB.
HUH?
YOUR FACE LOOKS RED.
THIS IS REVENGE!
I'LL *CRUSH* YOU!!!
SLAMM

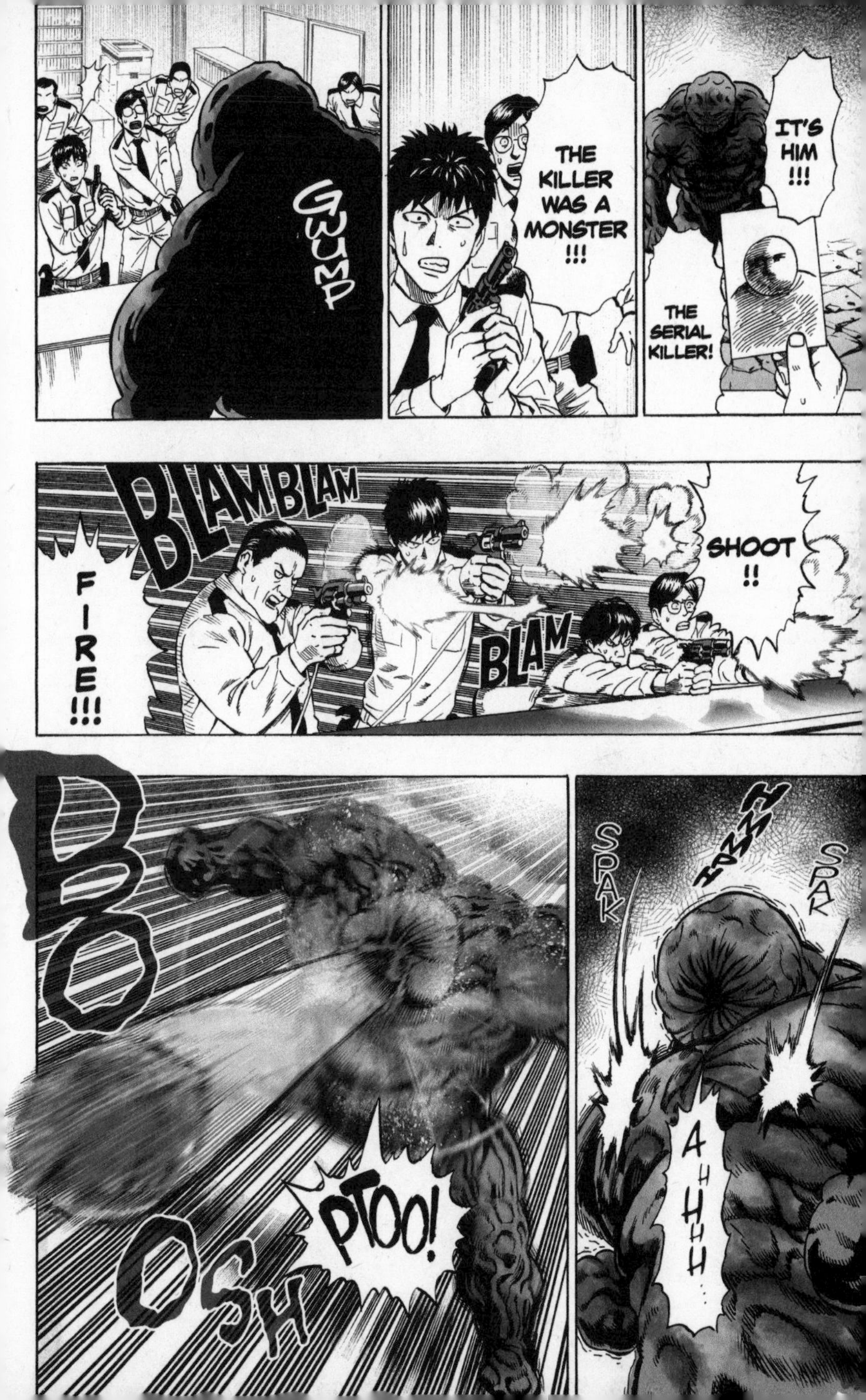
IT'S HIM !!!
THE SERIAL KILLER!
THE KILLER WAS A MONSTER !!!
GWUMP
SHOOT !!
BLAMBLAM
FIRE!!!
BLAM
HMMPH
SPAK
SPAK
AHHHH...
BOO
OSH
PTOO!

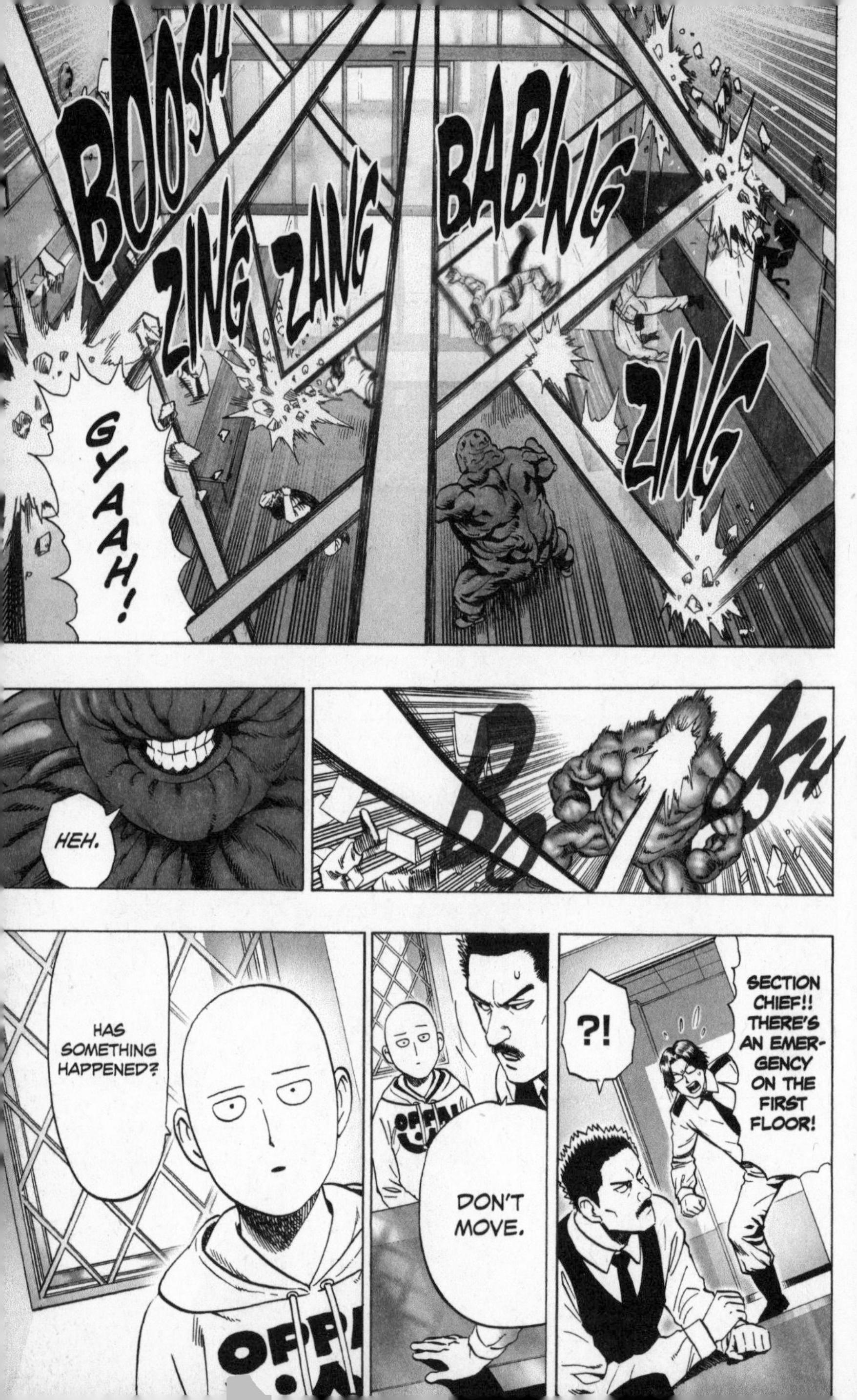
BABING
BOOSH
ZING
ZANG
ZING
GYAAH!
HEH.
SECTION CHIEF!! THERE'S AN EMERGENCY ON THE FIRST FLOOR!
?!
DON'T MOVE.
HAS SOMETHING HAPPENED?

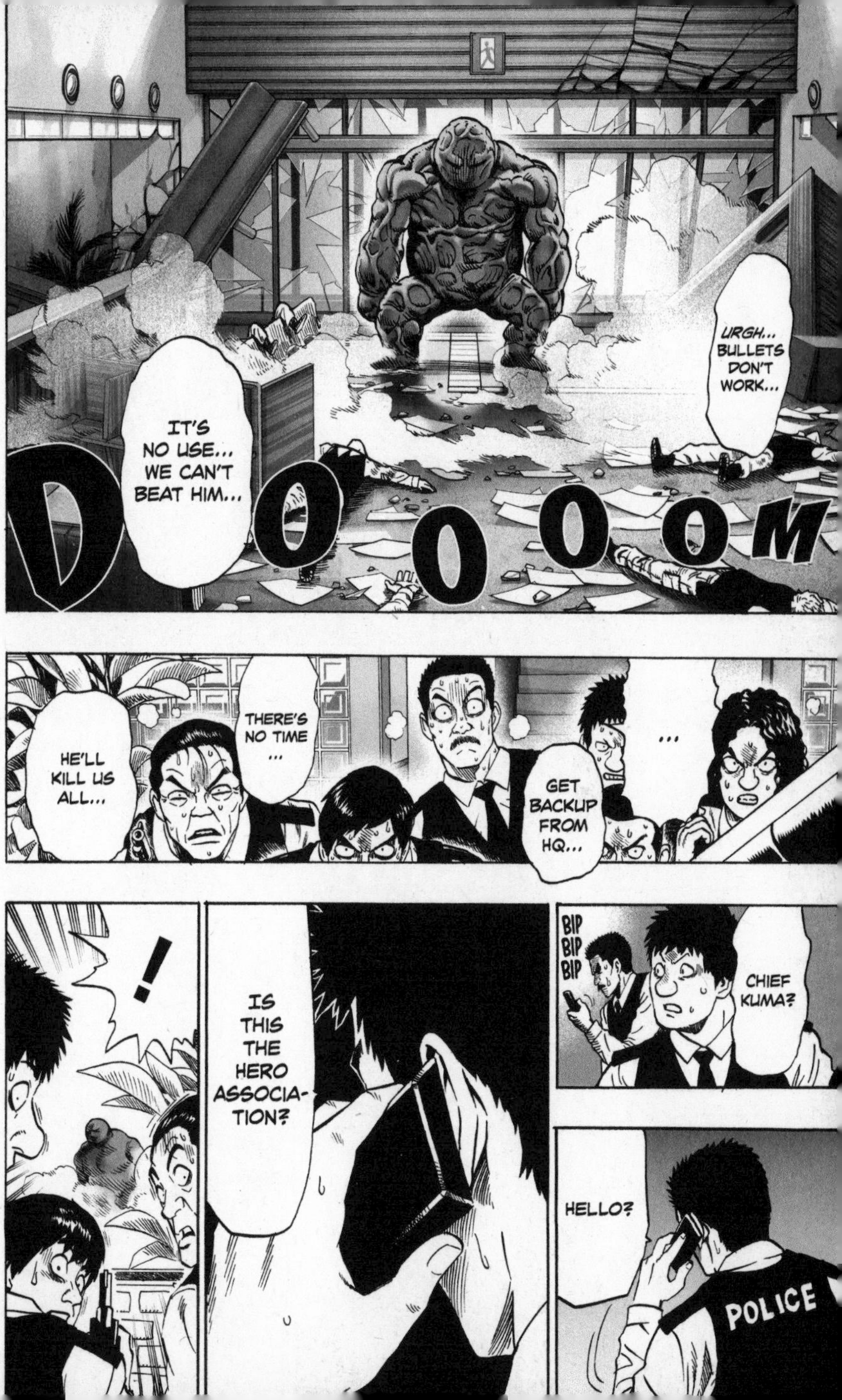
URGH... BULLETS DON'T WORK...
IT'S NO USE... WE CAN'T BEAT HIM...
DOOOOOM
...
GET BACKUP FROM HQ...
THERE'S NO TIME ...
HE'LL KILL US ALL...
BIP BIP BIP
CHIEF KUMA?
HELLO?
POLICE
IS THIS THE HERO ASSOCIATION?
!

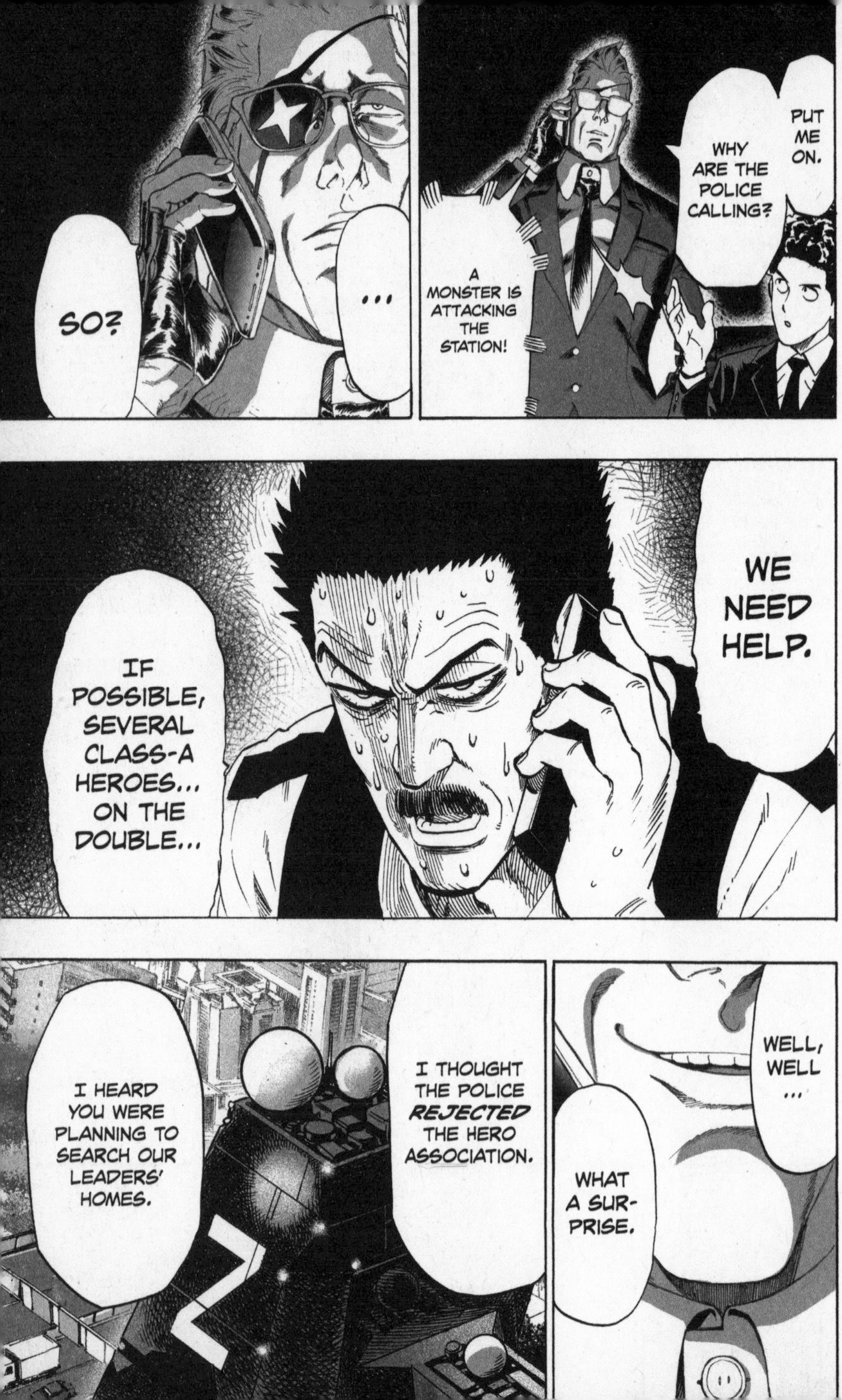
PUT ME ON.
WHY ARE THE POLICE CALLING?
A MONSTER IS ATTACKING THE STATION!
...
SO?
WE NEED HELP.
IF POSSIBLE, SEVERAL CLASS-A HEROES... ON THE DOUBLE...
WELL, WELL ...
WHAT A SUR-PRISE.
I THOUGHT THE POLICE *REJECTED* THE HERO ASSOCIATION.
I HEARD YOU WERE PLANNING TO SEARCH OUR LEADERS' HOMES.

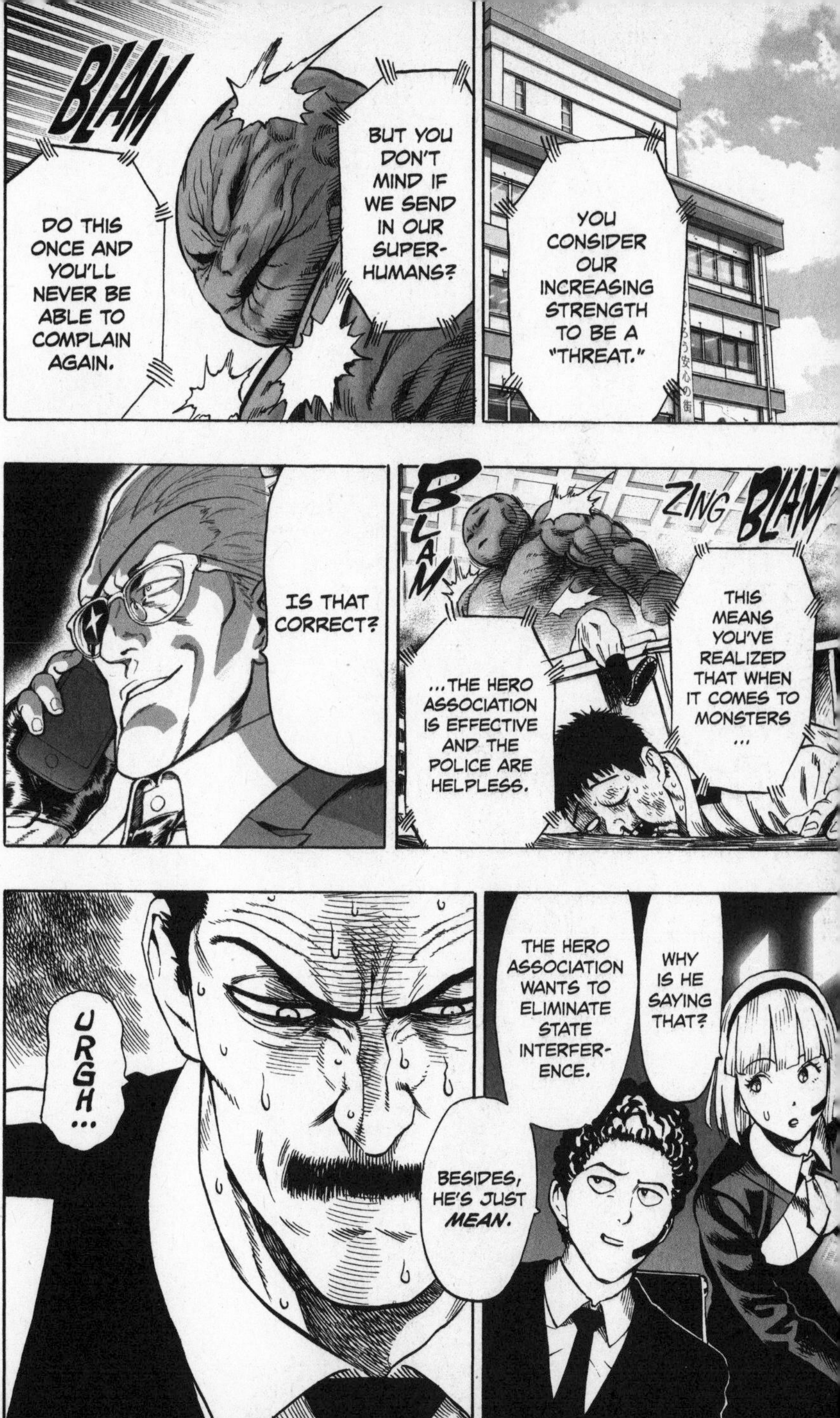
YOU CONSIDER OUR INCREASING STRENGTH TO BE A "THREAT."
BLAM
BUT YOU DON'T MIND IF WE SEND IN OUR SUPER-HUMANS?
DO THIS ONCE AND YOU'LL NEVER BE ABLE TO COMPLAIN AGAIN.
BLAM
ZING
BLAM
THIS MEANS YOU'VE REALIZED THAT WHEN IT COMES TO MONSTERS...
...THE HERO ASSOCIATION IS EFFECTIVE AND THE POLICE ARE HELPLESS.
IS THAT CORRECT?
WHY IS HE SAYING THAT?
THE HERO ASSOCIATION WANTS TO ELIMINATE STATE INTERFERENCE.
BESIDES, HE'S JUST *MEAN*.
URGH...

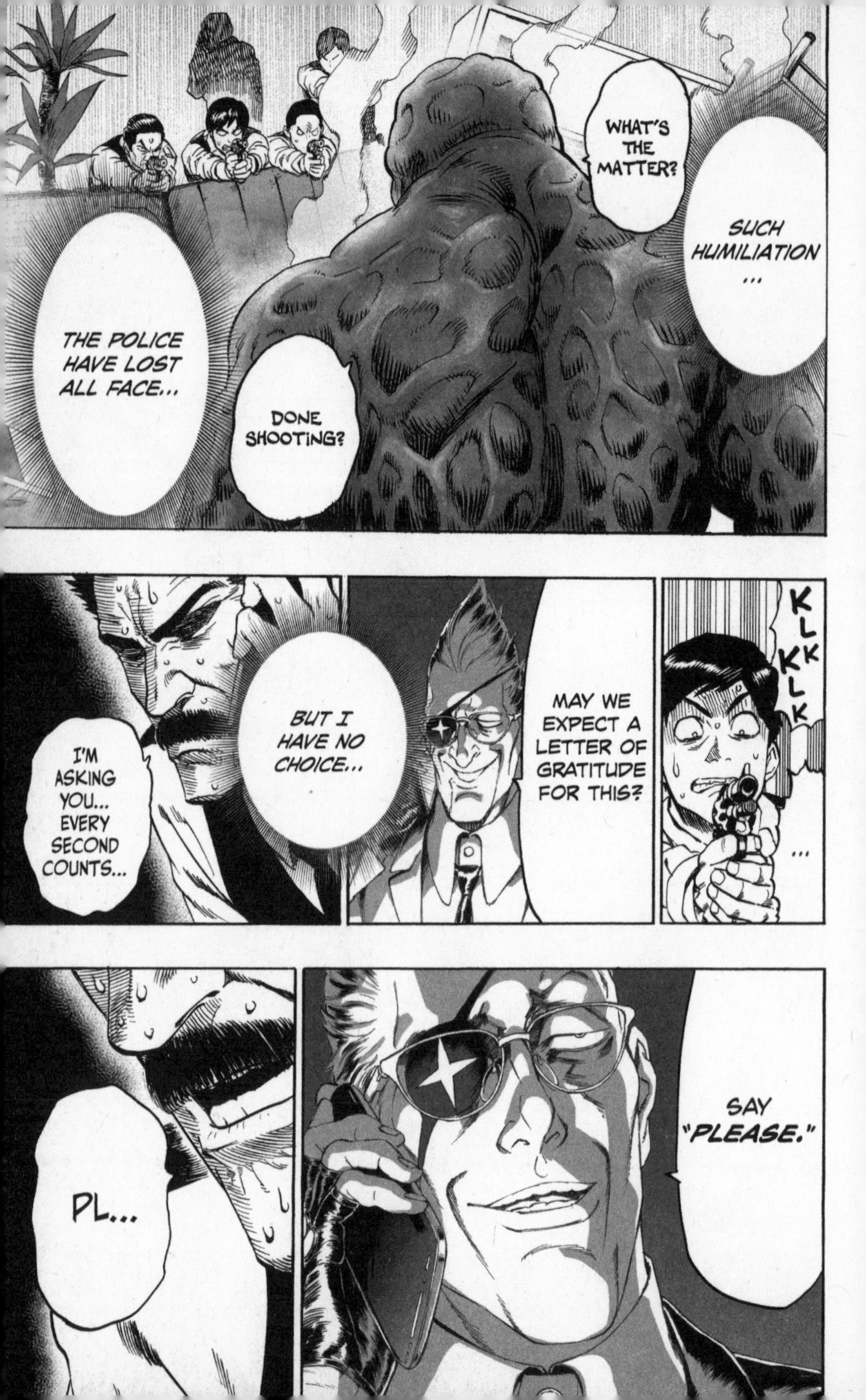
WHAT'S THE MATTER?
SUCH HUMILIATION...
DONE SHOOTING?
THE POLICE HAVE LOST ALL FACE...
KLK KLK
...
MAY WE EXPECT A LETTER OF GRATITUDE FOR THIS?
BUT I HAVE NO CHOICE...
I'M ASKING YOU... EVERY SECOND COUNTS...
SAY "PLEASE."
PL...

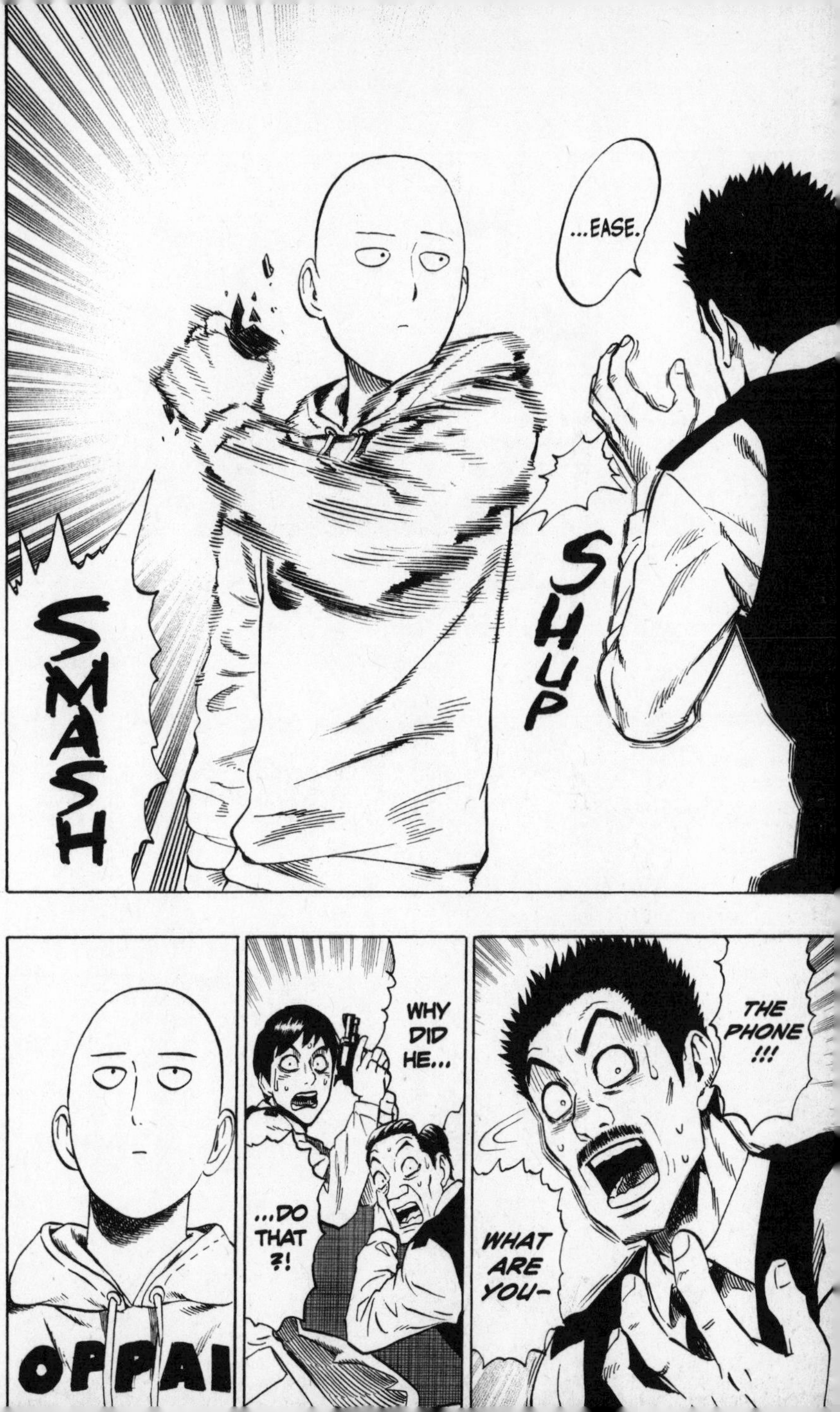
...EASE.
SHUP
SMASH
THE PHONE !!!
WHAT ARE YOU-
WHY DID HE...
...DO THAT ?!
OPPAI

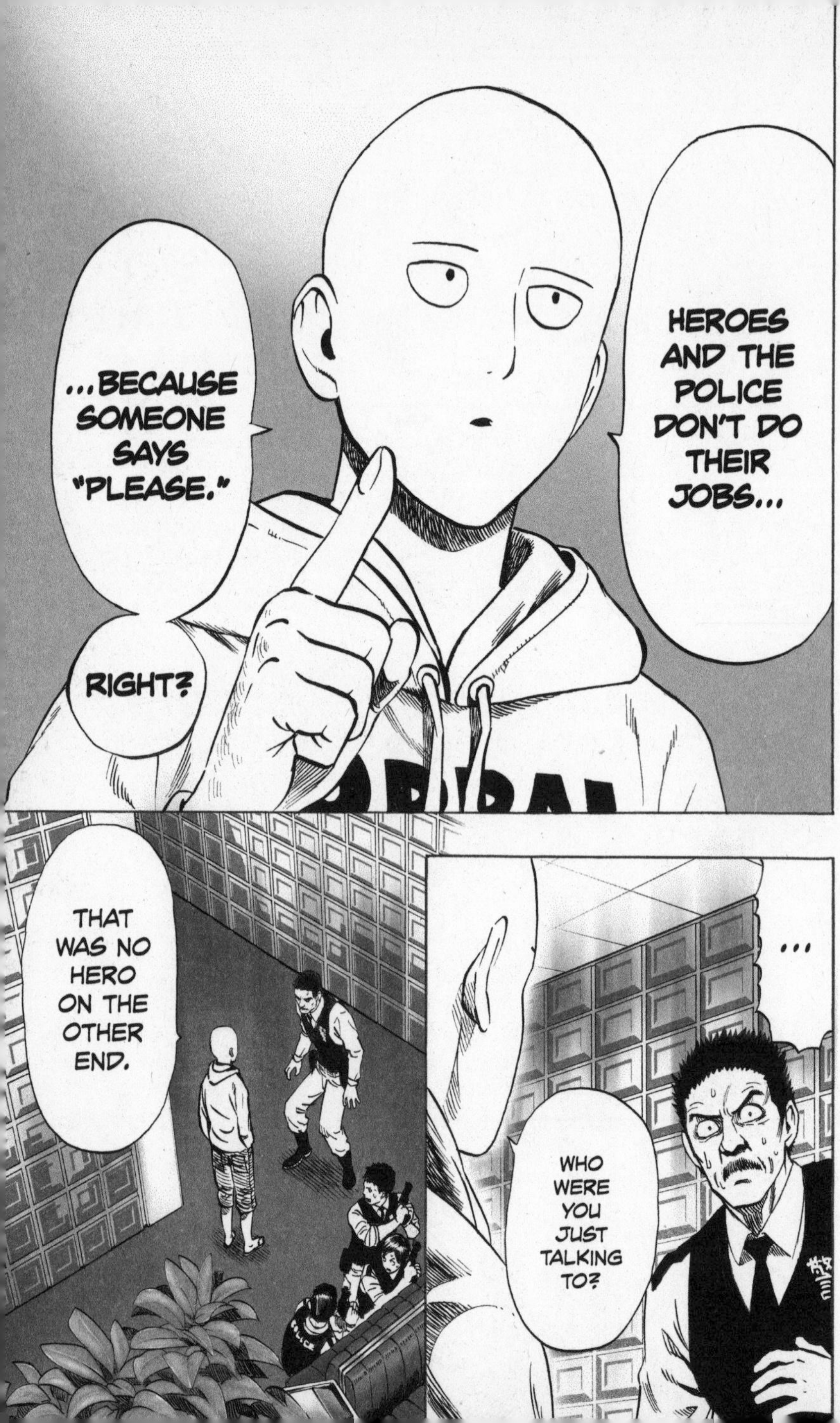
HEROES AND THE POLICE DON'T DO THEIR JOBS...
...BECAUSE SOMEONE SAYS "PLEASE."
RIGHT?
...
WHO WERE YOU JUST TALKING TO?
THAT WAS NO HERO ON THE OTHER END.

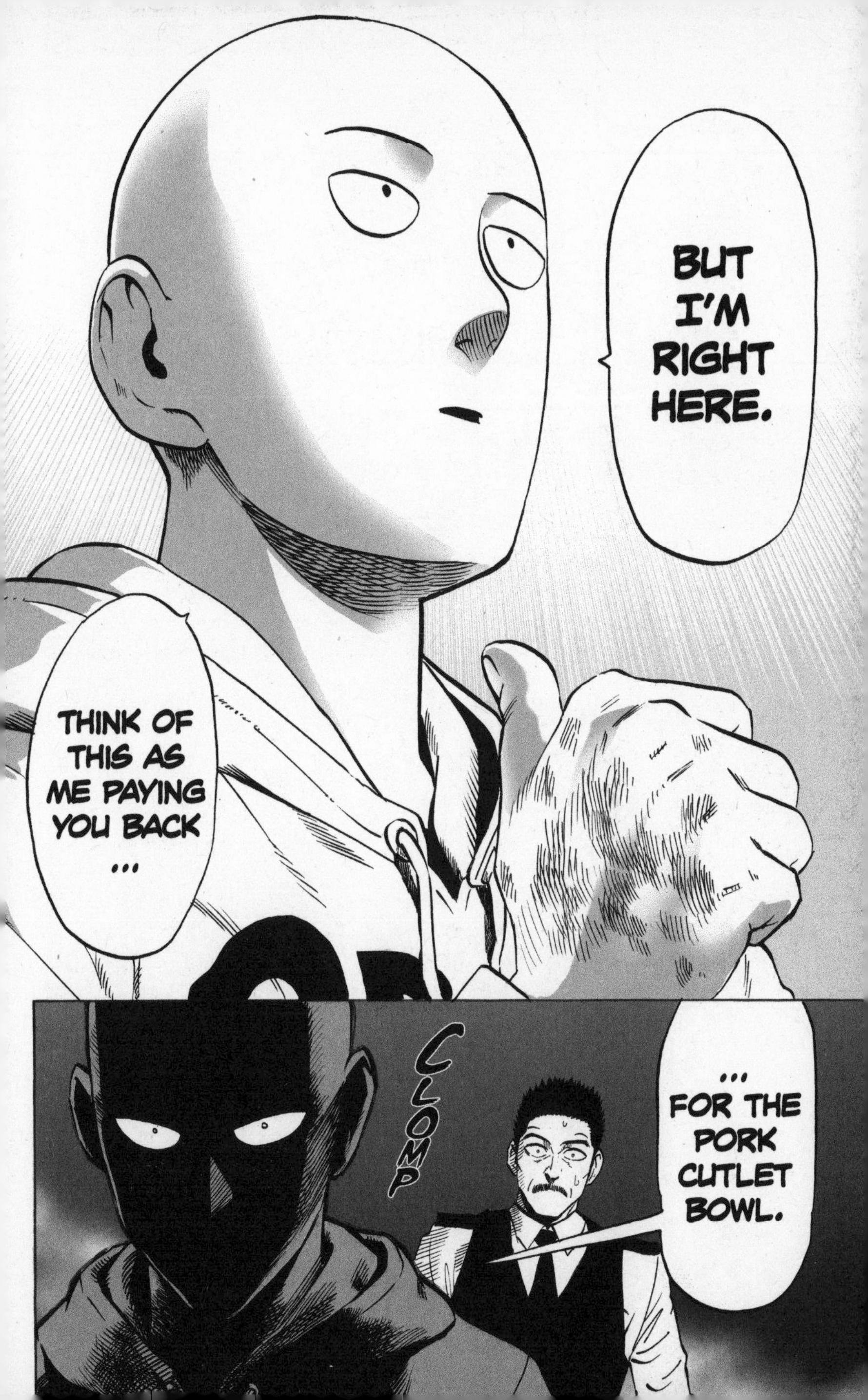
BUT I'M RIGHT HERE.
THINK OF THIS AS ME PAYING YOU BACK ...
... FOR THE PORK CUTLET BOWL.
CLOMP

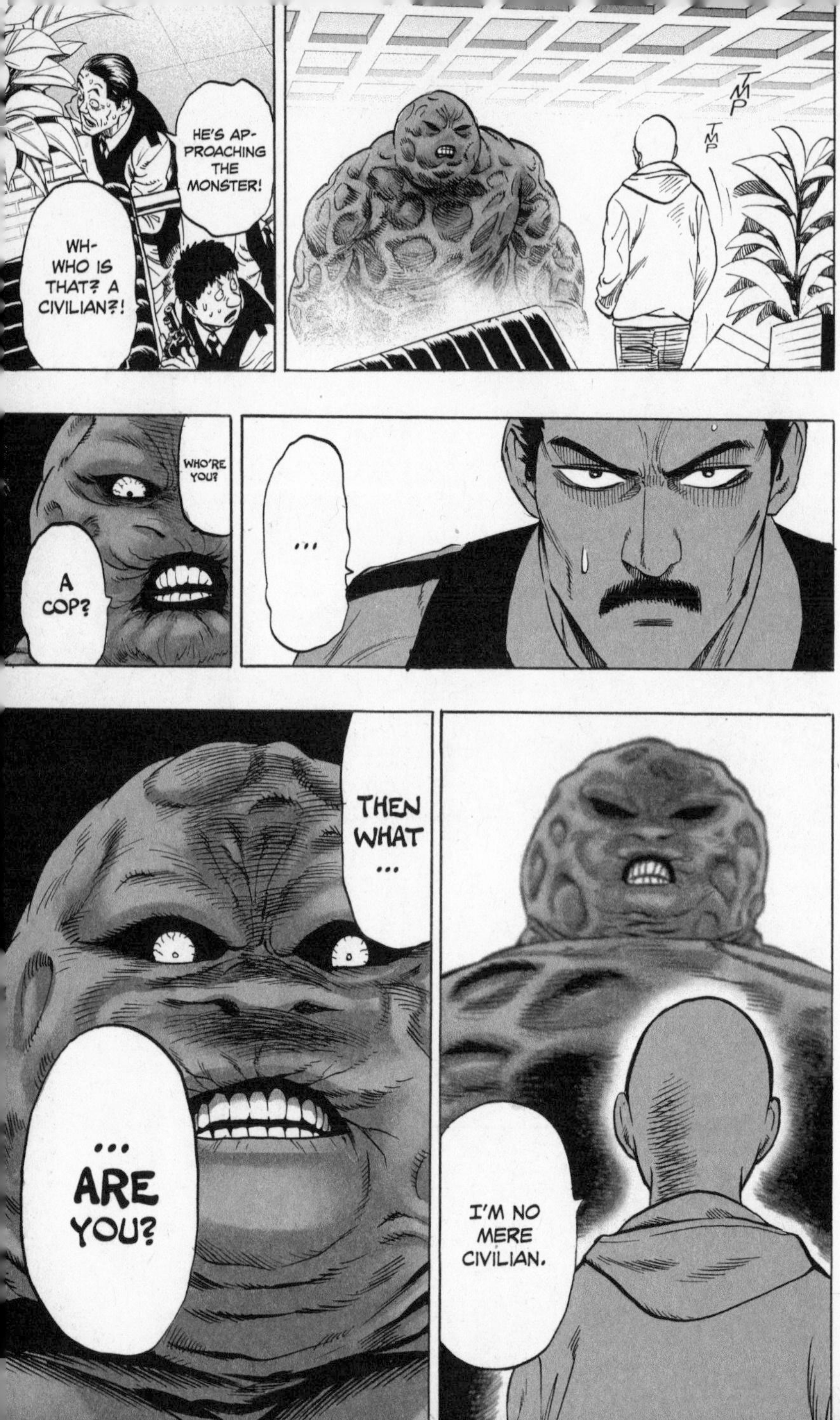
TMP
TMP
HE'S AP-PROACHING THE MONSTER!
WH-WHO IS THAT? A CIVILIAN?!
...
WHO'RE YOU?
A COP?
I'M NO MERE CIVILIAN.
THEN WHAT ...
... ARE YOU?

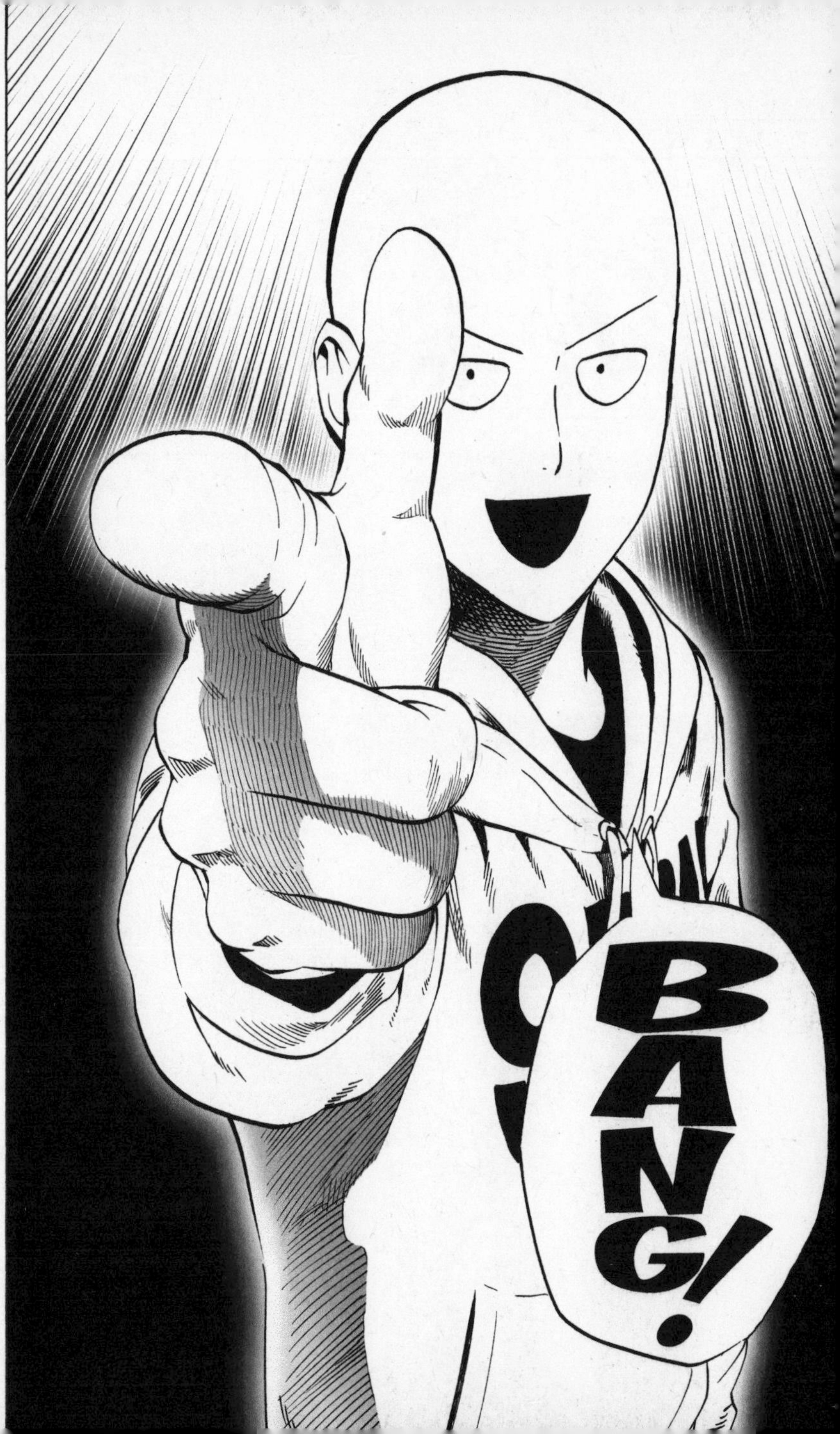
BANG!

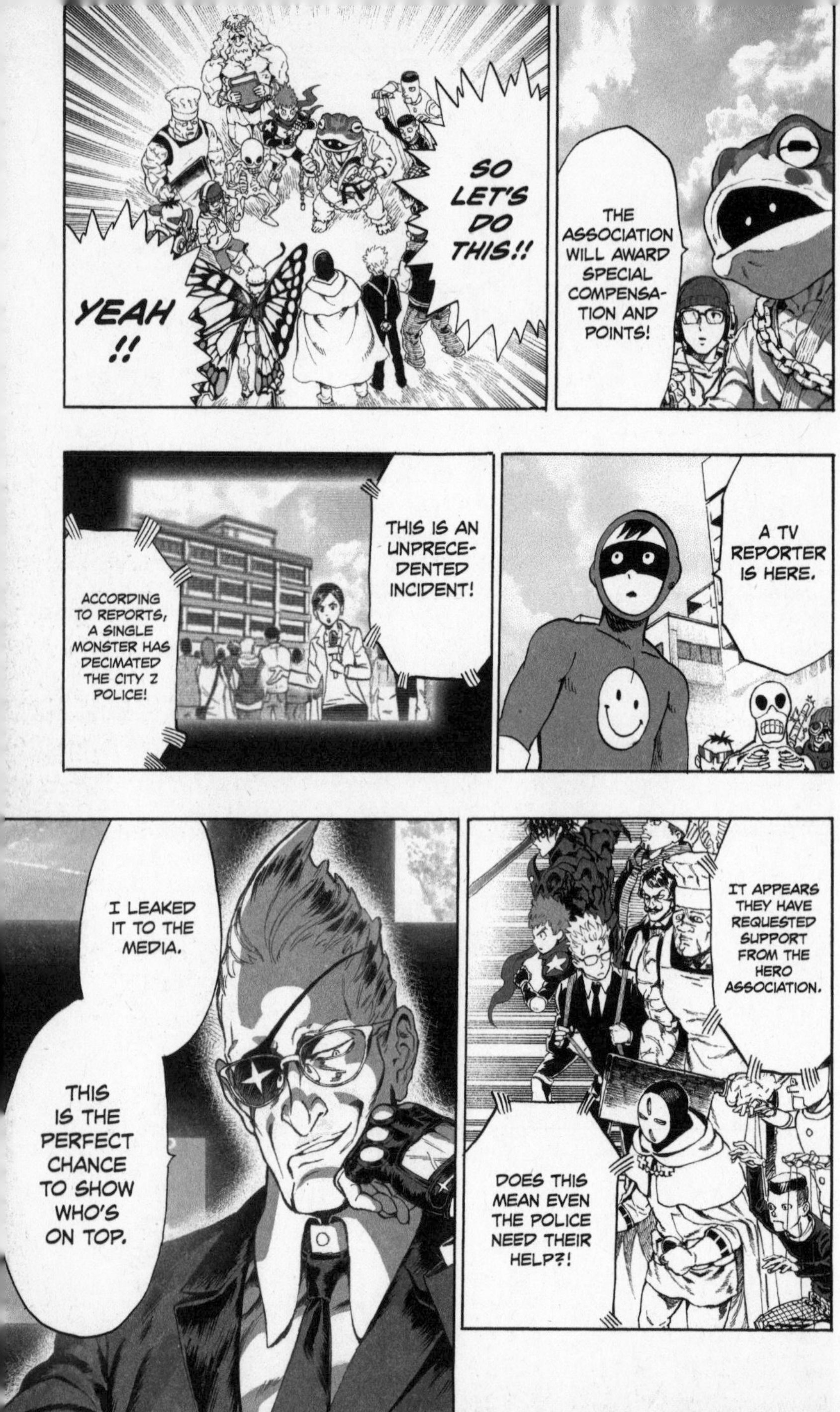
THE ASSOCIATION WILL AWARD SPECIAL COMPENSATION AND POINTS!
SO LET'S DO THIS!!
YEAH!!
A TV REPORTER IS HERE.
THIS IS AN UNPRECEDENTED INCIDENT!
ACCORDING TO REPORTS, A SINGLE MONSTER HAS DECIMATED THE CITY Z POLICE!
IT APPEARS THEY HAVE REQUESTED SUPPORT FROM THE HERO ASSOCIATION.
DOES THIS MEAN EVEN THE POLICE NEED THEIR HELP?!
I LEAKED IT TO THE MEDIA.
THIS IS THE PERFECT CHANCE TO SHOW WHO'S ON TOP.

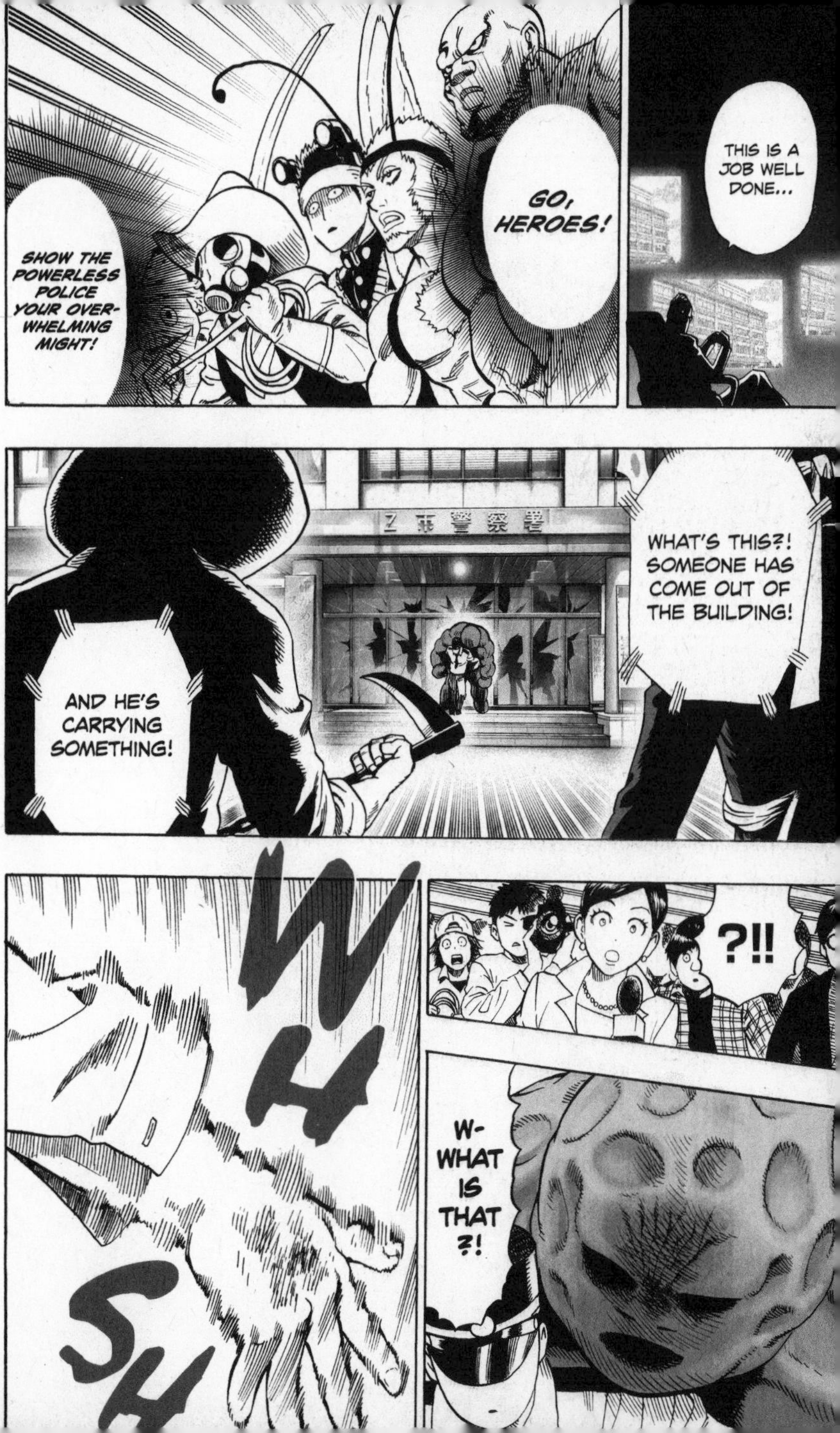
THIS IS A JOB WELL DONE...
GO, HEROES!
SHOW THE POWERLESS POLICE YOUR OVER-WHELMING MIGHT!
Z市警察署
WHAT'S THIS?! SOMEONE HAS COME OUT OF THE BUILDING!
AND HE'S CARRYING SOMETHING!
?!!
W- WHAT IS THAT?!
WH
SH

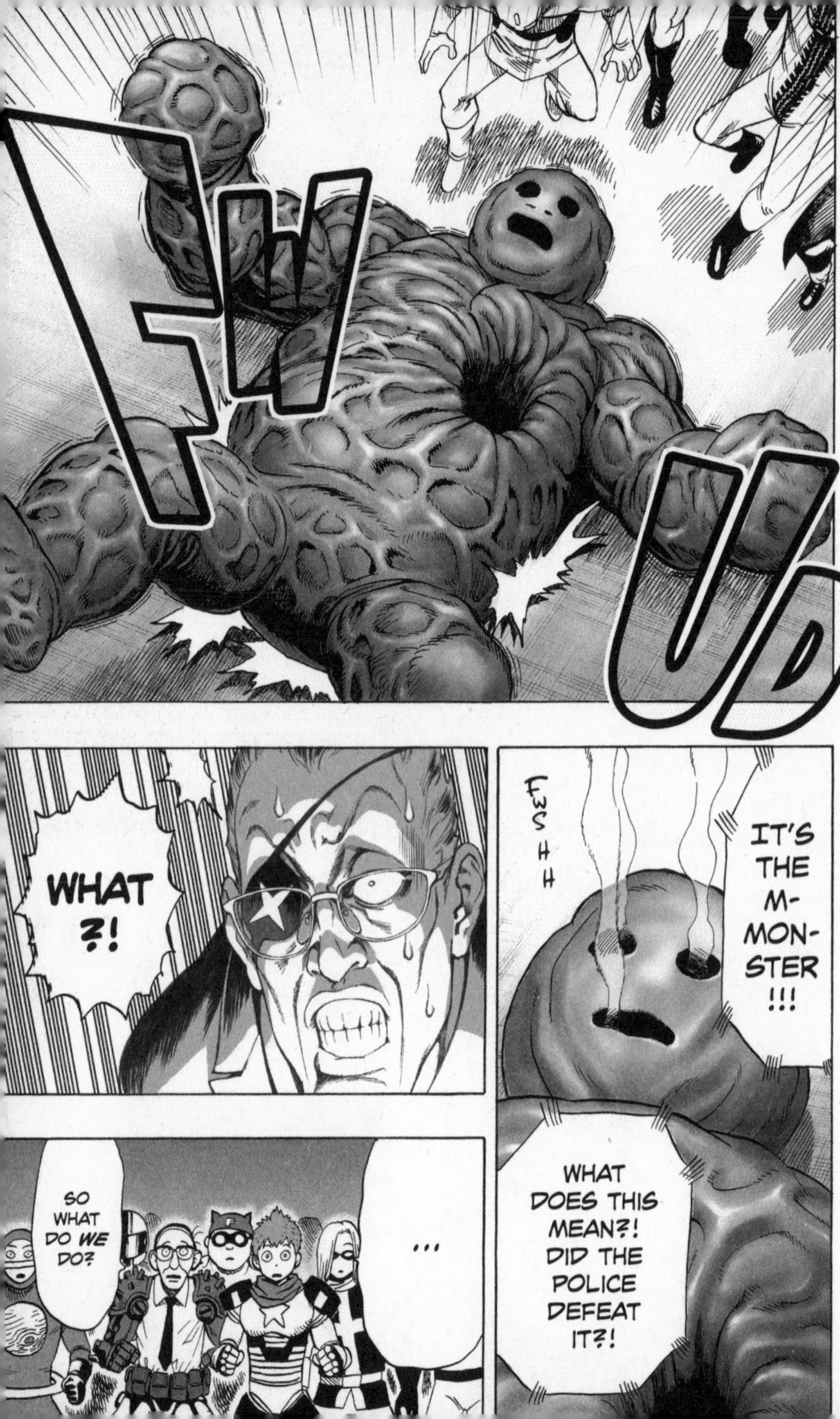
FW
UD
FWSHH
IT'S THE M-MONSTER!!!
WHAT DOES THIS MEAN?! DID THE POLICE DEFEAT IT?!
WHAT?!
...
SO WHAT DO WE DO?

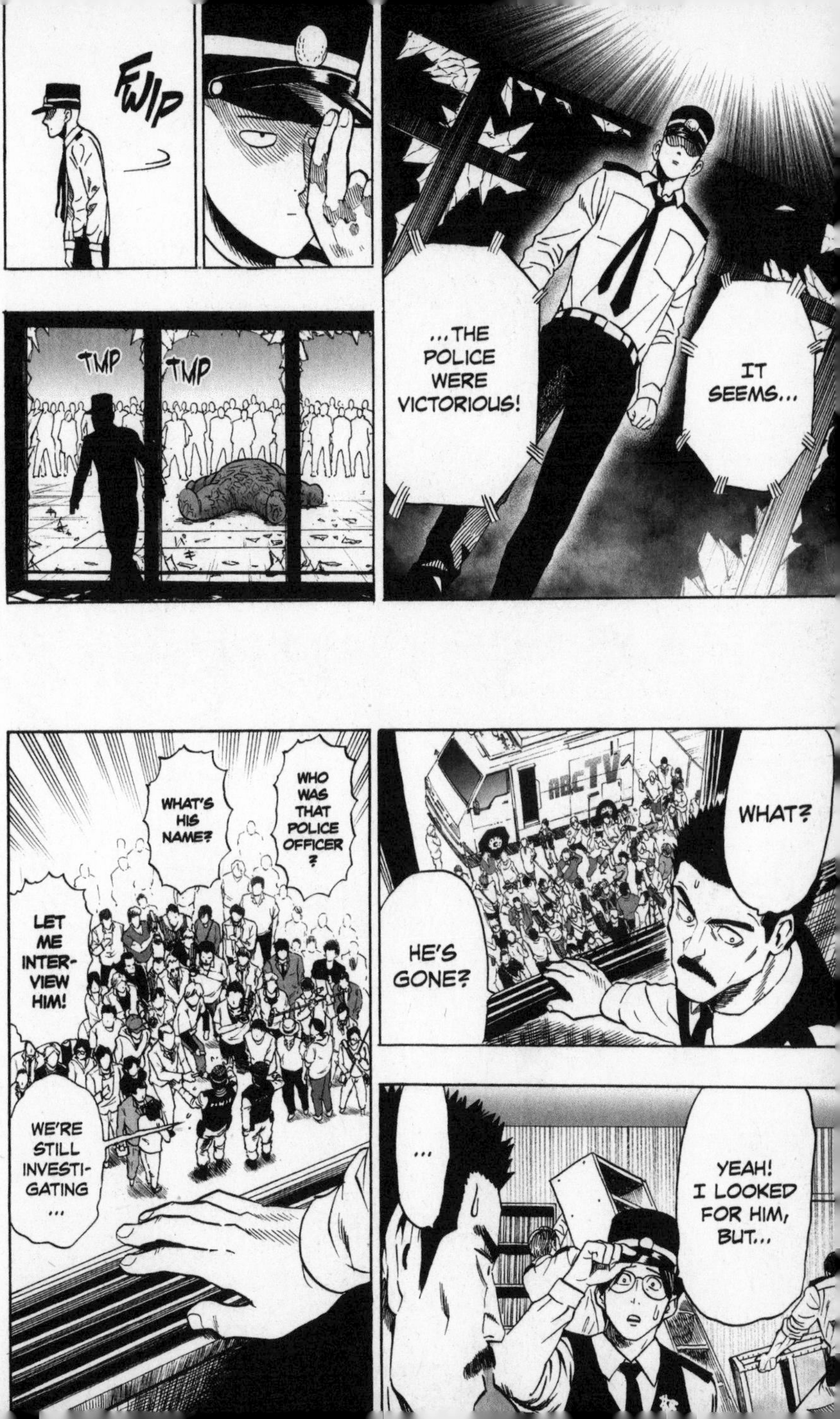
IT SEEMS...
...THE POLICE WERE VICTORIOUS!
FWIP
TMP
TMP
WHAT?
HE'S GONE?
YEAH! I LOOKED FOR HIM, BUT...
...
WHO WAS THAT POLICE OFFICER?
WHAT'S HIS NAME?
LET ME INTER-VIEW HIM!
WE'RE STILL INVESTI-GATING...

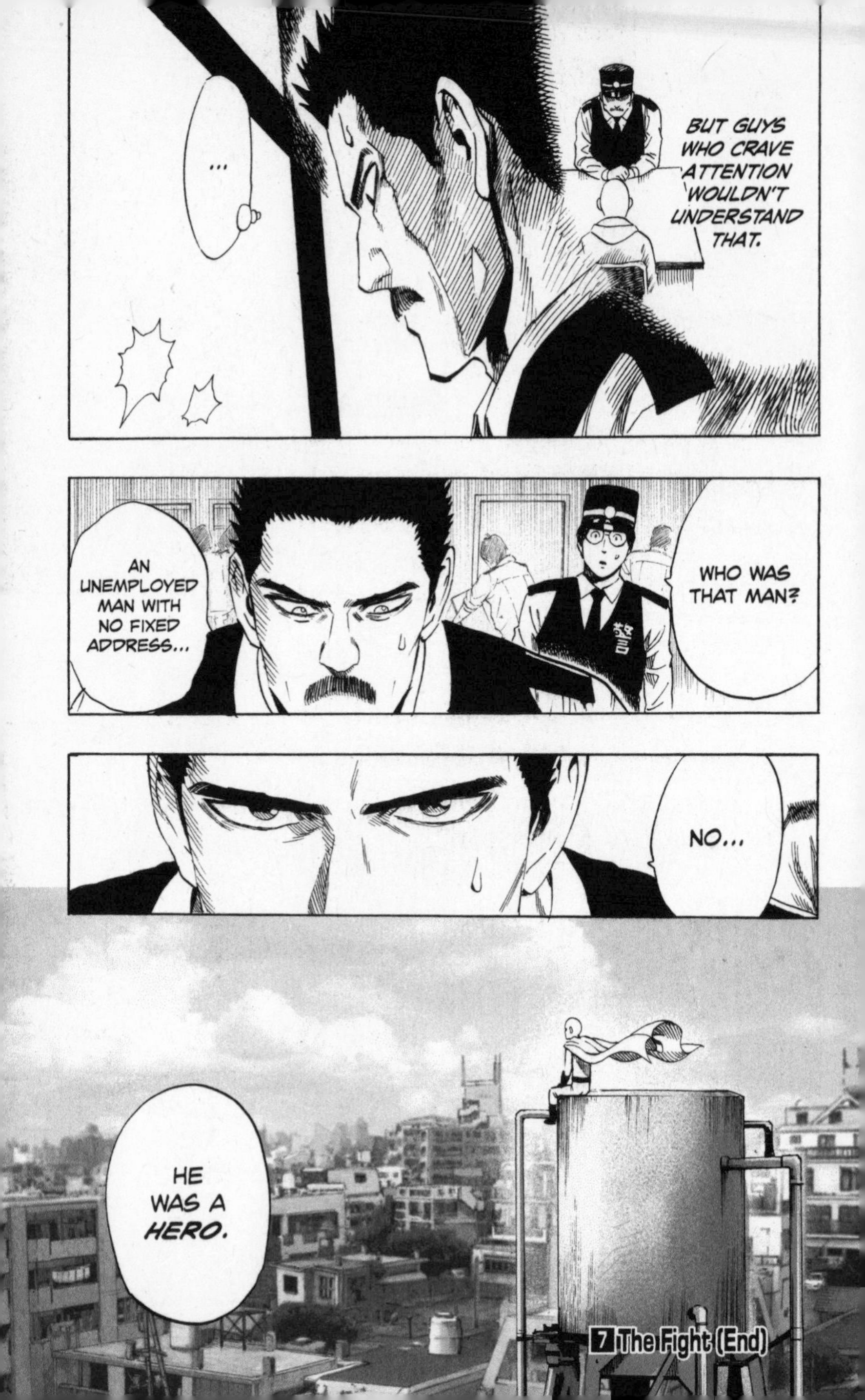
BUT GUYS WHO CRAVE ATTENTION WOULDN'T UNDERSTAND THAT.
...
WHO WAS THAT MAN?
AN UNEMPLOYED MAN WITH NO FIXED ADDRESS...
NO...
HE WAS A HERO.
7 The Fight (End)

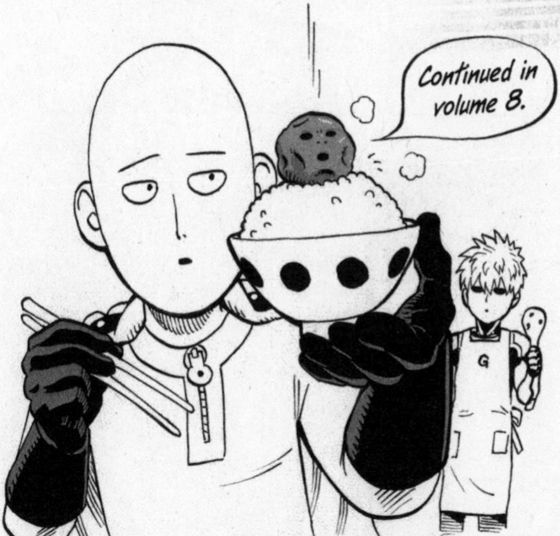
Continued in volume 8.

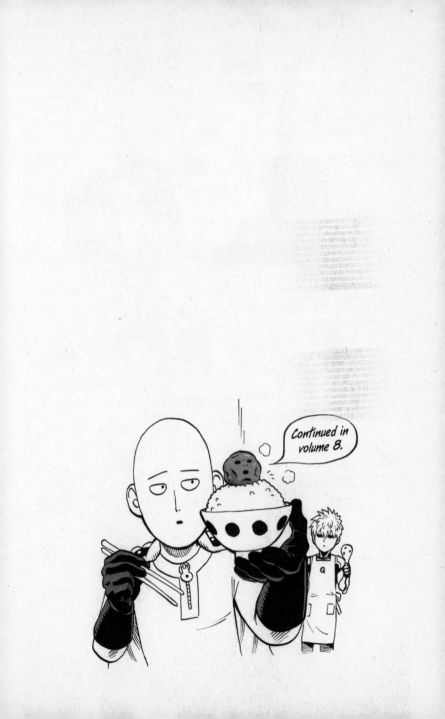

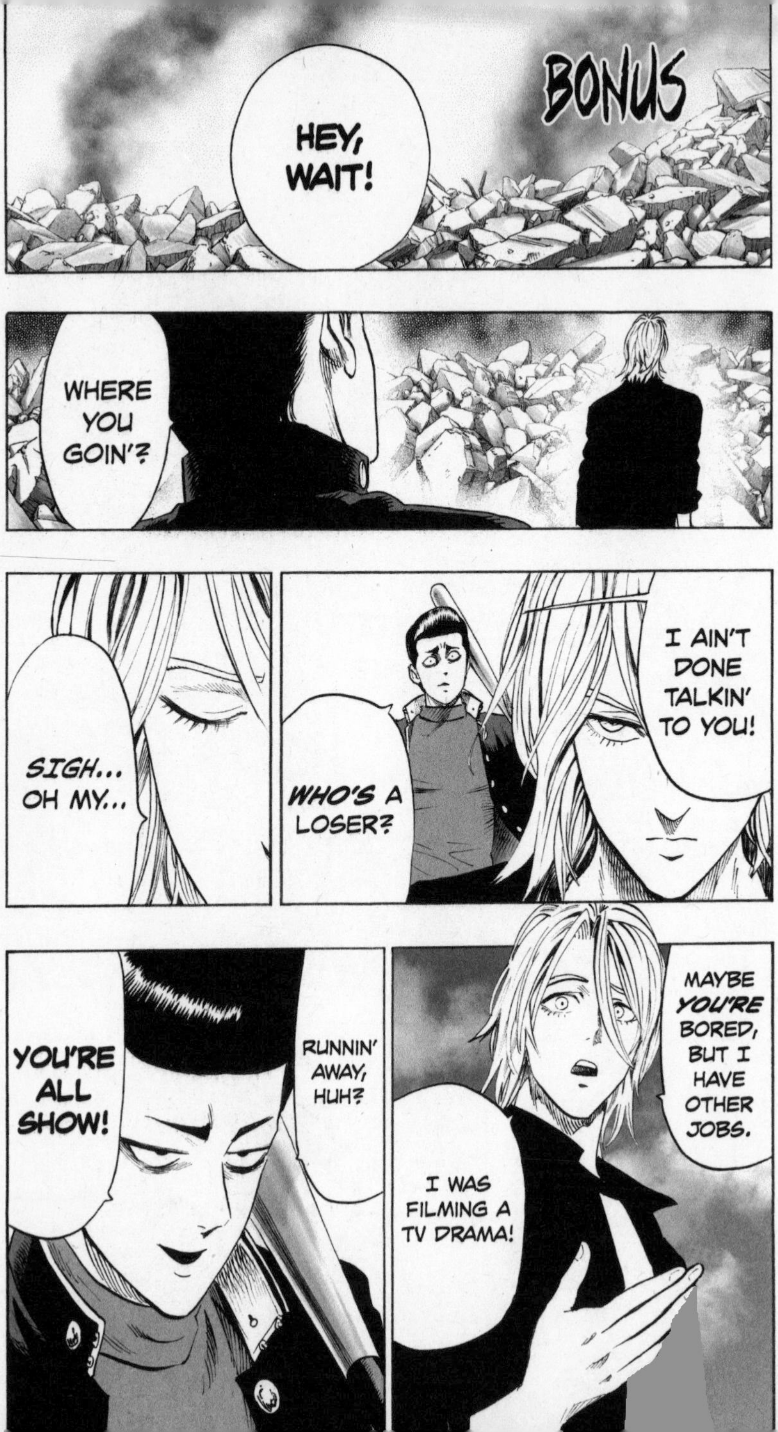
BONUS
HEY, WAIT!
WHERE YOU GOIN'?
I AIN'T DONE TALKIN' TO YOU!
WHO'S A LOSER?
SIGH... OH MY...
MAYBE *YOU'RE* BORED, BUT I HAVE OTHER JOBS.
I WAS FILMING A TV DRAMA!
RUNNIN' AWAY, HUH?
YOU'RE ALL SHOW!

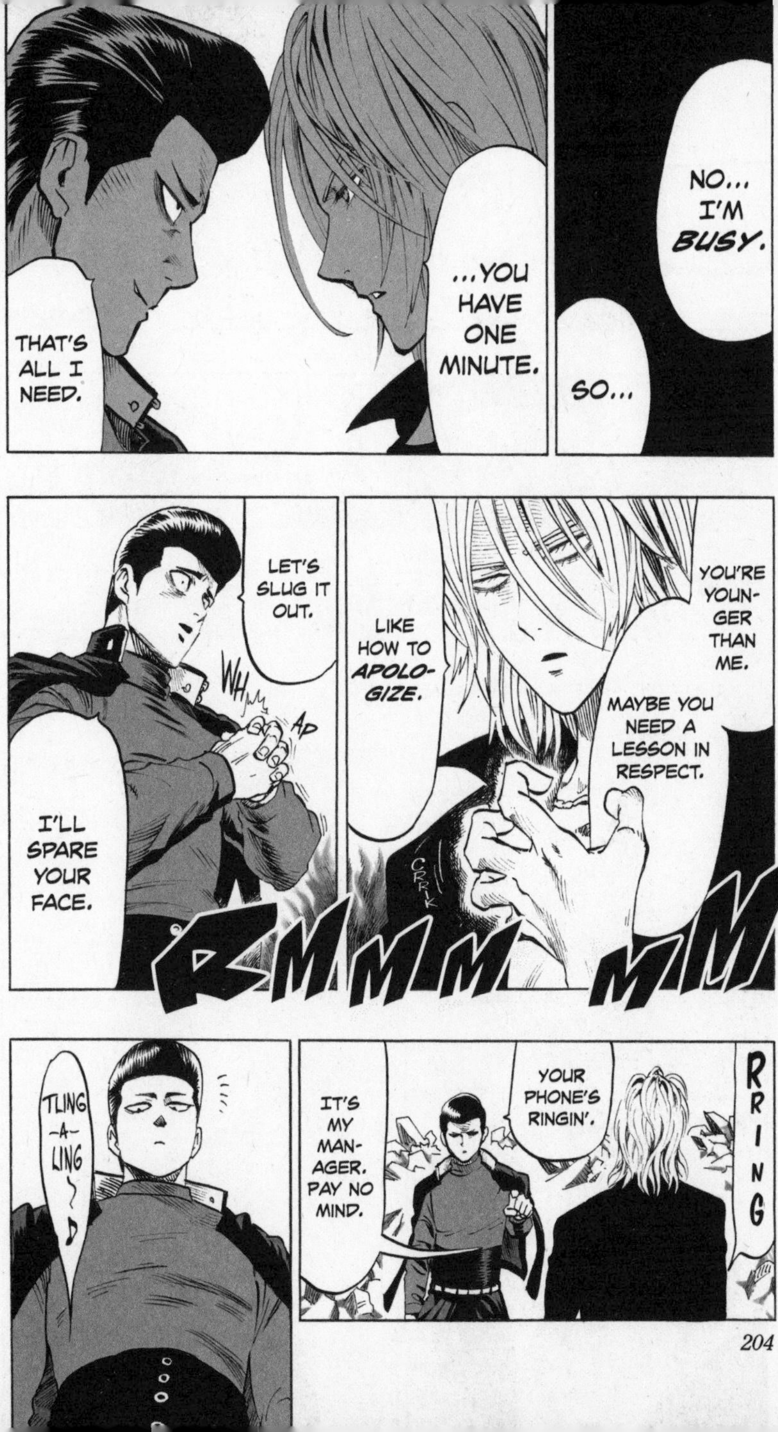
NO... I'M *BUSY*.
SO...
...YOU HAVE ONE MINUTE.
THAT'S ALL I NEED.
YOU'RE YOUNGER THAN ME.
MAYBE YOU NEED A LESSON IN RESPECT.
LIKE HOW TO *APOLOGIZE*.
CRRIK
LET'S SLUG IT OUT.
WHAP
I'LL SPARE YOUR FACE.
RMMMM MM
RRING
YOUR PHONE'S RINGIN'.
IT'S MY MANAGER. PAY NO MIND.
TLING-A-LING ♪

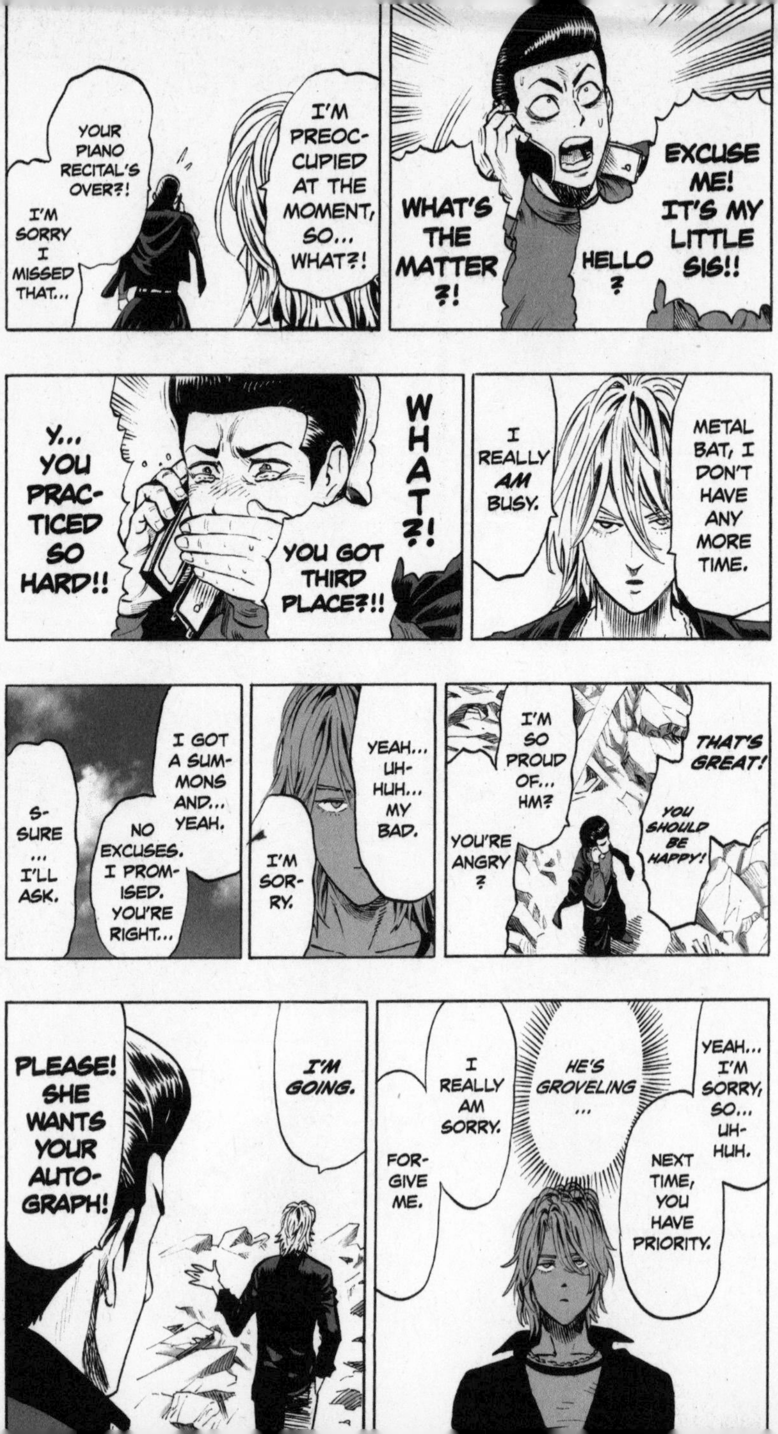
EXCUSE ME! IT'S MY LITTLE SIS!!
HELLO?
WHAT'S THE MATTER?!
I'M PREOCCUPIED AT THE MOMENT, SO... WHAT?!
YOUR PIANO RECITAL'S OVER?!
I'M SORRY I MISSED THAT...
METAL BAT, I DON'T HAVE ANY MORE TIME.
I REALLY *AM* BUSY.
WHAT?!
YOU GOT THIRD PLACE?!!
Y... YOU PRACTICED SO HARD!!
THAT'S GREAT!
YOU SHOULD BE HAPPY!
I'M SO PROUD OF... HM?
YOU'RE ANGRY?
YEAH... UH-HUH... MY BAD.
I'M SORRY.
I GOT A SUMMONS AND... YEAH.
NO EXCUSES. I PROMISED. YOU'RE RIGHT...
S-SURE... I'LL ASK.
YEAH... I'M SORRY, SO... UH-HUH.
HE'S GROVELING...
I REALLY AM SORRY.
NEXT TIME, YOU HAVE PRIORITY.
FORGIVE ME.
I'M GOING.
PLEASE! SHE WANTS YOUR AUTOGRAPH!

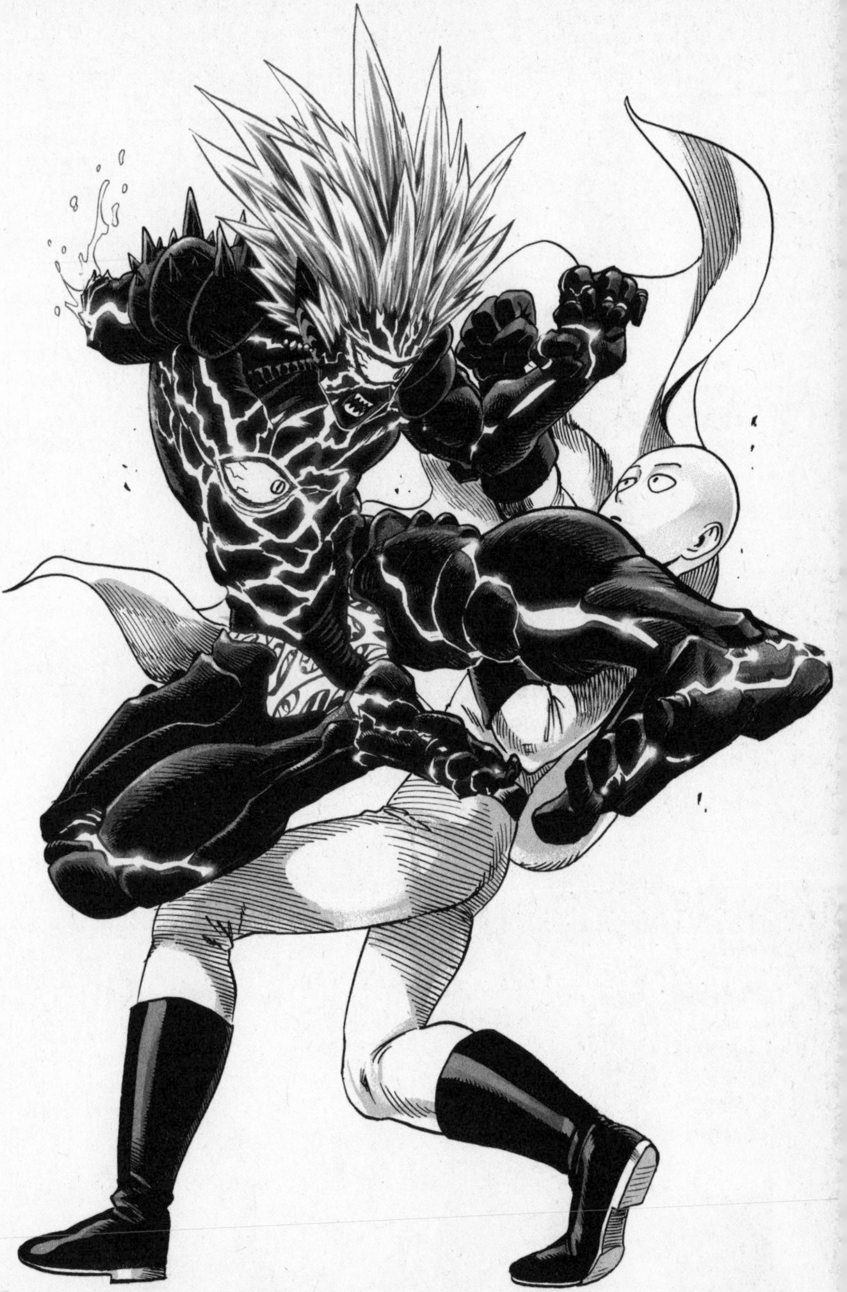

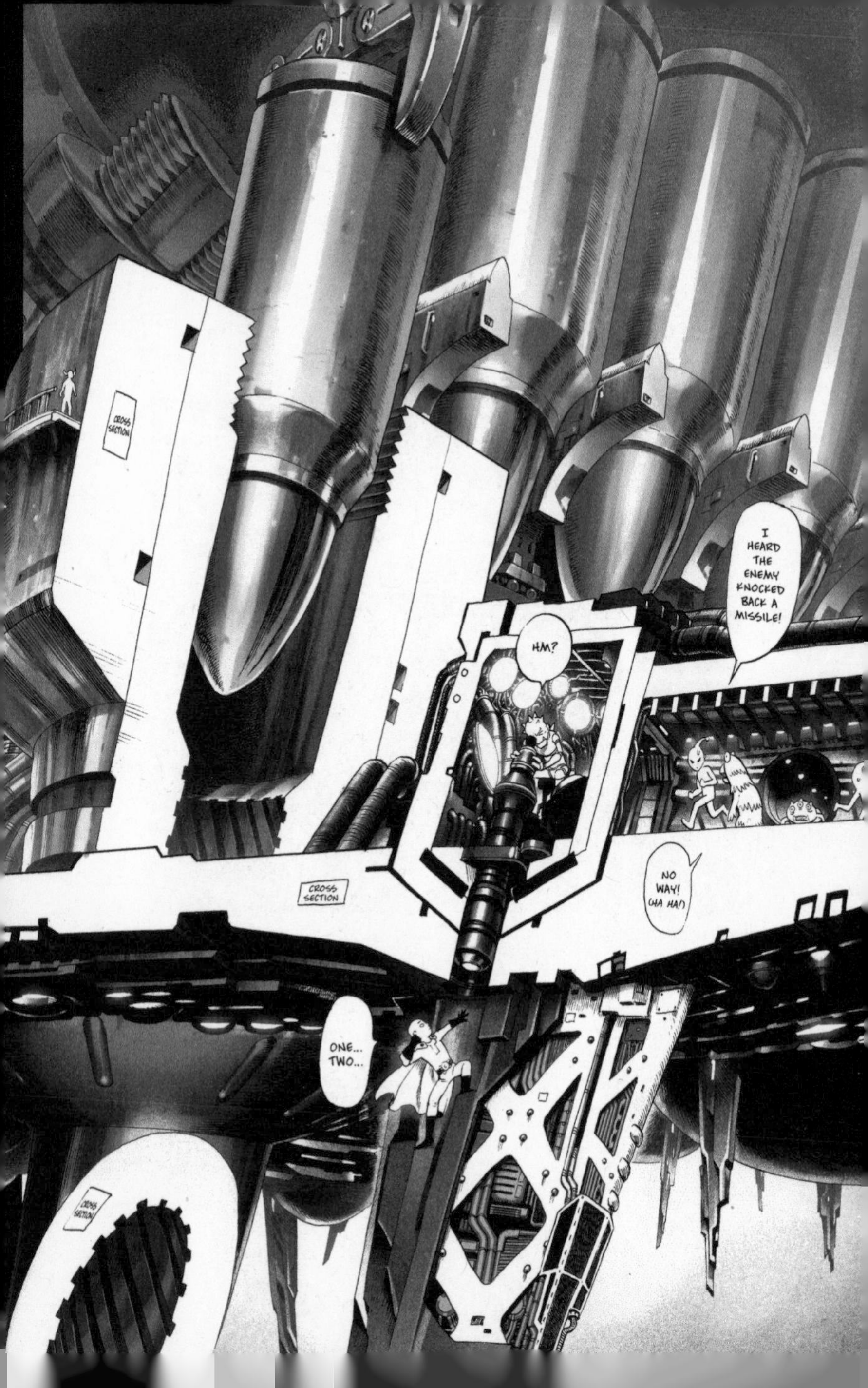
CROSS SECTION
I HEARD THE ENEMY KNOCKED BACK A MISSILE!
HM?
NO WAY! (HA HA!)
CROSS SECTION
ONE... TWO...
CROSS SECTION

END NOTES

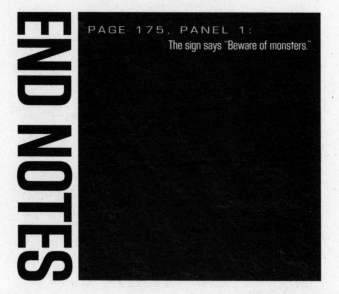

PAGE 175, PANEL 1:

The sign says "Beware of monsters."

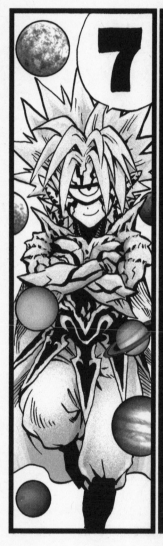

ONE-PUNCH MAN
VOLUME 7
SHONEN JUMP MANGA EDITION

STORY BY | ONE
ART BY | YUSUKE MURATA

TRANSLATION | JOHN WERRY
TOUCH-UP ART AND LETTERING | JAMES GAUBATZ
DESIGN | FAWN LAU
SHONEN JUMP SERIES EDITOR | JOHN BAE
GRAPHIC NOVEL EDITOR | JENNIFER LEBLANC

ONE-PUNCH MAN © 2012 by ONE, Yusuke Murata
All rights reserved.
First published in Japan in 2012 by SHUEISHA Inc., Tokyo.
English translation rights arranged by SHUEISHA Inc.

The stories, characters and incidents mentioned in this
publication are entirely fictional.

Printed in the U.S.A.

Published by VIZ Media, LLC
P.O. Box 77010
San Francisco, CA 94107

10 9 8 7 6 5 4 3 2 1
First printing, July 2016

www.viz.com

www.shonenjump.com

★ EYESHIELD 21

STORY BY **RIICHIRO INAGAKI**
ART BY **YUSUKE MURATA**

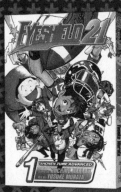

From the artist of *One-Punch Man!*

Wimpy Sena Kobayakawa has been running away from
bullies all his life. But when the football gear comes
on, things change—Sena's speed and uncanny ability
to elude big bullies just might give him what it takes to
become a great high school football hero! Catch all the
bone-crushing action and slapstick comedy of Japan's
hottest football manga!

www.viz.com   www.shonenjump.com

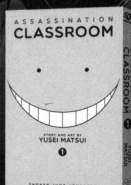

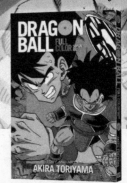

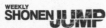

IN A SAVAGE WORLD RULED BY THE PURSUIT OF THE MOST DELICIOUS FOODS, IT'S EITHER EAT OR BE EATEN!

"The most bizarrely entertaining manga out there on comic shelves. *Toriko* is a great series. If you're looking for a weirdly fun book or a fighting manga with a bizarre take, this is the story for you to read."

—*ComicAttack.com*

TORIKO

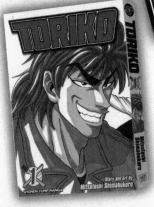

Story and Art by Mitsutoshi Shimabukuro

In an era where the world's gone crazy for increasingly bizarre gourmet foods, only Gourmet Hunter Toriko can hunt down the ferocious ingredients that supply the world's best restaurants. Join Toriko as he tracks and defeats the tastiest and most dangerous animals with his bare hands.

ratings.viz.com

www.shonenjump.com

www.viz.com

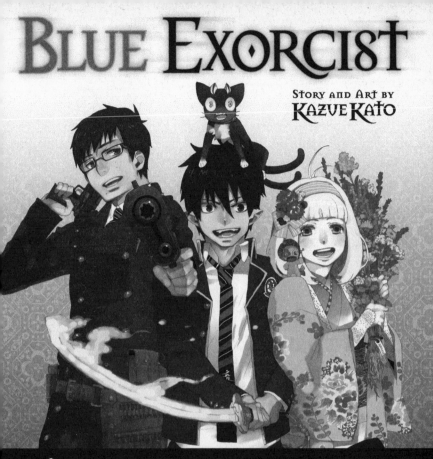
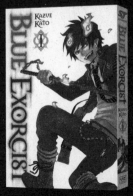

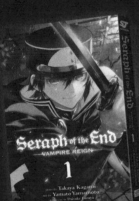

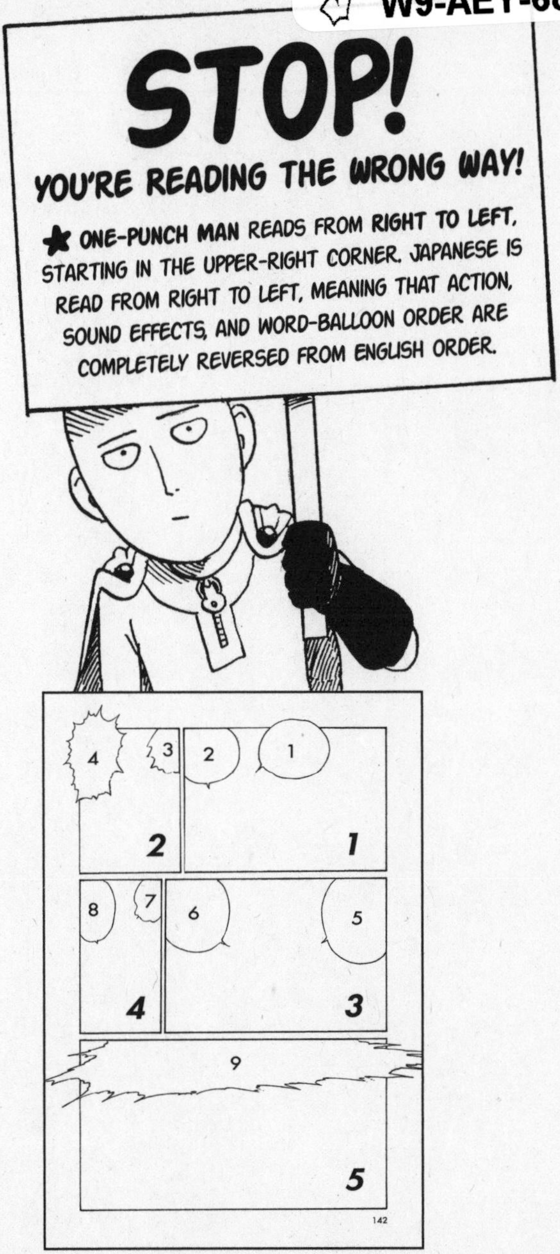
STOP!
YOU'RE READING THE WRONG WAY!
★ ONE-PUNCH MAN READS FROM RIGHT TO LEFT, STARTING IN THE UPPER-RIGHT CORNER. JAPANESE IS READ FROM RIGHT TO LEFT, MEANING THAT ACTION, SOUND EFFECTS, AND WORD-BALLOON ORDER ARE COMPLETELY REVERSED FROM ENGLISH ORDER.